Space in Mind

Space in Mind

Concepts for Spatial Learning and Education

Daniel R. Montello, Karl Grossner, and Donald G. Janelle, editors

The MIT Press
Cambridge, Massachusetts
London, England

MIT Press books may be purchased at special quantity discounts for business or sales promotional use. For information, email special_sales@mitpress.mit.edu

Set in ITC Stone Serif Std 9/13pt by Toppan Best-set Premedia Limited. Printed and bound in the United States of America.

Library of Congress Cataloging-in-Publication Data

Space in mind : concepts for spatial learning and education / edited by Daniel R. Montello, Karl Grossner, and Donald G. Janelle.
    pages cm
Includes bibliographical references and index.
ISBN 978-0-262-02829-5 (hardcover : alk. paper)
1. Space perception. I. Montello, Daniel R., 1959– II. Grossner, Karl, 1950–
III. Janelle, Donald G., 1940–
QP491.S66 2014
152.14'2—dc23
2014016284

10 9 8 7 6 5 4 3 2 1

Contents

Preface

This book is about research on human learning and education that focuses on thinking and reasoning about space and spatiality. The three of us share a professional interest in space and spatiality as central components in understanding the natural and cultural worlds, as well as in the abstract or metaphorical worlds of art, literature, and mathematics. Furthermore, we believe that promoting spatial thinking in educational curricula is worthwhile and that intellectual questions about such a profound property of reality—so concrete and pervasive yet so abstract and suited to metaphor—are utterly fascinating.

The book originated in an interdisciplinary workshop organized by the three of us and held on September 12, 2011 during the tenth biennial Conference on Spatial Information Theory (COSIT) at Belfast, Maine. The title of the workshop was Ontology of Spatial Thinking and Reasoning: Multi-Disciplinary Reconciliation. Owing to our particular interest in spatial learning and education, we further refined the topic and issued a call for chapter proposals. Only some of the proposals we received came from people who had attended the COSIT workshop. The three of us evaluated all the proposals independently. The edited collection consists of thirteen chapters by scholars from a variety of disciplinary fields, an introductory chapter by the editors, and a two-chapter epilogue graciously authored by two top scholars of spatial thinking and education, Michael F. Goodchild and Nora S. Newcombe.

We extend special thanks to the participants who encouraged us to proceed with an edited book on themes related to the discussions that took place during the COSIT workshop, and to the authors for their contributions. We are grateful to Mike and Nora for reading all the manuscripts and for their insights into the potential value of embedding spatial thinking in curricula. We thank Philip Laughlin, Katie Persons, Paul Bethge, and Christopher Eyer at the MIT Press for their interest in the project and their patience in shepherding the book to completion. Finally, we thank one another for challenging and respectful discussions and for the sharing of expertise as this project was brought to fruition.

Daniel R. Montello
University of California, Santa Barbara
Karl Grossner
Stanford University
Donald G. Janelle
University of California, Santa Barbara

I Introduction and Conceptual Foundations

1 Concepts for Spatial Learning and Education: An Introduction

Daniel R. Montello, Karl Grossner, and Donald G. Janelle

This book discusses concepts and conceptualization relevant to the emerging field of spatial learning and education. Spatial learning and education is learning and education about (and with) space and spatiality, both informally and in formal educational settings, such as those involving classrooms, textbooks, or workbooks for K–16 education (that is, from kindergarten to a bachelor's degree). The three of us share a professional interest in space and spatiality as central components in understanding the natural and cultural worlds, as well as the abstract or metaphorical worlds of art, literature, and mathematics. Furthermore, we believe that promoting spatial thinking in educational curricula is worthwhile and that intellectual questions about such a profound property of reality—so concrete and pervasive yet so abstract and suited to metaphor—are utterly fascinating. We recognize there is increasing interest across several disciplines and problem domains in the role of space and spatiality in thinking, learning, reasoning, and communication, and in the possibility of explicitly educating students about space and spatiality (Liben 2006; National Research Council 2006; Newcombe and Frick 2010). There has recently occurred what has been termed a "spatial turn" in many disciplines (Bodenhamer, Corrigan, and Harris 2010; Dear, Ketchum, Luria, and Richardson 2011; Goodchild and Janelle 2010; Scholten, van de Velde, and van Manen 2009; Warf and Arias 2009), quite possibly motivating a desire to develop educational curricula specifically focusing on spatiality. This spatial turn may also have encouraged an emerging focus by researchers and educators on understanding spatial conceptualization, language, learning, and problem solving more generally, across various academic and non-academic contexts. In this introductory chapter, we draw on the emerging interest in spatial thinking and (1) set forth the intellectual context of ideas and challenges that have guided the editors and chapter authors, (2) present problems associated with spatial-concept learning and education, (3) pose opportunities for advancing research on spatial concept understanding and use, and (4) present an overview of the book's content, highlighting how the authors of specific chapters augment our understanding of spatial thinking in different disciplines and contribute to spatial learning and education.

We believe this education focus on spatiality should be informed by the various research activities involving spatial thinking and reasoning that have been ongoing for several decades in such research fields as spatial cognition, geographic information systems, spatial econometrics, spatial humanities, data visualization, and other areas of innovation. We see obvious connections among the goals of these different communities, but they have been fairly separate thus far. We believe that bringing them together and exploring similarities and differences among their work will potentially benefit them all. We especially support the idea that effective spatial education must be based on a thorough understanding of how people conceptualize and learn space and spatiality in a broad range of problem domains, including design, communication, optimization, navigation, and others that relate to daily-life experiences and behavior and to spatial tasks associated with different professions.

Spatial learning and education pose definite intellectual and empirical challenges for researchers and educators. Its multi-disciplinary nature makes communication across disciplines confusing at times, with multiple terms and frameworks that are not easily translated or that are used differently by different communities. The tension between empirical and theoretical approaches (possibly most pronounced in comparing the humanities and the sciences, and in the sometimes incompatible goals of basic and applied research) is particularly challenging for this area, in part because spatiality is so ubiquitous but also so abstract. It has often been noted that simple, unambiguous definitions of terms such as "spatial thinking," "spatial learning," and "spatial intelligence" are hard to come by; just defining "spatiality" in the first place without invoking space is infamously difficult, as we consider further below. But at the same time we recognize these challenges, we want to develop education programs that enhance "spatial literacy" (itself an ambiguous term). Furthermore, a correlation between spatial reasoning skills and educational and professional performance in many scientific and technological fields has been demonstrated. If spatial intelligence or spatial thinking ability can be improved in the course of education and/or professional practice, where and how will it happen in the contexts of educational curricula and professional development? Although the editors and chapter authors offer evidence and speculate on possible answers to this question, readers are encouraged to approach these findings and suggestions with a critical mind, recognizing that there remain substantive research and institutional challenges to effective implementation of spatial curricula for education and lifelong learning. In the balance of this introduction, we address (1) questions about the meaning and possible interpretations of space and spatiality, (2) the importance of spatial concepts and conceptualizations, and (3) the case for spatial learning and education.

What Are Space and Spatiality?

We consider first the thorny problem of defining space and spatiality (Sklar 1974; van Fraassen 1985). It is thorny in part because space and spatiality is ubiquitous in experience and reality. Avoiding circularity in the definition is therefore quite difficult, perhaps impossible. The circularity is evident in any dictionary definition, where one finds "space" in the general sense we mean here—much broader than the common lay use of the term to refer to *outer* space—defined as something like "the dimensions of height, depth, and width within which all things exist and move" (source: http://www.oxforddictionaries.com/definition/english/space). Although we cite a specific dictionary definition here, others are similarly circular, using words like "extent," "extension," "area," "depth," "boundless," or "dimensions," all of which require the concept of space for their interpretation. Similarly, "spatial" is typically defined by an expression like "of or relating to space" (source: *Webster's Third New International Dictionary of the English Language*, 1986). Montello and Raubal (2012, p. 249) proposed to define spatiality as the "property of reality that reflects the fact that everything is not at one location," which is only slightly tongue-in-cheek and may be a little less circular than many other definitions.

Fully appreciating how difficult it is to generate a clear and non-circular definition of space and spatial, we nonetheless feel it is worthwhile and important to try. Among other reasons, having a clear understanding of what constitutes space and spatiality is necessary for delimiting what the focus and purpose of spatial education should be (although not sufficient by itself, of course). Indeed, we have frequently encountered broad uses of terms like "spatial thinking" or "spatial learning" that seem appropriate only because they involve some phenomenon that exists in space. Surely we do not want to classify any learning or education involving entities in space or entities with spatial properties as "spatial learning" or "spatial education." After all, all learning, certainly including formal education, occurs in space, involving materials with spatial properties and pedagogical content that concerns entities in space and with spatial properties, at least implicitly (even if it is some form of imaginary or fictional space). Learning literature or arithmetic involves entities that have spatial extent and are accessed in part through their spatiality (e.g., the left to right interpretation of sentences or equations, the orthography of perceiving letters and other symbols, etc.). Instead, we suggest restricting spatial learning and education to learning and education that is primarily, or at least centrally, about spatiality—that focuses on problems that engage spatial properties and their manipulation as a core component, as for example in architectural design, wayfinding, or graph interpretation.

One could explicate (without defining) the meaning of spatiality by listing spatial properties, which would include location, size, distance, direction, shape, connectivity, overlap, dimensionality, hierarchy, and more. Such a list would be large and diverse, although not unlimited. Presumably, it would be useful to organize this list into related terms, such as those reflecting properties of the same dimensionality, of the same discreteness or continuity, at the same scale (relative size), at the same level of geometric sophistication (i.e., topological, projective, affine, or metric geometry), etc. In chapter 11 in this book, Grossner and Janelle take this approach of exploring lists of spatial concepts in different domains as a way to approach the problem of understanding what is the domain of spatial learning and education.

What Are Concepts and Conceptualization?

In addition to the meaning of spatiality, we can consider the question of what concepts are. This too is an abstract question, with a long history of diverse answers (Margolis and Laurence 1999), although it does not beg the question nearly so much as defining spatiality does. We can say in a fairly straightforward way that concepts are the semantic ideas that constitute our understanding of the world and the objects and events that exist in it (whether represented in words or other sign systems). A little more specifically, human beings universally organize the world into categories of entities sharing some form of similarity, and concepts are the intellectual bases for defining the similarity (this is not to say that all humans or human groups necessarily organize in the same way). A little more abstractly, in semiotic terms, concepts are the interpretants that connect sign-vehicles to referents in the world, whether real or hypothetical (MacEachren 1995) or, alternatively, to referents in cognitive models of the world (Kuhn, Raubal, and Gärdenfors 2007). For example, the concept of a dog connects the verbal sign-referent "dog" to the hairy four-legged creature that barks and wags its tail (or to our understanding of that creature).

That said, there have been and still are many trenchant questions about the meaning and nature of concepts, questions that are at the foundation of established research programs in philosophy, psychology, linguistics, and other disciplines. Many have claimed that concepts are to be limited to propositional statements—claims about something that can be phrased in the form of "it is true that ... ," but others do not want to limit concepts in this way, presumably because such a limitation excludes forms of thinking and understanding we want to include, such as sensory imagery or emotionality. Clearly, we have propositional knowledge about spatiality (e.g., "objects that overlap must partially exist in the same space") but we also experience or reason with spatiality in ways we could not or do not express propositionally. More fundamentally, there has long been the question as to whether concepts are properties of the world (abstracta) or only properties of mental representations of the world, or perhaps that they always arise from an interaction of mind and world (i.e., the nature of concepts has been a prominent arena for arguing the mind-body question). Some scholars reject a propositional approach to understanding concepts because they believe no meaning is captured well in terms of the truth of a concept's correspondence to a reality, but instead meaning refers to the way a concept expresses a person's or culture's cognitive model of reality (Kuhn, Raubal, and Gärdenfors 2007). Other questions about the nature of concepts involve whether the form of their mental representation is more like a natural or formal language, a mental image, a spatial model, or something else; how concepts relate to spoken or written natural language, and thus how concepts do or do not vary across cultural groups; whether concepts are necessarily decomposable into primitive or elemental concepts; and more. Additionally, a given spatial concept is seldom used in isolation of other spatial concepts. An example is the application of the overlay concept in geographic information systems, where the concept "overlay" relates to the areal coverage of distinct phenomena in space (soil types, vegetation, hydrology, and so on) to identify regions (another spatial concept) based on overlaps among phenomena as displayed cartographically.

Several different theories of the composition of concepts have been explored in the literature, ranging from the classical idea that concepts delimit a modestly-sized finite set of necessary and sufficient conditions for something to be an example of some type or member of a category (a mostly untenable view, except for formal entities such as those defined in geometry); to the idea of prototype theory that concepts are sets of properties related with varying degrees of similarity to a "good" or "best" schematization of the core meaning of the concept; to the idea of concepts as theories of essential identity that explain why entities have the properties they have or act as they do. Various shades of all these exist, as well as other theoretical approaches altogether (Margolis and Laurence 1999).

We feel comfortable recognizing that concepts and conceptualization are real and are important to learning, knowledge, and reasoning, even if we grant that their ultimate nature is still a matter of debate. We note, however, that much of the academic literature in psychology and philosophy (as in Margolis and Laurence 1999) seems to focus on concepts as categories of entities, such as dogs, chairs, or events, and not on concepts as categories of properties and relations. Properties and relations would be central in spatial education, for example the spatial concepts of distance, location, and scale. We are not certain how straightforward it is to extend models of concepts of entities to models of spatial properties of entities and relations between them. Is it important that concepts as entities are bounded while concepts as properties or relations are relatively unbounded? Perhaps we are really touching here on thinking explicitly with concepts versus thinking with properties and relations, only implicitly with concepts. After all, when one imagines the directions to various places when deciding which way to travel, one is thinking with the spatial property of direction but not *about the concept* of direction.

Thus, we recognize that while concepts and conceptualization are important to human cognition and behavior, they are not all that is relevant to learning and education. Besides conceptual knowledge, humans make decisions and in general interact with the world on the basis of perceptual and motor activity. Much coordinated behavior reflects automatized habits and skilled behavior—I did not employ conceptualization in order to drive home this evening, but I (or my nervous system interacting with the world) definitely processed spatial information in order to pull this off effectively. Thinking, or cognition more broadly, involves low-level and high-level mental processes, implicit and explicit processes (varying in their degree of conscious awareness), and processes that are both bottom-up and top-down. Formal education perhaps most frequently involves relatively high-level tasks, such as those that engage reasoning, communication, imagination, symbolic representation and interpretation, and the like— tasks that are thought to incorporate internally represented spatial knowledge that is potentially accessed explicitly. The relative focus of spatial learning and education on explicit conceptual knowledge vs. other, more implicit forms of spatial knowledge is a substantial question for designers of spatial education and is addressed in several chapters in this book, especially in parts II and IV.

A word about ontologies

The goal of making spatial concepts explicit has been shared over many years by diverse and largely unconnected groups of researchers, and in the next section of this chapter we review some of that work having a particularly pedagogical focus. In the last couple of decades, however, another multi-disciplinary group of researchers, loosely grouped in the field of information theory (including spatial and geographic information), have also attempted to enumerate and in cases organize spatial concepts, under the rubric of *ontology*. Much of this work has been driven not by educational objectives, but by software application requirements.

In the traditional philosophical sense, ontology can be thought of as answering the question "What *is* there?"—i.e., the question of what is the nature of reality, including all types of phenomena and their properties and relations. Those prominently included spatial properties and relations, typically expressed in terms of topology, mereology (the study of parts and wholes), or some type of metric geometry (Smith 1998). Throughout much of the twentieth century, in contrast, various theories within philosophy and the behavioral and cognitive sciences have promoted approaches to comprehending reality and our understanding of reality that see our understanding as reflecting our mental models of reality rather than the reality itself (Kuhn, Raubal, and Gärdenfors 2007).

Such cognitivist approaches to semantics have dovetailed with a desire to understand computational systems and improve their usability for humans. It was recognized that digital representations of reality in computational systems are also essentially models of reality. This led to the burgeoning fields of theoretical and applied formal ontology, which attempt to express ontologies in the formal languages of mathematics, symbolic logic, and the like. Smith (1998) has pointed out that the idea of formal ontology was first proposed by Husserl more than a hundred years ago. A number of researchers within the communities of computational intelligence and information systems, including artificial intelligence (AI), computational linguistics, and database design in various domains (biomedical information, geographic information, etc.), have developed an active interest in formal ontology, including the formal ontology of space and spacetime (Guarino 1998; Uschold and Gruninger 1996).

Computational ontologists have recognized the difficulty or even impossibility of capturing all relevant models of the world within a single kind of ontology (Guarino 1998). Very general aspects of reality that should hold across disciplines and topic areas have been proposed to make up a "top-level" (or foundation) ontology. Examples would be space, time, matter, object, and event. Aspects of some reality that would be appropriate for particular domains, or for particular tasks and not others, are subsumed under top-level ontologies and are known as "domain" and "task" ontologies. Subsumed under these are "application" ontologies that apply to particular tasks within the context of particular domains.

The idea that some ontologies and ontology patterns apply very broadly, perhaps universally, and others apply very narrowly or only in specific contexts, presages the question we raise below as to the advisability or viability of developing a domain-general spatial education versus only domain-specific versions. In a way, this book could be considered an ontological investigation into the nature of space and spatiality. We have asked researchers with quite diverse backgrounds and interests, all deeply concerned with spatial concepts and conceptualization, to contribute their own perspectives and priorities in order to inform our collective effort to improve spatial learning and education.

Spatial Concepts, Spatial Thinking, Spatial Learning, and Spatial Education: Why Are They Important?

Spatial concepts are important because they are the basis for much of what we consider to be spatial thinking. Spatial thinking is important because of the critical function it plays in so many tasks—whether specialized or generic, mundane or extraordinary, performed by experts or by novices. Spatial learning in educational and everyday settings is important because it holds the promise of improving spatial thinking, which in turn holds the promise of contributing to a host of desirable outcomes, including generating economic development, making more user-friendly and functional technology, fostering equitable access to employment, and generally helping people realize their potential. To the extent that these claims are valid, there is little doubt that spatial concepts, thinking, and learning are quite important and worthy of our attention as academics, researchers, and educators (National Research Council 2006; Newcombe and Frick 2010).

We can expand on this argument a little. As we have seen, spatial concepts are the structured beliefs people (individually or collectively) hold about the spatial properties of individual and classes of entities, and of the relations among sets of entities and classes of entities. These entities may be real, imagined, or metaphorical. Notwithstanding the caveat that humans frequently act in space in a coordinated manner without invoking conceptual knowledge, conceptual thinking about space and spatiality provides a basis for reasoning about spatiality, playing a central role in numerous human activities and helping to solve numerous problems (Montello and Raubal 2012). It is difficult to overstate the importance and ubiquity of spatial conceptual thinking. People think spatially in order to orient themselves and find their way efficiently to their destinations. Activity planning is part of this, such as when people decide the sequence of their activities based on their beliefs about the relative locations of activity settings. People think spatially as they experience their surroundings, comprehending the meaning of events and objects in part based on the spatial context of the places where the events and objects are encountered; this spatial (or "placial") context becomes a fundamental organizing basis for storing experience in memory (Burgess, Maguire, and O'Keefe 2002) and is of special significance in the humanities where "sense of place" plays a crucial role in establishing meaning to life and human activities (Bodenhamer, Corrigan, and Harris 2010). People think spatially when they choose mechanical tools and manipulate them appropriately, whether in cooking, carpentry, or surgery. People think spatially when they design efficient, functional, or aesthetic relationships between physical entities and environmental settings, whether designing buildings to take advantage of sun directions or *chi* flow, or just packing luggage into a car's trunk so it all fits efficiently without crushing anything. People think spatially when they interpret maps and other geographic information displays, graphs, paintings, and other semiotic entities that express information literally or metaphorically via spatial properties of the symbols and their relations. People also think spatially when they interpret spatiality described in written or spoken natural language, and when they transmit spatiality themselves in verbal descriptions. Such verbal spatiality is not limited to explicit spatial instructions, such as how to put together a toy or find a restaurant—it is replete in narrative fiction and is a key to understanding and enjoying many novels, short stories, and poems.

In sum, we have offered a case for the importance of spatial concepts in the worlds of science and art, and in the planning and organization of human landscapes and human activities. However, if there is a case for embedding explicit opportunities for spatial learning within formal education, then it is also critical that we address the intellectual and institutional contexts of education, drawing on grounded research about spatial concept understanding and its uses across disciplines and in practical applications.

Spatial Education

We believe the emerging development of explicit spatial education should be informed by the research on spatial thinking, learning, and reasoning that has been ongoing for several decades. Behavioral and cognitive scientists have conducted research on human conceptualizations of space for many decades, primarily in the fields of psychology (Newcombe and Huttenlocher 2000), linguistics (Bloom, Peterson, Nadel, and Garrett 1996), and anthropology (Sheets-Johnstone 1990). Spatial researchers in disciplines like geography, geology, and architecture have also shared an interest in understanding and improving how people learn and use spatial concepts to think about spatial problems in their respective domains. More recently, computer and information scientists have become interested in how their databases and computer systems instantiate models of reality, including its spatiality, and how they can design such databases and systems to be compatible with human understanding. In essence, the book we introduce in this chapter is based on the premise that spatial thinking should become an explicit focus of education, promoting it from a subject of incidental and sporadic treatment in uncoordinated disciplinary lessons into a coherent and fundamental push coordinated across disciplines. To put it another way, we endorse Montello's (2008) proposal to add a fourth R to the three educational R's (Reading, 'Riting, and 'Rithmetic): *Räumlichkeit*, the German word for "spatiality." (There is no English word for "space" or "spatial" that begins with an R, and, after English, German may be the most common language of research relevant to research on spatial learning and education.) In advancing this fourth R, we examine briefly its foundations in cognitive and behavioral sciences and in geography and geographic information systems (GIS) education, elaborate on its importance to STEM (science, technology, engineering, and mathematics) learning, and consider its potential as a catalyst for transdisciplinary and collaborative problem solving.

Roots in Psychometrics and Differential Psychology

One of the earliest scholarly efforts to develop spatial education came from psychologists interested in measuring spatial thinking ability (or abilities) and how they differed across individual people. This research started in the nineteenth century and was especially prominent during the early to mid twentieth century (Eliot 1987; Fruchter 1954; Lohman 1996). Measuring spatial abilities was part of the earliest traditions of *psychometrics*, the subdiscipline of psychology that attempts to measure mental responses that do not correspond in a direct way to any objectively measurable stimulus or property of a person or of the world. General aptitude tests such as the SAT and the GRE include spatial thinking items, although these items are typically aggregated with nonspatial logical and mathematical items when used to make admissions decisions. This psychometric work had the basic-science goal of understanding human mental abilities and the practical goal of selecting people for particular tasks or professions. If an activity requires spatial thinking for its successful completion, then people who think better spatially should be more likely to succeed at it. These scholarly pursuits continue today; tests of spatial thinking are sometimes used, for example, to select from applicants to dental or medical schools (Hegarty, Keehner, Cohen, Montello, and Lippa 2007).

Of course, researchers are quite interested in *explaining* patterns of individual and group differences, not just describing them (McGee 1979). Efforts to measure spatial abilities focus first on treating each individual person as potentially different from other individuals, but scholars (and laypeople) often want to organize and interpret these variations in terms of groups of individuals, most commonly groups based on sex or age (Newcombe and Huttenlocher 2000; Voyer, Voyer, and Bryden 1995), but also those based on professional experience, scholastic major, language, or other aggregating factors. Presumably, identifying group patterns suggests something about the genesis of the variations, but this causal link is quite ambiguous to make, largely because variables such as sex, age, and culture cannot be experimentally manipulated. An excellent discussion of these issues is found in appendix C of the report by the National Research Council's Committee on Support for Thinking Spatially (2006). One common misunderstanding in this regard is the notion that just because some trait is genetically determined, it is necessarily immutable, and that because some trait is modifiable, it must be caused by experiences after birth (or conception) rather than by genetics. Neither of these complementary claims are true. Everyone accepts that body weight is substantially genetically determined at the same time they accept that body weight is also quite modifiable (for those of us with will power, anyway).

Although the validity of using measures of spatial abilities to select personnel would hold to some degree no matter how stable these differences were, it would be more valid to do so if the differences were relatively unmodifiable by training or other experiences. In contrast, if the performance of spatial tasks is not particularly stable and can be substantially modified by explicit training or other experiences, the traditional notion of abilities as stable traits becomes weakened. Of course, if the performance of spatial tasks is readily modifiable, it would be critically important to know that and to know how best to modify them, how long-lasting such modifications would be, and so on. There is an emerging body of research showing that some forms of spatial abilities are trainable, at least to some extent (Lohman and Nichols 1990; Newcombe and Frick 2010), but these are ongoing questions that are actively being researched. For example, the field of medical education continues debating the degree to which the abilities involved in, for example, learning anatomy or performing surgery are modifiable (Hegarty, Keehner, Cohen, Montello, and Lippa 2007).

Over the course of more than a hundred years, psychometric researchers developed and published more than a hundred tests to measure one or another component of spatial thinking. Performance on these spatial intelligence tests were typically developed and interpreted by factor analyzing their patterns of scores; the resulting summary factors have been described by terms such as "spatial visualization" or "spatial orientation." Evidence of distinct components or factors of spatial abilities has long made it clear that we should not conceive of spatial thought as a unitary, monolithic ability. But even this long-standing insight from psychometrics may undersell the multifarious nature of spatial thought (Hegarty and Waller 2005). The components of spatial thinking derived from the psychometric tradition are almost entirely based on "pictorial" tests—two-dimensional, abstract spatial problems presented on pieces of paper or computer screens. But spatial thinking, as we have seen, is much more than this, involving a rich variety of tasks and situation contexts at different spatial scales, dimensionalities, and levels of geometric sophistication. Increasingly, researchers are recognizing limits to the generality of current forms of psychometric spatial tests.

Roots in Geography and Geographic Information Science

A second effort to develop spatial education has come from researchers and teachers interested in educating students about geography, particularly when conceived of as primarily a "spatial" science. Although this is not the only way to think of geography, the spatial tradition in geography has ancient origins, displayed prominently in the cartographic achievements of Claudius Ptolemy (circa 100–178 AD). Later, geo-spatial concepts were at the core of what Bernhardus Verenius described as "general geography" in his 1650 publication of Geographia Generalis—a volume that was republished several times with updates by notable editors, including one by Isaac Newton in 1681 for teaching geography at Cambridge University; these edited versions of Varenius' work were standard texts in the leading early colonial colleges of America for more than 100 years (Warntz 1989). This spatial tradition was revived in geography's quantitative revolution in the 1950s, and became the focus of research and teaching programs structured around such themes as theoretical geography (Bunge 1962), general spatial systems theory (Coffey 1981), spatial analysis, GIS, and geographic information science (GIScience) (Goodchild 1992).

A specific focus on spatial reasoning about geographic problems emerged gradually but simultaneously with mid-twentieth-century developments in spatial approaches to geography, typically through attempts to distill a finite set of basic or fundamental spatial concepts relevant to geographic education. Nystuen (1968) discussed the idea of understanding geographic analysis in terms of "fundamental spatial concepts." Golledge (1992) further developed the idea of basic spatial concepts, specifically offering them as a rational basis for the design of geographic education curricula. Plumert (1993) explored the implications for geographic education of spatial knowledge development in children. Among the others who have explored an explicit link between spatial concepts and educational development are Gersmehl and Gersmehl (2006) and Golledge, Marsh, and Battersby (2008).

Golledge, Marsh, and Battersby (2008) proposed that spatial concepts could be arranged into five levels defined in terms of the abstractness and complexity of their relationship to a small set of "Level I" primitive spatial concepts, proposed here to include identity (not itself spatial but thematic), location, magnitude, and space-time (the idea of dynamic spatial phenomena). Building on the Level I Primitives, according to these authors, are Level II Simple concepts (e.g., direction, distance), Level III Difficult concepts (e.g., center, growth), Level IV Complicated concepts (e.g., connectivity, scale), and Level V Complex concepts (e.g., central place, projection). The authors empirically investigated the lowest three levels of their taxonomy by asking grade-school children to perform various tests designed to assess their spatial comprehension. For instance, one test required students to generate spatial terms corresponding to concepts depicted pictorially.

Linked to this push from geographic education has been the notion that GIS technology would be an especially effective way to teach spatial concepts and foster spatial reasoning skills, at all levels of formal education from kindergarten through a bachelor's degree. This notion has ranged from the idea that simply using a generic GIS will stimulate spatial thinking to the idea that GIS can be specially designed to support the effective teaching of spatial concepts and reasoning (Lee and Bednarz 2009; National Research Council 2006). Several scholars have advocated, and continue to advocate, for the incorporation of GIS technologies into the classroom at all grade levels. In fact, a handful of courses have been developed around understanding and using GIS as the basis for spatial thinking curricula (Sinton 2009; Spatial Literacy in Teaching, http://www.le.ac.uk/gg/splint/). It is interesting to note that using GIS to stimulate and improve spatial thinking is somewhat converse to one of the original insights of GIScience that we should understand how humans think spatially (and otherwise) so we can improve GIS technologies (Mark and Frank 1991; Montello 2009).

However, some scholars have cast doubt on the advisability of using GIS as the primary tool to teach spatial thinking. For examples, see the position papers of participating researchers and educators in the 2012 Specialist Meeting on "Spatial Thinking Across the College Curriculum" at http://www.spatial.ucsb.edu/events/STATCC/participants.php. Various concerns arise here, including the fact that not all spatiality is geographic and not all geography is spatial (Ishikawa 2013). Perhaps of more concern is that spatial technologies as they exist now work mostly by replacing spatial thinking, rather than enhancing it. In many cases, for instance, technology turns a thinking problem into a perception problem—one enters a command and then reads the answer off the screen. Consider, for example, how GPS vehicle navigation has displaced the use of maps and the reasoning process involved in navigation between locations. Recognizing this and other problems with basing spatial education on GIS technology (hardware and maintenance costs, need for teacher training), some voices promoting GIS for spatial education recommend it play a supporting role only: "Taken alone, GIS is not the answer to the problem of teaching spatial thinking in American schools; however, it can play a significant role in an answer." (National Research Council 2006, p. 8)

The attempt to incorporate GIS technology into spatial education is certainly going to continue. We believe the best bet for the success of this effort is to design systems with spatial education as their goal, not simply shoehorning generic systems into this purpose. This echoes Marsh, Golledge, and Battersby's (2007) proposal to develop a "Minimal GIS" with grade-appropriate pedagogy as its driving inspiration. That is, instead of trying to build systems that will most efficiently solve geospatial problems, appealing to other kinds of bottom lines, we need to build systems designed first and foremost to stimulate mental activity and learning about space and place.

Roots in Science Literacy and STEM Education

A third, more recent effort to develop explicit spatial education has come from a push to improve training in natural science and engineering fields in the United States. In the early 2000s, the National Science Foundation coined the acronym to highlight the need for better educational outcomes in those fields and provide material support for research activities that would ostensibly contribute to that goal. The advent of the acronym manifests a growing urgent concern about science literacy (Laugksch 2000) and American competitiveness in the increasingly global landscape driving so much of the world economy (Gonzalez and Kuenzi 2012). The American Association for the Advancement of Science, a primary initiator of this discussion, has promoted science literacy as "what all students should know and be able to do in science, mathematics, and technology by the time they graduate from high school" (AAAS 1993, p. xi) and specified its conceptual content in a progression of increasing complexity in application through grade levels K–12. At this writing, the STEM learning focus continues to grow, evidenced by two major learning standards initiatives for schools in the United States, Common Core State Standards Initiative (CCSS; http://www.corestandards.org/) and Next Generation Science Standards (NGSS; http://www.nextgenscience.org/).

Improving spatial learning and developing spatial education has emerged as a major focus of the push to improve STEM education and increase the supply of U.S. trained scientists and engineers. This is based on the proposed importance of spatial thinking in STEM fields and the idea that improving spatial skills will improve training in STEM fields and increase access of STEM professions to underrepresented groups, including women and some ethnic minorities. *Learning to Think Spatially* (National Research Council 2006) argued this case forcefully. (See also Uttal and Cohen 2012.) The report recommended that a program of scientific research be supported to better understand the link between spatial thinking and STEM and to experimentally evaluate instructional practices in the spatial domain. The same year this report was published, the National Science Foundation funded a program exactly along those lines, the Spatial Intelligence Learning Center, headquartered at Temple University; it has recently been refunded through 2016. The stated mission of the center is "to develop the new science of spatial learning and to use this knowledge to transform STEM educational practice."

As Gonzalez and Kuenzi (2012) observe, STEM originally (and still, for many people and institutions) referred to biophysical sciences only (as well as math and engineering). However, for the National Science Foundation, STEM now includes behavioral and social sciences. Presumably, spatial thinking is not equally involved in the reasoning and problem solving of all these scientific disciplines. A more dramatic development that has garnered interest from NSF and from industry is the transition from STEM to STEAM, the A standing for Art; the intent here is to highlight the potential for innovation by bringing together the cultures of art and science. Art programs focus on creativity in a broad range of disciplines that are spatial in their conceptions and execution. A partial list includes apparel design and textile art, architecture, ceramics, digital media (film, animation, video), furniture design, glass, graphic design, history of art and visual culture, illustration, industrial design, interior architecture, jewelry and metalsmithing, landscape architecture, painting, photography, printmaking, and sculpture. It is possible that a broad integration of STEM with art will help to foster an implicit spatial frame of mind for learning, potentially encouraging creativity that could benefit society.

Multi-Disciplinary, Inter-Disciplinary, and Trans-Disciplinary Visions

Besides the disciplinary-specific motivations we have just reviewed (differential psychology, geography/GIScience, STEM/STEAM education), one can identify other contributions to the emergence of explicit spatial education. Child and developmental psychologists have long studied the development of spatial thinking skills, strategies, and mental representations in children (Newcombe and Huttenlocher 2000). Scholars within several other disciplines have shown interest in the idea that educating students specifically in spatial thinking will improve learning of their subject. Prominent examples include geology and other earth sciences (Kastens and Ishikawa 2006), chemistry (Wu and Shah 2004), physics (Pallrand and Seeber 1984), astronomy (Taylor, Barker, and Jones 2003), mathematics (Battista 2007; Bishop 1980), medicine and dentistry (Hegarty, Keehner, Cohen, Montello, and Lippa 2007), and architecture (Roberts 2007). But education in spatial thinking is not relevant only to academic or scientific pursuits. It applies to many non-academic pursuits, such as carpentry, sewing, auto mechanics, interior decorating, taxi driving, athletics, and more (Gauvain 1993; National Research Council 2006). Whether academic, technical, or otherwise, spatial thinking in these domains is relevant to thinking about phenomena that make up the domain of interest itself (such as the spatial arrangement of molecules or furniture) as well as thinking *with* symbolic representations that encode spatial properties of the phenomena, such as maps, graphs, photographs, verbal descriptions, or physical models (Card, MacKinlay, and Schneiderman 1999; Hegarty and Just 1993; MacEachren 1995).

Spatial education is clearly a very multidisciplinary endeavor. We hope with this book to push it toward *inter*disciplinarity, implying the emergence of at least some common vocabulary and methods concerning spatial teaching and research that is shared across disciplines. Sometimes the term *trans*disciplinary is used to imply studies that don't merely combine disciplines but transcend them; a truly general spatial education that we can imagine would not be contained within any single discipline or even any single set of related disciplines. We see the potential audience for discussions of spatial learning and education as spanning many scientific and educational research communities concerned with spatial and spatio-temporal learning and education. It should also interest scholars in philosophy and in many engineering and design professions, including art, and dance.

Overview of the Book

This book presents a sampling of some of the major approaches to understanding the concepts, principles, and methods people with different backgrounds, disciplines, and purposes use to think, learn, and reason about spatial aspects of problems and situations, specifically exploring the implications of these approaches for educating people about space and spatiality. We hope the book contributes to advancing ongoing efforts to design and evaluate curricula to foster spatial thinking in the sciences, humanities, and other fields. It is intended to highlight broad aspects of our basic understanding of spatial thinking, learning, and reasoning, and to help bring together diverse disciplines and research communities, summarizing some of the work to date, exploring connections, and pointing toward future progress and potential for integration.

We have been guided in developing this book by several overarching questions. Can spatial ability and reasoning skills be improved by instructional practice, and presuming that it can, how? Are there spatial concepts, principles, and reasoning tasks that are general across all fields? If there are, what are they and how can they be characterized? What are useful or appropriate ways to organize these concepts and reasoning processes? Promising candidates include spatial scale (from nano to cosmic), the mental processes involved (mental rotation, pattern recognition, etc.), the context of activity (i.e., cognition in space, about space, with space), and the knowledge domain involved (e.g., the natural sciences, engineering, social sciences, art, mathematics, history). Can we identify and explicate the correct or most useful spatial conceptual distinctions within and across disciplines? Is a unified conceptual system (ontology) for spatial thinking and reasoning a feasible and worthwhile goal? If so, for what purposes? Or will it ultimately prove more productive to focus on discipline-specific approaches to spatial education? Of course, this book does not definitively answer these central questions, but we do believe it helps bring them into focus.

There are sixteen chapters, some of them focused particularly on education and others on spatial learning more generally. The chapters are organized in five parts, each of which we introduce with a short discussion.

Chapters 1–3 make up part I of the book. These chapters look at some of the philosophically broadest and most fundamental issues surrounding research on spatial learning and education.

In this introductory chapter, we present the topic of the book and its motivation. We consider broad issues concerning the meaning of space and spatiality, of concepts and conceptualization, and of spatial thinking in the context of learning and education. This chapter also lists some of the fundamental questions facing those who wish to construct explicit spatial curricula.

In chapter 2, Christian Freksa and Holger Schultheis of the Cognitive Systems Group at the University of Bremen argue that generic or universal approaches to spatial learning and education will fall short, because specific problem domains are so determinative of how people think about and reason with spatiality. Freksa and Schultheis present three approaches to spatial problem solving that differentially employ explicit or implicit mental representations of spatial properties, based on (1) knowledge in the world, or acting in space, (2) knowledge in the head, or solving spatial problems mentally, and (3) knowledge distributed between the world, the body, and the mind, or embodied and situated cognition. Clearly, many effective and efficient approaches to spatial problem solving exploit the specific spatial and temporal structures of a problem situation without explicitly representing them mentally. Spatial learning and education should not be constructed only around explicit, conceptual knowledge of space and spatiality, but recognize the role of spatial structure in the mind, in the body, and in objects and environmental surrounds. As a case in point, people often "think" spatially by directly interacting with and manipulating their physical spatial environment rather than by interacting with mental representations or external symbolic representations, such as verbal descriptions, graphs, or maps.

In chapter 3, John Bateman of the Department of Applied Linguistics at the University of Bremen and Sander Lestrade of the Department of Language Typology at the University of Amsterdam discuss the common role of spatial thinking of various types in almost all human activities. In many situations, however, spatial beliefs must be shared among individuals, and this most often occurs through natural language (English, German, etc.). Understanding how spatial language expresses meaning—expresses a spatial ontology—is very complex and involves a host of thorny issues concerning the mind and body, the mind and language, cross-linguistic similarities and differences, and more. In particular, there is no straightforward translation between spatial language and spatial meaning. This chapter highlights some of the subtle complexities of expressing and interpreting spatiality in language, a common format by which people learn spatial information, especially in formal educational settings.

The chapters in part II look at the role of visualization, both external (graphs, diagrams, maps) and internal (visual imagery and other mental spatial representations), in spatial learning and education.

Chapter 4 is authored by Mary Hegarty of the Department of Psychological & Brain Sciences at the University of California at Santa Barbara, Mike Stieff of the Department of Chemistry at the University of Illinois at Chicago, and Bonnie Dixon of the Department of Chemistry and Biochemistry at the University of Maryland. External and internal spatial representations are clearly critical to spatial learning and education, and this chapter contributes to our understanding of how the two types of spatial representations operate singly and in combination. The authors provide a novel framework for classifying strategies people use to solve spatial problems that distinguishes whether the strategy (1) recruits spatial versus nonspatial information, (2) relies primarily on internal versus external representations, and (3) involves modification of representations. As an example, the framework is applied to the domain of spatial problem solving in organic chemistry.

In chapter 5, Scott R. Hinze of the Department of Psychology and School of Education and Social Policy at Northwestern University,

Vickie M. Williamson of the Department of Chemistry at Texas A&M University, Mary Jane Shultz of the Department of Chemistry at Tufts University, Ghislain Deslongchamps of the Department of Chemistry at the University of New Brunswick, Kenneth C. Williamson of the Department of Construction Science at Texas A&M University, and David N. Rapp of the Department of Psychology at Northwestern University also discuss the role of external spatial representations (often called visualizations) in education, specifically science and engineering education. Such visualizations have long been used in science education, in part because of their power to depict spatial relationships, including those showing parts of reality that are too small or large, too slow or fast, or otherwise exist in reality in an obstructed, unobservable manner. However, an important question is how and how well these visualizations work for people of varying spatial abilities. The authors summarize literature on this question and present empirical evidence from their own work.

In chapter 6, Ranxiao Frances Wang of the Department of Psychology at the University of Illinois at Urbana-Champaign considers the fascinating possibility that humans can directly intuit spaces of four dimensions, and that the classic idea (as espoused by Kant and others) that human spatial apprehension is limited to three dimensions is not true. Phenomenological reports of four-dimensional spatial imagination have long been met with skepticism, and it is very difficult to evaluate such claims conclusively from systematic empirical exploration. But Wang attempts to do so and claims that such "extra-dimensional" spatial thought can be demonstrated. If so, we may need to expand our understanding of fundamental limits on spatial learning and education.

The chapters in part III expand on the theme set forth in chapter 2 by Freksa and Schultheis by providing perspectives from behavioral science on embodied spatial learning and education. Embodied cognition recognizes that humans usually interact "corporeally" with spatial properties of reality, and that this corporeal interaction is essential to how people understand space and learn about it.

David Waller of the Department of Psychology at Miami University lays out many of these conceptual issues in chapter 7. Waller advocates for understanding spatial learning and thinking not as mental spatial representations of the environment employing symbolic and arbitrary codes but as the mental structures and processes involved in perceiving and acting in the world. This is a novel conceptualization of spatial learning compared to a traditional cognitivist perspective—it does away with symbolic mental representation and makes it easier to explain a continuity between the thinking of humans and other animals. Waller applies his embodied approach to an analysis of spatial reference systems in thought.

In chapter 8, Evie Malaia of the Department of Linguistics at the University of Texas at Arlington and Ronnie B. Wilbur of the Department of Speech, Hearing, and Language Sciences at Purdue University remind us that spatial language is not only spoken or written, but exists for many people in a "manual" form, wherein static and dynamic spatial patterns of the hands and arms convey rich content about spatial properties and relations in the world. According to Malaia and Wilbur, sign language has profound effects on how its users perceive and conceive of spatiality in the world. An interesting implication for general spatial education is that some of the positive intellectual effects of using sign language can even be promoted in students without auditory impairments, when sign language is taught as a second language.

In chapter 9, Kinnari Atit and Thomas F. Shipley of the Department of Psychology and the Spatial Intelligence and Learning Center at Temple University and Basil Tikoff of the Department of Geology at the University of Wisconsin at Madison look at embodied spatial learning and education. Focusing not on sign language (a fully grammatically developed natural language) but on more common manual gestures used to convey spatial relations, they consider the notoriously difficult spatial problem of teaching students about the spatial properties of geological strata. They extend a previous framework for understanding spatial discourse and apply it to understanding gestures in spatial education in the geosciences.

In chapter 10, Alycia M. Hund of the Department of Psychology at Illinois State University discusses spatial strategies used during wayfinding, which consists of the orientation and decision-making components of coordinated travel through the environment. The strategy choice Hund specifically examines concerns thinking of the environment from a route perspective or a survey perspective. The route perspective is like a mental tour of the environment from a first-person, terrain-level perspective. It is conceptualized as embodied travel. In contrast, the survey perspective is like a disembodied, third-person view from above the environment. The distinction between route and survey strategies has emerged as one of the fundamental contrasts between different strategies for thinking spatially about the environment; it differentiates individuals, females and males, and approaches to problems phrased in different ways. The author advocates the value of promoting flexibility and adaptability in spatial strategy use as a way to improve spatial performance in a variety of problem-solving contexts.

Part IV consists of chapters 11–14, which examine the development and explicit instruction of spatial thinking and reasoning within and without the contexts of various disciplines.

In chapter 11, Diana S. Sinton, Executive Director of the University Consortium for Geographic Information Science, lays out many of the basic considerations for those who would design explicit spatial curricula. Although initially motivated within the context of geography and GIS, Sinton's efforts have gone beyond that to designing, implementing, and evaluating generic spatial curricula. She provides a working definition of spatial thinking as the ability to visualize and interpret location, position, distance, direction, movement, change, and relationships over space. The chapter concludes with specific advice for designing effective spatial curricula.

Chapter 12, by Karl Grossner of Stanford University Libraries and Donald G. Janelle of the Center for Spatial Studies at the University of California at Santa Barbara, is a wide-ranging investigation of spatial concepts and principles as they are used in many different disciplinary contexts, then organized into several categories in a speculative undergraduate course outline. The authors present empirical methods for identifying spatiality in the academic writing of various disciplines. The richness and heterogeneity of spatial concepts is nowhere on display more in this book than in this chapter.

In chapter 13, Thora Tenbrink of the Department of Linguistics and English Language at Bangor University, Christoph Hölscher of the Program in Cognitive Science at the Swiss Federal Institute of Technology, Dido Tsigaridi of the School of Design at Harvard University, and Ruth Conroy Dalton of the Department of Building Usability and Visualization at Northumbria University examine communicating about spatial and other properties of built spaces within another very spatial discipline: architecture. Interestingly, spatial conceptualization is different for the architect, the client, and a building's users. The variable spatial worldviews should be incorporated into spatial education, in this case, architectural education.

In chapter 14, Roger M. Downs of the Department of Geography at Pennsylvania State University uses a clever task to get at people's geo-spatial thinking in a way that avoids the pitfall of asking people to explicitly state their thoughts. The task, first suggested several decades ago by the geographic theorist William Bunge, provides people with part of a simple map-like representation of a landscape (including natural and cultural features) and asks them to predict what the neighboring landscape will look like. Downs analyzes possible responses to this task in terms of various levels of geo-spatial expertise, demonstrating the specialized nature that spatial learning can take with professionals who have spent many years thinking in particular spatial problem domains.

Part V contains two complementary epilogue chapters, one by Michael F. Goodchild, Emeritus Professor of Geography and Past Director of the Center for Spatial Studies at the University of California at Santa Barbara and one by Nora S. Newcombe of the Department of Psychology and the Spatial Intelligence and Learning Center at Temple University. These chapters nicely address fundamental issues concerning prospects and problems for developing effective spatial education and the role that spatial technologies play in spatial learning and education now and in the future.

Although no volume of modest size could capture more than a small fraction of the potential work and authors that might appropriately contribute to a book on this topic, we believe the chapters represent an interesting and important collection of multi-disciplinary scholarly thought on spatial conceptualization with implications for learning and education.

References

AAAS. 1993. *Benchmarks for Science Literacy*. ERIC Clearinghouse.

Battista, M. T. 2007. The development of geometric and spatial thinking. In *Second Handbook of Research on Mathematics Teaching and Learning*, ed. F. K. Lester Jr. Information Age.

Bishop, A. J. 1980. Spatial abilities and mathematics education—A review. *Educational Studies in Mathematics* 11: 257–269.

Bloom, P., Peterson, M. A., Nadel, L., and Garrett, M. F., eds. 1996. *Language and Space*. MIT Press.

Bodenhamer, D. J., Corrigan, J., and Harris, T. M., eds. 2010. *The Spatial Humanities: GIS and the Future of Humanities Scholarship*. Indiana University Press.

Bunge, W. 1962. *Theoretical Geography*. Department of Geography, Royal University of Lund

Burgess, N., Maguire, E. A., and O'Keefe, J. 2002. The human hippocampus and spatial and episodic memory. *Neuron* 35: 625–641.

Card, S. K., MacKinlay, J. D., and Schneiderman, B. 1999. *Readings in Information Visualization: Using Vision to Think*. Morgan Kaufmann.

Coffey, W. J. 1981. *Geography: Towards a General Spatial Systems Approach*. Methuen.

Dear, M., Ketchum, J., Luria, S., and Richardson, D., eds. 2011. *GeoHumanities: Art, History, Text at the Edge of Place*. Routledge.

Eliot, J. 1987. *Models of Psychological Space: Psychometric, Developmental, and Experimental Approaches*. Springer.

Fruchter, B. 1954. Measurement of spatial abilities: History and background. *Educational and Psychological Measurement* 14: 387–395.

Gauvain, M. 1993. The development of spatial thinking in everyday activity. *Developmental Review* 13: 92–121.

Gersmehl, P. J., and Gersmehl, C. A. 2006. Wanted: A concise list of neurologically defensible and assessable spatial-thinking skills. *Research in Geographic Education* 8: 5–38.

Golledge, R. G. 1992. Do people understand spatial concepts: The case of first-order primitives. In *Theories and Methods of Spatio-Temporal Reasoning in Geographic Space*, ed. A. U. Frank, I. Campari, and U. Formentini. Springer.

Golledge, R. G., Marsh, M., and Battersby, S. 2008. A conceptual framework for facilitating geospatial thinking. *Annals of the Association of American Geographers* 98: 285–308.

Gonzalez, H. B., and Kuenzi, J. J. 2012. Science, technology, engineering, and mathematics (STEM) education: A primer. Congressional Research Service, August 1.

Goodchild, M. F. 1992. Geographical information science. *International Journal of Geographical Information Systems* 6: 31–45.

Goodchild, M. F., and Janelle, D. G., eds. 2010. Toward critical spatial thinking in the social sciences and humanities. *GeoJournal* 75: 3–13.

Guarino, N. 1998. Formal ontology and information systems. In *Formal Ontology in Information Systems*, ed. N. Guarino. IOS Press.

Hegarty, M., and Just, M. A. 1993. Constructing mental models of machines from text and diagrams. *Journal of Memory and Language* 32: 717–742.

Hegarty, M., Keehner, M., Cohen, C. A., Montello, D. R., and Lippa, Y. 2007. The role of spatial cognition in medicine: Applications for selecting and training professionals. In *Applied Spatial Cognition: From Research to Cognitive Technology*, ed. G. L. Allen. Erlbaum.

Hegarty, M., and Waller, D. 2005. Individual differences in spatial abilities. In *The Cambridge Handbook of Visuospatial Thinking*, eds. P. Shah and A. Miyake. Cambridge University Press.

Ishikawa, T. 2013. Geospatial thinking and spatial ability: An empirical examination of knowledge and reasoning in geographical science. *Professional Geographer* 65: 636–646.

Kastens, K. A., and Ishikawa, T. 2006. Spatial thinking in the geosciences and cognitive sciences: A cross-disciplinary look at the intersection of the two fields. In *Earth and Mind: How Geologists Think and Learn about the Earth*, ed. C. A. Manduca and D. Mogk. Geological Society of America.

Kuhn, W., Raubal, M., and Gärdenfors, P. 2007. Editorial: Cognitive semantics and spatio-temporal ontologies [Special issue]. *Spatial Cognition and Computation* 7: 3–12.

Laugksch, R. C. 2000. Scientific literacy: A conceptual overview. *Science Education* 84: 71–94.

Lee, J., and Bednarz, R. 2009. Effect of GIS learning on spatial thinking. *Journal of Geography in Higher Education* 33: 183–198.

Liben, L. S. 2006. Education for spatial thinking. In *Handbook of Child Psychology*, sixth edition, volume 4: *Child Psychology in Practice*, ed. K. A. Renninger and I. E. Sigel. Wiley.

Lohman, D. F. 1996. Spatial ability and g. In *Human Abilities: Their Nature and Measurement*, ed. I. Dennis and P. Tapsfield. Erlbaum.

Lohman, D. F., and Nichols, P. D. 1990. Training spatial abilities: Effects of practice on rotation and synthesis tasks. *Learning and Individual Differences* 2: 67–93.

MacEachren, A. M. 1995. *How Maps Work: Representation, Visualization, and Design*. Guilford.

Margolis, E., and Laurence, S., eds. 1999. *Concepts: Core Readings*. MIT Press.

Mark, D. M., and Frank, A. U., eds. 1991. *Cognitive and Linguistic Aspects of Geographic Space*. Kluwer.

Marsh, M., Golledge, R., and Battersby, S. E. 2007. Geospatial concept understanding and recognition in G6–college students: A preliminary argument for minimal GIS. *Annals of the Association of American Geographers* 97: 696–712.

McGee, M. 1979. Human spatial abilities: Psychometric studies and environmental, genetic, hormonal, and neurological influences. *Psychological Bulletin* 86: 889–918.

Montello, D. R. 2008. Review of *Learning to Think Spatially*. *Journal of Environmental Psychology* 28: 104–106.

Montello, D. R. 2009. Cognitive research in GIScience: Recent achievements and future prospects. *Geography Compass* 3; 1824–1840.

Montello, D. R., and Raubal, M. 2012. Functions and applications of spatial cognition. In *Handbook of Spatial Cognition*, ed. D. Waller and L. Nadel. American Psychological Association.

National Research Council. 2006. *Learning to Think Spatially*. National Academies Press.

Newcombe, N. S., and Frick, A. 2010. Early education for spatial intelligence: Why, what, and how. *Mind, Brain, and Education* 4: 102–111.

Newcombe, N. S., and Huttenlocher, J. 2000. *Making Space: The Development of spatial representation and reasoning*. MIT Press.

Nystuen, J. D. 1968. Identification of some fundamental spatial concepts. In *Spatial Analysis: A Reader in Statistical Geography*, ed. B. J. L. Berry and D. F. Marble. Prentice-Hall.

Pallrand, G. J., and Seeber, F. 1984. Spatial ability and achievement in introductory physics. *Journal of Research in Science Teaching* 21: 507–516.

Plumert, J. M. 1993. The development of children's spatial knowledge: Implications for geographic education. *Cartographic Perspectives* 16: 9–18.

Roberts, A. S. 2007. Predictors of future performance in architectural design education. *Educational Psychology* 27: 447–463.

Scholten, H. J., van de Velde, R., and van Manen, N., eds. 2009. *Geospatial Technology and the Role of Location in Science*. Springer.

Sheets-Johnstone, M. 1990. *The Roots of Thinking*. Temple University Press.

Sinton, D. S. 2009. Roles for GIS within higher education. *Journal of Geography in Higher Education* 33: S7–S16.

Sklar, L. 1974. *Space, Time, and Spacetime*. University of California Press.

Smith, B. 1998. Basic concepts of formal ontology. In *Formal Ontology in Information Systems*, ed. N. Guarino. IOS Press.

Taylor, I., Barker, M., and Jones, A. 2003. Promoting mental model building in astronomy education. *International Journal of Science Education* 25: 1205–1225.

Uschold, M., and Gruninger, M. 1996. Ontologies: Principles, methods and applications. *Knowledge Engineering Review* 11: 93–136.

Uttal, D. H., and Cohen, C. A. 2012. Spatial thinking and STEM education: When, why and how. In *Psychology of Learning and Motivation*, volume 57, ed. B. H. Ross. Academic Press.

van Fraassen, B. C. 1985. *An Introduction to the Philosophy of Time and Space*, second edition. Columbia University Press.

Voyer, D., Voyer, S., and Bryden, M. P. 1995. Magnitude of sex differences in spatial abilities: A meta-analysis and consideration of critical variables. *Psychological Bulletin* 117: 250–270.

Warf, B., and Arias, S. 2009. *The Spatial Turn: Interdisciplinary Perspectives.* Routledge.

Warntz, W. 1989. Newton, the Newtonians, and the Geographia Generalis Varenii. *Annals of the Association of American Geographers* 79: 165–191.

Wu, H. K., and Shah, P. 2004. Exploring visuospatial thinking in chemistry learning. *Science Education* 88: 465–492.

2 Three Ways of Using Space

Christian Freksa and Holger Schultheis

By three methods we may learn wisdom:
first, by reflection, which is noblest;
second, by imitation, which is easiest;
and third, by experience,
which is the most bitter.

Confucius

Spatial and Temporal Structures Impose Constraints

Spatial structure is omnipresent in the physical world. This is true for the internal structure of physical objects, for their external relations to one another, for their relation to their environment, and for their relation to an observer inside or outside this environment. Spatial structure also is omnipresent in perception systems across a large variety of modalities, in biological memories, and in the motor mechanisms that cognitive agents and artifacts use for locomotion and for other types of motion, including motion of perceptual organs and motion of information-carrying signals inside and outside the cognitive agents. When motion or other forms of dynamics enter the picture, time and temporal structure are additionally involved: Temporal structure is omnipresent in processes, and the structure of time places additional constraints on top of the constraints imposed by spatial structures. Constraints impose limitations; they restrict what cognitive systems (e.g., humans or autonomous robots) can do. For example, because of spatio-temporal constraints, humans and robots cannot reach two different places at the same time with the same hand. Likewise, it is impossible to arrange three objects A, B, and C on a tabletop such that A is to the left of B, C is to the left of A, and B is to the left of C, from a given perspective. Does this mean that we should seek to avoid the constraints of spatial and temporal structures in order to avoid these limitations? In fact, in mathematics this has been the predominant and widely accepted view: More abstract approaches may be more general, and more general approaches are considered superior as they characterize a larger class of situations. In the tradition of mathematics and engineering, computer science and informatics have adopted the approach of seeking highly abstract, general ways of describing specific systems. (See, e.g., Kowalski 1980; Nilsson 1998.)

In this chapter we challenge the view that general approaches are generally to be preferred over specialized approaches. We will argue that—especially for many cognitive tasks—the specifics of the problem situation must be taken very seriously. We discuss three different approaches to solving spatial problems that differ in the extent to which they employ explicit or implicit representations of problem properties. We argue that approaches that exploit the specific spatial and temporal structures of the problem situation without explicitly representing them are crucial for obtaining cognitively plausible and performance-efficient solutions to spatial problems. Our result implies that spatial education should be built on students' experience from directly interacting with and manipulating their physical spatial environment rather than exclusively on the interaction with virtual models of physical space.

Spatial Problem Solving and Spatial Reasoning

In our terminology, the term *spatial problem solving* refers to solving problems of spatial nature or problems in space. Typical problems are navigation in space, rearranging spatial configurations, or locating objects in space. These problems are problems on the so-called *object level* of the spatial domain, the level at which space has physical and geometrical extension and structure. Purely mathematical geometric or algebraic statements, which may have a correspondence in extended space, are not spatial in the strong sense of the meaning.

For solving spatial problems with the help of computers, we need to transform the object-level properties of space into a form that is suitable for computers—for example into geometric or algebraic statements—as we cannot enter truly spatial entities themselves into the electronic brain. Thus, we put knowledge *about* the navigation task, *about* the spatial configurations, or *about* the object locations into the computer. Based on this knowledge, the computer can reason about the spatial entities and configurations. In order to meaningfully reason about space, the computer not only requires knowledge about the spatial entities and configurations in question; it also needs knowledge about the general properties of space and possibly also about properties of time. Knowledge about problems or about a domain addresses the problems or the domain on the *knowledge level*.

We could say that the knowledge about properties of space and time provides the computer with some understanding of spatial entities and configurations that enable it to solve problems on the meta level of the object domain, as it does not have direct access to the object level. Solving spatial problems on the knowledge level of course does not solve the original spatial problem; it only informs us about what a solution would look like. A knowledge-based solution may not inform us how to obtain the solution on the object level, as reasoning on the knowledge level of the problem may pursue a different route to solving the problem than would be possible on the object level. Even worse, we may be able to determine a solution only on the knowledge level but not on the object level. For example, our problem may be to divide an angle α into three equal parts. On the knowledge level of algebra the solution to this problem is $\alpha/3$. On the object level of space no method of geometric construction exists to divide arbitrary angles into three equal parts. In other words, the knowledge about what can be done in the spatial domain may abstract from the details of the physical problem-solving process. This shows that *understanding a domain* is necessarily limited to the level and detail of knowledge that is available; but it also shows that we may have knowledge about a spatial problem solution that cannot actually be generated.

Understanding a domain in which we want to solve problems is a great asset; it is an approach that is worthy of scientists. However, many situations confronting cognitive agents call for approaches long before the agents understand the domain sufficiently well to adequately represent and use knowledge for reasoning about them—long before they become scientists. For example, children learn to roll a ball toward another person before they know the physics of ball motion. This insight has led to comments on computer science approaches to building cognitive systems such as "It has long been recognized that it is much easier to write a program to carry out abstruse formal operations than to capture the common sense of a dog" (Winograd and Flores 1986, p. 98), alluding to the fact that formal (scientific) knowledge is much better suited for formalization for computers than is practical knowledge about physical entities. One approach to narrowing the gap between the knowledge about a domain and the domain itself has been to limit the knowledge to be formalized to naive knowledge about a domain (Davis 1990) rather than formalizing scientific knowledge. In this way, we may get a bit closer to commonsense reasoning that people without detailed understanding of a given domain are able to carry out; but using naive knowledge still deals with spatial problems on the meta level of knowledge, albeit knowingly with deficient knowledge.

In the following, we discuss the principal approaches to spatial problem solving and take a brief look at how problem-solving capabilities may develop. The aims of this discussion are to establish a better understanding of the requirements for natural (e.g., humans) and artificial (e.g., robots) cognitive systems and to provide criteria for deciding which kind of approach is suitable for a given purpose.

The Role of Knowledge in Solving Spatial Problems?

Do all spatial problems get solved entirely by the use of knowledge, i.e., by reflecting about them? Certainly not! Children, corvids (Bird and Emery 2009), and even adult humans solve spatial problems by accident, by imitation, by being told, by habit—and only in some cases by reflection and understanding. Although intellectually we may prefer solutions that are well-understood and well argued, solving problems by understanding and reflection may not yield a solution within a reasonable time frame, because the knowledge about the problem domain may be incomplete, because reasoning tools for using the knowledge may be missing, or because the solution on the knowledge level cannot (or cannot easily) be transformed into a solution on the object level.

As an example, consider a child learning to solve a jigsaw puzzle or an adult exploring ways to solve a Sudoku puzzle (Delahaye 2006). Both are spatial puzzles as certain spatial configurations of given elements will constitute solutions to the "problems." In the case of the jigsaw puzzle, the solution is perceptually evident to every human being who has developed a sense of shapes and pictures; in the case of a Sudoku puzzle, the correctness of a solution can be easily verified or falsified by checking the applicability of very simple rules. In both cases, learners will typically start with trial-and-error approaches; they will consequently detect certain regularities concerning successful problem-solving steps, and will then develop some heuristics to proceed in a more goal-oriented fashion.

In other cases, students—in particular, smaller children—will try out certain operations by imitation without being told what to do (or perhaps even with being told not to do it). They will acquire certain skills in dealing with properties of space and with physical entities in space that would be almost impossible to convey in terms of words. This suggests that knowledge is not a prerequisite to spatial problem solving; rather, it may be an intermediate or final product of reflecting on observed solutions to spatial problems.

Once certain knowledge has been acquired—in case of the jigsaw puzzle, this might be the insight that the border of the puzzle requires straight edges and that straight edges exclusively belong to the border of the puzzle—this knowledge can be employed as a strategy to look for and select only pieces with straight edges, during a certain phase of the problem-solving process. The knowledge required on the mental level is factual knowledge about the presence of a straight edge; the precise shapes of the puzzle pieces need not to be mentally represented. The task of checking for straight edges can be "outsourced" to perception on the object level; here the focus of attention can be set such that features other than straight edges will not be noticed and will not have to be dealt with in the problem-solving process.

Similarly for other spatial features of jigsaw puzzle pieces: We may know that protrusions of a certain kind will match inversions of the same shape. But we may not be willing or able to represent all details of these shapes mentally such that we would be able to determine with certainty whether or not the pieces match perfectly; we may only represent a few characteristics about the shapes to determine whether it is worth trying to find out whether the pieces *actually* fit in the object domain of the puzzle pieces. In short, very little knowledge about the domain may be sufficient to improve spatial problem solving considerably. Once a knowledge procedure has been established, it may be compiled into an object-level procedure where the knowledge "behind it" is no longer accessible. For example, a jigsaw puzzle solver may routinely first search for straight edges, but no longer know why this is a good strategy.

Reconsidering the Knowledge-Based Approach

As we suggested in the previous section, the recognition of regularities may lead to insights that enable us to develop heuristics that may help us to solve problems in a more goal-directed manner. Heuristics can be viewed as a form of belief or unconfirmed knowledge that may help us to see new regularities, to construct better heuristics, and to obtain better knowledge about the nature of a problem and approaches to its solution. Thus, knowledge about the nature and structure of the problem and its solutions certainly can be very helpful in spatial problem solving.

Natural knowledge processing takes place predominantly in brains; artificial knowledge processing takes place predominantly in computers. We have argued that for *spatial* problem solving, substantial support for people and animals comes directly from spatial structures and configurations on the object level of the problem domain. As we discussed in the second section, computers are confined to processing spatial knowledge on the meta level of the spatial problem domain, and current artificial intelligence (AI) systems solve spatial problems by representing all knowledge about spatial structures in the computer, solving the entire problem by reasoning about that knowledge.

This raises the interesting question of whether we are confined to solving spatial problems on the meta level of the problem domain when employing computers for spatial problem solving. Certainly not. Computers contribute only the brain part of solving spatial problems. But just as humans have a body with considerable spatial perception and spatial interaction abilities (embodied cognition), we are able today to give computers a body with considerable spatial perception and interaction abilities. Autonomous mobile robots that directly interact with their spatial environment (situated cognition) may serve as examples of such embodied computers. Thus, the role of the computer that had to do all the work in a classical AI system can be restricted to just one part of a more multifaceted spatial problem-solving system.

In order to solve problems closer to the spatial domain, we will have to reconsider the distribution of labor between the body and the mind of an embodied cognitive system. In particular, in order to exploit spatial structures in the object domain, we will not have to represent all the knowledge we may have about space; we can directly employ spatial structures to benefit from their properties.

The idea of replicating biological mechanisms through implementing perception-actuator systems connected to electronic circuits is not new; before computers became widely available, cybernetic turtles (Eichler 1955a,b; Oettel 1964; Zemanek 1955) were constructed that exhibited simple sensor-based navigation behavior in space. Braitenberg (1984) used cybernetic turtles to demonstrate that very simple, well-understood structures can exhibit surprisingly complex behavior in space and time. He used this insight to advocate a research strategy ("synthetic psychology") to investigate complex systems in nature. Braitenberg's thought experiments involve "vehicles" such as cybernetic turtles that interact with spatial objects and environments via sensors and actuators directly on the object level. Hardware and software simulations of these vehicles have been implemented (Hutchison and Garnock-Jones 1993).

In autonomous robotics it was recognized that it is impossible to extract all relevant spatial features of the environment to represent it for computer processing and path planning in the computer (Thrun et al. 2005, p. 488). A plan to move on a straight line based on the knowledge of the spatial layout of the environment fails as a result of microscopic spatial features that cause the robot to deviate from the prescribed route. Whereas for physical interactions with the environments, it is state of the art to involve perception and feedback control to correct for unaccounted-for deviations and to ensure that the robot is on the intended path; for other aspects of space, a shared approach between the knowledge and object levels of space is not being employed.

Interesting epistemic issues arise when we connect the knowledge level with the object level; for example, it may not always be clear where to draw the line between knowledge level and object level when both levels interact. When we *use* a computer that implements a feedback circuit between sensors and actuators, we tend to ignore the knowledge level on which the circuit is programmed and consider it an object-level entity. When we *program* a computer to act as this feedback circuit, we are dealing with the circuit on the knowledge level. Thus, it depends on the specific operations we are considering (feedback operations vs. program operations) that decide on the epistemic status of a given activity.

Is it worthwhile for scientists to study spatial problem solving that takes place on the unreflected object level rather than on the meta level of knowledge and understanding? Certainly. If we really want to understand the principles of cognition, then engineers and scientists must make an effort to implement these principles *directly* in technical systems. It is a good start for scientists to reflect about such principles on the meta level of the spatial domain, but in the end we want to see a technically implemented proof of concept whose method of operation and performance can be compared on a par with biological systems.

Solving spatial problems on the physical object level does not mean that we should abandon reflection about spatial problem solving on the meta level of knowledge and understanding. On the contrary. We know very well how problem-solving abilities can be greatly enhanced by reasoning about them. Reasoning helps to select appropriate actions for solving spatial problems; thus object-level problem solving with a powerful knowledge component may be a goal worthwhile pursuing. Furthermore, the division of labor between the levels may vary depending on the specific spatial and temporal situation. We know this very well from daily experience: When we are searching for a specific object in our immediate vicinity, we tend to employ an object-level approach and simply look for the object; however, if the object is presumed not to be in our immediate vicinity, we may employ a knowledge-level approach and reason about where the object must be located, based on our knowledge of the history of that object.

Does this mean we can stick with the knowledge-level descriptions of spatial problem solutions and put an object-level component beneath it? This may be a good start, but we doubt that this approach will work in the long run when we will require real-time interactions between cognitive agents and complex environments. Nature seems to have chosen a different approach for good reasons: Beginners solve problems in an unsophisticated way; intermediate and advanced players employ considerable amounts of knowledge; experts have gained such substantial experience with the object domain and with the knowledge associated with it that they can compile their expertise into object-level abilities ("gut feelings"), which make them highly effective and efficient.

Three Ways of Solving Spatial Problems

There are at least three epistemologically distinct types of approaches asso-ciated with *spatial problem solving* or *spatial reasoning*.

Knowledge in the world: Acting in space

We can solve many spatial problems simply by taking some action or action sequence. For example, children (and some dogs) open doors by pushing the door handle down, long before they may understand the mechanisms that unleash the lock and open the door. They may have seen others take such action and imitated them until they achieved the desired effect. Simi-larly, they may be able to "navigate" to some place without reflecting about the specific steps to be taken. Even solving puzzles is first achieved by small children through planless action that accidentally leads to success. The attraction of children to certain objects and their drive to grasp and play in combination with the affordances of the spatial structures involved (Gibson 1977) can make it likely that the solution state will be achieved (Norman 1988).

In these examples, only the result counts; a problem can be considered solved when a desired state has been achieved (door is open; agent is at destination; puzzle is solved).

Knowledge in the head: Solving spatial problems mentally

Once we comprehend the domain of a particular problem sufficiently well to map its essence into a mental representation—usually by means of perception—we can detach the mind from the spatial environment and infer implications of the spatial situation on the knowledge level. Different forms of knowledge have been proposed; they may include subconscious motion patterns as encoded by mirror neurons (Rizzolatti, Fadiga, Gallese, and Fogassi 1996) and highly reflected theories about spatial relations. Mental representations provide a means to escape physical space by reflecting about it. We give up exploiting the affordances of space (or conversely, enduring the constraints of space) and replace the laws of spatial environments by affordances of mental operations. Knowledge processing may result in veridical simulations or implications; that is, it may correctly reflect the represented situations and operation, but it also may result in purely imaginary implications, which have no correspondence in the spatial environment.

If the knowledge is to be used by an artificial head, a computer, it has to be formalized in a computer-processable form. The computer offers a seemingly unconstrained abstract formal space in which to consider spatial structures and the restrictions that come along with them. In this abstract space, the affordances are given by the algorithms that process the formal structures; these affordances may or may not have a correspondence to the affordances in the spatial environment. In this abstract formal world we can describe the states and state transitions that are physically possible in spatial environments; we can associate features and properties with states and state transitions and reason about them. We also can describe imaginary domains, worlds that are physically or spatially impossible, as they transcend the constraints of the physical realm. Assuming complete and correct knowledge about the properties of physical space, we should be able to derive the same final solutions that we could obtain through actions in physical space.

Depending on the level of abstraction used for reasoning about spatial properties and configurations, the formal operations employed may be completely different from physical operations in physical space. For example, any motion from the physical location A to the physical location B transits through a very large number of intermediate locations; in a qualitative simulation, this motion may be represented in the computer by a direct transition from a state A' to the state B'. However, we may attempt to preserve certain relations (or properties of relations) in order to apply analogical operations that follow the same structural principles as the corresponding spatial operations. In principle, we could try to construct a detailed model of the spatial environment that would take into account all the knowledge we have about this environment on macroscopic levels as well as on subatomic levels. We must be aware, however, that it may not be possible to consider all the properties of physical space simultaneously, as the act of formally representing the knowledge disintegrates the underlying spatial structures into separate aspects about them.

As a consequence, we may not be able to preserve the time course of spatial actions in detail. This, however, may be a crucial demand on our cognitive system, for example, if we want the system to be able to interact with real-world entities in real time. (We could try to overcome this particular problem by developing a system architecture for our spatial knowledge machine in which each aspect is dealt with separately in real time and interacts with the modules that are responsible for the other aspects; however, this approach could only be feasible if the number of aspects to be considered is limited and if we understand their interactions in detail.) In cases where real-time capability is of less importance and not achievable jointly with other aspects of the cognitive system (e.g., computing some future state in a provably correct way), real-time capability requirements may be relaxed.

Knowledge distributed among the world, the body, and the mind: Embodied and situated cognition

When humans or smart animals experience random successes in spatial problem solving, they develop a partial understanding of the conditions under which their spatial problems can be solved and they learn to distinguish different qualities of problem solutions. For example, they may discover different ways in which doors can be opened and closed; they may know about different routes that lead to their goals, and these different routes may be associated with different attributes, such as shortest, fastest, prettiest, safest, loneliest, and least familiar—attributes that may or may not be desirable in specific situations.

In contrast with the first two ways of spatial problem solving, here the attention is not on the final state, the problem solution, or on specific correspondences between the spatial environment and its mental representation. In the distributed and combined approach, a high degree of synchronization through real-time interaction is required. In particular, perception and action depend on the actual availability of the respective spatial configuration. Some abstract knowledge about the features of different approaches to solving spatial problems has to be represented in the head (or computer) of the perceiving and acting cognitive agent in order to select one or the other approach. Knowledge about the nature or structure of space and time is not required; the affordances of space and time can take care of the actual spatial solution.

None of these three ways of solving spatial problems is generally superior or inferior to the respective other two ways. Rather, each of these three ways of solving spatial problems comes with distinct advantages or disadvantages that render it more or less suitable for specific problems and problem situations.

Epistemological Issues in Building Cognitive Systems

We now argue in more detail that the three approaches address different issues. The reason why different issues are addressed is that in each approach different knowledge is involved, and different knowledge corresponds to different levels of understanding. In the first approach to solving spatial problems—"knowledge in the world" (Norman 1988)—no knowledge is involved on the part of the cognitive agent; problems are solved on the basis of spatio-temporal affordances (Gibson 1977) in the problem domain that are exploited through spatio-temporal affordances on the part of the cognitive agent. There are driving forces acting in the agent and in the environment that probably can be better described by the words 'instinct', 'desire', or 'gravity', respectively, than by 'knowledge'; all function is implicitly provided by the environment. A random action generator might solve the problem similarly well under these affordances. Under epistemological considerations, the first way to a solution is of little interest.

From the knowledge point of view, the second approach ("knowledge in the head") is far more sapid: Specific aspects of the spatial problem that are deemed important for solving it are made explicit. Making explicit means turning states of affairs or processes into knowledge about these states of affairs or processes. The states of affairs and processes are on the object level of the problem; knowledge about them is on the meta level of the object domain. Knowledge is selective. Only what is represented can be reasoned about. In some cases, the approach aims at getting to know everything about the world and representing this knowledge in such a way that computers can do everything on the knowledge level. The object level of the original environment completely disappears in this approach. The knowledge level becomes the new reality and is treated as if it was the reality. Although it has been a wonderful dream of humanity (since the days of the library of Alexandria) to make all the knowledge in the world accessible, it is not clear how this approach relates to cognitive reality; here continuous interaction with the environment and selective extraction of features and relations seems to be of crucial importance.

The third approach ("knowledge distributed between the world and the head") makes implicit facts and relations selectively explicit and thus creates a hybrid approach: One part of the structures and processes remains implicit and guarantees on the object level that their properties are maintained, while another part is made explicit and thus adds knowledge about the domain to the meta level of the object domain. An everyday example of such a hybrid approach to knowledge representation would be if we were to use our living environment (e.g., a village) "as is" and add street signs that make the names of streets explicit. By doing so, we add knowledge about the village to the village. The conceptual separation between the object level of the village and the meta level of the knowledge about the village is important from an epistemological point of view, but, of course, the street sign, the name of the street, and the villagers' knowledge of the name of the street become parts of the (object level of the) village. Whether we need to draw the distinction between the levels and where to draw it will depend on the specific problem we have to solve and on the approaches available to solve it.

Cognitive Systems and Commonsense Problem Solving

Different approaches to building cognitive systems can be characterized by the extent to which they implement the three different ways of solving (spatial) problems. Classical AI approaches have been trying for quite some time to implement the second way ("knowledge in the head") in artificial brains (e.g., Feigenbaum 1992). Partly stemming from a dissatisfaction with the success of this approach, starting with the seminal work of Brooks (1991; see also Pfeifer and Scheier 1999), systems implementing the first way ("knowledge in the world") have been developed and successfully applied in certain contexts. While the first and the second way of solving spatial problems have thus been explored in existing cognitive systems, the third way (distributed knowledge) has received little or no attention as a general approach to knowledge processing. We believe that this is a serious shortcoming in research on cognitive systems. Accordingly, one major aim of this chapter is to raise awareness of this approach and to propose its thorough investigation.

We are not arguing that the distributed approach is generally superior to the other two approaches. Rather, the success of a cognitive system will depend on how well the respective problem-solving approach matches the combination of (a) the problems the cognitive system needs to solve, (b) the properties of the environment, and (c) the means of representing the environment available to the system. The distributed knowledge approach seems particularly interesting when one strives to understand and implement the cognitive processes that allow for efficient problem solving that may involve real-time interactions with the physical world. Taking the "knowledge in the head" approach in such a situation would mean to formalize all relevant aspects of the physical environment and the cognitive systems' interaction with it, as well as maintaining numerous spatial relations in dynamic environments. Because of the high computational effort associated with such an approach, real-time problem solving will quickly become infeasible. In contrast, the distributed knowledge approach relies on the (interactive) use of information implicitly provided by the physical environment rather than only on an explicit representation of this information and accordingly remains capable of real-time problem solving where the meta-level approach fails.

To further clarify the differential advantages of the two approaches, consider the following example. If one needs to determine the aerodynamic drag of car designs, there are two fundamentally different approaches to do this. First, one can build a—perhaps small-scale—prototype of the possible design and measure drag in a wind tunnel. Second, one can build a mathematical model that can be applied more generally to various different designs. In the first approach, properties and features intrinsic to the domain implicitly carry over to the prototype without having to worry about correctly modeling their properties, and the drag can be measured directly without extensive computation. In the second approach, considerable effort may be required to construct (i.e., extract and make explicit the general regularities that govern aerodynamic drag) as well as to simulate the model, but the resulting model may be more easily varied in the design process.

The "knowledge in the world" and "knowledge in the head" approaches are analogous to the use of a prototype and the use of a mathematical model, respectively, in the aerodynamic drag example. While the "knowledge in the world" approach will often be better capable of real-time performance thanks to the use of information implicitly provided by the environment, the "knowledge in the head" approach may provide greater generality and reflects a certain level of understanding of the domain.

Consequently, to develop and understand cognitive systems that solve spatial problems and interact with their environment in real time, the distributed knowledge approach may be advantageous. In fact, from work in robotics, we know that it is virtually impossible to adequately model the physical behavior of a robot in a given environment by an entirely software-based approach. Today, computer scientists employ physical robots rather than computer models thereof. Similarly, we propose to use embodied cognitive agents in physical environments to investigate cognitive processes in everyday real-world settings.

Note that this is different from a line of research in cognitive science that equips existing robot hardware and software with additional processes and representations developed in AI. (See, for example, Hertzberg and Saffiotti 2008.) Essentially, this amounts to adding "knowledge in the head" solutions of spatial problems without addressing the division of labor with the knowledge in the world.. Although this approach can be considered an interesting way toward embodying artificial intelligence, it does not seem to speak to the questions of how cognition can change, and be more effective and efficient when you have a body to solve problems. In contrast, our proposal addresses these questions by suggesting that it is the felicitous combination of explicit knowledge in the head and implicit knowledge in the environment that contributes substantially to the efficiency with which embodied cognitive agents are capable of solving spatial problems.

Implications for Spatial Education

Spatial abilities and factual knowledge appear to be complementary assets of human cognition. Without either of them our cognitive abilities are considerably restricted; to a certain extent one ability may compensate for a lack of the other. But an important question is whether or to what extent one of the abilities depends on the other. Can we improve our general abstract reasoning capabilities by training our more concrete perceptual and hands-on skills with spatial objects and configurations, or do we prevent abstract reasoning capabilities from developing if we focus training on the concrete skills? Conversely, we may ask whether we can improve practical spatial reasoning skills by training general abstract reasoning abilities or whether we prevent the practical skills from developing if we focus education on abstract reasoning abilities.

Developmentally speaking, perceptual and motoric experience of space certainly precedes factual knowledge about space—this applies to a larger extent the more children grow up with spatial objects and toys they can physically manipulate than with images thereof. Motor-perceptual experience is quite concrete and involves the whole body, whereas factual knowledge can be rather abstract and concerns mainly the mind. This insight has been used to banish concrete visual examples from school education, as it was claimed that students' elaborate preoccupation with concrete physical entities in topics such as calculus may prevent them from developing abstract thinking abilities. As a consequence, rather abstract ways of teaching math were promoted (a focus on set-theoretic approaches, for example). In our own experience and based on the analysis expounded in this chapter, concrete examples and specific problem solutions precede generalization and abstraction, and promote rather than prevent more abstract cognition. This idea receives support from a number of sources: First, anecdotally, some of the best abstract thinkers (e.g., Einstein) claimed they needed to visualize their concepts and ideas by means of sketches or other perceptual tools in order to be able to formulate abstract theories. Similarly, we do not know of good theoretical mathematicians who were not first skilled in calculus. Second, further support comes from empirical investigations of inductive reasoning (Hayes and Heit 2013) in both adults and children. Hayes, Fritz, and Heit (2013), for example, have found that preschool children are apt at and show a strong propensity to generalize object properties of experienced exemplars to new exemplars. Interestingly, this propensity was significantly stronger in children than in adults. Third, recent research in educational psychology stresses the importance of concrete instantiations in the acquisition of enduring and generalizable (abstract) knowledge. A study by McNeil and Fyfe (2012), for example, showed that undergraduates learned mathematical concepts more robustly if the learning material consisted of concrete instantiations of the concepts that were "faded" into abstract symbols during learning. Moreover, in an extensive analysis of teacher classroom behavior, Richland, Zur, and Holyoak (2007) found that the superior math skills of Japanese compared to American students are related to the fact that Japanese teachers more often employed good analogies than American teachers, where good analogies are analogies that (a) comprise (concrete) familiar source domains and (b) use "appropriate visual and spatial cues [to] aid comprehension of abstract relations."

In the light of these observations, it seems unlikely that good spatial cognitive abilities prevent people from becoming good abstract thinkers. Our recommendation is to adjust to students' individual receptiveness and interest for dealing with spatial entities and topics. This requires, of course, that students be offered opportunities to dealing with spatial environments that are commensurate with their cognitive development.

Conclusion

In a thought experiment, we presented three ways of relating cognitive agents with spatial objects and configurations from a knowledge-processing perspective. In the first approach, the agent has no knowledge about the spatial environment; playful actions in conjunction with physical affordances ("knowledge in the world") enable desired changes in the spatial configuration of the environment. In the second approach, all the knowledge in the world is represented in the agent's mind as *knowledge in the head*; associations or reasoning processes replace the cognitive agent's interaction with the spatial environment. The third approach, *knowledge distributed between the world and the head*, enables the agent to decide on actions to be taken in the spatial environment.

While it is an intellectual challenge to identify the properties and relations of spatial environments as well as the knowledge of cognitive agents, and to formalize it for use by computers for different problem classes, the *knowledge in the head* approach alone is not a suitable approach to develop efficiently performing cognitive systems. The characteristic strength of cognitive systems is in simultaneously using multiple modalities to interact with a multitude of highly integrated aspects of the physical world in form of its structures, properties, and relations. The challenge we need to address is how we can construct cognitive agents with *limited* knowledge about the world that can interact in smart ways with all the knowledge in the world and selectively extract just those features that they need in order to solve a given task.

Should cognitive scientists use the *knowledge in the head* approach to build spatial problem solvers? Yes and no! Yes: as analytic tools to understand the potential, the limitations, and the characteristics of spatial reasoning mechanisms. No: as substitutes for object-level cognitive mechanisms. Spatial reasoning approaches that are adapted to the structures and processes of the spatial domain may be particularly effective and efficient for solving spatial problems. The added generality of general logic problem solvers comes at the expense of accounting for hypothetical worlds, which cannot be fully exploited by cognitive agents that are restricted to a spatial world and spatial actions. However, if one wants to address the capabilities of cognitive agents to include non-spatial dimensions, for example color or sound, or if one wants to address metaphorical reasoning (Lakoff and Johnson 1980), which relates different dimensions and structures to one another, the consideration of more general meta-reasoners may be beneficial for cognitive tasks that go beyond analytical exploration.

Among other aspects, in line with recent results in educational psychology, our analysis stresses the importance of concrete instances for spatial education. Instead of attempting to teach abstract spatial knowledge directly, spatial education should start with giving students the opportunity to explore spatial concepts and relations by interacting with and manipulating concrete instances of spatial problems. Abstract knowledge can then (more) easily arise by generalization from the experience with the concrete instances.

References

Bird, C. D., and Emery, N. J. 2009. Rooks use stones to raise the water level to reach a floating worm. *Current Biology* 19: 1410–1414.

Braitenberg, V. 1984. *Vehicles: Experiments in Synthetic Psychology*. MIT Press.

Brooks, R. A. 1991. Intelligence without representation. *Artificial Intelligence* 47: 139–159.

Davis, E. 1990. *Representations of Commonsense Knowledge*. Morgan Kaufmann.

Delahaye, J.-P. 2006. The science behind Sudoku. *Scientific American* 294: 80–87.

Eichler, E. 1955a. Die künstliche Schildkröte. Ein umweltabhängiger Automat. *Radiotechnik* 5/6: 173–179.

Eichler, E. 1955b. Aufbau und Verhalten der künstlichen Schildkröte. *Radiotechnik* 7/8: 239–244.

Feigenbaum, E. A. 1992. A personal view of expert systems: Looking back and looking ahead. *Expert Systems with Applications* 5: 193–201.

Gibson, J. J. 1977. The theory of affordances. In *Perceiving, Acting, and Knowing*, ed. R. E. Shaw and J. Bransford. Erlbaum.

Hayes, B. K., and Heit, E. 2013. Induction. In *Oxford Handbook of Cognitive Psychology*, ed. D. Reisberg. Oxford University Press.

Hayes, B. K., Fritz, K., and Heit, E. 2013. The relationship between memory and inductive reasoning: Does it develop? *Developmental Psychology* 49: 848–860.

Hertzberg, J., and Saffiotti, A. 2008. Using semantic knowledge in robotics. *Robotics and Autonomous Systems* 56: 875–877.

Hutchison, L., and Garnock-Jones, T. 1993. *Braitenberg Vehicles: An Electronic Model of Neural Behavior.* CREST Report.

Kowalski, R. A. 1980. Contribution to SIGART newsletter No. 70, *Special Issue on Knowledge Representation.*

Lakoff, G., and Johnson, M. 1980. *Metaphors We Live By.* University of Chicago Press.

McNeil, N. M., and Fyfe, E. R. 2012. "Concreteness fading" promotes transfer of mathematical knowledge. *Learning and Instruction* 22: 440–448.

Nilsson, N. 1998. *Artificial Intelligence: A New Synthesis.* Morgan Kaufmann.

Norman, D. A. 1988. *The Design of Everyday Things.* Basic Books.

Oettel, R. 1964. Kybernetisches Fahrmodell (Schildkröte). *Funkamateur* 8–10: 256–353.

Pfeifer, R., and Scheier, C. 1999. *Understanding Intelligence.* MIT Press.

Richland, L. E., Zur, O., and Holyoak, K. 2007. Cognitive supports for analogies in the mathematics classroom. *Science* 316: 1128–1129.

Rizzolatti, G., Fadiga, L., Gallese, V., and Fogassi, L. 1996. Premotor cortex and the recognition of motor actions. *Brain Research. Cognitive Brain Research* 3: 131–141.

Thrun, S., Burgard, W., and Fox, D. 2005. *Probabilistic Robotics.* MIT Press.

Winograd, T. A., and Flores, F. 1986. *Understanding Computers and Cognition.* Ablex.

Zemanek, H. 1955. Die künstliche Schildkröte von Wien. *Radio-Magazin mit Fernseh-Magazin* 9: 275–278.

3   The Linguistic Ontology of Space: General Methods and the Role of Comparative Linguistic Evidence

John Bateman and Sander Lestrade[1]

Problems involving spatial reasoning, spatial perception, and spatial representation are present in almost all human activities. Spatial skills and intelligence in general appear to be closely related and "spatial thinking" as such is increasingly considered an important enabler for many of the skills that are essential for life today. Spatial skills are not only evident as cognitive processes, however. Whenever spatial problems are addressed as cooperative tasks, drawing on the knowledge, abilities, or even position(s) of different parties, it becomes necessary to add into this complex of issues considerations of *spatial language*. This has been approached in several ways, broadly varying according to the role that linguistic organizations of space are seen to play over and above conceptual, or other non-linguistically derived, representations and processes.

At one extreme, spatial language can be seen to be a more or less straightforward labeling of (some aspects of) conceptual structure. Spatial behavior is then largely independent of how any particular language or linguistic practice deals with space. At the other extreme, linguistic con-structions of language may be taken to exert considerable influence on cognitive representations, even determining just which conceptualizations are made and which not. The extent to which such a position of strong relativism can be upheld is at present again a hotly contested issue, the strongest sources of evidence being taken from cross-linguistic and cross-cultural studies (Levinson 1996; Levinson, Kita, Haun, and Rasch 2002; Li and Gleitman 2002).

In attempting to achieve a robust position from which to attempt tri-angulation on the complex interplay of spatial phenomena at work, we argue, it is beneficial to consider more precisely the organizations of spatial information that language(s) themselves impose when communi-cating spatial information. The more accurately the particular contribu-tion of language can be characterized, the more focused experimental hypotheses and formal models of spatial activities and problem solving are possible, and the better the complex of linguistic and non-linguistic factors can be teased apart. To that end, we describe how the semantics of spatial language can be approached employing methods developed within the field of formal ontology. In essence, we consider the semantics of natural language to be describable in terms of an additional "ontologically organized" level whose function is to mediate between concrete linguistic forms and those forms' contexts of use. This view posits that interpretation and production of natural spatial language, in all contexts of application, relies on a relationship being drawn between at least two ontologies, or *ontological levels*: one characterizing the linguistic semantics of space and another capturing the situated context of an agent or group of agents jointly interacting and communicating in and about space—i.e., spatial aspects of the corresponding social and physical reality. "Understanding" spatial language is then seen as a process of building a flexible mapping between these levels—an architecture that invites application of fundamental principles from ontological engineering, such as modularity and distributed ontology alignment; Bateman (2010a) summarizes this use of ontological engineering for distinct ontologies of space from the formal ontological perspective.

Relating real, naturally occurring spatial language to its situated interpretation and contexts of use has proved itself to be a considerable challenge. Even though the analysis and formalization of the meaning of spatial expressions continues as an extremely active area of research (for extensive literature reviews, see Bateman 2010b; Carlson and van der Zee 2005; Coventry, Tenbrink, and Bateman 2009; Tenbrink 2007), significant problems in formulating effective mechanisms remain. The adoption of a two-level ontological approach to the problem appears to promise several benefits of both a practical and theoretical nature. Practically, it becomes possible to apply ontology-based methods for integrating natural-language technology with applications such as autonomous, mobile assistance systems or dialogic navigation systems (e.g., Jian, Zhekova, Shi, and Bateman 2010; Ross, Mandel, Bateman, Hui, and Frese 2006; Ross, Shi, Vierhuff, Krieg-Brückner, and Bateman 2005). Theoretically, it provides a means of pinpointing precisely the commitments a particular selection of linguistic expressions brings to the interpretation process.

Studies of the use of spatial language in natural dialogic settings show a remarkable flexibility: Spatial terms appear to be able to adjust themselves to diverse situations that are often difficult to group together on the basis of their non-linguistic spatial properties alone. Thus, spatial linguistic expressions appear to structure their construction of space in ways that are not immediately evident in considerations of space made independently of language. Providing a natural-language semantics directly in terms of a non-linguistic external representation is therefore problematic: If the connection between contextualization and linguistic form is too direct, problem cases are created that make the use of spatial language appear more vague and underspecified than is actually the case.

Even though natural dialogue seldom contains the explicit disambiguating spatial information that might appear necessary from a non-linguistic perspective (Tenbrink 2007), spatial expressions in most cases receive appropriate interpretations—which strongly suggests that additional information is being brought to bear. The overall structure and motivation of this approach to space have been set out in Bateman 2010c, while detailed characterizations and evaluations of the linguistic spatial ontology resulting are provided in Bateman, Hois, Ross, and Tenbrink 2010.

Although this method offers a cleaner architecture within which the extreme flexibility of spatial natural-language usage can be explored, there are significant issues to resolve. In particular, questions of the relation between fine-grained descriptions of linguistic data and the semantic representations proposed to cover such data remain. Moreover, the degree to which proposed representations will need to vary across languages and language families is unknown at this time. These issues, coupled with further challenges in language acquisition across cultures and the uses of spatial language in diverse communicative situations, together define a constellation of inter-related research questions still awaiting answers.

In this chapter we pick up particularly the question of cross-linguistic variation and comparison as one keystone to take our exploration of spatial language further within this overall framework. In the next section, therefore, we first give a brief review of the problems raised by spatial communication using natural language, introducing the notion of a linguistic ontology as a way of approaching those problems, and then, in the section following, move on to consider the crucial importance of cross-linguistic comparison when establishing such ontologies. We offer in particular a case study demonstrating just how detailed cross-linguistic investigation helps pinpoint the modeling decisions that need to be made.

The kind of separation of issues that we motivate then suggests several new angles on traditional concerns raised by treatments of space, spatial representations, and spatial problem solving. By pulling apart the linguistic and the non-linguistic contributions to spatial representation and reasoning as we suggest, it may be possible to characterize more finely those skills contributing to spatial intelligence in the performance of cooperative, communicatively mediated tasks, which may in turn allow for more focused educational practices and diagnostics concerning the challenges faced by human spatial problem solvers. Moreover, our focus on sources of cross-linguistic evidence may provide ways of investigating potential sources of difficulty (and beneficial opportunities for transfer) that could arise when natural-language spatial semantics differ across languages and cultures.

The chapter as a whole is, then, a synthesis of the ontological approach taken in Bateman et al. 2010 and the cross-linguistic methods and insights developed in Lestrade 2012, which itself can be seen as a further revision of Lestrade 2010 on the basis of Bateman et al. However, we assume no familiarity with either of these papers and introduce and define each new technical term as required.

Linguistic Ontologies

In this section, we briefly review the particular problems raised by spatial communication and set out the notion of a linguistic ontology as one way of approaching the issues. We have already noted the extreme flexibility of spatial-language usage and the challenge that this raises for finding appropriate levels of semantic abstraction for accounting for the phenomena—on the one hand, we need to capture the contribution of linguistic expressions to spatial interpretations but, on the other, we must avoid overcommitment that would prematurely rule out possible interpretations in context.

As a simple example, consider the interpretation of expressions involving the spatial linguistic term *left*. One common interpretation would be as an area of high probability along an axis situated 90° counterclockwise with respect to some reference object and a given orientation. But, in different contexts, the word 'left' can equally well denote the entire "left-hand" half-plane, a reorientation by an angle of contextually determined size, a redirection of movement or, in the case of a street network, some intersection of the left-hand half-plane with the actual turnings available (Klippel, Tappe, Kulik, and Lee 2005). Even more challenging variation is easy to find. Bateman et al. (2010) offer an example with the linguistic term 'between'. Although often seen as picking out a (narrow) space between two reference objects, the term appears without problem in phrases such as "swim only between the flags" even when the referenced flags are placed in a location where swimming cannot occur, such as in the middle of a sandy beach.

An extensive collection of interpretative problems of this kind is given by Herskovits (1986). The specification of English *in*, for example, only in terms of geometrical containment can be argued to be an overcommitment, because we can also use it when containment does not apply—e.g., *a light bulb in a socket*—and need not use it when containment does apply, e.g., *a potato is in the bowl* vs. *a potato is under the bowl*, where the geometrical relationship is the same across the two cases. Moreover, whenever containment does apply, the question as to which part of the located object is exactly included in which region with respect to the reference object can often only be answered post hoc.

Such examples compellingly suggest that the flexibility required in interpreting spatial language is a pervasive feature of spatial language rather than a result of isolated occurrences. Therefore, any approach that attempts to see such spatial usage as involving "exceptions," or spatial cases requiring idiosyncratic treatment, is in danger of missing a fundamental property of spatial language as such. We need to ensure that flexibility of this kind is engineered into the accounts we build from the ground up.

Approaches that "outsource" their treatments of spatial semantics to nonlinguistic concerns, such as for example, sensor measurements or other data obtained more directly from a spatial environment, also face considerable problems when adopted for explaining the use of natural language. For example, the human user of a geographic information system might want to find "rivers near but not entering or leaving lakes" or "all houses facing the lake but on the other side of the road" but may be uninterested in offering precise metrical characterizations of 'near', 'facing', 'other side', and so on. Although this may seem to be a question of vagueness, in the sense of just leaving out precise information, linguistic statements involving non-metrical characterizations often express precisely the degree of generalization *desired to identify the situations of interest.*

A superficially more "exact" characterization may then easily become over-specific with respect to the user's goals. That is, there are situations where we need to "precisely" preserve the semantic import of the linguistic descriptions given and not relate these prematurely to particular locations in the world. Here again, therefore, precisely what the linguistic expressions are committing to and what they are not must be a major concern. As a consequence, the semantics offered for spatial language will generally demand a *qualitative* treatment. It is this level of semantics that is acquired when children (and others) learn to use spatial language appropriately and so it is this level that we need to capture in our accounts—both from a linguistic, theoretical perspective and for concrete educational practices involved with the use of spatial language for mediating and communicating spatial tasks. Assessment of the adequacy or otherwise of the use of spatial language therefore needs to incorporate awareness of both the specific meanings contributed by linguistic spatial constructions and the natural flexibility with which such constructions are related to context. Education may need to target each of these component skills individually as well as in combination in order for an accurate picture of "spatial thinking" in action to result.

More extensive discussion both of the theoretical descriptive problems and of the approaches that have been taken in research on spatial language to solve them is given in Bateman 2010c. We need then to characterize in detail the semantic contributions of linguistic spatial descriptions *and only then* relate this semantics to contextualized geometric (or other) specifications of locations as given in a spatial situation or environment. Moreover, the application of some basic principles from ontological engineering provides precisely such a characterization and so offers many suggestions for dealing with space and spatial language.

Within our earlier work on "space" more generally, for example, we found a clear need for ontological "multi-perspectivalism" and modularity. (See Bateman, Borgo, Lüttich, Masolo, and Mossakowski 2007; Hois, Bhatt, and Kutz 2009.) This involves a rejection of more traditional views of ontology in which one overarching and general descriptive framework of categories and relationships is sought to cover all possible domains of interest. Instead, it appears more beneficial to allow different perspectives to co-exist. This "multi-perspectivalism" allows different communities to characterize their worlds in very different ways. For example, whereas for the transport specialist a road might be a component of a route in a navigation network (that is, a "graph link"), for the ecologist that same road might be a habitat border (a boundary of a spatial region). These two kinds of entities have very different formal properties and so forcing them together is more likely to produce confusion and inconsistency rather than a useful description. Indeed, adopting the wrong spatial conceptualization for a particular task may make certain problems difficult, or impossible to solve and so *choice* of spatial conceptualization needs itself to be seen as part of the set of skills one must learn in order to perform effective spatial reasoning.

Research on spatial representations has even isolated distinct *formal* characterizations of space, each with its own benefits and drawbacks. Often these alternatives cannot be sensibly reduced to one common scheme, just as with the two perspectives on 'road' above. Consider, for example, the question of "foundational units" for formalizing an account of space. Both points and regions can play this role—each can be used to build up a mathematical axiomatization of the other (cf. Borgo, Guarino, and Masolo 1996). Insisting that one should then be "more" foundational than the other risks enforcing an arbitrary decision that is, moreover, unnecessary given an appropriate multi-perspectival formalization. The view best taken will often depend on the task and so as long as there are well-defined ways of relating theories and descriptions building on one framework to those building on the other, there is no need to choose. Choosing one rather than the other would again be an example of what we mean by overcommitment.

Similar results obtain across the very broad range of spatial calculi now known (cf. Bateman and Farrar 2004; Cohn and Hazarika 2001). Moreover, it also appears that a very similar state of affairs can be considered to hold for the use of spatial language. In previous work, therefore, we have been led to characterize the linguistic contribution to spatial construal as an *additional layer* of ontological information, whose particular responsibility is to formalize the "semantic commitments" entered into by any linguistic construction. This perspective is then "additional" to any other perspectives on space and its modeling that may be established following other criteria, such as cognitive modeling, psychological experimentation, or formal axiomatization.

We term this additional layer a *linguistically motivated ontology*, or *linguistic ontology* for short. Ontologies of this kind take on the task of mediating between linguistic form and contextualized interpretation, just as other ontological perspectives on space take up other tasks, such as modeling the formal properties of regions and boundaries, the connectivity properties of navigation networks, the principles of measurement and approximation when treating sensor data, and many more. The methodology for constructing such specifically linguistic ontologies has been pursued in some detail. Essentially it is necessary to examine lexico-grammatical patterns in a given language and their use in context. The semantic description constituting the linguistic ontology can then be seen as a set of *generalizations* over those patterns.

The linguistic phenomena considered vary in their power to suggest appropriate generalizations. For example, whereas lexical items provide structure in various specific domains relevant for a culture—and so readily embody idiosyncratic solutions to communicative needs—grammatical constructions evolve to be reusable across such domains. It is then grammatical patterns that provide the strongest evidence for general semantic organization. In developing a linguistic ontology, therefore, we are interested mostly (if not only) in the structure provided by the grammatical analyses.

Such a view can be found in diverse approaches to linguistic semantics. Similarities can be drawn in particular with Jackendoff's (1999) discussion concerning distinct components of the overall "cognitive architecture," the motivations for their contents, and relations between them. Jackendoff argues that distinctions be drawn between levels of description by relying on a *criterion of grammatical effect* (ibid., p. 13). This states that only information that is grammaticized should be placed in the linguistic conceptual structure. This is very similar to the methodology adopted for mapping out the semantic import of a lexico-grammatical system that we employ here.

Moreover, it is also at this level of descriptions that generalizations across languages can be expected. And the challenge remains to explore this for a far broader range of languages than has been done to date. This also raises fundamental linguistic questions concerning just what we are going to include among the grammatical phenomena addressed. Different languages draw rather different boundaries between areas of grammar and this itself may give us useful insights into the semantic generalizations that we need to draw when constructing linguistic ontologies. In the next section, we address this with respect to a particularly challenging area of cross-linguistic variation.

Evidence from Language Comparison: The Ontology of Mode

As we explained above, a spatial linguistic ontology is a formal specification of the semantic commitments of spatial constructions, setting out the uses of such constructions without overcommitting with respect to the physical or conceptual situations for which they are used. It should be motivated solely by the requirements of linguistically expressed spatial meaning, and be free of nonlinguistic, contextually dependent additions (Bateman et al. 2010, p. 1029). It should not overcommit in terms of the possible contextualizations posited for linguistic expressions, as each such overcommitment threatens to restrict the flexibility of the account in ways not supported by data. In other words, a crucial requirement is that the semantic description of an item in our ontology allows for its application to all and only those situations it may describe. We saw several examples above involving the linguistics terms *left, between,* and *in.*

Following the methodology of linguistic motivation, semantic distinctions are introduced in the ontology only if they are necessary to distinguish between situations that are distinguished by a relevant (grammatical) linguistic construction—a procedure also described in detail by Talmy (1985) and others. However, and quite crucially, *it can be difficult on the basis of evidence from single languages to see just where overcommitment might be occurring*. To solve this problem, therefore, cross-linguistic evidence in the formulation of distinct spatial linguistic ontologies for different languages can be of considerable benefit. So far, however, linguistically motivated ontological work has been very restricted in terms of the range of languages that it has been able to draw on. Our own linguistic ontology, for example, has been limited primarily to evidence from English and/or German.

Here we discuss concretely how the cross-linguistic perspective can now take us further. As an illustration, we show how drawing on a broader linguistic basis provides strong evidence that the previous treatment of paths (or "routes") within our spatial linguistic ontology needs to be changed. By these means, we demonstrate how detailed attention to grammatical evidence can sharpen a linguistic ontology, providing a progressive refinement of our understanding of the construal of space in and by language(s) applicable to all situations where spatial language is employed.

Paths

The notion of path or route can be found in virtually all semantic analyses of spatial meaning. Consider the following examples:

(1) a. He is standing to the right of the chair.
   b. He goes to the right of the chair.

In both sentences the same region is defined with respect to a chair, namely the region to its right. In the terminology of Bateman et al. (2010, pp. 1045–1046), this region is called a *generalized location* and is the result of applying a spatial modality (*to the right of*) to a relatum (*the chair*). The ontology as a whole provides a rich classification of such "spatial modalities," which generally characterize linguistically constructed "regions" of concern. The emphasis on "linguistic" construction here indicates the status of these "regions"—they operate more as spatial discourse referents than actual spatial regions in the world, and so the task of relating them to regions in the world remains. Their semantic descriptions then bring constraints to bear on just what kinds of regions in the world the process of discourse interpretation can anchor them to.

For the examples under discussion here, the difference between the two sentences lies in the way in which the constructed generalized location participates in the spatial situation being expressed. In example 1a, the generalized location functions as a *placement*; in example 1b, however, it functions as a *route*. More specifically, in example 1b the generalized location is assigned a role by means of participation in one *route component* of a *GeneralizedRoute*, namely its destination. The next example will make this clearer.

The sentence following describes a more complex spatial situation (Bateman et al. 2010, p. 1046, example 19):

(2) The deer ran from the hill to the stream.

This sentence is analyzed in table 3.1. The notation here is one standard form for writing ontologies within the formalism employed—in this case, the Web Ontology Language (OWL). Words in italics in the table are formal variables serving as place holders for showing co-reference, and so have no formal status in the ontology itself. The variables introduced specifically by the sentence at hand are those given in the **Individual** slots in the representation. The categories given under **Types** are concepts defined in the linguistic ontology, and so are available for all sentences involving

Table 3.1
Ontological analysis of *The deer ran from the hill to the stream.*

Individual:	*NADM*	
Types:	NonAffectingDirectedMotion	
Facts:	actor	*Deer*
	processInConfiguration	*running*
	route	*GenRoute*
Individual:	*GenRoute*	
Types:	GeneralizedRoute	
Facts:	source	*GLsource*
	destination	*GLdest*
Individual:	*GLsource*	
Types:	GeneralizedLocation	
Facts:	relatum	*Hill*
	hasSpatialModality	GeneralDirectionalDistancing
Individual:	*GLdest*	
Types:	GeneralizedLocation	
Facts:	relatum	*Stream*
	hasSpatialModality	GeneralDirectionalNearing

spatial expressions. These concepts also generally determine which roles can occur—for example, the *NonAffectingDirectingMotion* (second line) states that some *actor* moves in some way along some optionally specified *route*, and so on. In prose, this specification says that some deer is running along a route, the source of which is at a hill, and the end of which is at a stream.

Now, it may well be that we indeed construct something like a path of motion in our pragmatic, contextualized interpretation of example 2—but the question for our current linguistic-ontological purposes is whether this should be attributed to any of the linguistic components or, instead, be part of our conceptual representation defeasibly deduced during discourse interpretation. Although the notion of paths and the analysis in example 2 certainly make sense intuitively, we will argue here that the identification of a GeneralizedRoute in examples such as examples 1b and 2 is in fact another case of overcommitment. This means that the analysis identifies paths where there are none—there is mention of a starting and an end point only; there is no *linguistic* need to already commit to the set of points in between. As we show below, however, this only becomes evident when we adopt a suitably broad linguistic basis for comparison.

The analysis in example 2 shows an additional problem, as will also become evident in the discussion of the cross-linguistic data in the next section. As can be seen, *GeneralDirectionalNearing* and *GeneralDirectional-Distancing* are classified as spatial modalities. This implies they are similar to such meanings as *Support* (e.g., *on*) and *Inclusion* (e.g., *in*), which are also defined as spatial modalities according to the scheme given in full in Bateman et al. 2010. As our discussion in the next section will show, however, the two are operating at different levels that we need to represent and distinguish in our analysis accordingly.

In particular, as was noted above, we create GeneralizedLocations by means of "applying" the semantics of spatial modality expressions. Linguistically, however, there is evidence for a finer discrimination. There are also **mode** distinctions that then say something *about* these created regions. These directly mark the way in which GeneralizedLocations participate in the spatial situation, *replacing* the need to explicitly stipulate Generalized-Routes in the ontology. The presence of GeneralizedRoutes is then also revealed to have been an overcommitment. The revised linguistic ontological analysis of example 2 that we propose here is then as set out in table 3.2, the prose version of which reads "some deer is running, starting from a hill and going to a stream."

Table 3.2
Revised analysis of *The deer ran from the hill to the stream.*

Individual:	*NADM*	
Types:	NonAffectingDirectedMotion	
Facts:	actor	*Deer*
	processInConfiguration	*running*
	GeneralizedLocation	*GL1, GL2*
Individual:	*GL1*	
Types:	GeneralizedLocation	
Facts:	relatum	*Hill*
	hasMode	Source
Individual:	*GL2*	
Types:	GeneralizedLocation	
Facts:	relatum	*Stream*
	hasMode	Goal

Distinguishing between Mode and SpatialModality in this way makes possible the straightforward analysis of expressions such as *into, in, out of, onto, on,* and *off.* Rather than being six different GeneralizedLocations, as the previous analysis would force us to say, these form the product of the Mode distinctions *Goal, Place,* and *Source* with the SpatialModalities Inclusion and Support. As we will see below, Goal, Place and Source (or *GPS* for short) in fact seem to be three basic distinctions of Mode. Also, we will deal with a question that still needs to be answered: What exactly is Mode about if not about paths?

Evidence from spatial-case systems

We ended the previous section with two closely related claims. First, paths are not inherent to the linguistic description of motion events, and second, there is an additional level of analysis marking the way in which *GeneralizedLocations* participate in a spatial situation. In this section we will look into the spatial case systems of a number of languages to motivate and corroborate these claims. We will first show how the two levels (Mode and SpatialModality) indeed seem to be two different dimensions morphologically.

As we said above, linguistic-ontological distinctions should be reusable across meaning domains. Whereas lexical items are often situationally restricted, grammatical items are reused, by definition. For example, whereas the noun *ontology* probably appears less frequently in an average newspaper edition than it does in this chapter, the use of grammatical items such as articles (*a* and *the*) or the plural marker *-s* will not differ significantly between the two.

Morphological case, if present in a language, is among the most strongly grammatical resources a language has available, hence its interest for the development of a linguistic ontology. Morphological case is the use of suffixes to mark the syntactic or semantic role of a more lexical item in a clause. For example, where English uses word order to communicate who does what to whom, Latin and German (mostly) use case markers. More specifically, and of central concern to us here, *spatial case* is the use of dedicated morphological case markers to express spatial meaning. Whereas a language may have dozens of (spatial) adpositions, it typically has very few (spatial) case markers. As a result, the distinctions that are made by spatial case are generally of a more systematic and fundamental type. As we will see below, virtually all spatial-case systems distinguish between the three basic types of mode of GPS. In richer case systems, however, additional meaning distinctions can be made, and it is these additional distinctions that show the combinatorial possibilities of Mode and SpatialModalities we are after.

Consider the spatial-case paradigm of Hungarian in table 3.3.[2] The three Mode distinctions Goal, Place, and Source form a Cartesian product with the SpatialModalities ON, AT, and IN (unlike the terminative case 'up to'). This is reflected in the formal structure to some degree, as the two dimensions can partly be distinguished at the submorphological level. The IN cases start with *-b*, the ON cases start with *-r*, the Place cases end with *-n*, and the Source cases end with *-l*.

Table 3.3
Hungarian spatial case paradigm.

	Mode			
Configuration	Place	Source	Goal	TOWARD
ON	superessive	delative	sublative	terminative
	-on/-en/-ön/-n	*-ról/-röl*	*-ra/-re*	*-ig*
AT	adessive	ablative	allative	terminative
	-nál/-nél	*-tól/-töl*	*-hoz/-hez/-höz*	*-ig*
IN	inessive	elative	illative	terminative
	-ban/-ben	*-ból/-böl*	*-ba/-be*	*-ig*

Table 3.4
The case paradigm of Hungarian postpositions.

	Mode		
SpatialModality	Place	Goal	Source
OVER	fölött	fölé	fölül
UNDER	alatt	alá	alól
IN FRONT	elött	elé	elől
BEHIND	mögött	mögé	mögül
IN BETWEEN	között	közé	közül

The semantic and morphological structure becomes even clearer when one considers the case paradigm of Hungarian postpositions, shown in table 3.4. Here, only a three-way distinction is made. (The forms go back to the Old Hungarian spatial case system; see Creissels 2006 and Stolz 1992.) The different stems of Hungarian postpositions express more fine-grained SpatialModality distinctions comparable to English prepositions, their case forms make an additional Mode distinction.

Hungarian is an example of a language with a large case inventory. Consider the following examples from Dyirbal (Dixon 1972, p. 57), illustrating a more basic variety. Allative case marks Goal (3a), the ablative marks Source (3b), and locative case marks *Place* (3c), which, as will be shown, is the third logical Mode option.

(3) a. miãa-gu   b. miãa-Nunu   c. miãa-Nga
       camp-ALLATIVE   camp-ABLATIVE   camp-LOCATIVE
       'to the camp'   'from the camp'   'at the camp'

Studying a sample of 32 spatial-case inventories, Lestrade (2010) argues that these three distinctions are the standard ones made by spatial cases cross-linguistically. (See the table in the appendix below for an overview; see Creissels 2009; Kilby 1983; Stolz 1992 for similar enterprises, with consistent results; see Lestrade 2011, 2012 for further discussion). The existence of this basic set will figure prominently in our second claim, which is still to be developed. For if we accept the cross-linguistic morphological evidence as suggesting a distinction between the ontological levels SpatialModality and Mode (ignoring terminological issues; see for example Jackendoff 1983; Kracht 2002; Pantcheva 2010; Schank 1973; Svenonius 2008; Wunderlich 1991; and Zwarts 2005 for similar proposals), with GPS as the latter's basic distinctions, the question still remains as to what precisely the nature of Mode is.

If Mode concerned paths, the predominance of Goal, Place, and Source in spatial-case paradigms would actually be rather hard to explain. As argued in detail in Lestrade (2012), different path analyses come up with different classifications, but from none of these does it follow that Goal, Place, and Source are basic. Instead, one would expect meanings such as VIA, THROUGH, TOWARD, ALONG, and UP TO to be equally attested in spatial-case paradigms (e.g., Jackendoff 1983; Zwarts 2005). Under a path analysis, if Goal meant something like 'path ends in *GeneralizedLocation*' THROUGH, for example, could similarly be characterized as 'path goes through *GeneralizedLocation*' and UP TO as 'path that ends just before *GeneralizedLocation*'. As can be seen in the inventory given in table 3.5, however, these meanings only show up once the basic distinctions are made, if at all, and so cannot at all be considered to be as basic or primary as the GPS categories.

Table 3.5
Mode distinctions made by spatial case inventories. Abbreviations: P for Place, S for Source, G for Goal.

Language	Mode(-like)	Language	Mode(-like)
Ainu	P, G, S, 'via'	Ket	P1, P2, S, G, 'via'
Alamblak	P, P/G, G, 'via'	Koasati	P(/G), G
Aymara	P, G, S	Lithuanian	P
Basque	P, G, S, 'up to'	Malayalam	P/G, G
Cahuilla	P, G, S	Mangarrayi	P(/G), G
Dyirbal	P, G, S	Maricopa	P/G, 'via'
ES Nivkh	P/S, G, 'up to'	Meithei	P/G, S
Evenki	P, G, S, 'toward', 'via', 'along', 'from the direction of'	Mundari	P/G, S, 'up to'
Finnish	S, P, G	Nez Perce	P, G, S
Harar Oromo	P/G, S	P-Maliseet	
Hua	P/G, S	Tarma Quechua	P, G, S, 'via', 'up to'
Hungarian	S, P, G, 'toward'	Tswana	
Hunzib	P, G, S, 'via'	Tundra Yukaghir	P/G, P, G, S, 'via'
Ika	Warao	P, G/'via', S	
Imonda	P, G, S	West Greenlandic	P, G, S, P/'via'
Kanuri	P/S/'via', G	Yasin-Burushaski	P, G, S

Figure 3.1
Subeventual structure (adapted from Pustejovsky 1995).

As an alternative, we propose to think of mode as providing the link between the *GeneralizedLocation* and the subinterval of the event at which it is said to hold true. If we adopt the approach of Pustejovsky (1995) or the subeventual structure of Moens and Steedman (1988), the three Mode distinctions follow for free, as we will now show.

Some events can be analyzed as consisting of two ordered subevents. Formalities aside, this can be represented as in figure 3.1, in which a matrix event *e3* is decomposed into a first subevent *e1* and a final subevent *e2*. This structure is established independently from Mode concerns, for example to analyze such events as 'building a house', in which a building process (*e1*) precedes a state in which there is a house (*e2*).

If we think of Mode as exploiting this organization, then linking *GeneralizedLocations* to different parts of the structure allows the three basic modes to follow for free without special stipulation: Goal links a *GeneralizedLocation* to the final subevent, Source links it to the first one, and Place says a *GeneralizedLocation* holds true for the entire matrix event (or, equivalently, a non-decomposed simple event).

This section has argued that Mode is to be distinguished from Spatial-Modality—both are independent dimensions in the semantics of spatial situations. There seem then to be three basic mode distinctions only, viz. Goal, Place, and Source. This set automatically follows if we analyze Mode as providing the link between event time and GeneralizedLocation, an analysis which has the advantage of dispensing with spatial entities that are not encoded linguistically (i.e., paths).

Additional evidence for the ontology of mode
Suggestive as the evidence from language comparison already may be, there is more to discuss. In some languages, motion does not seem to be lexicalized as a moving object traversing a path, but as a discrete location change instead. For example, Bohnemeyer (2007) argues that in Yukatek Maya the traversal of a corresponding path is left for the hearer to infer. If in psycholinguistic experiments the subject/relatum does not move but the

ground is moved instead (for example a box covering a ball), change of location verbs, which in English would suggest motion of the subject/relatum, are applicable. Thus, whereas it is evidently the box that is moving, this would be expressed as *the ball goes into the box* nevertheless. (For similar observations about Japanese, see Kita 1999.) Also, and more important, if in similar experiments an object is "beamed" into a ground, one can say that it *entered* it in Yukatek Maya. Crucially, in both cases there is no course of motion of a moving figure and hence no path of motion.

Note that this is not at all as exotic as it may sound. In English too we can use Goal and Source expressions in situations in which there is no motion path. Consider the following quotation from the Wikipedia entry for *teleportation* (consulted on October 11, 2013; emphasis added):

(4) Teleportation is the transfer of matter **from one point to another** without traversing the physical space between them.

Obviously, our point is not about the physical possibility of this phenomenon, but about the naturalness with which Source and Goal expressions are used here in the explicit absence of a path. No speaker of English is going to stumble on the construction selected here involving 'from' and 'to' and the stated lack of traversal between the endpoints as involving a non sequitur. This is very different to the usual response to violations of necessary pre-conditions. Consider, for example, "he went from Paris to London but was never anywhere near Paris." This self-contradictory statement will be considered anomalous because basic presuppositions inherent to the semantics of the sentence have been violated. Evidently, no such violation is felt to be present in our teleportation example—not, we would suggest, because of what 'teleportation' means, but rather because giving Source and Goal information does not entail the presence of a path.

Now one could argue that uses as the above are in fact nothing but a metaphor, so let us consider this possibility. When we use a metaphor, we highlight a common structure in two different domains. We use something we know about a well-understood domain (the *vehicle*), to understand something else. If the essence of mode was about paths, we should be able to identify a metaphorical path in non-spatial uses of mode expressions too. This is not what we find however, as shown in the following example:

(5) The traffic light turned from red to green.

Rather than following a continuous path, the transition between red and green in (5) is very discrete. At one interval some state does not apply; at another it does. Obviously, if Goal and Source mode are understood as a change of location instead of paths, this non-spatial use is straightfor-wardly explained as a metaphorical change of location, i.e., from "being in a red state" to "being in a green state." But irrespective of whether one analyzes the above examples as metaphors, a unified semantics for these and core spatial uses of *from* and *to* suggests a discrete change rather than a continuous development along a path.

Where did paths come from (and where do they go)?

We stated above that it is not always clear on the basis of evidence from single languages where overcommitment might be occurring, and that cross-linguistic evidence is of crucial relevance in the formulation of dis-tinct spatial linguistic ontologies. Indeed, the reason that people did not question a path analysis of mode before is probably the focus on English prepositions (but see Bohnemeyer 2007; Fong 1997; Kracht 2002; Lestrade 2011). As Bateman et al. (2010, p. 1035) argue, however, languages can be expected to vary at more lexical levels of spatial organization, combining semantic features from domains that are not necessarily basic to the actual domain of interest.

Although, in comparison with nouns, prepositions are rather gram-matical, they probably still are too lexical a category to give a clean picture of the mode domain: Since languages generally have dozens of non-synonymous prepositions, they necessarily make more than just the five-way mode distinction that theories of mode allow at the maximum. (See Lestrade 2012.) As a result, a semantic characterization of mode on the basis of prepositions is likely to be obscured by meaning contrasts that do not belong to the domain proper.

In the proposal of Jackendoff (1999), for example, TOWARD belongs to the type of paths called *directions*, which, unlike a *bounded* path such as TO, do not include (the region with respect to) the reference object but would do so if the path were extended by some unspecified distance. In a non-trivial sense, we probably only want to allow for extensions in approxi-mately the same direction (otherwise, any direction could be turned into a TO path).[3]

Now, consider an enclosure around point A with an opening at its south side and point B to its north, as illustrated in figure 3.2. Because of the enclosure, one can only go from *A to B* going southwards, through the opening. To go from *A toward B*, however, one should go north. Crucially, the TOWARD path in this situation cannot be extended in the same direc-tion to become a bounded *to B* path. It is proposed here that *toward* expresses something categorically different from *to*. Instead of mode,

Figure 3.2
TO vs. TOWARD.

toward expresses orientation. When modifying a motion event with an orientation, the moving object generally ends up closer to the ground in which direction it is moving. And by continuing along this direction, the moving object will probably end up at this ground too. But this need not be, as this example shows.

We have argued above that Paths do not establish the ontological domain often attributed to them. This does not mean we should dispense with them altogether, however. In the revised ontology we envisage, they are a subclass of spatial modality. Differently from most other regions, however, they are elongated entities. Because of their semantics, they easily combine with motion expressions in situations in which the course of motion follows the path of the SpatialModality. This need not be, however, as it is just as well possible to occupy a path when no motion applies (e.g., *the people were standing around the fire*).

Conclusion

This chapter introduced the notion of a linguistically motivated ontology as one means of modeling the flexibility of natural spatial language. The distance between linguistic expressions and their contextualized interpretation was suggested to involve a mediating layer which allows semantics for spatial expressions to be formulated without overcommitting to meanings that might prevent possible and valid contextualized interpretations being found. Linguistic ontologies of this kind must be motivated on the basis of grammatical distinctions but it cannot always be guaranteed that one particular language will provide sufficient sources of information to constrain modeling choice at the semantic level. On the basis of previous work on English and German, for example, a particular ontological configuration for treating paths appeared plausible and this was built into our first versions of the linguistic ontology of spatial language.

However, more general linguistic treatments show that other possibilities might have been considered. To address this more systematically, this chapter showed how a broad cross-linguistic approach can provide the necessary points of triangulation to focus in on more appropriate modeling decisions. We also showed how useful insight can be taken from the limiting case of grammatical distinctions—grammatical case. Many languages show considerable sophistication in this area concerning their construction of space, spatial relationships and changes in spatial relationships.

We set out the treatment of paths in considerable detail. Attending to spatial case across languages allowed us to argue for a specific modeling decision that differs from the previously proposed account. The new construction is then claimed to be more adequate—*also for the languages previously treated*. In short, analysis in terms of paths is often an overcommitment. We therefore needed to revise the linguistic ontology and distinguish between mode and path as a further type of SpatialModality. Mode is then a discrete change of state/location, and only motion trajectory may be analyzed in terms of paths.

Providing increasingly fine-grained distinctions concerning the precise contribution of linguistic semantics of the kind illustrated here we then see as an important component of any broader understanding of spatial reasoning and communication skills in general.

Notes

1. The order of the authors' names is alphabetical.

2. The different case variants are driven by vowel assimilation and are phonologically predictable.

3. Thanks to Emar Maier for this observation.

References

Bateman, J. A. 2010a. Ontological diversity: The case from space. In A. Galton and R. Mizoguchi (eds.), *Formal Ontology in Information Systems*. IOS Press.

Bateman, J. A. 2010b. Situating spatial language and the role of ontology: Issues and outlook. *Linguistics and Language Compass* 4: 639–664.

Bateman, J. A. 2010c. Language and space: A two-level semantic approach based on principles of ontological engineering. *International Journal of Speech Technology* 13: 29–48.

Bateman, J. A., Borgo, S., Lüttich, K., Masolo, C., and Mossakowski, T. 2007. Ontological modularity and spatial diversity. *Spatial Cognition and Computation* 7: 97–128.

Bateman, J. A., and Farrar, S. 2004. Spatial ontology baseline. SFB/TR8 Internal Report I1-[OntoSpace]: D2, Collaborative Research Center for Spatial Cognition, University of Bremen.

Bateman, J., Hois, J., Ross, R., and Tenbrink, T. 2010. A linguistic ontology of space for natural language processing. *Artificial Intelligence* 174: 1027–1071.

Bohnemeyer, J. 2007. The pitfalls of getting from here to there: Bootstrapping the syntax and semantics of motion event expressions in Yucatec Maya. In M. Bowerman and P. Brown (eds.), *Cross-Linguistic Perspectives on Argument Structure: Implications for Learnability*. Erlbaum.

Borgo, S., Guarino, N., and Masolo, C. 1996. A pointless theory of space based on strong congruence and connection. In L. Aiello and J. Doyle (eds.), *Principles of Knowledge Representation and Reasoning*. Morgan Kaufmann.

Carlson, L. A., and van der Zee, E. 2005. *Functional Features in Language and Space: Insights from Perception, Categorization and Development*. Oxford University Press.

Cohn, A., and Hazarika, S. 2001. Qualitative spatial representation and reasoning: An overview. *Fundamenta Informaticae* 43: 2–32.

Coventry, K., Tenbrink, T., and Bateman, J. 2009. *Spatial Language and Dialogue*. Oxford University Press.

Creissels, D. 2006. Suffixes casuels et postpositions en hongrois. *Bulletin de la Société de Linguistique de Paris* 101: 225–272.

Creissels, D. 2009. Spatial cases. In A. Malchukov and A. Spencer (eds.), *The Oxford Handbook of Case*. Oxford University Press.

Dixon, R. 1972. *The Dyirbal Language of North Queensland*. Cambridge University Press.

Fong, V. 1997. The Order of Things: What Directional Locatives Denote. Doctoral thesis, Stanford University.

Herskovits, A. 1986. *Language and Spatial Cognition: An Interdisciplinary Study of the Prepositions in English*. Cambridge University Press.

Hois, J., Bhatt, M., and Kutz, O. 2009. Modular ontologies for architectural design. In R. Ferrario & A. Oltramari (eds.), *Formal Ontologies Meet Industry*. IOS Press.

Jackendoff, R. 1983. *Semantics and Cognition*. MIT Press.

Jackendoff, R. 1999. The architecture of the linguistic-spatial interface. In P. Bloom, M. A. Peterson, L. Nadel, and M. F. Garrett (eds.), *Language and Space*. MIT Press.

Jian, C., Zhekova, D., Shi, H., and Bateman, J. 2010. Deep reasoning in clarification dialogues with mobile robots. In *Proceedings of the 2010 Conference on ECAI 2010: 19th European Conference on Artificial Intelligence*. IOS Press.

Kilby, D. 1983. Universal and particular properties of the Ewenki case system. *Papers in Linguistics (Edmonton)* 16: 45–74.

Kita, S. 1999. Japanese enter/exit verbs without motion semantics. *Studies in Language* 23: 307–330.

Klippel, A., Tappe, T., Kulik, L., and Lee, P. U. 2005. Wayfinding choremes—A language for modeling conceptual route knowledge. *Journal of Visual Languages and Computing* 16: 311–329.

Kracht, M. 2002. On the semantics of locatives. *Linguistics and Philosophy* 25: 175–232.

Lestrade, S. 2010. The Space of Case. Doctoral thesis, Radboud University, Nijmegen.

Lestrade, S. 2011. Analyzing directionality: From paths to locations. In Proceedings of the Second Workshop on Computational Models of Spatial Language Interpretation and Generation, Boston.

Lestrade, S. 2012. A linguistic ontology of mode: The use of locations in spatial language. In C. Stachniss, K. Schill, and D. Uttal (eds.), *Spatial Cognition 2012*. Springer.

Levinson, S. C. 1996. Relativity in spatial conception and description. In J. J. Gumperz and S. C. Levinson (eds.), *Rethinking Linguistic Relativity*. Cambridge University Press.

Levinson, S. C., Kita, S., Haun, D. B., and Rasch, B. H. 2002. Returning the tables: Language affects spatial reasoning. *Cognition* 84: 155–188.

Li, P., and Gleitman, L. 2002. Turning the tables: Language and spatial reasoning. *Cognition* 83: 265–294.

Moens, M., and Steedman, M. 1988. Temporal ontology and temporal reference. *Computational Linguistics* 14: 15–28.

Pantcheva, M. 2010. The syntactic structure of locations, goals, and sources. *Linguistics* 48: 1043–1082.

Pustejovsky, J. 1995. *The Generative Lexicon*. MIT Press.

Ross, R. J., Mandel, C., Bateman, J., Hui, S., and Frese, U. 2006. Towards stratified spatial modeling for communication and navigation. Presented at IROS Workshop "From Sensors to Human Spatial Concepts," Beijing.

Ross, R., Shi, H., Vierhuff, T., Krieg-Brückner, B., and Bateman, J. 2005. Towards dialogue based shared control of navigating robots. In C. Freksa, M. Knauff, B. Krieg-Brückner, B. Nebel, and T. Barkowsky (eds.), *Spatial Cognition IV: Reasoning, Action, Interaction*. Springer.

Schank, R. 1973. Identification of conceptualizations underlying natural language. In R. Schank and K. Colby (eds.), *Computer Models of Thought and Language*. Freeman.

Stolz, T. 1992. *Lokalkasussysteme: Aspekte einer strukturellen Dynamik*. Gottfried Egert Verlag.

Svenonius, P. 2008. Projections of P. In A. Asbury, J. Dotlačil, B. Gehrke, and R. Nouwen (eds.), *The Syntax and Semantics of Spatial P*. John Benjamins.

Talmy, L. 1985. The fundamental system of spatial schemas in language. In B. Hampe (ed.), *From Perception to Meaning: Image Schemas in Cognitive Linguistics*. Mouton de Gruyter.

Tenbrink, T. 2007. *Space, Time, and the Use of Language: An Investigation of Relationships*. Mouton de Gruyter.

Wunderlich, D. 1991. How do prepositional phrases fit into compositional syntax and semantics? *Linguistics* 29: 591–621.

Zwarts, J. 2005. Prepositional aspect and the algebra of paths. *Linguistics and Philosophy* 28: 739–779.

II Visualization in Spatial Learning and Education

4 Reasoning with Diagrams: Toward a Broad Ontology of Spatial Thinking Strategies

Mary Hegarty, Mike Stieff, and Bonnie Dixon

Recently there has been much interest in the importance of spatial thinking, especially in science, technology, engineering, and mathematics (STEM) disciplines, and in fostering this type of thinking in our educational system. But what is spatial thinking? For many psychologists this question brings to mind classic tasks such as mental rotation (Shepard and Metzler 1971), scanning (Kosslyn, Ball, and Reiser 1978), and paper folding (Shepard and Feng 1972). These tasks are theoretically important in providing evidence that spatial inferences can be made by analog mental simulations that operate on mental images. Some of these tasks have also been adapted by psychometricians to develop measures of spatial abilities (Hegarty and Waller 2005). For example, two of the most commonly used tests of spatial ability are the Vandenberg and Kuse (1978) Mental Rotation Test and the Paper Folding Test (Ekstrom, French, Harman, and Dermen 1976).

In considering the role of spatial thinking in STEM disciplines, many psychologists and educators have focused on these classic tasks. They have shown that performance on mental rotation and paper folding tasks is correlated with performance in STEM disciplines (e.g., Casey, Nutall, and Pezaris 1997; Coleman and Gotch 1998; Orion, Ben-Chaim, and Kali 1997; Wai, Lubinski, and Benbow 2009). Most attempts to train spatial thinking have also concentrated on these tasks. (For a recent meta-analysis, see Uttal et al. 2013.) But a possible negative consequence of focusing on these tasks is that it might lead to the assumption that all spatial thinking depends on internal transformations of mental images. If we assume too narrow an ontology for spatial thinking, and concentrate on educating only one type of spatial thinking, we might miss opportunities for fostering spatial thinking that in the long term might bring more success.

Rather than concentrating exclusively on classic spatial tasks, in this chapter we consider how people solve a range of spatial problems in domains such as chemistry, mathematics, and mechanics. We examine problems in which scientists must consider the transformation of objects in three-dimensional space and in which the objects, phenomena, and concepts are represented by diagrams. We also revisit some of the classic tests of spatial ability to consider what strategies are actually used in taking these tests. We find that, in solving these problems, scientists and students frequently report using strategies that include generating, transforming, and inspecting mental images using spatial information. However, we also find that the strategies applicable to these problems are not limited to those that recruit imagistic thinking. In addition, they also include more analytic rule-based approaches and approaches that depend on modifying external representations. We develop a taxonomy of strategies for solving spatial problems and examine its applicability to understanding strategies in both organic chemistry problems and psychometric tests of spatial ability.

Strategies in Scientific Reasoning Tasks

Scientists in a variety of fields must consider both the structure of objects and the processes that bring about their transformation. For example, ecologists reason about the migration of species across geographic areas, physicists reason about the motion of light through different media, and chemists reason about the structure of molecules. Scientists often report the use of visual imagery in thinking about these structures and processes. Indeed, several key scientific discoveries have been attributed to insights gained from visual imagery (Ferguson 1977; Rothenberg 1995; Shepard 1978; Watson 1968).

However, cognitive science research has also revealed that in scientific problem solving, mental imagery is often augmented by other strategies and processes (Hegarty 2004; Schwartz and Black 1996; Stieff 2007). First, such problems can often be solved analytically. For example, when Schwartz and Black (1996) asked people to solve gear problems in which they had to determine which direction a particular gear in a gear chain would move (see figure 4.1a), their gestures indicated that they initially mentally simulated the motion of each gear; however, on the basis of these simulations, they discovered an analytic rule that any two interlocking gears move in opposite directions. After discovering this rule, people switched from imagery to a rule-based strategy. They shifted from internally representing and transforming all of the spatial information in the problem to just representing the number of gears between the crank and the gear in question to apply a simple parity rule.

a. When the driver turns clockwise, in which direction will gear 5 turn?

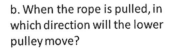

b. When the rope is pulled, in which direction will the lower pulley move?

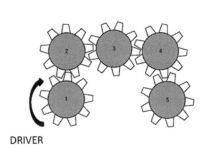

DRIVER

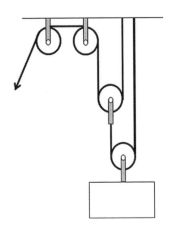

Figure 4.1
Examples of diagrammatic reasoning problems in the domain of mechanics.

Similarly, in the domain of organic chemistry, Stieff (2007) examined how novices and experts in organic chemistry solved a problem in which they were shown two molecular diagrams and asked if the two diagrams represented the same molecule or a mirror image pair. Such judgments are critical in organic chemistry, because two molecules composed of the same atoms with different spatial configurations have very different properties. Novices used mental rotation to solve this task. In contrast, experts were able to determine that two diagrams were identical if either of the two diagrams was symmetrical around a central axis. The differences in strategy use indicate that as chemistry expertise increases, a shift occurs from internally representing and transforming all of the given spatial information to making a judgment based on the a subset of the spatial information in the diagram.

Another type of analytic strategy, task decomposition, can be used when reasoning about complex systems from diagrams. Using task decomposition, participants mentally simulate the behavior of a relatively complex mechanical system piecemeal rather than holistically (Hegarty 1992, 2004). This strategy is especially effective when problem solvers are allowed to alter the diagram. For example, Hegarty and Steinhoff (1997) allowed one group of students to annotate external diagrams while they solved pulley systems problems such as the one in figure 4.1b. Another group was not allowed to make any notes. Interestingly, only some of the students in the notes group annotated the diagram. These students drew an arrow on each pulley and rope as they inferred how it moved. Although the inference process is likely to have involved imagery (see Hegarty 2004), only a small amount of the information in the problem (e.g., one pulley and its surrounding rope) had to be internally represented and transformed at a time, with other relevant information being added to the external diagram as it was computed.

Finally, translating between different representations can also be an effective problem-solving strategy (Ainsworth 2006, Kozma and Russell 2005). As pointed out by the Gestalt psychologists (Duncker 1945), re-representing a problem can often make a seemingly difficult problem almost trivial to solve. Scientists and engineers have capitalized on this fact and invented different unique diagrams for different purposes. For example, engineers might show the structure of a machine in an exploded view, a series of orthogonal cross sections, or an isometric view (Ferguson 1977). Diagrams not only provide an external representation, but they schematize or abstract from the reality that they represent so that they highlight some spatial aspects of the referent but not others. Depending on what they highlight, different diagrams are suited to solving different problems. For example, in chemistry, the three-dimensional structure of molecules is often shown in a dash-wedge diagram (figure 4.2a) in which the wedges represent bonds coming toward the viewer and the dashes represent bonds projecting away. Limited by the affordances of this diagram, Newman (1952) created an alternative diagram (figure 4.2b), to illustrate that any given molecule could assume unique spatial conformations to demonstrate to the scientific community that changes in spatial conformation produces strain on chemical bonds. Today, if a chemist has to reason about strain on chemical bonds, translating the dash-wedge diagram in figure 4.2a into the Newman projection diagram in figure 4.2b can be an effective strategy that highlights the task-relevant information and reduces the demands on internal processing. Examples of the invention or adaptation of diagrams for problem solving are commonplace in the history of STEM disciplines and often precede major scientific developments (Goodwin 2008; Kaiser 2008).

In summary, both experts and novices use a variety of strategies to make inferences about the spatial information represented in domain-specific diagrams. Interestingly, although tests of spatial ability typically include tasks such as mental rotation or mental paper folding, which are assumed

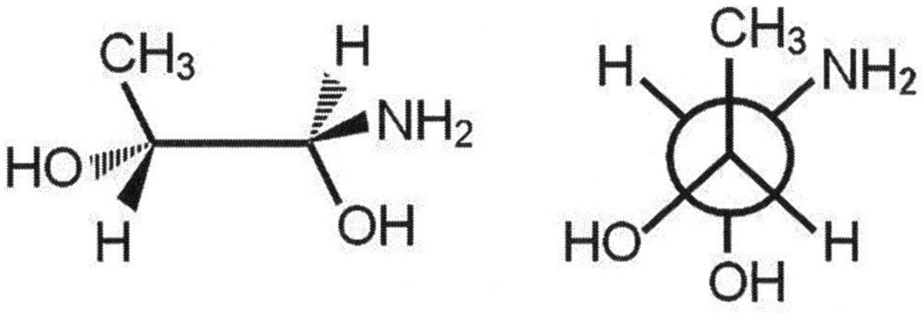

Figure 4.2
Left: Dash-wedge diagram of a molecule. Right: Newman projection representing the same molecule.

to measure ability to construct and transform mental images, there is also a history of studies showing that people use a variety of strategies on these tests, including piecemeal strategies and analytic strategies that do not involve imagery (Geiser, Lehmann, and Eid 2006; Just and Carpenter 1985; Lohman 1988). This raises questions about the enabling conditions for using different types of strategies in diagrammatic problems and whether the choice of strategy for a problem reflects a consistent cognitive style (Kozhevnikov 2007) or is dependent on problem type. Although the roles of alternative strategies for problem solving with diagrams have been discussed for some time, we need a framework that systematically characterizes the features of each strategy.

A Proposed Framework for Characterizing Spatial Reasoning Strategies with Diagrams

Stieff, Hegarty, and Dixon (2010) proposed a preliminary framework for defining and distinguishing the range of strategies that problem solvers employ in spatial reasoning with diagrams. This framework was derived from the analysis of verbal protocols, experiments, and informal observations of people working with diagrams on psychometric measures of spatial ability and organic chemistry problems (Hegarty 2010; Stieff 2011; Stieff and Raje 2010). A diagram is defined as an external visual-spatial representation (e.g., printed on a page or displayed on a computer monitor) that we can inspect with our eyes. By spatial reasoning with diagrams we mean any mental process that infers new spatial information from information encoded from a diagram or infers new spatial information in order to produce a diagram. We limit our framework (for now) to problems in which the diagram represents an entity that has spatial extent (although it may not be visual). For example, it can include representations of forces that are spatially distributed but not visible, or entities such as molecules that are too small to see. We set aside here the issue of how our framework might apply to entities that are only meta-phorically spatial, such as information "spatializations" (Skupin and Fabrikant 2003). We also limit our framework to tasks that involve infer-ences from static diagrams, although gestures, models, and animated dia-grams can also be important external representations in problem solving (Alibali 2005; Keehner, Hegarty, Cohen, Khooshabeh, and Montello 2008; Stull, Hegarty, Dixon, and Stieff 2002).

We classify problem solvers' spatial reasoning strategies according to three dimensions: (1) the locus of the primary representation (in the mind or in the world), (2) the amount of spatial information in the external diagram that is drawn upon, and (3) if and how the relevant representa-tion is modified. The first dimension places any spatial reasoning strategy on a continuum defined by the extent to which the solver relies upon internal versus external representations. On one end of the continuum, the problem solver might construct a mental image from the external representation and then transform that image to solve the problem. On the other end, the problem solver might rely primarily on the diagram in the problem statement, for example by translating it into a different diagram and reading the answer off that new external diagram. We acknowledge that both internal and external representations and pro-cesses are always used to some degree in solving problems in this class, but we propose that strategies differ in the degree of emphasis on internal versus external processing.

The second dimension identifies the amount of spatial information in the problem statement that is recruited by the strategy. At one end of this dimension, a problem solver might use a strategy that relies on all of the spatial information in the given diagram (e.g., the location, shape, and connectivity of entities depicted in the diagram). At the other end, he or she might focus on non-spatial information in the diagram, such as counting parts of the diagram. Finally, the framework includes a third dimension that defines how the problem solver modifies any relevant representation This dimension ranges from strategies that involve exten-sive modification, such as the construction of new external or internal representations, to those that involve no modification, such as strategies that read information off an unmodified representation. Figure 4.3 illus-trates the potential interactions between each of these three dimensions. Situating the axes orthogonally demonstrates the power of the framework to capture many strategies involved in spatial reasoning with diagrams.

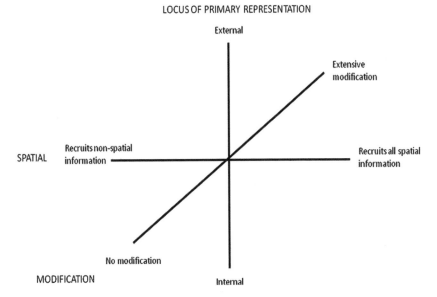

Figure 4.3
Framework for distinguishing the range of strategies used in spatial reasoning with diagrams.

However, whether the axes are fully orthogonal is an empirical question that is addressed below.

Using this framework, we have identified several common strategies used by problem solvers in chemistry and in the psychology laboratory during spatial reasoning with diagrams (Stieff et al. 2010). We developed "strategy assessments" for both typical end-of-chapter organic chemistry problems and common spatial ability tests (Hegarty 2010; Stieff, Ryu, Dixon, and Hegarty 2012). In these assessments, students first solve some problems and then choose from a set of strategy descriptions the method(s) they used to solve each problem (Lean and Clements 1981). In pilot studies, we determined that strategies chosen by students in these assessments were very consistent with strategies they were classified as using on the basis of think-aloud protocols on the same problems.

Here, we describe a study in which we classified students' self-reported strategies for organic chemistry problems and spatial abilities tests, according to the framework. We consider the range of strategies, how different strategy dimensions were related to problem-solving success, whether they were related to spatial abilities and instruction in organic chemistry, and whether an individual systematically chooses strategies of the same kind when solving problems in organic chemistry and when taking tests of spatial abilities.

The Study

Participants
Fifty chemistry students (25 female) at a research university participated in the study. They varied in the amount of instruction they had received in organic chemistry: 18 students (10 female) had taken one organic chemistry class, 17 students (8 female) had taken two classes, 11 students (6 female) had taken three classes, and 4 (1 female) were graduate students. They were paid $25 for their participation. One student (female, who had taken two organic chemistry classes) was not included in the analyses because her scores on two of the spatial tests were below chance.

Materials
Measure of organic chemistry problem solving and strategy choice
The organic chemistry problem-solving test consisted of twelve problems that assessed student understanding of spatial relationships relevant to organic molecules and organic transformations. (See the sample item in figure 4.4). Each item required students to (1) identify spatial relationships between molecules or structures within a molecule and (2) self-report one or more strategies used to solve each problem immediately after solving the problem. The measure of problem-solving success was the total number

Please indicate the stereochemical relationship between the two molecules.

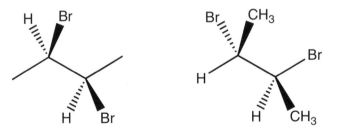

Figure 4.4
Item 1 from the test of organic chemistry problem solving, which can be solved via multiple strategies. Straight lines indicate bonds between atoms in the plane of the page, dashed lines indicate bonds projecting behind the plane of the page, and bold lines indicate bonds projecting above the plane of the page. These molecules are diastereomers that contain identical atoms arrayed in unique spatial arrangements.

of problems answered correctly. Participants were asked to report the strategy (or strategies) they used to solve each item by selecting from a fixed list of applicable strategies, adapted from previous studies (Stieff 2011; Stieff and Raje 2010). They were allowed to report more than one strategy per problem and to write in their own strategy if no choice matched it.

Measures of spatial ability and strategy choice
Students were tested on three measures of spatial ability, the Mental Rotation Test (Vandenberg and Kuse 1978), the Paper Folding Test (Ekstrom et al. 1976), and a modified version of Guay's Visualization of Views Test (Guay and McDaniels 1976). Sample test items are shown in figure 4.5.

a. Mental rotation

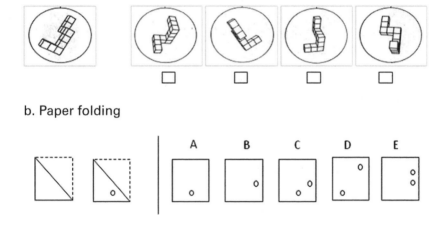

b. Paper folding

c. Visualization of views

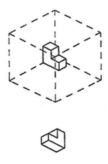

Figure 4.5
Examples of items from tests of spatial ability.

After completing the three spatial tests, students were given a strategy choice questionnaire for each test. Questionnaires showed a sample item from the test and a list of applicable strategies adapted from previous studies (Hegarty 2010). Students were allowed to report more than one strategy per test and to write in their own strategy if no choice matched it.

Procedure

Students participated in groups (four maximum). They first completed the measure of organic chemistry problem solving and strategy choice at their own pace. Then they were administered the three spatial ability tests, with the usual time limits for these tests. Finally they completed the strategy choice questionnaires for the spatial ability measures at their own pace. The study took approximately 90 minutes.

Coding of strategies

The self-reported strategies for chemistry problems were coded according to the three dimensions of our framework. (See figure 4.3.) Figure 4.4 illustrates a representative item from the chemistry task, which requires students to determine the spatial relationships between two molecules. The student must identify the internal spatial relationships between atoms in each molecule and determine if their relative geometries are identical. In the figure, the second molecule differs from the first with respect to the geometry of the atoms on the right half of the structure: the bromine (Br) and the methyl group (CH_3) are in opposite locations in the two structures. The atoms on the left half of each molecule have the same geometric relationships despite an internal rotation around the central axis. Thus, a student must notice (and disregard) the internal rotation on the left side while simultaneously recognizing that the atoms on the right side are transposed.

A partial list of strategies applicable to this item are listed in table 4.1. The first involves visualizing the spatial relationships depicted in the given diagram using mental imagery to predict the outcome of a rotation without modifying the external diagram. The strategy was coded as relying on an internal representation that involves a high degree of spatial information that is not modified. The second strategy has similar features, but involves shifting the viewer's perspective as opposed to rotating either of the molecular diagrams for comparison. These are both imagistic strategies.

In contrast, the third strategy relies on annotating the given diagram to compare the relative geometries. Using this strategy the student can

Table 4.1
Applicable strategies for solving item 1 on the chemistry assessment.

	Primary representation	Spatial information	Representation modification
I tend to imagine the molecule and rotate it "in my head."	Internal	High	Low
I tend to imagine myself moving into the paper or around the molecule.	Internal	High	Low
I tend to assign R/S designations to each asymmetric center (on the diagram).	External	Medium	Medium
I tend to first draw a basic skeletal structure and then make changes as I go.	External	Medium	High

apply verbal labels to each of the atoms according to a disciplinary algorithm and then draw vectors between the labels. This strategy makes evident that the bromine atom (Br) is located counterclockwise from the hydrogen atom (H) in the diagram on the left; in the diagram on the right, the bromine is located clockwise from the hydrogen. This strategy involves adding information to an existing representation to highlight spatial relationships so it is classified as relying on an external representation with medium modification and medium spatial information. The final strategy involves constructing a completely new representation of the given structure to support problem solving and modifying the novel representation in route to the problem solution. It is classified as relying on an external representation that involves high modification and medium spatial information.

Using this approach we coded each of 79 strategies (excluding guessing and direct recall) applicable across the 12 items. Each strategy was given a code of 1, 2, or 3 for each of the three dimensions. For the locus of representation dimension, a code of 1 indicated a strategy that depended primarily on manipulating an internal representation, a code of 2 indicated a piecemeal strategy that involved interplay between internal and external representations, and a code of 3 indicated that the strategy depended primarily on external representations. For the spatial dimension, we assigned a code of 1 for a strategy that recruited nonspatial information, 2 for a strategy that used a subset of the spatial information given, and a code of

3 for a strategy that used all of the spatial information given. For the representation modification dimension, a code of 1 was assigned if the student did not modify the given diagram in any way, 2 if they added some information to the representation, and 3 if they re-represented the given diagram (i.e., translated it into a different diagram). If students reported more than one strategy for a problem, the codes for the reported strategies were averaged for that problem. Finally, the three codes were averaged for the 12 problems, yielding a single score (range 1 to 3) for each student for each of the three strategy dimensions.

The Vandenberg Mental Rotation Test

Examples of items from the three psychometric tests of spatial abilities are shown in figure 4.5, and representative strategies for these items with their codes, are given in table 4.2. In the Mental Rotation Test (5a), people are shown a standard object on the left and four rotated items on the right. Their task is to decide which of the four objects on the right have the same shape as the standard object. The first two strategies in table 4.2 are imagistic and it was presumed that they involved internally representing the whole

Table 4.2

Common strategies for solving items on the Mental Rotation Test.

Strategy	Primary Representation	Spatial Information	Representation Modification
I imagined myself being stationary and the whole object rotating with respect to me.	Internal	High	Low
I imagined the objects being stationary as I moved around them to view them from different perspectives.	Internal	High	Low
I first imagined rotating a part of the object and then checked whether the rest of the object could be rotated in the same way to match the target.	Both	Medium	Low
I counted the number of cubes in the four straight segments of the object.	Both	Low	Low
I examined the directions of the two end segments with respect to each other.	Both	Medium	Low

object. The first, mental rotation, involves imagining the object move, whereas the second, perspective taking, involves imagining oneself moving around the object. Both strategies were classified as depending primarily on internal representations, as high in recruitment of spatial information, and as low in modification of the given representation. The third strategy describes piecemeal rotation, coded as involving an interplay between internal and external representations, medium reliance on spatial information (because only a part of the object was rotated), and low modification.

The next strategy, comparing arm axes involved abstracting a subset of the spatial information—the directions of the different segments or "arms" of the figures and comparing the relative directions of the two end arms in the standard figure to each of the four answer choices (Geiser et al. 2006). It was classified as involving interplay between internal and external representations, as medium in recruitment of spatial information, and as low in modification of the given representation. Another common strategy, counting the cubes in each segment of the object, recruits even spatial information from the problem statement, so it was classified as low in recruitment of spatial information. (See table 4.2.)

The Paper Folding Test

Table 4.3 lists representative strategies for the Paper Folding Test and how they were classified. The first strategy involved visualizing the folding of the paper and figuring out where the holes would be. This imagistic strategy depended primarily on internal representations, was high in recruitment of spatial information, and low in modification of the given representation. Some students who reported this strategy drew the holes on the test booklets (despite instruction not to), and in these cases we classified their strategy as relying on both internal and external representations and as medium on the modification dimension. Students also used a number of analytic strategies. Examples of these strategies and how they were classified are given in the table.

The Visualization of Views Test

Table 4.4 lists the classification of strategies for the Visualization of Views Test. The first two strategies correspond to holistic mental rotation and perspective taking, respectively, and they were coded as depending primarily on internal representations, high in spatial information, and low in modification. The next strategy uses mental rotation, but focused on only a part of the object, so was coded as medium in recruitment of spatial information. The last strategy listed involved two operations on the

Table 4.3
Common strategies for solving items on the Paper Folding Test.

Strategy	Primary Representation	Spatial Information	Representation Modification
I imagined folding the paper, punching the hole, and unfolding the paper in my mind. (If holes drawn)	Internal Both	High High	Low Medium
I figured out how many folds/sheets of paper were punched through and/or how many holes there would be in the paper at the end.	Both	Low	Low
I figured out where one of the holes would be and then eliminated answer choices that did not have a hole in that specific location.	Both	Medium	Low

Table 4.4
Common strategies for solving items on the Visualization of Views Test.

Strategy	Primary Representation	Spatial Information	Representation Modification
I imagined rotating the whole glass box with the object inside.	Internal	High	Low
I imagined myself moving around the object to view it from different corners of the glass box.	Internal	High	Low
I focused on a distinctive part of the object inside the cube (e.g., a triangle, a corner, a missing chunk) and imagined rotating the object while keeping track of that distinctive part.	Internal	Medium	Low
I first figured out the general direction of the view (e.g. top, bottom, left or right) and then figured out the specific corner from which I would see the view.	Both	Medium	Low

externally represented information, first considering the general direction of the view and then focusing in on the specific corner from which one would see the view, so they were coded as involving the interplay between internal and external representations and medium in spatial information, as they did not recruit all of the given spatial information.

Results

Descriptive statistics

Table 4.5 gives descriptive statistics for the measures of chemistry problem solving, spatial abilities, and strategy choice. The problems were challenging and the maximum score attained was 10 out of 12. The mean chemistry strategy scores were at about the center of the possible range for locus of representation (internal vs. external) and recruitment of spatial information, but students tended not to modify the representations extensively.

Scores on the spatial ability measures were somewhat higher than those observed in previous studies with college students, reflecting the fact that

Table 4.5
Descriptive statistics for the measures of chemistry problem solving, spatial abilities, and strategy choice.

Measure	Possible range	Mean	SD
Chemistry Problem Solving Score	0–12	5.2	2.1
Mental Rotation (MR) Score	0–80	44.2	19.4
Paper Folding (PF) Score	0–20	12.5	3.7
Visualization of Views (VoV) Score	0–24	13.1	7.7
Chemistry: Locus of Representation	1–3	2.0	0.4
Chemistry: Spatial Information	1–3	2.2	0.2
Chemistry: Representation Modification	1–3	1.4	0.3
MR: Locus of Representation	1–3	1.7	0.2
MR: Spatial Information	1–3	2.1	0.3
MR: Representation Modification	1–3	1.0	0.2
PF: Locus of Representation	1–3	1.5	0.3
PF: Spatial Information	1–3	2.3	0.5
PF: Representation Modification	1–3	1.1	0.3
VoV: Locus of Representation	1–3	1.3	0.2
VoV: Spatial Information	1–3	2.3	0.2
VoV: Representation Modification	1–3	1.0	0.0

STEM students (and chemistry students in particular) tend to have somewhat higher spatial abilities (Wai et al. 2009). The strategy scores for these measures indicated that participants depended primarily on internal representations in taking these tests and were relatively high in recruitment of spatial information. In general, very few students modified the representations. Only four students reported any representation modification for the Mental Rotation Test, and none of the strategies reported for the Visualization of Views Test involved any modification of the representation. A minority of the participants (15, or 30.6 percent) modified the representation for the Paper Folding Test, typically by drawing in the locations of the holes on the printed test. Because representation modification was rare on the spatial tests, this strategic aspect is not analyzed further for the spatial ability measures.

Correlations among strategies and performance on the chemistry problems
Correlations among the strategy dimensions for the chemistry problems, shown in table 4.6, were high. The very high correlation between the representation and modification strategies indicates that these strategies are not distinguishable for the chemistry problems considered here. A possible explanation is that the spatial information depicted by the diagrams was so complex that, because of limitations of working memory, it could not be transformed to a new representation internally, and as a result all modification of representations must occur externally. Furthermore,

Table 4.6
Correlations among the strategy dimensions for solving chemistry problems, and between these strategy dimensions and measures of performance.

	Locus of Representation	Recruitment of Spatial Information	Representation Modification	Chemistry Problem Solving
Recruitment of Spatial Info.	−.60**			
Representation Modification	.92**	−.51**		
Chemistry Problem Solving	.28*	−.13	.13	
Mental Rotation	−.20	.36*	−.26	.19
Paper Folding	−.05	−.01	−.17	.34*
Visualization of Views	−.10	.12	−.15	.43**

recruiting more spatial information was negatively correlated with relying on external representations and modifying the given representation. This suggests that when external representations are modified, they tend to be schematized (become more abstract) so that less spatial information is tracked.

As table 4.6 shows, use of external representations was marginally correlated with problem-solving success, but the other two strategy dimensions were not significantly correlated with success. This table also indicates that recruitment of more spatial information in one's strategy for solving chemistry problems was correlated with performance on the Mental Rotation Test but not the other two spatial tests. In contrast, success on the chemistry problem-solving test was correlated with the Paper Folding and Visualization of Views Tests but not the Mental Rotation Test.

Correlations among strategies and performance on the spatial tasks

Correlations among the spatial ability strategy dimensions and spatial scores are presented in table 4.7. As in the case of chemistry problem solving, when students depended more on external representations in their problem solving, they tended to recruit less spatial information in their solutions. It is notable that the strategy dimensions were not correlated across the different spatial ability tests. For example, there was no significant correlation between recruitment of spatial information on the Mental Rotation Test and recruitment of spatial information on the other two tests. Accuracy scores on the three spatial tests were moderately correlated, as expected. It is notable that none of the strategy dimensions for the spatial tests was significantly correlated with performance on that test.

Table 4.7 also shows correlations between the strategy dimensions for the spatial ability tests and those for the chemistry problems. These were somewhat consistent. Specifically, recruitment of spatial information on the Visualization of Views Test and chemistry problems were significantly correlated, and dependence on external representations in the Paper Folding Test and the chemistry problems were significantly correlated.

Domain-specific instruction

Previous research has found that students tend to switch from imagistic to analytic strategies with experience in a domain (Hegarty et al. 2013; Schwartz and Black 1996; Stieff et al. 2012). Table 4.8 shows trends in chemistry strategies as a function of the number of organic chemistry classes taken by students. Students relied more on external representations and recruited less spatial information with more knowledge of organic

Table 4.7
Correlations among the spatial ability strategy dimensions and test scores.

	MRT Rep	MRT Spatial	PF Rep	PF Spatial	VoV Rep	VoV Spatial	MRT	PF
MRT Spatial	−.85**							
PF Rep	−.17	.25						
PF Spatial	.08	−.13	−.57**					
VoV Rep	.07	−.07	.28	−.20				
Vov Spatial	−.24	.10	−.07	−.06	−.55**			
Chem Spatial	−.16	.21	−.03	−.03	−.20	.33*		
Chem Rep	−.17	.17	.41**	−.22	.14	−.10		
MRT	−.02	.16	−.18	.03	.00	.18		
PF	.19	−.15	−.15	.09	.01	−.02	.39**	
Vov	−.02	.02	−.39**	.19	−.04	−.02	.56**	.44**

Table 4.8
Means and standard deviations for the three strategy dimensions on chemistry problems for students who had taken different numbers of organic chemistry classes.

	Classes			
	One	Two	Three or more	
	Mean (SD)	Mean (SD)	Mean (SD)	F (2, 46)
Locus of Representation	1.8 (.42)	2.1 (.39)	2.2 (.28)	3.7, $p < .03$
Recruitment of Spatial Information	2.3 (.25)	2.2 (.17)	2.1 (.15)	3.2, $p < .05$
Modification	1.3 (.27)	1.4 (.24)	1.5 (.21)	2.0, $p = .15$

chemistry. Post hoc (Bonferroni) tests indicated that in both cases, students who had taken three or more classes differed significantly from those who had taken only one organic chemistry class; students who had taken two courses did not significantly differ from these groups.

Discussion

In this chapter we examined the plausibility of a new framework for characterizing and classifying problem-solving strategies for spatial reasoning with diagrams. We classified strategies for solving spatial problems according to three unique characteristics: use of internal versus external representations, recruitment of spatial information, and modification of representations. A first important result of our study is that many different strategies are used to solve organic chemistry problems and items from tests of spatial ability; these strategies vary across all three dimensions of our framework. A second important result is that problem-solving success was almost never associated with the specific type of strategy used. While success on the chemistry problems was marginally correlated with use of external representations, none of the other strategy dimensions were correlated with performance on either the chemistry or spatial measures. All types of strategies, as defined by our framework, can contribute to success. None is privileged, nor does any type of strategy guarantee success. These results argue for a broad ontology of spatial thinking processes and against the idea that effective spatial thinking is always based on internal manipulation of mental images.

Stieff et al. (2010) placed strategies on a multi-dimensional space with three orthogonal dimensions. Having applied the framework in an empirical study, we can now ask whether all three dimensions of the framework are necessary to classify strategies, and whether the dimensions are in fact orthogonal. For all four problem types considered here (chemistry problems and the three spatial tests), recruitment of spatial information was negatively correlated with use of external representations, suggesting that these two dimensions, although not identical, are probably not orthogonal. Rather, it seems that external representations of spatial entities tend to be more schematic and recruit less spatial information than internal representations. One likely reason for this relationship is that external representations on paper are two-dimensional, whereas the entities they represent in these problems are often three-dimensional. Furthermore, at least in chemistry, external representations are conventional representations of the discipline, which are often deliberately schematized to emphasize only a subset of the information that is relevant to solving a specific problem. Finally there is a cost to generating extensive external representations of a problem: The act of externalizing the representation may induce the problem solver to consider only the most relevant information and to schematize.

Modification of representations was very highly correlated with use of external representations in the case of the organic chemistry problems and was rare for spatial ability problems. These results initially suggest that modification is not a necessary dimension of our framework. However, it would be premature to conclude this based on the domains considered in this study. As suggested earlier, the molecular structures considered in our chemistry problems are quite complex, so it is unlikely that students would be able to modify them internally given working memory limits, and in the case of the spatial ability tests, the instructions often discourage students from making any external modifications. Internal modification of representations also appears to be rare on these types of tests. However, when we consider a broader set of problems, it becomes clear that both internal and external modification may be important in other domains. For example, research on linear reasoning problems (e.g., "A is smarter than B, C is dumber than B, who is smartest?") has revealed that people often translate the given verbal representation into an internal spatial representation (Knauff 2013), and research on abstract arithmetic and algebra problem solving indicates that solvers often translate the external abstract representation into an internal spatial representation (Dehaene, Bossini, and Giraux 1993; Goldstone, Landy, and Son 2010).

We found that students who had taken more classes in organic chemistry depended less on internal representations and recruited less spatial information. These results are consistent with the spatial-to-abstract shift documented in other domains, that naive strategies tend to be primarily imagistic, while strategies become more abstract with experience (Schwartz and Black 1996; Stieff 2007; Stieff et al. 2012). We suggest that imagistic strategies are effortful and demanding of working memory resources, even for high-spatial students, so that students switch to more analytic problem-solving methods when they can. With more knowledge of the domain, students are better able to abstract the critical spatial information in a problem and have also been exposed to more disciplinary algorithms, which depend more on external manipulations of spatial information.

Finally, there was only weak evidence that dimensions of people's strategies correlated across problem types. Students who recruited more spatial information on the Visualization of Views Test also recruited more spatial information on chemistry problems, and there was a significant correlation between use of external representations on the Paper Folding Test and chemistry problems; however none of the strategy dimensions correlated across the spatial tests. While research on cognitive style has attempted to classify individuals as preferring imagistic or more abstract problem-solving methods across a range of problems (see Kozhevnikov 2007 for a review), our results suggest that strategy choice may depend more on the specific demands of a problem or the knowledge of the problem solver than on a domain general cognitive style.

Our research argues for a broad ontology of strategies for solving problems with spatial representations. Although internal transformation of mental images is an important aspect of spatial thinking, spatial thinking strategies are broader than this and include extensive use of external representations and spatial-analytic processes that make inferences from spatial representations on the basis of rules and heuristics rather than imagistic simulations. These conclusions raise obvious questions about whether strategies can be taught and how strategy training might impact performance in real classroom settings. We addressed these questions in a recent educational intervention study, in which we trained three different cohorts of students (over 100 students in each cohort) to use either imagery strategies, analytic problem-solving strategies, or their combination in the context of a college chemistry course (Stieff, Dixon, Ryu, Kumi, and Hegarty 2014). As predicted, students were more likely to adopt analytic strategies after analytic training, indicating that we had successfully influenced their strategies. Moreover, training in the combined use of imagery and analytic strategies resulted in significantly better performance on both our problem-solving test and on class assessments, compared to training in the use of either imagery or analytic strategies alone. This study provides an initial demonstration of the effectiveness of attending to diverse problem-solving strategies in an educational context. As we consider how to educate spatial thinking, it is important that we teach students to employ the full range of spatial thinking strategies.

Acknowledgments

We thank Bailey Bonura, Krista DeLeeuw, Bryna Kumar, Jana Ormsbee, Minjung Ryu, and Andrew Stull for contributing to data collection, coding, and analysis activities as well as input on the framework. This work was supported by the National Science Foundation under grants DRL-0722333 and 0723313.

References

Ainsworth, S. 2006. DeFT: A conceptual framework for considering learning with multiple representations. *Learning and Instruction* 16: 183–197.

Alibali, M. W. 2005. Gesture in spatial cognition: Expressing, communicating and thinking about spatial information. *Spatial Cognition and Computation* 5: 307–331.

Casey, M. B., Nuttall, R. L., and Pezaris, E. 1997. Mediators of gender differences in mathematics college entrance test scores: A comparison of spatial skills with internalized beliefs and anxieties. *Developmental Psychology* 33: 669–680.

Coleman, S. L., and Gotch, A. J. 1998. Spatial perception skills of chemistry students. *Journal of Chemical Education* 75: 206–209.

Dehaene, S., Bossini, S., and Giraux, P. 1993. The mental representation of parity and number magnitude. *Journal of Experimental Psychology. General* 122: 371–396.

Duncker, K. 1945. On problem solving. *Psychological Monographs* 58 (5): i–113.

Ekstrom, R. B., French, J. W., Harman, H. H., and Dermen, D. 1976. *Kit of Factor-Referenced Cognitive Tests*. Educational Testing Service.

Ferguson, E. S. 1977. The mind's eye: Non-verbal thought in technology. *Science* 197: 827–836.

Geiser, C., Lehmann, W., and Eid, M. 2006. Separating "rotators" from "non rotators" in the Mental Rotations Test: A multivariate latent class analysis. *Multivariate Behavioral Research* 41: 261–293.

Goldstone, R. L., Landy, D., and Son, J. Y. 2010. The education of perception. *Topics in Cognitive Science* 2: 265–284.

Goodwin, W. M. 2008. Structural formulas and explanations in organic chemistry. *Foundations of Chemistry* 10: 117–127.

Guay, R., and McDaniels, E. 1976. *The Visualization of Viewpoints*. Purdue Research Foundation.

Hegarty, M. 1992. Mental animation: Inferring motion from static diagrams of mechanical systems. *Journal of Experimental Psychology. Learning, Memory, and Cognition* 18: 1084–1102.

Hegarty, M. 2004. Mechanical reasoning as mental simulation. *Trends in Cognitive Sciences* 8: 280–285.

Hegarty, M. 2010. Components of spatial intelligence. In *The Psychology of Learning and Motivation*, volume 52, ed. B. H. Ross. Academic Press.

Hegarty, M., and Steinhoff, K. 1997. Use of diagrams as external memory in a mechanical reasoning task. *Learning and Individual Differences* 9: 19–42.

Hegarty, M., Stieff, M., and Dixon, B. L. 2013. Cognitive change in mental models with experience in the domain of organic chemistry. *Journal of Cognitive Psychology* 25: 220–228.

Hegarty, M., and Waller, D. 2005. Individual differences in spatial abilities. In *Handbook of Visuospatial Thinking*, ed. P. Shah and A. Miyake. Cambridge University Press.

Just, M. A., and Carpenter, P. A. 1985. Cognitive coordinate systems: Accounts of mental rotation and individual differences in spatial ability. *Psychological Review* 92: 137–172.

Kaiser, D. 2008. Physics and Feynman's diagrams. *American Scientist* 93: 156–165.

Keehner, M., Hegarty, M., Cohen, C. A., Khooshabeh, P., and Montello, D. R. 2008. Spatial reasoning with external visualizations: What matters is what you see, not whether you interact. *Cognitive Science* 32: 1099–1132.

Knauff, M. 2013. *Space to Reason*. MIT Press.

Kosslyn, S. M., Ball, T. M., and Reiser, B. J. 1978. Visual images preserve metric spatial information: Evidence from studies of image scanning. *Journal of Experimental Psychology. Human Perception and Performance* 4: 47–60.

Kozhevnikov, M. 2007. Cognitive styles in the context of modern psychology: Toward an integrated framework of cognitive style. *Psychological Bulletin* 133: 464–481.

Kozma, R. B., and Russell, J. 2005. Students becoming chemists: Developing representational competence. In *Visualization in Science Education*, ed. J. K. Gilbert. Springer.

Lean, C., and Clements, M. A. 1981. Spatial ability, visual imagery, and mathematical performance. *Educational Studies in Mathematics* 12: 267–299.

Lohman, D. F. 1988. Spatial abilities as traits, processes, and knowledge. In *Advances in the Psychology of Human Intelligence*, ed. R. J. Sternberg. Erlbaum.

Newman, M. A. 1952. A useful notation for visualizing certain stereospecific reactions. *Record of Chemical Progress* 13: 111.

Orion, N., Ben-Chaim, D., and Kali, Y. 1997. Relationship between earth-science education and spatial visualization. *Journal of Geoscience Education* 45: 129–132.

Rothenberg, A. 1995. Creative cognitive processes in Kekulé's discovery of the structure of the benzene molecule. *American Journal of Psychology* 108: 419–438.

Schwartz, D. L., and Black, J. B. 1996. Shuttling between depictive models and abstract rules: Induction and fall-back. *Cognitive Science* 20: 457–497.

Shepard, R. N. 1978. Externalization of mental images and the act of creation. In *Visual Learning, Thinking and Communication*, ed. B. S. Randhava and W. E. Coffman. Academic Press.

Shepard, R. N., and Feng, C. 1972. A chronometric study of mental paper folding. *Cognitive Psychology* 3: 228–243.

Shepard, R. N., and Metzler, J. 1971. Mental rotation of three-dimensional objects. *Science* 171: 701–703.

Skupin, A., and Fabrikant, S. I. 2003. Spatialization methods: A cartographic research agenda for non-geographic information visualization. *Cartography and Geographic Information Science* 30: 99–119.

Stieff, M. 2007. Mental rotation and diagrammatic reasoning in science. *Learning and Instruction* 17: 219–234.

Stieff, M., and Raje, S. 2010. Expert analytic and imagistic problem solving strategies in advanced chemistry. *Spatial Cognition and Computation* 10: 53–81.

Stieff, M. 2011. When is a molecule three-dimensional? A task-specific role for imagistic reasoning in advanced chemistry. *Science Education* 95: 310–336.

Stieff, M., Ryu, M., Dixon, B., and Hegarty, M. 2012. The role of spatial ability and strategy preference during spatial problem solving in organic chemistry. *Journal of Chemical Education* 89: 854–859.

Stieff, M., Hegarty, M., and Dixon, B. 2010. Alternative strategies for spatial reasoning with diagrams. In *Diagrammatic Representation and Inference*, ed. A. K. Goel, M. Jamnik, and N. H. Narayanan. Springer.

Stieff, M., Dixon, B. L., Ryu, M., Kumi, B., and Hegarty, M. 2014. Strategy training eliminates sex differences in spatial problem solving in a STEM domain. *Journal of Educational Psychology* 106: 390–402.

Stull, A. T., Hegarty, M., Dixon, B. L., and Stieff, M. 2012. Representational translation with concrete models in organic chemistry. *Cognition and Instruction* 30: 404–434.

Uttal, D. H., Meadow, N. G., Tipton, E., Hand, L. L., Alden, A., Warren, C., et al. 2013. The malleability of spatial skills: A meta-analysis of training studies. *Psychological Bulletin* 139: 352–402.

Vandenberg, S. G., and Kuse, A. R. 1978. Mental Rotations: A group test of three dimensional spatial visualization. *Perceptual and Motor Skills* 47: 599–601.

Wai, J., Lubinski, D., and Benbow, C. P. 2009. Spatial ability for STEM domains: Aligning over 50 years of cumulative psychological knowledge solidifies its importance. *Journal of Educational Psychology* 101, 817–835.

Watson, J. D. 1968. *The Double Helix*. Penguin.

5 Spatial Ability and Learning from Visualizations in STEM Disciplines

Scott R. Hinze, Vickie M. Williamson, Mary Jane Shultz, Ghislain Deslong-champs, Kenneth C. Williamson, and David N. Rapp

Students in science, technology, engineering and math (STEM) courses are often exposed to pictures, animations, and displays that are intended to convey complex concepts and interactions. These types of presentations have been termed visualizations, which embodies the idea they are external representations that convey information in an interpretable form. In many cases, well-designed visualizations help make visible the kinds of processes and relationships that normally are unobservable to the naked eye. Much of the content of STEM coursework proves inaccessible in this way, either because the critical elements under study are so microscopic or temporally expanded that seeing them is impossible (e.g., cellular structure or geophysical development), or because the elements are abstracted from reality or associated with imagined objects (e.g., scientific formulas or hypothetical situations). As such, visualizations have become indispensable in STEM fields, both for students and scientists. Successful scientific understanding, in classrooms, laboratories, and conference settings, requires fluent interpretations of information that cannot be directly observed. And such fluency proves a challenge because these unobservable constructs and processes often run counter to peoples' experiences with objects and interactions in the observable world (Sanger, Phelps, and Fienhold 2000; Williamson and Jose 2009). For these reasons, visualizations present a means of providing valid experiences with fundamental scientific content.

Despite peoples' endorsements of visualizations, as exemplified by their frequent implementation in textbooks, classrooms, online courses, and news media, it remains an open question as to when and for whom visualizations might prove more or less effective at supporting student understandings. One way to begin addressing this issue is by considering whether and how students of differing spatial abilities with differing goals approach and learn from visualizations. Determining whether visualizations prove differentially effective as a function of learner abilities (aptitude-treatment-interactions: Cronbach and Snow 1977; Snow 1989) would prove informative both in identifying conditions for which they might be usefully employed and for considering the kinds of supports that are necessary for scaffolding their use with particular groups of learners. Our goal in this chapter is to outline evidence from our own research and the work of others that examines how spatial abilities relate to learning from and with visualizations. Our interest in this set of issues derives precisely from investigations of whether spatial skills influence comprehension of STEM visualizations.

Spatial skills can include a variety of abilities and processes, including speeded identification of features, robust construction and manipulation of mental models (see Pellegrino and Kail 1982), imagining an object from multiple angles, and visualizing a cross-section through a three-dimensional object (see Hegarty and Waller 2005). Although these are separable skills, they are sometimes grouped together as a general construct termed *spatial ability* (see Carroll 1993 for discussion). Previous work has employed this general construct, with predictions in a variety of literatures hypothesizing that spatial skills can support the efficient construction and manipulation of mental models encoded as a function of the spatial features of visualizations (e.g., Cohen and Hegarty 2007; Huk 2006; Mayer and Sims 1994). This general processing advantage should therefore lead to greater visualization benefits for individuals with higher as compared to lower spatial abilities, which is consistent with what has been termed the *ability-as-enhancer hypothesis*. A recent meta-analysis (Höffler 2010) found general support for this hypothesis across 27 experiments, identifying a positive relationship between spatial abilities and learning from visualizations ($r = 0.34$). However, the relationships between spatial abilities and learning from visualizations, we have found, are more complex than is implied by the observation that spatial abilities and learning from visualizations are positively related. This complexity is precisely the focus of the current chapter.

We begin with evidence for two possible relationships. On one hand, as discussed, visualizations may be most useful for learners with *high* spatial abilities, because these learners have the requisite skills to comprehend and utilize the spatial information conveyed in the visualizations (Mayer and Sims 1994). By this account, students' spatial abilities should support their learning from visualizations. On the other hand, some visualizations can be particularly useful for learners with *low* spatial abilities, scaffolding their understandings of complex spatial information (e.g.,

Höffler and Leutner 2011). This might suggest that pre-existing spatial abilities are less crucial for supporting students' learning from well-designed visualizations. So these two accounts offer contrasting views, reflecting either a crucial role for spatial abilities in helping people comprehend visualizations, or indicating that visualizations can help overcome any inherent difference in learners' spatial abilities. Understanding when these or other relationships obtain is crucially important for educators and instructional designers for developing and implementing visualizations intended to convey spatial relationships in STEM content areas. In this chapter, we propose that predicting when these possible relationships will obtain for a given visualization depends on a number of factors including visualization design, task demands, a learner's domain knowledge, and their processing strategies.

To support this discussion, we briefly review earlier research demonstrating that visualizations can be designed to enhance learning for individuals with lower spatial abilities, in contrast to generally assisting participants with high abilities. We then review previous research as well as ongoing work from our own lab demonstrating that the relationships between spatial ability and comprehension of visualizations are more complex than previously characterized. Importantly, this complexity helps to identify methods for scaffolding learners' understandings of the representations, which we consider relevant given the ubiquity of visualizations in formal and informal educational settings.

Designing Visualizations to Compensate for Spatial-Ability Limitations

One important role for visualizations is that they externalize representations that would otherwise be difficult to mentally conceptualize. By some accounts, visualizations help support the construction of spatial mental models (Rapp 2005; Rapp and Kurby 2008). Although learners with strong spatial abilities seem to construct such models easily, external visualizations may be crucial for individuals with weaker spatial abilities, helping to compensate for processing difficulties (i.e., identifying important features of a visualization; making spatial connections and inferences; converting from two- to three-dimensional representations). Of course, not all visualizations are identical, and some features may be more or less useful for participants with lower spatial abilities. Effective visualizations are often designed to target particular challenges for learners and succeed better when characteristics of their displays are more obviously visible so as to support identification and inference.

For example, in the geosciences, learners often struggle with visualizing dynamic relationships (e.g., plate tectonics) as provided by text descriptions (Gobert and Clement 1999) or presented in static pictures (Jee, Gentner, Forbus, Sageman, and Uttal 2009). As one demonstration, the functional spatial and temporal relationships that underlie interacting plates may not be obvious from a static visual representation, requiring the mental visualization of the relevant processes and their products (see Hegarty 1992). Participants who score low on tests of spatial visualization ability may have particular difficulty with the demands of this mental activity. One way to address this difficulty is to animate the visualizations, making critical dynamic relationships salient in a display. Research has indicated that animations can help low-spatial learners perform more like high-spatial learners (Sanchez and Wiley 2010), because the mental visualization of dynamic relationships is not required if those dynamic relationships are explicitly presented. Precisely because animations make particular features of visualizations more obvious, one line of reasoning is that spatial abilities are less important for understanding animated displays than for static displays (Höffler and Leutner 2011). Similarly, spatial abilities appear to be less important for learning from three-dimensional displays than from two-dimensional displays, at least based on differences in effect sizes across experiments (Höffler 2010). Presumably, three-dimensional displays make readily apparent features of a model that would otherwise need to be mentally derived from a two-dimensional display (Rapp, Culpepper, Kirkby, and Morin 2007), effectively reducing spatial demands. In addition, visualizations with which students can make notes or that explicitly denote features and relationships serve as external memory aids, helping low-spatial participants offload memory demands (Hegarty and Steinhoff 1997). The result is that learners can utilize their mental resources more effectively to engage with the displays.

The design features described above are specifically hypothesized to reduce some of the burdens placed on learners. As such, these types of design features (see also Ainsworth 2006; Mayer 2001) can help reduce the demands of spatially intensive comprehension tasks, especially for participants who might typically struggle with spatial thinking. This suggests that visualization designs can have a strong influence on whether spatial abilities will predict performance, as those abilities might be more or less crucial or relevant depending on the particular design affordances available during attempts at understanding the depicted information. In the next section, we discuss how task demands might recruit different *types* of spatial skills.

Spatially Relevant Task Demands

Visualizations are often presented to students in their coursework, in textbooks and on tests, to help them learn about fundamental STEM concepts. For example, in physics classes students may be required to translate graphical representations of velocity over time into explanations about the operation of objects in the real world (Kozhevnikov, Motes, and Hegarty 2007); in biology classes, students may be asked to use multiple visualizations of population dynamics to observe and test models for how predators and prey interact (Wilensky and Reisman 2006). These are but two examples of the kinds of visualizations that are commonly employed as part of students' STEM lessons. One way to evaluate the utility of STEM visualizations for participants with high and low spatial abilities is to identify the particular spatial demands of a learning task, and outline how the demands might align or misalign with the spatial abilities necessary for completing them. A form of this approach is actually utilized in the development of standard tests of spatial abilities (e.g., Bodner and Guay 1997; Guay and McDaniels 1976; Vandenberg and Kuse 1978) although in a slightly different way; these tests intentionally require specific types of spatial processes, meaning that some spatial skills are requisite for task performance while others are not. Standard tests are typically designed to focus in on single abilities as a measurement goal. Researchers can apply this classic approach to the study of learning from visualizations by identifying, bottom-up, the various spatial abilities that might be part of a learning experience, and then determining whether the demands associated with completing the task necessitate or influence use of those abilities.

Consider, for example, the task of memorizing navigational routes from maps with the goal of later reproducing those routes from memory (Sanchez and Branaghan 2008). Performance on this task is positively related to spatial tests thought to reflect the ability to visualize or imagine complex spatial information (e.g., the Paper-Folding Test), but is unrelated to tests thought to reflect the ability to rotate mental representations (e.g., the Cube Comparisons Test). One explanation for this finding is that the recall task required mental visualization of the spatial relationships conveyed by the map, as associated with performance on the former tests, but did not specifically require mental rotation of the map features to complete successfully, as measured by performance on the latter tests. This illustrates a basic tenet of this approach: Generally speaking, relationships between spatial abilities and visualization comprehension will be strongest when the demands of spatial-abilities tests align with the demands of the learning task. (For particular examples of tests and the processes necessary for completing them, please see Carroll 1993 and Uttal et al. 2013.)

Even with this tenet in place, it is not always obvious when particular learning demands might align or misalign with a skill or test, which presumably could be overcome in a relatively arduous way by analyzing spatial tests and visualization features on a case-by-case basis. To help guide these predictions and explanations in a more principled way (while also avoiding "fishing expeditions" for particular relationships), formal taxonomies of spatial skills can be used to identify potential alignments between task demands and spatial skills. Several informative taxonomies have been derived based on process and psychometric analyses of spatial tasks, in order to differentiate the cognitive demands of spatial tasks on one or more dimension (see Carroll 1993; Hegarty and Waller 2005; Linn and Petersen 1985; Pellegrino and Kail 1982). For example, some tasks require individuals to identify simple spatial relationships between objects, and measure performance based on speeded judgments, while others require individuals to visualize complex spatial relationships and rely on accuracy measures (Lohman 1979; Pellegrino and Kail 1982; Pellegrino, Alterton, and Shute 1984). As a more recent example, a taxonomy offered by Newcombe and Shipley (Newcombe and Shipley 2012; see also Uttal et al. 2013) differentiates tasks on two dimensions, each based on earlier experimental and theoretical work: On one dimension, tasks can focus on characteristics that are *intrinsic* to an object (its shape, size, and constituent parts), or characteristics that are *extrinsic* to an object (its relationship to another reference point, such as another object or the observer). The second dimension, which we focus on here, differentiates processes that are "static," requiring the coding of shapes and identifying embedded objects, from processes that are "dynamic," requiring the mental manipulation of imagined objects, as in Mental Rotation or Paper Folding tests. This dimension appears consistent with earlier work differentiating [static] spatial perception tasks from [dynamic] mental rotation tasks (Linn and Petersen 1985) or [static] visual closure tasks from [dynamic] spatial relations tasks (see Carroll 1993). One implication of this static-dynamic distinction is that the skills associated with dynamic spatial-abilities tests (e.g., Mental Rotation) should prove most crucial to performance on visualization tasks that require the manipulation of spatial features, but matter less for performance on tasks focused on the decomposition of shapes. In contrast, skills associated with static spatial-abilities tests (e.g., tests requiring the identification of embedded figures, such as the Hidden Patterns Test) should relate to performance on visualization tasks that require the decomposition or identification of shapes, but not to performance on tasks that require the manipulation of spatial features. Thus, depending on how we measure and conceptualize spatial abilities and the spatial demands of the learning task, spatial-ability metrics can be evaluated with respect to their implications for deriving learning outcomes.

Recent work from our own lab has obtained evidence consistent with the taxonomic distinction between static and dynamic spatial skills, indicating that matches between visualization tasks and spatial skills prove important for predicting any visualization benefits for performance (Hinze, Rapp, Williamson, Shultz, Deslongchamps, and Williamson 2013). We presented first-semester students of organic chemistry with static images of molecules in two formats. One format presented familiar ball-and-stick images displaying atoms as colored balls connected via "sticks" representing the bonds between atoms. Students were familiar with these types of models given their traditional and routine implementation in formal classroom settings. The other format presented unfamiliar, color-coded, space-filling models termed *electrostatic potential maps* (EPMs). The students were unfamiliar with the EPMs, having never encountered them in explicit instruction at the college level (or likely previous to attending college). Participants were asked to use one or both of the visualization formats to answer questions about features of the molecules or chemical interactions. Importantly, the unfamiliar EPM models were particularly useful for molecular interaction questions that were of interest in the visualized lesson. Our goal was to determine whether and when students would begin relying on the novel EPMs for reasoning about molecular interactions, and whether patterns of reliance were related to different types of spatial or other cognitive abilities. For this reason, we assessed students' static and dynamic spatial skills along with their domain knowledge and performance on logical reasoning tasks. For participants to answer questions regarding molecular interactions, they needed to reason about features of the static molecules (e.g., identifying atoms and relative electrostatic charges; perhaps mapping features of the two types of models). But answering these questions did not require them to mentally rotate or manipulate the components of the visualizations. Thus, reasoning on this STEM task should not be strongly related to performance on *dynamic* spatial-abilities tests, but should be related to performance on *static* spatial-abilities tests.

This is precisely the pattern we found. Student accuracy on inferential judgments that necessitated focus on the interactions between molecules correlated significantly with performance on the Hidden Patterns Test ($r(30) = 0.37$, $p < 0.05$), a speeded static task requiring the identification of embedded shapes (Ekstrom, French, and Harmon 1976). Inference accuracy, in contrast, was *not* related to performance on dynamic tests such as the Mental Rotation Test (Ekstrom et al. 1976), the Visualization of Views Test (Guay and McDaniels 1976), or the Visualization of Rotations Test (Bodner and Guay 1997; all *r*'s < 0.18). These data provide an example in which the relationship between spatial ability and visualization comprehension depends on the specific spatial-ability tests of interest.[1] If we had only assessed dynamic spatial skills, we would have concluded that spatial abilities did not relate to performance in this scenario. And, in fact, it does not seem surprising that mental rotation or complex visualization skills did not predict performance for this specific task: Students were only required to decode and infer relationships from the visualizations, without the explicit requirement to mentally manipulate the representations in any way. In contrast, quickly and accurately identifying components of a complex display is a key skill for many standard spatial tasks, including the Hidden Patterns Test (see Mumaw, Pellegrino, Kail, and Carter 1984), and individual differences in these skills were necessarily important for the chemistry task that students were asked to complete.

The above findings indicate that taxonomic classifications of task demands can be useful for considering the role of spatial skills in learning from visualizations. Given the array of processing demands across everyday and lab-based learning and spatial-ability tasks, careful consideration of how these demands may influence performance can inform the selection of appropriate spatial skills tests. Additionally, post hoc assessments of which spatial skills relate to particular types of performance may help determine the corresponding demands required by a learning task (e.g., inferring that speeded static skills but not complex visualization skills are required for learning to utilize EPMs). These types of taxonomic considerations may be particularly useful for instructors and designers in determining whether and how certain visualizations will influence participants with different levels of spatial skills, and for considering the types of spatial skills that may be most relevant given the demands of a task.

Strategic Application of Domain Knowledge

Researchers may be interested in isolating the role of spatial skills in learning from novel visualizations in specific content areas. But real-world STEM education involves ongoing, long-term interactions with content of ever-increasing complexity, ideally with learners integrating new information and experiences with existing domain knowledge (see National Research

Council 2007). Developing domain knowledge can have a direct influence on learning from visualizations because comprehension regularly necessitates accessing relevant knowledge that can inform any experienced content. Fundamentally, the kinds of external visualizations we are focusing on here are *representations* of the real world rather than exact copies, meaning that they require some knowledge to map the features of the representations to their referents (see Uttal and O'Doherty 2008), and to fill in missing information. Knowledge within a domain facilitates this integration of visualization features with their domain-specific referents (see Hinze et al. 2013). As evidence of the importance of such a role for domain knowledge, research demonstrates that domain experts consider visual representations within their domain more effectively than do novices (Cook 2006; Gegenfurtner, Lehtinen, and Säljö 2011). But here is another potential benefit. In our experiments involving EPMs described above (Hinze et al. 2013), we found that prior knowledge was a strong predictor of learning to utilize novel visualizations. Students with more domain knowledge in chemistry (all participants were novice first-semester organic chemistry students, but were selected to represent high-knowledge and low-knowledge groups with respect to their prior knowledge based on a pre-test) were more likely to adopt the novel visualizations, as indicated by eye-tracking and verbal-explanation data. Moreover, high-knowledge students were more accurate when making inferences based on the visualizations. These differences based on domain knowledge were correlational in nature, but we have reason to believe that the relationships were due to domain knowledge, rather than other factors. First, domain knowledge was more predictive of behavior and performance than were measures of spatial abilities or logical reasoning abilities, suggesting that the results probably were not due to differences in general intelligence. Second, the finding is consistent with other experimental work demonstrating that even short instructional manipulations can influence learners' understanding and inferences based on visualizations (Hegarty, Canham, and Fabrikant 2010). In sum, whereas complex visualization ability tests did not predict performance on our novel visualization task, relatively subtle differences in domain knowledge did, suggesting an independent role for domain knowledge in learning from visualizations.

While spatial abilities and domain knowledge can independently relate to performance, as was the case with our EPM studies, in many instances spatial abilities and domain knowledge can interact (see Uttal and Cohen 2012 for a review). Consider a study in which geology students with a range of domain expertise engaged in a field study, collecting samples of different rock units in different locations of a specified geographic area (Hambrick et al. 2012). Based on their observations, the students constructed geological bedrock maps identifying the spatial locations of different layers of rock. The maps were scored based on how closely their constructions depicted rock layers as aligned with a scientifically valid key. This task appears to rely on spatial visualization abilities, given the demands of constructing a cross-sectional map relating features reflecting geological breadth and depth (see Rapp et al. 2007). And as expected, a general spatial-ability factor correlated with accuracy scores on the constructed maps. But this correlation only held for participants with low geological domain knowledge. Experts, in contrast, revealed no relationship between their spatial abilities and the accuracy of their maps. Presumably experts were able to draw on their knowledge about geology to generate expectations about the relationships between geological features, helping them to construct the map without need for relying on spatial thinking. Based on these findings, the authors hypothesized that domain knowledge can reduce the need to rely on spatial skills for interpreting and organizing spatial visualizations, which can help to circumvent any potential limitations a learner may have with respect to applying such skills. More generally, these findings indicate that spatial abilities may predict a novice's comprehension or construction of visualizations, but that this relationship should decrease as individuals gain domain knowledge and become ever more expert.

Further evidence for interactions between prior knowledge and spatial thinking come from tasks that can be completed using *either* a spatial strategy, requiring the visualization and manipulation of spatial features, or a knowledge-based strategy, employing analytical reasoning with a reduced regard for spatial thinking (see Hegarty 1992; Schwartz and Black 1996). Research on spatial-abilities tasks has shown that individuals can utilize a variety of strategies to complete them, and that these strategies can alter the skills applied to the task (see Just and Carpenter 1985; Lohman 1979). Similarly, differences in "spatial" and "analytical" strategy use should influence the types of skills applied to learning from visualizations. One task on which these two strategies can both be applied involves identifying the similarities between stereochemistry visualizations (Stieff 2007; Stieff, Ryu, Dixon, and Hegarty 2012). For the specific tasks of interest here, learners are presented with two molecular visualizations that are either identical or mirror images of each other. The visualizations can be rotated on an axis anywhere between 0° and 180°. Participants are asked to identify whether the two molecules, one rotated on its axis differently from the other, are the same or different (i.e., mirror images). This design makes stereochemistry problems look quite similar to classic mental rotation tasks involving abstract three-dimensional figures (Shepard and Metzler 1971). Results from those classic tasks typically demonstrate a linear relationship between the speed of identification and the degree of rotation of the two objects, suggesting that the objects must be mentally transformed to accurately compare them.

For stereochemistry problems, as with abstract three-dimensional figures, Stieff (2007) found similar relationships between the degree of rotation and participant response time specifically for chemistry novices. This suggests that chemistry novices used a mental rotation strategy to solve the problems, which it turns out, they identified on a subsequent survey as the explicit strategy they used for completing the task. Chemistry experts, in contrast, more often reported using a knowledge-based strategy for solving stereochemistry problems with symmetrical molecules. This strategy required a simple heuristic to compare certain ions between the two visualizations, necessitating no need for mental rotation. Consequently, experts revealed no relationship between the necessary degree of mental rotation and their response times for solving the problems. Participants' domain knowledge provided alternative, non-spatial strategies for effectively reasoning with the problems. This indicates that the relationship between spatial abilities and performance can change with expertise, but this shift may reflect strategic choices that downplay a role for spatial thinking, instead emphasizing other kinds of analytic strategies. Even for tasks with features that clearly align with spatial skills tests, such as comparing the angles of two molecules or two abstract objects, relationships between spatial abilities and performance can be influenced by the strategic approaches an individual utilizes for solving problems.

These interactions between domain knowledge and spatial skills complicate the relationship between spatial abilities and any knowledge acquisition from visualization experiences. Intriguingly, the above patterns for experts suggest that domain knowledge can, in some cases, overwhelm or circumvent any limitations that learners might exhibit if they rely solely on spatial skills. Thus, interventions aimed at promoting domain knowledge, or encouraging non-spatial strategies for problem solving (Stieff 2013), may be beneficial for learners with lower spatial abilities.

Strategic Application of Spatial Skills

In the previous section, we reviewed evidence that it is possible for students to decide *whether or not* they apply their spatial skills, especially when more analytical domain-knowledge-based strategies are available. Equally important may be whether individuals effectively direct their spatial skills when they put them to use on visualization comprehension tasks. Recently, we found evidence that spatial abilities can guide both effective and ineffective learning strategies (Hinze, Williamson, Shultz, Williamson, Deslongchamps, and Rapp 2013). Participants in these experiments included general chemistry students whose dynamic spatial visualization abilities varied based on scores on the Mental Rotation Test, the Visualization of Views Test, and the Visualization of Rotations Test. We presented these students with three "simulated experiments" included in previous studies in chemical education (Velázquez-Marcano, Williamson, Ashkenazi, Tasker, and Williamson 2004; Williamson et al. 2012). These simulated experiments displayed a video on one side of a computer screen showing water or gas reaching equilibrium in different situations. Appearing simultaneously on the other side of the screen was a schematic animation depicting the movement of molecules in the same system. The participants were asked to view the visualizations and select and construct explanations for why the result shown in the video occurred. That explanation needed to be informed by the animation, as the animation provided the necessary detail to correctly explain these results in a manner consistent with the particulate nature of matter (see Johnstone 1993). For example, in one set of displays the animation depicted the random motion of gas molecules within one container. When another container was connected to create a greater volume, the random motion of the molecules continued throughout the larger space. Thus, the random motion depicted in the animation can be used to explain why gases diffuse to apparently fill a container, as related to activities shown in the video.

One adaptive strategy for viewing these simultaneous displays is to transition back and forth between them to integrate the molecular and real-world information. We allowed one group of participants ($n = 41$) to view the two displays in anticipation of explaining the results while we tracked their eye movements. The number of transitions that participants performed between the two displays was positively related to explanation accuracy, which suggests that an integration strategy was helpful. We also found that the relationship between transitions and accuracy was moderated by spatial visualization abilities, with integration attempts *more* helpful for participants with high spatial ability, and *less* helpful for participants with low spatial ability. In other words, we observed little in the way of a general advantage for participants with high spatial abilities, but those spatial skills were beneficial when participants attempted to integrate the displays. We concluded that spatial visualization skills help participants to more effectively construct and relate information provided in multiple displays, but only if participants direct their attention toward such integrating activity.

An alternative strategy for viewing the visualizations could involve concentrating on one display (e.g., the video only) at the expense of the other. We noted that typical procedures (Velázquez-Marcano et al. 2004) can subtly encourage just such a focusing strategy, as when participants are required to predict the results of a simulated experiment at the macroscopic level. These instructions convey to participants the need for attending to real-world depictions and information. Across two of our experiments, we specifically asked participants ($n = 83$) to complete just such a prediction task and noted they spent most of their time looking at the video rather than the animation, making relatively few transitions between the two displays. Interestingly, spatial visualization abilities seemed to enhance this focusing strategy, correlating with more time viewing the video and less time viewing the animation! Thus it seems as though spatial skills were associated with attending to certain kinds of spatial information. Interestingly, this strategy was ineffective in one experiment and apparently detrimental to learning in the other experiment, as focus and spatial abilities *negatively* correlated with explanation accuracy.

These results illustrate that pre-study tasks, like the predictions we asked participants to generate, can sometimes encourage an ineffective application of spatial skills. The results also support a more general (and perhaps unsurprising but important) point: Spatial thinking must be directed in effective ways to support performance. Most studies have examined situations in which spatial skills should enhance the effective use of spatial strategies for comprehending visualizations. However, the appropriate application of such strategies is far from guaranteed in everyday learning experiences, and as we have shown, depend on complex relationships between cognitive abilities and task demands (see Hinze, Bunting, and Pellegrino 2009). We reiterate: Instructors and educational designers should carefully consider the types of instructions, pre-study tasks, and available cues that may bias processing approaches. The strategies that people rely upon as they interact with visualizations can have positive *or* negative consequences with respect to guiding spatial considerations and supporting accurate understandings.

Conclusions

The goal of this chapter was to consider how individual differences in spatial abilities relate to the use of and learning from STEM visualizations.

Previous work has generally identified a positive relationship between spatial abilities and learning from visualizations. Spatial abilities *should* support learning from visualizations, given the spatial demands required to comprehend and use these often complex displays. (See Höffler 2010.) Our focus here was on factors that might complicate this generally positive relationship. We began by describing how particular design decisions can benefit low-spatial participants, helping to level the playing field for learners of differing abilities. Next, we identified a critical role for task demands, both with regard to visualizations, and with regard to spatial-abilities tests associated with learning. We indicated that taxonomies identifying different types of spatial abilities can prove useful for determining when the exigencies of a learning task may rely on a particular spatial skill (likely leading to positive relationships between measures of this skill and performance), and when the demands may misalign (likely leading to no or even a negative relationship). A crucial element of this discussion focused on how learners can use domain knowledge to supplement or circumvent limitations in their spatial abilities through the use of non-spatial strategies. We then offered evidence from our own work that highlighted implications of the above issues by demonstrating situations for which spatial skills can be directed in effective or ineffective ways.

Each of the factors we discussed (visualization design, alignments between task demands, domain knowledge interactions, and learner strategies) complicate the notion of a simple, positive relationship between spatial abilities and learning from visualizations. We do not wish to claim based on these findings that spatial abilities are *unimportant* for learning from STEM visualizations. Rather, we believe that outlining these factors can help clarify and specify the types of spatial thinking involved for specific learning experiences, allowing for more nuanced theoretical and applied considerations of spatial thinking and visualization comprehension.

We also add that the factors reviewed in this paper are by no means an exhaustive list, as other influences can no doubt interact with spatial ability. For example, other relevant considerations likely include learner motivation (e.g., Dweck 1986) and the learner's level of interest in a particular visualization (Goldstone and Son 2005). Another important factor that has been severely understudied relates to the types of high-stakes environments in which learners often find themselves (Sarason and Sarason 1990). Research has demonstrated that pressure to perform on STEM tasks in high-stakes as compared to low-stakes situations can hurt performance (e.g., Beilock and Carr 2001). Interestingly, these decrements appear to most strongly influence participants with high working-memory capacity.

Presumably, high-ability participants' cognitive resources, normally allocated effectively for task performance, are diverted to dealing with performance-related worry in high stakes situations (Beilock and Carr 2005). One intriguing question is whether pressure could similarly influence participants' performance on spatial visualization tasks, and whether such pressure would have a disproportionate influence on participants with stronger spatial abilities.

Earlier research demonstrated that spatial abilities predict success and long-term involvement in STEM fields (Shea, Lubinski, and Benbow 2001; Wai, Lubinski, and Benbow 2009). In apparent contrast to these general findings, the work reviewed here intriguingly demonstrates a certain amount of flexibility with regard to individual differences in a critical area of STEM learning. That is, for visualization comprehension, there appear to be a number of possible routes to success. Aided by careful considerations of spatially relevant task demands, visualization designers could build in supports that might offload difficult task demands for low-spatial participants, or reduce cognitive demands more generally. Guided by strategy training or effective pre-task activities, learners may be directed toward effective implementations of spatial thinking. Interventions could thus help learners more effectively apply their spatial skills and attention, perhaps through dynamic interactions intended to direct attention toward information that is particularly relevant for understanding specific topics (Rapp 2006). Domain knowledge can also facilitate competencies or strategies with regard to visualization use to help learners overcome limitations related to their spatial abilities. Similarly, explicit strategy training could reduce differences between participants for tasks that recruit spatial thinking. (See Stieff 2013.) Continued research in this area will further inform the types of design decisions, educational interventions, and learning strategies that can support learners of varying abilities to comprehend and learn from visualizations.

Acknowledgments

This work was funded by the National Science Foundation under REESE grants 0907780 and 0908130 to Dr. David N. Rapp and Dr. Mary Jane Shultz.

Note

1. Astute readers will note that we assessed only one measure of static spatial skill, but several measures of dynamic skills. The reason for this is that our taxonomic distinction was applied after selecting standard spatial-abilities tasks from the

psychometric literature (but before data analysis), and that selection included only one measure that could be characterized as a static task. More careful analyses related to this or other taxonomies could select multiple measures a priori, representing different spatial skills, along with multiple target tasks that might be relevant to those different skills. (See Newcombe and Shipley 2012.)

References

Ainsworth, S. 2006. DeFT: A conceptual framework for considering learning with multiple representations. *Learning and Instruction* 16: 183–198.

Beilock, S. L., and Carr, T. H. 2001. On the fragility of skilled performance: What governs choking under pressure? *Journal of Experimental Psychology. General* 130: 701–725.

Beilock, S. L., and Carr, T. H. 2005. When high-powered people fail: Working memory and "choking under pressure" in math. *Psychological Science* 16: 101–105.

Bodner, G. M., and Guay, R. B. 1997. The Purdue visualization of rotations test. *Chemical Educator* 2: 1–18.

Carroll, J. B. 1993. *Human Cognitive Abilities: A Survey of Factor Analytic Studies*. Cambridge University Press.

Cohen, C. A., and Hegarty, M. 2007. Individual differences in use of external visualisations to perform an internal visualisation task. *Applied Cognitive Psychology* 21: 701–711.

Cook, M. P. 2006. Visual representations in science education: The influence of prior knowledge and cognitive load theory on instructional design principles. *Learning* 60: 1073–1091.

Cronbach, L., and Snow, R. 1977. *Aptitudes and Instructional Methods: A Handbook for Research on Interactions*. Irvington.

Dweck, C. 1986. Motivational processes affecting learning. *American Psychologist* 41: 1040–1047.

Ekstrom, R. B., French, J. W., and Harmon, H. H. 1976. *Manual for Kit of Factor-Referenced Cognitive Tests*. Educational Testing Service.

Gegenfurtner, A., Lehtinen, E., and Säljö, R. 2011. Expertise differences in the comprehension of visualizations: A meta-analysis of eye-tracking research in professional domains. *Educational Psychology Review* 23: 523–552.

Gobert, J. D., and Clement, J. J. 1999. Effects of student-generated diagrams versus student-generated summaries on conceptual understanding of causal and dynamic knowledge in plate tectonics. *Journal of Research in Science Teaching* 36: 39–53.

Goldstone, R., and Son, J. Y. 2005. The transfer of scientific principles using concrete and idealized simulations. *Journal of the Learning Sciences* 14: 69–110.

Guay, R., and McDaniels, E. D. 1976. *The Visualization of Viewpoints.* Purdue Research Foundation.

Hambrick, D. Z., Libarkin, J. C., Petcovic, H. L., Baker, K. M., Elkins, J., Callahan, C. N., et al. 2012. A test of the circumvention-of-limits hypothesis in scientific problem solving: The case of geological bedrock mapping. *Journal of Experimental Psychology. General* 141: 397–403. doi:10.1037/a0025927.

Hegarty, M. 1992. Mental animation: Inferring motion from static diagrams of mechanical systems. *Journal of Experimental Psychology. Learning, Memory, and Cognition* 18: 1084–1102.

Hegarty, M., Canham, M. S., and Fabrikant, S. I. 2010. Thinking about the weather: How display salience and knowledge affect performance in a graphic inference task. *Journal of Experimental Psychology. Learning, Memory, and Cognition* 36: 37–53.

Hegarty, M., and Steinhoff, K. 1997. Individual differences in use of diagrams as external memory in mechanical reasoning. *Learning and Individual Differences* 9: 19–42.

Hegarty, M., and Waller, D. 2005. Individual differences in spatial abilities. In *The Cambridge Handbook of Visuospatial Thinking*, ed. P. Shah and A. Miyake. Cambridge University Press.

Hinze, S. R., Bunting, M. F., and Pellegrino, J. W. 2009. Strategy selection for cognitive skill acquisition depends on task demands and working memory capacity. *Learning and Individual Differences* 19: 590–595.

Hinze, S. R., Rapp, D. N., Williamson, V. M., Shultz, M. J., Deslongchamps, G., and Williamson, K. C. 2013. Beyond ball-and-stick: Students' processing of novel STEM visualizations. *Learning and Instruction* 26: 12–21.

Hinze, S. R., Williamson, V. M., Shultz, M. J., Williamson, K. C., Deslongchamps, G., and Rapp, D. N. 2013. When do spatial abilities support student comprehension of STEM visualizations? *Cognitive Processing* 14: 129–142.

Höffler, T. N. 2010. Spatial ability: Its influence on learning with visualizations—a meta-analytic review. *Educational Psychology Review* 22: 245–269.

Höffler, T. N., and Leutner, D. 2011. The role of spatial ability in learning from instructional animations—Evidence for an ability-as-compensator hypothesis. *Computers in Human Behavior* 27: 209–216.

Huk, T. 2006. Who benefits from learning with 3D models? The case of spatial ability. *Journal of Computer Assisted Learning* 22: 392–404.

Jee, B., Gentner, D., Forbus, K., Sageman, B., and Uttal, D. 2009. Drawing on experience: Use of sketching to evaluate knowledge of spatial scientific concepts. In Proceedings of the 31st Annual Conference of the Cognitive Science Society, Amsterdam.

Johnstone, A. 1993. The development of chemistry teaching: A changing response to changing demand. *Journal of Chemical Education* 70: 701–705.

Just, M. A., and Carpenter, P. A. 1985. Cognitive coordinate systems: Accounts of mental rotation and individual differences in spatial ability. *Psychological Review* 92: 137–172.

Kozhevnikov, M., Motes, M. A., and Hegarty, M. 2007. Spatial visualization in physics problem solving. *Cognitive Science* 31: 549–579.

Linn, M. C., and Petersen, A. C. 1985. Emergence and characterization of sex differences in spatial ability: A meta-analysis. *Child Development* 56: 1479–1498.

Lohman, D. F. 1979. Spatial Ability: A Review and Reanalysis of the Correlational Literature. Technical report 8, Aptitude Research Project, School of Education, Stanford University.

Mayer, R. E. 2001. *Multimedia Learning*. Cambridge University Press.

Mayer, R. E., and Sims, V. K. 1994. For whom is a picture worth a thousand words? Extensions of a dual-coding theory of multimedia learning. *Journal of Educational Psychology* 86: 389–401.

Mumaw, R. J., Pellegrino, J. W., Kail, R. V., and Carter, P. 1984. Different slopes for different folks: Process analysis of spatial aptitude. *Memory and Cognition* 12: 515–521.

National Research Council. 2007. *Taking Science to School: Learning and Teaching Science in Grades K–8*. National Academies Press.

Newcombe, N. S., and Shipley, T. F. 2012. Thinking about spatial thinking: New typology, new assessments. In *Studying Visual and Spatial Reasoning for Design Creativity*, ed. J. S. Gero. Springer.

Pellegrino, J. W., and Kail, R. V. 1982. Process analyses of spatial aptitude. In *Advances in the Psychology of Human Intelligence*, volume 1, ed. R. J. Sternberg. Erlbaum.

Pellegrino, J. W., Alderton, D. L., and Shute, V. J. 1984. Understanding spatial ability. *Educational Psychologist* 19: 239–253.

Rapp, D. N. 2005. Mental models: Theoretical issues for visualizations in science education. In *Visualization in Science Education*, ed. J. K. Gilbert. Springer.

Rapp, D. N. 2006. The value of attention aware systems in educational settings. *Computers in Human Behavior* 22: 603–614.

Rapp, D. N., Culpepper, S. A., Kirkby, K., and Morin, P. 2007. Fostering students' comprehension of topographic maps. *Journal of Geoscience Education* 55: 5–16.

Rapp, D. N., and Kurby, C. A. 2008. The 'ins' and 'outs' of learning: Internal representations and external visualizations. In *Visualization: Theory and Practice in Science Education*, ed. J. K. Gilbert, M. Reiner, and M. Nakhleh. Springer.

Sanchez, C. A., and Branaghan, R. J. 2008. The interaction of map resolution and spatial abilities on map learning. *International Journal of Human-Computer Studies* 67: 475–481.

Sanchez, C. A., and Wiley, J. 2010. Sex differences in science learning: Closing the gap through animations. *Learning and Individual Differences* 20: 271–275.

Sanger, M. J., Phelps, A. J., and Fienhold, J. 2000. Using a computer animation to improve students' conceptual understanding of a can-crushing demonstration. *Chemical Education Research* 77: 1517–1520.

Sarason, I. G., and Sarason, B. R. 1990. Test anxiety. In *Handbook of Social and Evaluation Anxiety*, ed. H. Leitenberg. Plenum.

Schwartz, D. L., and Black, Y. 1996. Shuttling between depictive models and abstract rules: Induction and fall-back. *Cognitive Science* 20: 457–497.

Shea, D., Lubinski, D., and Benbow, C. 2001. Importance of assessing spatial ability in intellectually talented young adolescents: A 20-year longitudinal study. *Journal of Educational Psychology* 93: 604–614.

Shepard, R. N., and Metzler, J. 1971. Mental rotation of three-dimensional objects. *Science* 171: 701–703.

Snow, R. 1989. Aptitude-treatment interaction as a framework for research on individual differences in learning. In *Learning and Individual Differences: Advances in Theory and Research*, ed. P. Ackerman, R. J. Sternberg, and R. Glaser. Freeman.

Stieff, M. 2007. Mental rotation and diagrammatic reasoning in science. *Learning and Instruction* 17: 219–234.

Stieff, M. 2013. Sex differences in the mental rotation of chemistry representations. *Journal of Chemical Education* 90: 165–170.

Stieff, M., Ryu, M., Dixon, B., and Hegarty, M. 2012. The role of spatial ability and strategy preference for spatial problem solving in organic chemistry. *Journal of Chemical Education* 89: 854–859.

Uttal, D. H., and Cohen, C. A. 2012. Spatial thinking and STEM education: When, why, and how? *Psychology of Learning and Motivation* 57: 147–181.

Uttal, D. H., and O'Doherty, K. 2008. Comprehending and learning from visual representations: A developmental approach. In *Visualization: Theory and Practice in Science Education*, ed. J. Gilbert, M. Reiner, and M. Nakhleh. Springer.

Uttal, D. H., Meadow, N. G., Tipton, E., Hand, L. L., Alden, A. R., Warren, C., et al. 2013. The malleability of spatial skills: A meta-analysis of training studies. *Psychological Bulletin* 139: 352–402.

Vandenberg, S. G., and Kuse, A. R. 1978. Mental rotations, a group test of three-dimensional spatial visualization. *Perceptual and Motor Skills* 47: 599–601.

Velázquez-Marcano, A. A., Williamson, V. M., Ashkenazi, G., Tasker, R., and Williamson, K. C. 2004. The use of video demonstrations and particulate animation in general chemistry. *Journal of Science Education and Technology* 13: 315–323.

Wai, J., Lubinski, D., and Benbow, C. P. 2009. Spatial ability for STEM domains: Aligning over 50 years of cumulative psychological knowledge solidifies its importance. *Journal of Educational Psychology* 101: 817–835.

Wilensky, U., and Reisman, K. 2006. Thinking like a wolf, a sheep, or a firefly: Learning biology through constructing and testing computational theories—an embodied modeling approach. *Cognition and Instruction* 24: 171–209.

Williamson, V. M., and Jose, T. J. 2009. Using visualization techniques in chemistry teaching. In *Chemists' Guide to Effective Teaching*, volume 2, ed. N. J. Pienta, M. M. Cooper, and T. J. Greenbowe. Prentice-Hall.

Williamson, V. M., Lane, S. M., Gilbreath, T., Tasker, R., Ashkenazi, G., Williamson, K. C., et al. 2012. The effect of viewing order of macroscopic and particulate visualizations on students' particulate explanations. *Journal of Chemical Education* 89: 979–987.

6   Can Humans Form Four-Dimensional Spatial Representations?

Ranxiao Frances Wang

Representations of space and time are deeply rooted in human thinking, reasoning, and perception of the world. Being one of the most concrete, well-experienced, and intuitive domains, spatial analogies are widely used to explain and comprehend more abstract, complex, and difficult non-spatial concepts, such as number, category, strategy set, and so on. Nearly all areas of science and engineering use spatial thinking as a tool for their theoretical and application development. For example, when plotting one variable (such as temperature) as a function of another (such as season) in a two-dimensional graph, the two non-spatial variables are each mapped to a spatial dimension (vertical and horizontal, respectively), so that the relationship between these non-spatial variables can be understood more intuitively.

Spatial representations are often preferred and highly valued for creative thinking and reasoning (Finke 1993), because they can provide unique insights in problem solving. For example, mentally visualizing an object can often help one identify its geometrical properties and find solutions to mathematical proofs. Since many mathematical objects are high-dimensional or embedded in high-dimensional space, it requires high-dimensional mental spatial representations to gain this type of insights in their properties. Moreover, as science and technology advance, complex data sets and models that have more than three dimensions become more and more common. Although these dimensions may be non-spatial themselves, a mental spatial model of high-dimensional data sets can help one grasp the relationship among different variables and understand the operation of complex models. Thus, it is of both theoretical and practical interests for scientific research and education to find out whether humans are able to have direct insights about the structural properties of high-dimensional objects without relying on the mathematical symbol systems.

Possibility of 4D spatial representations

Living in a physical world of three dimensions, human perceptual and cognitive systems have evolved for sensing, storing, transforming, and reasoning about three-dimensional objects. Nevertheless, the concepts of higher-dimensional space and higher-dimensional geometric objects have been conjectured on the basis of lower-dimensional space and examined extensively in mathematics. For example, a one-dimensional Euclidean space is the set of points on a straight line, which can be represented algebraically as a real number x. A two-dimensional Euclidean space is a flat plane, containing points that can be represented as two real numbers (x, y). Points in a three-dimensional space can be represented as three ordered numbers (x, y, z). Accordingly, an n-dimensional Euclidean space can be defined as the geometrical entity formed by a set of points, each corresponding to a sequence of n real numbers $(x_1, x_2, \ldots, x_n)$.

The development of high-dimensional geometry in mathematics proved that humans were able to break the conceptual barrier of spatial dimensions. People with mathematical training can generate symbolic representations of high-dimensional space using labels and equations, and perform sophisticated logical reasoning about these abstract spatial concepts. However, the symbolic systems in mathematics are generally not considered *spatial* representations.[1] In other words, these representations are not like mental images that allow people to inspect and manipulate an object as they do with ordinary 3D spatial representations. So the question of interest is whether humans are able to construct mental spatial representations similar to those for 3D objects and 3D environments, but with four spatial dimensions.

There are two schools of thoughts related to whether humans are capable of creating high-dimensional spatial representations, despite having evolved in a three-dimensional world. Some thinkers—among them Kant (1896)—believed that perception of objects and events is impossible without a priori representations of space and time. That is, to an individual human being, space has to be a pre-existing mental representation, and a rich and concrete representation of the world is built by "filling" this space with objects through experience. A natural extension of this view is that, people who are born with an a priori representation of 3D space may develop symbolic systems to conceptualize multi-dimensional entities which they call "high-dimensional space," but they can never overcome the innate constraint and add another dimension to the 3D mental space they are given a priori, because they can never figure out where that dimension could be put.

Other theorists—among them Berkeley, Hume, and Locke—emphasized the role of experience in shaping our cognitive systems (Berkeley 1901; Hume 1900; Locke 1948). According to this view, the concept of a three-dimensional world is obtained from perceptual experience and interactions with three-dimensional objects. Thus, the dimensionality of the space we are capable of mentally constructing is determined by our perceptual experience. If a child lives in a virtual world where all perceptual experience conforms to a space with four dimensions, the child might obtain a mental representation of 4D space. Moreover, given the plasticity of the human brain (e.g., Harris 1965; Luaute et al. 2006), even human adults may acquire such representations with sufficient perceptual exposure. That is, although there is nowhere to put a fourth dimension in the physical world, there is somewhere it can be created in the mental space.

There are also two corresponding contrasting predictions from the standpoint of neural physiology. On the one hand, objects of high dimensions have novel structural properties and produce novel transformations that 3D objects do not have. The biological structure of our visual-spatial system may have certain constrains on the type of perceptual structure and events it is capable of representing. As a result, humans may never be able to add a fourth dimension in order to represent and support judgments in four-dimensional space. On the other hand, representations of space are realized through neurons and neural connectivity. In principle, this type of construction does not have an intrinsic limit in dimensionality, and higher-dimensional space may be constructed through new connections within the existing brain structure similarly to how three-dimensional space is represented. Thus, existing theories from neurophysiology do not resolve the issue of the potential dimensional limitations of mental space.

Given these contradictory predictions, it is theoretically ambiguous whether human 4D spatial comprehension can go beyond the formal mathematical representation. Thus, the dimensionality limitation issue of human spatial representations should be examined empirically. The first step is to establish a more concrete definition of four-dimensional spatial representation.

What Counts as a 4D Spatial Representation?

The intuitive concept of a 4D spatial representation, i.e., something that one can "see" in one's mental eye, is not well defined. A concept of 4D representations may refer to the subjective experience of *feeling* that one can perceive or imagine what a 4D object is. The assessment of subjective experience relies primarily on subjective reports, which can provide useful information about mental representations and processes. However, subjective reports have their limitations. It is not always possible to describe one's perceptual and cognitive experience in language, especially when the experience is not shared. For example, someone with normal color vision may have a difficult time fully explaining to a color-blind person what he or she means by the word 'red'. Similarly, if someone can imagine a 4D object, it will be difficult to explain what that mental representation is to those who don't have the same types of experience. Thus, subjective reports on 4D intuitions are likely going to be vague, abstract, and puzzling to others.

In contrast, 4D spatial representations may be defined on the basis of what types of spatial inferences such a perceptual or cognitive representation can support. Measurements of spatial-reasoning abilities require demonstrations of certain task performance, such as path integration or judgments of spatial relations and properties. When evaluating objective evidence of 4D spatial representations, a number of important issues arise as to what counts as empirical evidence for 4D spatial representations. These issues have to be resolved before empirical studies of 4D spatial representations are possible.

Spatial vs. non-spatial dimensions

The first issue is what a *spatial* dimension in a mental representation means. Multi-dimensional representations are common in both perceptual and cognitive systems. For example, an object representation may include multiple feature dimensions such as color, size, shape, orientation, and so on, and many of these feature dimensions may be encoded metrically. Since there is no evidence that neural signals of spatial and non-spatial dimensions are physiologically different (Eichenbaum and Cohen 1988), a 4D object representation of color, size, shape, and orientation may look like the same thing as a 4D spatial representation. Moreover, an external stimulus dimension itself can be a representation of another dimension. For example, if we use a line (spatial dimension) to represent duration (time dimension), then a mental representation of the length of the line could be a spatial dimension, a time dimension, or both depending on the context. Because almost all non-spatial dimensions can be mapped onto a spatial dimension, it can be difficult to tell whether a feature representation also serves as a spatial dimension. So is there any real difference between spatial and non-spatial dimensions?

The answer is yes. One of the fundamental differences between spatial and non-spatial dimensions is that only spatial representations can support spatial operations such as distance, angle, area, and so on. For example, when one talks about the distance between red and yellow, one first has to (often implicitly) map the color dimension to a spatial dimension (such as a color circle) before the term *distance* can be defined. Similarly, an event representation (e.g., a movie) is a spatial-temporal mixed representation. However, if one wants to define and calculate the 3D distance between an object "5m to the left at 10am" and another object "3m in front at 4pm," one first has to convert the time dimension to a spatial dimension. As a result, the mixed 3D event representation becomes a pure 3D spatial representation. In other words, whether a dimension is spatial or not is primarily determined by the type of operations it can support. On the basis of this distinction, a spatial-judgment task across all dimensions of a representation provides sufficient (but not necessary) evidence that it is a *spatial* representation, regardless of the nature of the original stimulus dimension from which the representation is acquired.

Performance and systematic biases

The second issue concerns what level of performance counts as success in a spatial-judgment task. The dimensionality of the spatial representation primarily concerns whether a spatial dimension is represented, not how well it is represented. The performance level reflects the *quality* of the representation, not the *presence* of a representation. Thus, the criterion of the ability to perform a spatial-judgment task should be the chance level. Any performance that is significantly above chance may be considered success at the task and provide evidence for the underlying spatial representation (Wang and Street 2013).

A high-dimensional spatial representation is also not necessarily veridical. Systematic biases have been shown in spatial judgments of lower dimensions. For example, localization of a dot in a circle is usually biased toward the center of the quadrant to which it belongs (Huttenlocher, Hedges, and Duncan 1991; Sampaio and Wang 2009). Thus, systematic biases should not be considered evidence against high-dimensional spatial representations.

Lower-dimensional cues

The third issue is dimension reducibility. One of the common concerns about high-dimensional spatial representations is that a high-dimensional spatial-judgment task may be performed using lower-dimensional information in the sensory input, such as the speed and acceleration of a vertex, length of a line, area of a figure, etc. in the retinal image. These types of information in the sensory input are usually referred to as lower-dimensional cues. It is often believed that if an apparently advanced, challenging cognitive task such as high-dimensional spatial judgment can be performed using one of these lower-dimensional cues, then the task only requires a lower-dimensional spatial representation. Thus, in order to show evidence of high-dimensional spatial representations, one needs to prove that no such lower-dimensional cues can be used to perform the spatial-judgment task. This criterion will be referred to as the *absolute cue reducibility rule* of the spatial-dimensionality test.

Although the rule may sound reasonable intuitively, there are several problems when using it to determine the dimensionality of spatial representations. First, the absolute cue reducibility rule implies that the dimension of the spatial representation can never exceed the dimension of the sensory input, because if the spatial representation contains more dimensions than the sensory input, then those additional dimensions must have been created from the existing dimensions of the sensory input. In other words, any spatial dimensions exceeding those of the sensory input can be *reduced* to functions of the lower sensory dimensions, and therefore, according to the absolute cue reducibility rule, they are not valid, additional dimensions.

Consequently, it would not be possible by definition to acquire three-dimensional and higher-dimensional spatial representations from two-dimensional retinal images in visual simulations, because the dimension of the spatial representation cannot exceed that of the sensory input. For example, the distance of an object from the observer can be expressed as functions of the two-dimensional variables in the retinal input, such as its height in the visual field. That means according to the absolute cue reducibility rule, spatial representations of the environment acquired from visual inputs are of two dimensions or lower, even if the third-dimensional variable (depth) is computed and represented explicitly in the spatial representation in addition to the two retinal dimensions. This restriction on the dimensionality of mental representations by the dimensionality of the sensory input obviously contradicts the common notion of the dimension of spatial representations, and the absolute cue reducibility rule is generally not used in the research of 2D and 3D spatial representations.[2] Thus, there is no clear reason it has to be adopted for the examination of 4D spatial representations.

Second, a lower-dimensional cue defined without restrictions can be *any* possible functions of the sensory inputs, no matter how complex or meaningless they might be. As a result, it is not possible to prove that a high-dimensional spatial-judgment task is performed without using lower-dimensional cues, because there is an infinite number of functions that can be generated for a given stimulus, and it is always possible that some unknown cue (or cues) that has (or have) not been tested may account for the performance. Thus, the alternative hypothesis implied by the absolute cue reducibility rule—i.e., that performance in a spatial-judgment task relies on some unknown lower-dimensional cue(s)—is practically unfalsifiable and is not a meaningful rule to adopt in empirical research.

Nevertheless, a less extreme approach compatible with the cue usage framework may be adopted by specifying a priori what types of lower-dimensional cues need to be excluded as the basis for solving a high-dimensional spatial task. That is, a constraint will be placed on what counts as a "lower-dimensional solution" instead of including all possible functions of the sensory inputs. One approach is to define true lower-dimensional solutions on the basis of how difficult it is to identify a lower-dimensional cue that can be used to solve a high-dimensional spatial problem. For example, there is an infinite number of potential lower-dimensional cues that might be used to estimate a high-dimensional spatial property, and success in the task would suggest that the observer have used some appropriate cue(s). However, the difficulty of cue selection can vary. Under some conditions, a useful lower-dimensional cue is relatively easy to identify for a given task and there is no need to assume high-dimensional spatial comprehension. These should be considered true lower-dimensional solutions. Under other conditions, however, it is very difficult to find an appropriate lower-dimensional function among the infinite number of candidates without assuming advanced comprehension of higher-dimensional space. Therefore, it is reasonable to define such comprehension as a form of *high-dimensional representation* and performance in such tasks provides evidence for high-dimensional spatial representations. This approach will be referred to as the *restricted cue reducibility rule*.

Several conditions can be suggested in which the cue selection is relatively easy and task performance may be due to true lower-dimensional solutions (Wang 2014). First, some lower-dimensional cues can be directly derived from the basic mathematical definitions of the test variables. For example, the length of a path is mathematically defined as the sum of the length of the line segments of its partitions. On the basis of this definition, one can come up with a one-dimensional solution to estimate the path length by adding up the length of each step one makes, without having a mental representation of the path in 2D or 3D space. According to the restricted cue reducibility rule, this type of definition-based solution does not require a higher-dimensional spatial representation and should be excluded.

Second, cue selection is relatively easy when feedback is provided. For example, one can use a trial-and-error strategy by randomly choosing one cue and performing the task accordingly. If the results are inconsistent with the feedback, then try another cue, until by chance a useful cue is discovered. This trial-and-error strategy based on feedback allows one to find a solution to a high-dimensional spatial-judgment task without acquiring a high-dimensional spatial representation; therefore, studies of high-dimensional spatial representations must avoid using feedback training.

Cue selection can be very challenging when none of these conditions are provided, because the number of possible lower-dimensional functions is infinite. Moreover, most of these functions are not useful in predicting the correct answer to a spatial-judgment task, and there is generally no obvious reason that one cue is more promising than the others. When there are no definition-based solutions and no feedback to help test the validity of potential cues, successful selection of a solution probably is due to a high-dimensional spatial representation that allows one to identify the appropriate functions to perform the spatial judgments, even if these functions are based on lower-dimensional information.

An operational definition

Taken together, 4D spatial representations can be operationally defined as the perceptual or cognitive representation of a four-dimensional object or environment that can support judgments of novel 4D spatial relations or spatial properties without using definition-based lower-dimensional solutions, algebraic equations, and feedback training.[3] Under these conditions, the ability to identify the useful cues to perform the task provides evidence for some form of 4D spatial representations, whether or not lower-dimensional functions and variables are actually used.

4D Learning Methods

There are various methods to describe a four-dimensional object. The first method is a mathematical description using symbols and equations. For example, a random hyper-tetrahedron can be described by specifying the coordinates of its five vertices, each with four coordinate values (x, y, z, w).

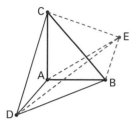

Figure 6.1
An example of a hyper-tetrahedron with its 3D "base" (tetrahedron ABCD) in the regular 3D space and the fifth vertex (E) out in the fourth-dimensional space. Vertices A(0, 0, 0, 0), B(1, 0, 0, 0), C(0, 1, 0, 0), and D(0, 0, 1, 0) form a tetrahedron within a 3D space at zero hyper-depth (i.e., $w = 0$). The fifth vertex E(0, 0, 0, 1) is at a hyper-depth of one unit, just "above" vertex A in the W direction. All solid lines are inside the 3D space, while all dashed lines are outside the 3D space.

(See figure 6.1 for an example.) Manipulations of an object can be described by mathematical operations, such as translation, rotation, reflection, folding, and so on. On the basis of these mathematical representations and operations, one can perform spatial reasoning on a hypothetical object, predict its geometric properties, and examine novel spatial relationships. This method is the foundation of high-dimensional spatial comprehension. However, it requires rigorous mathematical training, and it is generally difficult and non-intuitive.

To help people obtain a more intuitive understanding of high-dimensional objects, the method of analogy is often employed—for example, high-dimensional spatial properties are compared with the corresponding lower-dimensional properties. Abbott (1991) explained the construction of a 3D cube to a 2D creature by describing how a point moving in one direction makes a line; then describing how the line, moving in a second, orthogonal direction, makes a square; then describing, by analogy, how the square moving in a third direction makes a cube. By the same analogy, if the cube moves in a fourth (hypothetical) direction perpendicular to the first three, the trace of it will make a novel type of object called a hypercube (figure 6.2). Analogy is useful for insights and intuitive understanding. However, because rules of lower dimension do not always generalize to higher dimensions, conclusions drawn from analogies are not always reliable and can lead to erroneous judgments.

In addition to analogy, visual illustration is another common method used to explain high-dimensional spatial relations. Visual illustrations can provide certain perceptual aspects of the hypothetical object they depict;

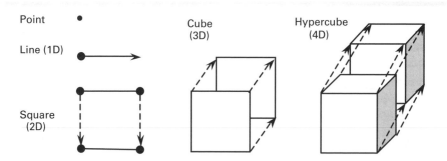

Figure 6.2
An explanation of how a four-dimensional object (a hypercube) is constructed by moving a dot in one dimension to create a line, then moving the line in the second dimension to form a square, then moving a square in the third dimension to form a cube, and finally moving the cube in a fourth dimension, which is orthogonal to the previous three, to form a hypercube.

therefore, they can potentially help the viewer construct a spatial representation and reason about its properties. However, visual illustrations are not necessarily veridical reproductions of the object, and the viewer needs to separate the genuine information belonging to the depicted object from the irrelevant/misleading aspects belonging to the specific illustration technique. (See figure 6.3.)

Traditional illustrations are 2D line drawings, and they are very useful in depicting 3D objects. However, owing to their low dimension, these illustrations usually have limited capability to portray the perceptual features of an object with four or higher dimensions. With the development of computer graphics technology, the quality and variety of visual illustrations have improved substantially, and human experience of space has taken a great leap. Various types of 4D objects and environments have been developed in virtual-reality simulations, both in static images and in dynamic movies (Banchoff and Strauss 1978; Francis 2005). Many of these programs allow the user to interact with high-dimensional objects in real time.

Display techniques using virtual-reality techniques

Most of the simulation techniques present a portion of a 4D object at a given moment, and then move the object to reveal its whole structure over time. There are three basic types of presentation schemes: slice translation, slice rotation, and projection rotation (D'Zmura, Colantoni, and Seyranian 2000; Wang 2009). Figure 6.4 shows an example of each technique used to display 3D objects in 2D planes.

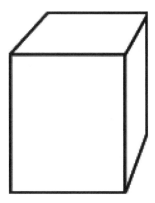

Figure 6.3

A 2D illustration of a cube using perspective projection technique. Some spatial information in the 2D illustration is veridical, such as the shape of the front surface (i.e., square). Some spatial information is not veridical in the 2D graph, such as the shape of the top surface.

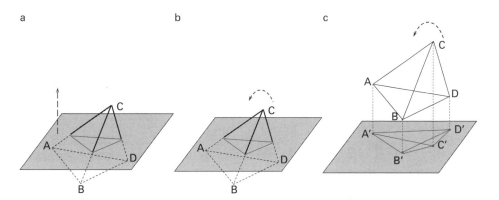

Figure 6.4

An illustration of displaying 3D objects in 2D planes using (a) slice translation, (b) slice rotation, and (c) projection rotation techniques. Panels (a) and (b): the 2D observation plane cuts through the tetrahedron in the middle, leaving one portion above the plane (solid lines) and the rest below the plane (dashed lines). The triangle is the cross-section that can be displayed within the 2D plane. When the observation plane (or the tetrahedron) moves (panel a) or rotates (panel b), different parts of the tetrahedron pass through the 2D plane, which can reveal its overall 3D structure. Panel (c): a shadow of the tetrahedron is casted on the 2D plane. When the tetrahedron rotates, the shape of the shadow changes, which can reveal the 3D structure of the tetrahedron over time.

Slice translation

In general, an n-dimensional object can be cut into a series of infinitesimally thin slices along one of its dimensions, each slice being an object of $n - 1$ dimensions. For example, a 3D object can be sliced into a series of 2D horizontal figures, and when we stack up these 2D slices along the vertical axis, we get the original 3D object (figure 6.4a). Because the slices are one dimension lower than the original object, they can be simulated and presented in a lower-dimensional space. The slice translation technique for 4D simulations first constructs a mathematical model of a 4D object in a virtual 4D space. According to the model, a series of 3D cross-sections of the object can be computed and presented in our three-dimensional space. Thus, an observer can examine the structure of the 4D object by looking at these slices in order, which is equivalent to moving along the fourth dimension in the virtual 4D space and observing the cross-sections of the 4D object from different depths in the fourth dimension. A full run from one side of the object to the other side can provide sufficient information to reconstruct the original 4D object.

Slice rotation

This technique is similar to the slice translation technique, except that the observer explores different parts of the object not by translating but by rotating the object around one of its axis (figure 6.4b). Again, at any moment the observer sees only a 3D cross-section of the 4D object. However, when the observer moves around the object for a full circle, the entire structure of the object may be fully revealed.

Projection rotation

Another approach to get a lower-dimensional portrait of a high-dimensional object is by projection. When lights shine along one direction of an n-dimensional object, they can generate an $(n - 1)$-dimensional shadow, which can be presented and examined by a creature living in the lower-dimensional space. For example, when lights shine from above a 3D wireframe object, we get a 2D figure on a screen below (figure 6.4c). A 2D creature living on the screen surface may study the structure of the 2D figure. However, depth information along the vertical dimension is missing in the 2D shadow. One way to provide the 3D depth information is by rotating the object around one of its axes. Similarly, a 4D hypothetical object can be presented in our 3D space by shining lights along the fourth dimension, and displaying its 3D shadows while it rotates.

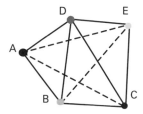

Figure 6.5
An illustration of a randomly shaped hyper-tetrahedron projected into 3D space. The darkness of the vertices represents their hyper-depth (i.e., their *w* coordinates).

Other techniques

All these basic techniques employ the time dimension one way or another in addition to 3D space to reveal the structure of a 4D object. Other feature dimensions have also been used in combination with some of the basic techniques (figure 6.5). For example, color was used to depict a point's hyper-depth, where red and blue represented the "hot" and "cold" directions of the fourth dimension (Aflalo and Graziano 2008). Some of the 3D depth cues, such as occlusion and relative size, may also be employed to indicate depth relationships in the fourth dimension. The effectiveness of these cues and presentation techniques in conveying the spatial structure of 4D objects has not been well examined.

Empirical Studies of 4D Learning

Initial psychological data attempting to demonstrate 4D mental spatial representations came from subjective reports. Davis, Hersh, and Marchisotto (1995) reported that a mathematician who actively interacted with computer-graphical simulations of 4D geometric objects obtained novel insights about higher-dimensional space, quoting the mathematician as follows:

"I tried turning the hypercube around, moving it away, bringing it up close, turning it around another way. Suddenly I could *feel* it! The hypercube had leaped into palpable reality, as I learned how to manipulate it, feeling in my fingertips the power to change what I saw and change it back again. The active control at the computer console created a union of kinesthetic and visual thinking which brought the hypercube up to the level of intuitive understanding."

These reports support the subjective experience notion of 4D spatial representations, and according to this criterion, humans are indeed able to obtain intuitions about four-dimensional space. However, the nature of this intuition is not clear. For example, it is possible that the subjective feeling of comprehension was a result of discovering a certain regularity of the stimuli, after getting familiar with the simulations. Furthermore, such experience is quite rare, and informal comments from observers who interact with simulations of high-dimensional space in virtual reality suggest that people generally have difficulty in apprehending the spatial meaning the visualizations are designed to convey.

To better understand the underlying mental representations, several recent studies examined human 4D spatial comprehension using objective measurements. Two general paradigms were adopted. The first one is path integration in 4D virtual space. This approach was inspired by the extensive research on navigation in both humans and other animals, in which the ability to perform novel short-cuts to return home after an outbound trip through 2D or 3D space is used as evidence of 2D or 3D spatial representations, respectively. The second paradigm uses judgments of spatial properties of a simulated 4D geometric object, where the ability to reason about spatial relationships in 4D virtual space is considered evidence of 4D spatial representations.

Path integration in 4D space

Seyranian (2001) reported two psychological experiments on navigation and spatial learning in four-dimensional space using objective methods. In experiment 1, people navigated from a fixed home room to various target rooms in 4D virtual space, and then returned home through the shortest path. They found that performance improved with repetition. In experiment 2, participants navigated from various target rooms to a given home, and then pointed to where they came from. Performance improved after an intervening training session with the same task in different, simpler 4D environments (transfer effect). Unfortunately, both experiments had methodological limitations that prevent useful conclusions to be drawn from these data. In experiment 1, the improvement might have been a result of learning route connectivity and avoiding circular detours through trial and error, without a spatial representation of the 4D space. In experiment 2, participants received explicit feedback about the correct direction for each target room. Thus, it is possible the improvement in the post-training session was due to residual memory of the feedback.

Aflalo and Graziano (2008) compared path integration in 2D, 3D, and 4D virtual tunnel mazes displayed on a computer monitor. Participants learned over multiple sessions to navigate along four-segment paths using a keyboard to translate along the path and select directions of rotation at the junctions. After they reached the end of the maze, participants were required to rotate using the keys until they were facing the origin. To see whether performance in the 4D mazes exceeded that predicted by the 3D task, they defined two ideal 3D navigators, one based on the participants' individual performance on the 3D maze tasks, and the other with perfect performance during the first three segments of the maze and random in the last segment in the fourth dimension. Aflalo and Graziano found that participants' performance improved over training in several stages, and in the end, performance in the 4D maze exceeded that predicted by either of the two 3D ideal-navigator models.

As in Seyranian's experiments, feedback was provided to participants after each trial; thus, improvements in the task could be a result of a trial-and-error strategy. Moreover, because the rotations were orthogonal, only two of the four dimensions are needed to update the home location within an egocentric reference frame after each rotation, which can be done algebraically without much difficulty (Wang 2014). Therefore, these data do not meet the criteria of no algebraic solutions and no feedback training.

Judgments of spatial properties of 4D objects

A study by Ambinder, Wang, Crowell, Francis, and Brinkmann (2009) examined judgments of distance and angles in 4D space. Observers studied 3D slices of random 4D objects (hyper-tetrahedron) in a virtual-reality cube by moving a 3D observation window along the fourth dimension. (Ambinder et al. called this the "slice translation technique.") Then they made spatial judgments about the hyper-tetrahedron, including the distance between two of its vertices and the angle between two of the line segments. A multiple-regression was run on the responses as a function of both the correct distance and angle and the 3D component of the correct distance and angle. The data showed a correlation between the responses and the correct distance and angle after controlling for the 3D strategy. The angle-judgment task met the criteria of no definition-based solution, no algebraic calculations, and no feedback training, suggesting that the observers were able to form 4D spatial representations that could support both distance judgments and orientation judgments about 4D objects.

A follow-up study examined whether human 4D spatial judgments could extend to completely novel properties unique to high-dimensional space, i.e., the hyper-volume of a random hyper-tetrahedron (Wang 2014). The observers studied the 3D orthogonal projection of a random wireframe 4D object rotating around the yz plane in virtual reality and adjusted the size of a hyper-block to match the hyper-volume of the target. The judgments correlated significantly with the correct hyper-volume, but not with other lower-dimensional variables such as the mean 3D volume of the projections. This study met all four criteria of the operational definition and provided evidence of 4D spatial representations that can support judgments of novel 4D spatial properties such as the hyper-volume.

Summary and Conclusions

The dimensionality limitation of human spatial representations has important implications for fundamental theories in perception, cognition, neuroscience, and philosophy of science. In this chapter we have examined theoretical issues related to definitions of high-dimensional spatial representations, techniques for visual simulations of high-dimensional objects, and empirical findings on human 4D spatial comprehension. Both anecdotal subjective reports and existing experimental data suggest that it is possible for humans to construct 4D mental spatial representations beyond mathematical definitions and algebraic equations. These representations can support judgments of novel spatial properties unique to high-dimensional space. However, the exact properties of the 4D mental spatial representations still need further investigation.

Another area that needs further research is the display techniques and their effectiveness in helping the observer obtain high-dimensional spatial representations. A better perceptual simulation of high-dimensional objects may improve the strength of the representations and make it easier for the observer to gain an intuitive understanding of these hypothetical entities. On the other hand, understanding how people develop representations of high-dimensional space may provide useful guidance for designing technological tools that can provide training and education in mathematics, physics, biology, medicine, and other fields in which visualization of high-dimensional spatial concepts and data sets is involved.

Notes

1. The term "symbolic representation" here refers to algebraic symbols and operations only. The distinction between a general symbolic system and visual-spatial representation can be fuzzy sometimes (Anderson 1978; Horst 1996; Kaufmann 1980; Kosslyn 1994; Pylyshyn 1973, 1981, 2002).

2. For example, the novel short-cut task is a common paradigm used to determine whether an animal has 2D spatial representations for navigation (Wang and Street

2013). However, this task generally does not meet the absolute cue reducibility criterion.

3. Note that these criteria are stricter than those used for the assessment of 3D spatial representations. For example, the no-feedback-training criterion is usually not required when determining whether an animal has 3D spatial representations. That is, an animal may acquire the depth cues through feedback information when interacting with the environment and use these cues to form 3D spatial representations. Also, the no-algebraic-solution criterion is not required to establish animal 2D and 3D spatial representations.

References

Abbott, E. A. 1991. *Flatland: A Romance of Many Dimensions*. Princeton University Press.

Aflalo, T. N., and Graziano, M. S. A. 2008. Four-dimensional spatial reasoning in humans. *Journal of Experimental Psychology. Human Perception and Performance* 34: 1066–1077.

Ambinder, M. S., Wang, R. F., Crowell, J. A., Francis, G. K., and Brinkmann, P. 2009. Human four-dimensional spatial intuition in virtual reality. *Psychonomic Bulletin and Review* 16: 818–823.

Anderson, J. R. 1978. Arguments concerning representations for mental imagery. *Psychological Review* 85: 249–277.

Banchoff, T. F., and Strauss, C. M. 1978. *Real-Time Computer Graphics Analysis of Figures in Four-Space*. Westview.

Berkeley, G. 1901. In *The Principles of Human Knowledge.* , ed. T. J. McCormack. Reprint: Open Court.

Davis, P. J., Hersh, R., and Marchisotto, R. A. 1995. Four dimensional intuition. In *The Mathematical Experience*. Birkhäuser.

D'Zmura, M., Colantoni, P., and Seyranian, G. 2000. Virtual environments with four or more spatial dimensions. *Presence* 9: 616–631.

Eichenbaum, H., and Cohen, N. J. 1988. Representation in the hippocampus: What do hippocampal neurons code? *Trends in Neurosciences* 11: 244–248.

Finke, R. A. 1993. Mental imagery and creative discovery. In *Imagery, Creativity, and Discovery: A Cognitive Perspective*, ed. B. Roskos-Ewoldsen, M. J. Intons-Peterson, and R. E. Anderson. North-Holland/Elsevier.

Francis, G. K. 2005. Metarealistic rendering of real-time interactive computer animations. In *Mathematics and Culture II*, ed. M. Emmer. Springer.

Harris, C. S. 1965. Perceptual adaptation to inverted, reversed, and displaced vision. *Psychological Review* 72: 419–444.

Horst, S. W. 1996. *Symbols, Computation and Intentionality: A Critique of the Computational Theory OF Mind*. University of California Press.

Hume, D. 1900. *An Enquiry Concerning Human Understanding*. Open Court.

Huttenlocher, J., Hedges, L. V., and Duncan, S. 1991. Categories and particulars: Prototype effects in estimating spatial location. *Psychological Review* 98: 352–376.

Kant, I. 1896. In *Immanuel Kant's Critique of Pure Reason*, ed. F. M. Muller. Macmillan.

Kaufmann, G. 1980. *Imagery, Language and Cognition*. Universitetsforlaget.

Kosslyn, S. M. 1994. *Image and Brain: The Resolution of the Imagery Debate*. MIT Press.

Locke, J. 1948. An essay concerning human understanding, 1690. In *Readings in the History of Psychology*, ed. W. Dennis. Appleton-Century-Crofts.

Luaute, J., Michel, C., Rode, G., Pisella, L., Jacquin-Courtois, S., Costes, N., et al. 2006. Functional anatomy of the therapeutic effects of prism adaptation on left neglect. *Neurology* 66: 1859–1867.

Pylyshyn, Z. W. 1973. What the mind's eye tells the mind's brain: A critique of mental imagery. *Psychological Bulletin* 80: 1–25.

Pylyshyn, Z. W. 1981. The imagery debate: Analogue media versus tacit knowledge. *Psychological Review* 88: 16–45.

Pylyshyn, Z. W. 2002. Mental imagery: In search of a theory. *Behavioral and Brain Sciences* 25: 157–237.

Sampaio, C., and Wang, R. F. 2009. Category-based errors and the accessibility of unbiased spatial memories: A retrieval model. *Journal of Experimental Psychology. Learning, Memory, and Cognition* 35: 1331–1337.

Seyranian, G. D. 2001. Human spatial perception in environments with four spatial dimensions. *Dissertation Abstracts International B* 62 (3-B): 1611.

Wang, R. F. 2009. A case study on human learning of four-dimensional objects in virtual reality: Passive exploration and display techniques. In Proceedings of the Fourth International Conference on Frontier of Computer Science and Technology.

Wang, R. F. 2014. Human four-dimensional spatial judgments of hyper-volume. *Spatial Cognition and Computation* 14: 91–113.

Wang, R. F., and Street, W. N. 2013. What counts as the evidence for 3-D and 4-D spatial representations? *Behavioral and Brain Sciences* 36: 567–568.

III Spatial Thinking and the Body

7 Embodiment as a Framework for Understanding Environmental Cognition

David Waller

The study of environmental cognition focuses on the relationship between the patterns and structures in the physical world and the mental patterns and structures that cause and are caused by them. Questions as to what information about the external environment is sensed, how that information is transduced and stored, and how it influences behavior have dominated empirical and theoretical approaches to this topic for many decades. In this chapter, I will sketch how cognitive science has begun to address these questions from an emerging perspective generally known as *embodied* or *grounded* cognition. Embodied cognition is often considered a recent reaction to the traditional *cognitivist* account of mental processing, but the dynamic between these approaches can also be seen as recapitulating a perennial interplay of ideas that can be traced at least as far back as ancient Greek philosophy. For example, in addressing the relationship among mind, body, and environment, Aristotle suggested that in thinking a mind becomes isomorphic to its contents. These notions contrasted with those of Plato, who postulated the existence of pure abstract forms and a clear duality between the realms of thought and matter—an idea whose expression reached its zenith centuries later with Descartes.

It is worth lingering for a moment on Descartes, whose ideas and influence put in sharp relief the ensuing discussion of embodied cognition and its connection to our understanding of environmental knowledge. It is hard to overstate the degree to which modern Western culture owes its everyday conceptualization of the relationship between mind and body to Cartesian philosophy. Indeed, our conception of the mind itself has probably been shaped more by Descartes than by any other philosopher. Although most present-day scientists probably would explicitly renounce Cartesian mind/body dualism, many remain enmeshed in a culture that assumes a qualitative difference between mind and body. Such dualism underlies everyday expressions such as "body and soul" as well as many modern societies' preoccupations with weight, weight loss, and body image. Indeed, even the phrase "my body" raises the question of who exactly is in possession of the body. Dualism underlies modern society's treatment of the relative importance (and differentiation) of physical and psychological distress, the delegation of psychology to university divisions that do not include biology, and the fractionation of perspectives on psychotherapy into biomedical and psychodynamic approaches. (I thank Jeffrey Schweitzer for pointing this out.) Cartesian dualism also is expressed in humanity's current relationship to other animal species, who are typically implicitly regarded as lacking the mental or spiritual capacities that could render our consumption of them problematic. Finally, the scientific treatment of human cognition certainly owes a debt to the Cartesian notion that the mind operates according to rules and principles rather than causal laws.

Since the middle of the twentieth century, the scientific treatment of cognition as a system of underlying rules has led to the mainstream scientific assumptions that human cognition is a variety of computation and that mental activity is essentially generated by a sophisticated biological computer. This computer metaphor of mental function generally regards the mind as analogous to software, operating under formal rules that take in, transform, and build mental representations of the world. The recent convergence of neuroscience and psychology has done little to fundamentally alter this conceptualization of the mind; in fact, it has generally served to provide plausible "hardware" to support this metaphor. The all-or-none mechanism of neuronal action potentials, for instance, nicely facilitates an understanding of cognition as analogous to the binary coding schemes that underlie digital computation. John Searle has eloquently pointed out, however, that essential features of this mainstream computer metaphor still exhibit a clear form of dualism:

If mental operations consist in computational operations on formal symbols, then it follows that they have no interesting connection with the brain; the only connection would be that the brain just happens to be one of the indefinitely many machines capable of instantiating the program. This form of dualism is not the traditional Cartesian variety that claims there are two sorts of substances, but it is Cartesian in the sense that it insists that what is specifically mental about the mind has no intrinsic connection with the actual properties of the brain. (1980, p. 424)

The widespread regard of the digital computer as a metaphor for the mind generally yields a view of cognition as the processing of information from low-level sensorimotor data to high-level thoughts and concepts. Successive processing stages transform concrete experience into increasingly abstract and symbolic representations of the world that ultimately bear no more resemblance to the events that they represent than ones and zeroes resemble an image on a computer display. The traditional cognitivist approach to environmental cognition has therefore focused on transforming information from the external environment through sensory and perceptual processing, and ultimately through further cognitive processing into an abstract mental representation of the environment (often referred to as a *cognitive map*). Nowhere is this position more clearly articulated than in Gallistel's outstanding book *The Organization of Learning* (1990):

What distinguishes the use of the term representation in this book is the insistence that there is a rich formal correspondence between processes and relations in the environment and the operations the brain performs. Brain processes and relations recapitulate world processes and relations. (p. 27)

The representation of the geometric relations among points and sets of points by means of metric position vectors and parameter vectors preserves all the geometric relations among the mapped entities, in the sense that any such relation is in principle recoverable from the position vectors that represent the points and the parameter vectors that represent the point sets. Whether a point does or does not fall on a given line is not explicitly given in the representation of the point and the line, but it may be recovered by testing whether the coordinates of the point satisfy the function that defines the line. (p. 103)

[The nervous system] no doubt has some process for representing the conformation and position of ... surfaces economically. Those familiar with drafting and illustration programs for microcomputers will know that shapes of remarkable complexity are coded in small files. For example, the Postscript™ encoding of [Gallistel's figure 4.13] takes only 1.4 kilobytes of disk memory; whereas the bitmapped file for the same image occupies 300 kilobytes. (p. 109)

In general, this cognitivist framework to environmental cognition has facilitated researchers' examination of reflective and memory-based phenomenon, and has fostered a conception of higher-level cognition as heavily supported by offline processing (e.g., recovering specific information that has been coded in an all-purpose representation). At the same time, it is fair to say that this focus on higher-level cognition has tended to downplay the role of the body in cognition, treating it primarily as a mechanistic vehicle through which the mind understands itself and its environment.

In recent decades, a growing number of cognitive scientists have challenged many of these ideas, pursuing the notion that high-level cognitive functions such as memory, categorization, language, and decision making are founded on—and indeed ultimately consists of no more than—the mental structures and processes involved in perception and action. The cluster of ideas associated with this pursuit is often referred to as "embodied" or "grounded" cognition. In this chapter, I provide a brief overview of some of the tenets of this approach to cognition. I then examine in detail its primary foundational assumption about the nature of mental representation, focusing on the types of mental representations that the embodied cognition approach posits to underlie our knowledge of and behavior in the environment. Finally, I will attempt to illustrate how an embodied cognition approach can be used to frame and understand the issue of reference systems in spatial memory.

Overview of the Embodied Cognition Framework

As with much current thought in the life sciences, Darwin's evolutionary theory provides a helpful starting point for understanding the embodied cognition approach. The lynchpin of Darwin's theory—the idea of a common ancestor—overturns a host of culturally ingrained assumptions about the privileged status of human cognition, and natural selection—the mechanism of change in evolutionary theory—forces cognition to overcome real-time situational pressures that do not lend themselves easily to offline processing. In what follows, I have selectively chosen three ideas that routinely emerge from the literature on embodied cognition and that ultimately owe their strength to evolutionary theory. The discussion does not attempt to be comprehensive or exhaustive, but rather illustrative of the relevance of embodied cognition to understanding how people acquire, store, and use knowledge about their environment. Attempts to define or organize more broadly the range of ideas associated with the embodied cognition framework have been made by Clark (1998), Anderson (2003), Barsalou (2008), and Shapiro (2011), and interested readers are encouraged to consult this literature.

Humans as animals

Darwin's treatment of the relationship between humans and other animals is an apt starting point for understanding the embodied cognition approach, for if nothing else Darwinian evolution can focus a cognitive theorist's attention on the biological basis and ecological context of human thought. But even more, the supposition of a common ancestor of all species forces the theorist to regard humans as ultimately connected to other animal species—different only to the extent that humans have adapted to a unique ecological niche. It is inarguable that many basic cellular, metabolic, physiological, and anatomical functions are shared by humans and other animals. As a result, basic perceptual and motor processes are also common among all species, and those that navigate over land or need to acquire knowledge about space would be expected to have similar biological bases.

Scholars sympathetic to an embodied cognition approach are quick to point out that it is exactly these shared sensory, perceptual, and motor functions that evolution has required the vast majority of its history to perfect. Brooks (1999), for example, notes that humans have existed in their present form for far less than 1 percent of the history of evolution on Earth, and that one implication of this fact may be that uniquely human mental capacities such as language and abstract reasoning are relatively simple adaptations once a basis of sensory, perceptual, and motor functions has evolved. For Brooks, these shared common "primitive" functions constitute the hard work of evolution. As I describe in greater detail below, a central tenet of the embodied cognition approach is that these evolutionarily perfected "primitive" functions provide the physical grounding necessary for abstract high-level cognition.

With respect to spatial cognition, the notion of common animal ancestry reminds us that, although different animal species may rely on and express knowledge that is derived from uniquely adapted sensory and motor systems, there are also common spatial properties of the world to which these systems have adapted. It thus seems quite plausible for humans to process environmental information with many of the same basic psychological mechanisms as do other animals. Although humans bring high-level artifacts such as language and symbolism to bear on their interaction with the environment, from an embodied cognition perspective these phenomena must, at a minimum, rely on underlying mechanisms that are more "primitive," and may in many cases be completely constituted by them.

Cognition and time

A second theme of the embodied cognition approach that may be particularly relevant to environmental cognition is a heightened appreciation of the role of time in cognition. As was noted above, the acceptance of the relevance of Darwinian evolution to human cognition constrains theories of mental functioning to explain behavior in time-pressured real-world situations. An embodied cognition approach generally pushes this idea further, emphasizing that cognition is not just constrained by time—it is wholly dependent on it. This theme echoes J. J. Gibson's (1979) realization that perception requires sensitivity to change over time, fostering a close association with and reliance on dynamic systems theory (e.g., Thelen and Smith 1996), and helping to emphasize the complementarity of perception and the actions that enable it and result from it.

An emphasis on cognition's reliance on time blurs the boundaries between action, perception, and cognition. Rather than discrete types of mental phenomena, action, perception, and cognition are conceptualized as complementary aspects of a unified whole, differentiated largely by their temporal properties and constraints. Action and perception are integrated, for example, by O'Regan and Noë's (2001) postulation that visual awareness is nothing more than expert knowledge of sensorimotor contingencies. On this view, knowledge of the perceptual consequences of one's actions is sufficient to account for the phenomenological experience of being surrounded by a rich, coherent world, and obviates the need to maintain an internal representation of the environment. Likewise, and perhaps more important for the theorist of environmental cognition, perception and cognition can be integrated by regarding cognition as potentially nothing more than an extension over time of basic perceptual functions. Just as O'Regan and Noë's (2001) theory of visual consciousness denudes perception of any representational content, an embodied cognition approach can regard "cognitive" phenomena as extensions of these same sensorimotor contingencies, simply played over grosser motor functions and over longer time frames. Heft, for example, has brilliantly described how a cognitive map—the ultimate abstract mental representation—can be conceptualized as principally a phenomenon of purposeful exploratory action:

The idea of perceiving information over time raises an intriguing question: What is the length of time over which information can be perceived? If talking about perceiving what is "presently" in view is problematic, can we specify some minimum duration over which information is detected? The invariant information specifying the shape of a small object might be detected over a few seconds of transformations in the ambient array as we move with respect to it or as we turn it in our hand. The invariant information specifying a larger object, such as a statue, or an even larger object, such as a building, might be detected over transformations lasting several minutes as we walk around the feature in question. ... The claim that perceiving can take place over such extended durations of time might seem fantastic. However, if perceiving environmental features involves the detection of invariant information over time, any a priori limit on the temporal duration over which this can take place is arbitrary. (1997, p. 96; see also Neisser 1976)

On this view, the temporal grounding of action, perception, and cognition unifies these functions in such a way that cognition can be conceptualized as a sophisticated variety of perceptual/motor activity.

Modal representation

I will devote the remainder of this section to discussing a third idea— indeed a central pillar—of an embodied cognition approach: a respect for the power of modal representations. Referring to a mental representation as modal emphasizes a non-arbitrary linkage between its form and content, stressing that the original sensory and perceptual qualities that helped to generate a mental representation are retained in it. In this sense, the representation is not symbolic or independent of these constitutive perceptual/motor characteristics. Barsalou's (1999) theory of perceptual symbols provides a specific account of how modal representations can potentially account for a great deal of abstract thought. Unlike Gibson's ecological framework, which attempts to eschew mental representations altogether, embodied cognition approaches to cognition accept the exis- tence of mental representation, but posit that such representations are generally nonsymbolic and retain a sensorimotor format.

There are two theoretical advantages to the supposition that mental representations are modal. The first is parsimony. Recognizing that infor- mation is acquired through our senses and that knowledge is expressed through our motor system, we see that the adoption of modal representa- tions means that there is no need to translate this information into an intermediate, symbolic, or multi-purpose format. Clearly, it is theoretically simpler to base high-level cognition on basic perceptual/motor mecha- nisms that are common across species, and to rely on uniquely human amodal representations to explain behavior only when observations compel us to do so. Of course, with this theoretical simplicity comes an attendant difficulty in accounting for the human use of abstract concepts— —a difficulty that sets the agenda for most current research with an embodied cognition approach. Second, by accepting the power of modal representations, one gains a foothold on the symbol grounding problem. If mental representations are entirely symbolic, their correspondence to the environment is arbitrary, and some method of connecting them to the entities that they represent would have to be specified. By connect- ing mental representations to their perceptual/motor bases, embodied cognition approaches can readily connect that which is represented to its representation.

It is worth noting that a full embrace of modal representations can have much stronger theoretical ramifications than are often attributed to the embodied cognition approach. Much of the recent empirical work seeking to support an embodied cognition framework has been used to conclude, for example, that the body is closely associated with cognition, or that online perceptual-motor activity can affect offline cognition in surprising or unintuitive ways. However, findings that sensorimotor experience affects thought are rarely controversial, and can be accommodated easily in both cognitivist and embodied cognition frameworks. Those who mistake such findings as providing compelling evidence for embodied cognition risk trivializing the framework. The much more powerful—and central—claim of the embodied cognition approach is not that bodily functions affect thought, but that they *constitute* it. In the following subsections, I briefly sketch how the assumption of modal representation can influence several areas of present-day research in cognitive psychology before focusing on specific research issues in environmental cognition.

Modal representations in high-level cognition

The idea of modal representations has found traction in many areas of cognitive psychology, and an embodied cognition approach to psychological function has been shown to be consistent with domains that are often considered uniquely human. For example, language is often regarded as a quintessentially human ability, involving the mental manipulation of abstract amodal symbols—words. Yet with respect to the comprehension of action-related sentences (e.g., "You gave Liz the toy"), Glenberg and Kaschak (2002) have shown that the physical actions that one takes in order to respond to a sentence affects the time required to judge its sensibility. Thus, for instance, reaching away from the body to respond facilitates the comprehension of sentences that depict forward actions, whereas reaching toward the body facilitates the comprehension of sentences about actions toward the subject. Such an effect would not clearly be predicted by cognitivist accounts of language and suggests that comprehension involves the recruitment of sensorimotor resources, probably through a simulation process. (For thorough theoretical accounts of these effects, see Glenberg and Gallese 2011 and Clark 2006.)

Findings in other areas of cognitive psychology, including decision making (DeCaro et al. 2009), memory (Rubin 2006), and social cognition

(Dijksterhuis and Bargh 2001), have also been interpreted within an embodied cognition framework. In addition, key insights of William James' theory of emotion, which involves a grounding of emotion on bodily states, are gaining empirical support from current research on emotion (Niedenthal, Mermillod, Maringer, and Hess 2010; see also Johnson 2007). Indeed, empirical demonstrations of the body's influence on emotion—such as the mood-altering effects of the activation of facial muscles (Strack, Martin, and Stepper 1988)—have become widely known as a hallmark effect of the embodied cognition framework. Yet, as was noted above, much of this research shows little more than a close connection between the body and cognition, and does not necessarily imply that sensorimotor structures and processes *constitute* mental representations.

Modal representations in learning and education

The idea that conceptual knowledge is grounded in modal representations has been useful to recent treatments of learning and education and has clear implications for the increasingly important area of spatial education (Newcombe and Frick 2010). Historically, the dominant models of education have tended to focus on cultivating conscious deliberate thought, and on the acquisition of abstract and sophisticated conceptual knowledge (which is typically expressed through verbal or symbolic media). By contrast, an embodied cognition approach to education recognizes the importance of incorporating low-level, online perceptual/motor experience in learning, as such functions are viewed to be the ultimate source of any more sophisticated conceptual knowledge. Thus, an embodied cognition approach to education will tend to focus on nurturing the practical, emotional, or imaginative states that are thought to undergird formal analytical thought.

This general approach has several specific implications for the theory and the practice of education. First, by recognizing the grounding of conceptual knowledge in perceptual-motor experience, the embodied cognition approach emphasizes the importance of learning through examples, rather than through deductions from general theory. If conceptual knowledge is necessarily grounded in basic perceptual and action-based functions, then a student's immediate sensorimotor experience with hands-on examples may be more effective than verbal (i.e., symbolic) discourse for acquiring it (Glenberg 2008). Second, another potential focus for educators with an embodied cognition perspective can involve the discovery, choice, and use of metaphors to ground and develop sophisticated conceptual knowledge (e.g., Lakoff 1990). Finally, sensitivity to an embodied cognition framework of education can remind educators of the importance of knowledge transmission by means of one's body, and can lead to an increased sensitivity to the conceptual understanding that is conveyed through students' and teachers' gestures (Alibali and Nathan 2012), postures (Riley, Mitra, Saunders, Kiefer, and Wallot 2012), facial expressions, and gazes (Mayer and DaPra 2012).

Modal representations for environmental knowledge

The incorporation of modal representations into research on environmental cognition has been comparatively slow. However, spatial thought may be an excellent venue for these ideas, and may be relatively better poised than many other research domains to provide evidence for the constitutive claims of embodied cognition. For example, pioneering work in object recognition by Shepard and Metzler (1971) that demonstrated a linear relationship between the angular disparity of a pair of depicted blocks and the time to determine whether they are the same or different, is readily interpreted as evidence for modal representations. A digital computer, for example, does not require more time to compute the cosine of 60° than to compute the cosine of 30°, and would not be expected to show such linear patterns of rotation. However, a manipulator of analog modal representations would. More recent research on mental rotation has shown that the motor system is closely connected to judgments of the relative orientations of objects such that, for example, hand movements can either facilitate or interfere with recognition performance, depending on whether the movements are in the same or different direction of mental rotation (Wexler, Kosslyn, and Berthoz 1998; Wohlschlaeger and Wohlschlaeger 1998). At present, however, the literature lacks a compelling demonstration that these motor systems necessarily and completely constitute the phenomenon of mental rotation.

With respect to "higher-level" spatial cognition, recent research examining people's comprehension of spatial descriptions has also shown a highly selective facilitative effect of body-derived auditory information on reading speeds (Brunyé, Mahoney, and Taylor 2010). In this research, participants were asked to read about environments that were described from either a ground level (route) or a bird's-eye (survey) perspective. As the participants read these descriptions, the researchers played sounds of either footsteps or a metronome, and both types of sounds were played at fast and slow rates. Faster metronome sounds were associated with faster reading for both route and survey descriptions, but faster footstep sounds led to faster reading only for route descriptions. The researchers interpreted this pattern of results as demonstrating the role of sensory information in guiding the generation of a mental simulation of space. By this account, the sounds of footsteps were readily used to generate a mental simulation of a walking tour of an environment (i.e., the route-perspective descriptions), but were not relevant for simulating space based on the bird's-eye (survey) descriptions. Of course, for those loyal to the embodied cognition approach, survey representations would also be considered to be embodied, but would be expected to be relatively more resistant to the walking sound manipulation because they are likely to be represented by other sensorimotor systems.

Embodiment and Spatial Reference Frames

A long-standing topic in the field of spatial cognition that may also benefit from an embodied cognition perspective is the study of reference frames (also referred to as reference systems) in human memory. Generally speaking, reference frames provide an organizational structure (e.g., reference axis, origin, or scale) that enables the coding of spatial relations. Distinct from the question of *what* is coded (e.g., self-to-object versus object-to-object relations), reference frames address the question of *how* spatial information is coded. For example, one can remember the location of a parked car with respect to a reference frame defined by features in the car's environment, such as signs, other cars, or the edges of the parking lot. Alternatively, one can remember its location relative to oneself—for example, "from this location, the car will be to my right, at about thirty paces." The differences between these examples highlight the historically important distinction between allocentric reference frames, which code spatial relations with respect to other objects or structures in the environment, and egocentric reference frames, which code spatial relations with respect to the observer.

Like many other distinctions in cognitive psychology, the contrast between egocentric and allocentric spatial representation captures the degree to which knowledge is either composed by instances of one's direct experience or abstracted from these experiences into a more general-purpose knowledge structure. Because allocentric reference frames are used to represent spatial information independently of a particular viewpoint, they are generally understood to involve abstraction from one's direct experience. Because of this, they are commonly thought to underlie "cognitive maps"—generalized mental representations that contain abstract (unexperienced, general, and all-purpose) information about an environment. In its most extreme form, an allocentric representation would be one so abstract that it does not involve a viewpoint at all, but rather codes relationships among objects that are invariant over viewpoint changes. Theorists who have developed models of allocentric spatial representation acknowledge that such representations may incorporate "preferred directions" (perspectives that are more accessible than others); however, according to these theories, a preferred direction need not be based on direct experience, especially if other directions enable a more efficient organization.

Over the past 20 years, much of the evidence for the types and qualities of the reference frames used to organize spatial memory has come from people's estimates of the relative directions among objects in a recently learned array of objects. In a typical experiment, a participant views an array of objects and is subsequently moved into another room in which he or she makes judgments of relative directions (JRDs) among the recently learned objects. Each judgment requires the participant to imagine standing at one of the learned objects, facing a second object, and then to point to a third. The orientations between the standing and facing objects are varied systematically, and researchers then examine the pattern of error (or latency) across these imagined headings. Imagined perspectives that are relatively error-free (or fast) are conceptualized as being "preferred" in spatial memory, and are hypothesized to underlie the reference system in memory.

An illustrative and influential use of such a task was published by Mou and McNamara (2002, Experiment 2), who asked people to view and remember a set of seven objects that had been laid on the floor in front of them (figure 7.1). The objects were arranged in salient rows and columns, and these rows and columns were misaligned with the participants' viewing perspective. Participants were asked to learn the relative locations of the objects, and were instructed to learn them with respect to the rows and columns—not with respect to their own view. Afterwards, participants made a series of JRDs that required imagining the array from a variety of different perspectives. Mou and McNamara found that the perspectives aligned with the rows and columns of the array were significantly easier to imagine than was the participants' previous viewing perspective. This finding was perhaps the first in the literature to demonstrate that a preferred direction in spatial memory was not necessarily aligned with one's earlier direct experience, but rather could be based on the structure of the environment (or instructions). Mou and McNamara used this finding to conclude more generally that spatial memory is coded with intrinsic

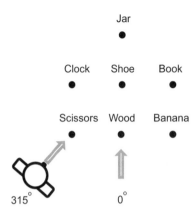

Figure 7.1
Schematic plan view of Mou and McNamara's (2002) experiment. Participants viewed an array of objects from the corner of the array (labeled 315°) and subsequently remembered the array best from imagined headings aligned with its rows and columns (labeled 0°).

reference frames—a type of allocentric reference frame that is based on the properties of the array itself.

From the perspective of embodied cognition, it is interesting to examine some of the assumptions that may underlie the use of JRDs to draw these and similar conclusions about allocentric coding of mental representations. Despite their common use in the literature on reference frames in memory, it is worth noting that JRDs, as they are commonly employed, give participants an underspecified problem. In particular, the typical instructions to adopt an imagined heading (e.g., "imagine you are at the X, facing the Y") do not instruct people to imagine how or whether this heading could be rolled about the vector that connects X and Y—being at 'X' and facing 'Y' specify only the yaw and pitch components of an imagined orientation. The researcher's interpretation of performance on such a task, correct responses and, presumably, participants' understanding of the procedure, are therefore based on an implied, unchanging "upright" perspective. Figure 7.2 illustrates plainly that "correct" answers to JRDs are not invariant over the roll component of the imagined heading. The observer's alignment with gravity is thus an unspoken assumption that underlies all the theoretical conclusions that have been based on JRD performance, including those of Greenauer and Waller (2008), Mou and McNamara (2002), Richard and Waller (2013), and Shelton and McNamara (2001). To my knowledge, this fact and its implications have gone unnoticed in

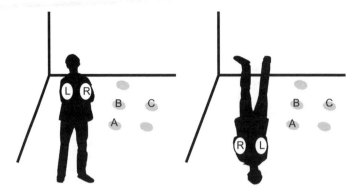

Figure 7.2
Illustration that correct answers to judgments of relative direction (JRDs) are not invariant over the roll component of the imagined viewing orientation. In both panels, the observer faces an array of objects. Left: From an upright perspective, a JRD that asks one to imagine being at A, facing B, and to point to C would require a turn to one's right of 45°. Right: The same judgment made from an inverted perspective would require a turn of 45° to the left. Perspectives with roll components between upright and inverted would require answers between 45° and –45°.

the literature. To many, the observation that spatial knowledge is tacitly measured and modeled with respect to the direction of gravity would, no doubt, seem trivial and without meaningful implications. Empirical evidence is clear that there are typically preferred directions in spatial memory, and the idea that an upright component is preferred should not be surprising. On the other hand, it is also possible that the trivialization of this observation provides further evidence for the pervasiveness and the depth to which knowledge of space is grounded in our experience. After all, to the extent that allocentrically framed spatial memories are abstracted from bodily experience and ascended to a Platonic realm of ethereal Form, the notion of "upright" is wholly meaningless. If mental representations of the locations of objects generally code interobject relations with respect to a non-egocentric reference frame, the notion of "upright" should be relatively arbitrary, and certainly not *necessarily* dependent on one's particular viewing perspective.

Yet empirically there is probably as strong a tendency for people to think of space with respect to gravitational upright as there is for researchers to fail to account for it through JRDs. Several years ago, Catherine Mello, Nathan Greenauer, and I conducted two experiments that examined people's ability to imagine spatial relations from an inverted perspective. We reasoned that if spatial memory fundamentally stores interobject relations with respect to a non-egocentric reference system, then the influence of cues such as gravity or the observer's posture, which emphasize the conventional upright direction, should be subject to overriding by instructional manipulations or visual cues. Much as instructions and salient environmental cues can serve to emphasize an upright non-egocentric view around which one can organize memory (e.g., Mou and McNamara 2002), these factors should similarly facilitate organizing memory around a non-upright view.

The data, however, were more consistent with an alternative conceptualization: that spatial memory relies on mental representations that are grounded in physical experience. Indeed, we found in our first experiment that participants were generally unable to encode an array from an imagined, inverted perspective. Despite clear instructions, helpful visual cues, and an array of objects without a salient vertical orientation, our participants were able to recall interobject relations only in a way that had been consistent with their learning experience (and with their lifetime experience of viewing the world with an upright perspective). In our second experiment, two groups of participants learned an array without instructions and were told at test to respond from either upright or inverted imagined perspectives. In this case, both groups' test performance indicated successful adoption of the cued perspectives; however, the participants who made judgments from an imagined inverted perspective required significantly more time (nearly five seconds) to respond. Consistent with the traditional interpretation of JRD effects, we regarded this effect as arising from mental processes that transformed an upright representation into a response that adequately accounted for the imagined inversion.

From an embodied cognition standpoint, most interactions between humans and their environment involve an upright perspective, and it would thus be expected that such a perspective would help compose one's memory of his or her environment. On the other hand, if spatial memory works to code relations among objects in an allocentric reference frame, there would be no necessary reason to privilege an upright perspective, and coding memory with respect to an equally efficient inverted perspective ought to be amenable to instruction. The data from our experiments were clearly consistent with a strong tendency to code space mentally with respect to an upright perspective, and were thus broadly consistent with an embodied cognition approach. In the end, our experiments served as a counterexample to the hypothesis that the mental representation of a recently learned array of objects is completely abstracted from one's experience. Of course our results do not provide particularly strong evidence against other forms of allocentric representation. Nonetheless, it is still notable that the assumption of an upright observer has remained an implicit feature of allocentric theories of spatial memory, and that participants whose data have led researchers to conclude that their memory was non-egocentric presumably had at least one element of egocentric experience—a gravitationally aligned perspective—as a part of their representation.

Conclusion

From Copernican heliocentrism to Darwinian evolution to Freud's unconscious, theories that have tended to demote a previously perceived "special" status of humanity have been enormously generative. By focusing on the role of perceptual/motor involvement in abstract thought, the framework of embodied cognition may offer the prospects of such a movement to the present-day study of environmental cognition. Rather than couching sophisticated behavior as depending on sophisticated representations of the environment, the embodied cognition approach suggests that basic and evolutionarily more primitive functions can, in many cases, be sufficient for understanding complex (and perhaps uniquely human) behavior. As with other animal species, human behavior evolved in a context that continues to demand real-time online actions, and thus it makes sense that the systems that evolved to enable these actions function by integrating information over time. The embodied cognition approach captures the critical role of time in cognition, as well as our relation to other animal species, and in so doing posits the power of modal representations that are grounded in one's immediate perceptual/motor experience. Although much of the empirical treatment of embodied cognition in the literature has demonstrated little more than a close connection between body and mind, the framework's more powerful claim—that perceptual/motor functions *constitute* thought—represents an important contribution to our understanding of mind, body, and environment.

References

Alibali, M. W., and Nathan, M. J. 2012. Embodiment in mathematics teaching and learning: Evidence from learners' and teachers' gestures. *Journal of the Learning Sciences* 21: 247–286.

Anderson, M. L. 2003. Embodied cognition: A field guide. *Artificial Intelligence* 149: 91–130.

Barsalou, L. W. 1999. Perceptual symbol systems. *Behavioral and Brain Sciences* 22: 577–660.

Barsalou, L. W. 2008. Grounded cognition. *Annual Review of Psychology* 59: 617–645.

Brooks, R. A. 1999. *Cambrian Intelligence: The Early History of the New AI.* MIT Press.

Brunyé, T. T., Mahoney, C. R., and Taylor, H. A. 2010. Moving through imagined space: Mentally simulating locomotion during spatial description reading. *Acta Psychologica* 134: 110–124.

Clark, A. 1998. *Being There: Putting Brain, Body, and World Together Again.* MIT Press.

Clark, A. 2006. Language, embodiment, and the cognitive niche. *Trends in Cognitive Sciences* 10: 370–374.

DeCaro, D. A., Bar-Eli, M., Conlin, J. A., Diederich, A., Johnson, J. G., and Plessner, H. 2009. How do motoric realities shape, and become shaped by, the way people evaluate and select potential courses of action? Toward a unitary framework of embodied decision making. In *Mind and Motion: The Bidirectional Link Between Thought and Action,* ed. M. Raab, J. G. Johnson, and H. Heekeren. Elsevier.

Dijksterhuis, A., and Bargh, J. A. 2001. The perception-behavior expressway: Automatic effects of social perception on social behavior. In *Advances in Experimental Social Psychology,* volume 33, ed. M. Zanna. Academic Press.

Gallistel, C. R. 1990. *The Organization of Learning.* MIT Press.

Gibson, J. J. 1979. *The Ecological Approach to Visual Perception.* Houghton Mifflin.

Glenberg, A. M. 2008. Embodiment for education. In *Handbook of Cognitive Science: An Embodied Approach,* ed. P. Calvo and A. Gomila. Elsevier.

Glenberg, A. M., and Gallese, V. 2011. Action-based language: A theory of language acquisition, comprehension, and production. *Cortex* 48: 905–922.

Glenberg, A. M., and Kaschak, M. P. 2002. Grounding language in action. *Psychonomic Bulletin and Review* 9: 558–565.

Greenauer, N., and Waller, D. 2008. Intrinsic array structure is neither necessary nor sufficient for nonegocentric coding of spatial layout. *Psychonomic Bulletin and Review* 15: 1015–1021.

Heft, H. 1997. The relevance of Gibson's ecological approach to perception for environment-behavior studies. In *Advances in Environment, Behavior, and Design*, volume 4, ed. G. T. Moore and R. W. Marans. Plenum.

Johnson, M. 2007. *The Meaning of the Body: Aesthetics of Human Understanding*. University of Chicago Press.

Lakoff, G. 1990. *Women, Fire, and Dangerous Things: What Categories Reveal about the Mind*. University of Chicago Press.

Mayer, R. E., and DaPra, C. S. 2012. An embodiment effect in computer-based learning with animated pedagogical agents. *Journal of Experimental Psychology. Applied* 18: 239–252.

Mou, W., and McNamara, T. P. 2002. Intrinsic frames of reference in spatial memory. *Journal of Experimental Psychology. Learning, Memory, and Cognition* 28: 162–170.

Neisser, U. 1976. *Cognition and Reality: Principles and Implications of Cognitive Psychology*. Freeman.

Newcombe, N. S., and Frick, A. 2010. Early education for spatial intelligence: Why, what, and how. *Mind, Brain, and Education* 4 (3): 102–111.

Niedenthal, P. M., Mermillod, M., Maringer, M., and Hess, U. 2010. The simulation of smiles (SIMS) model: Embodied simulation and the meaning of facial expression. *Behavioral and Brain Sciences* 33: 417–480.

O'Regan, J. K., and Noë, A. 2001. A sensorimotor account of vision and visual consciousness. *Behavioral and Brain Sciences* 24: 939–1031.

Richard, L., and Waller, D. 2013. Towards a definition of intrinsic axes: The effect of orthogonality and symmetry on the preferred direction of spatial memory. *Journal of Experimental Psychology. Learning, Memory, and Cognition* 39 (6): 1914–1929.

Riley, M. A., Mitra, S., Saunders, N., Kiefer, A. W., and Wallot, S. 2012. The interplay between posture control and memory for spatial location. *Experimental Brain Research* 217: 43–52.

Rubin, D. C. 2006. The basic-systems model of episodic memory. *Perspectives on Psychological Science* 1: 277–311.

Searle, J. R. 1980. Minds, brains, and programs. *Behavioral and Brain Sciences* 3: 417–457.

Shapiro, L. 2011. *Embodied Cognition*. Routledge.

Shelton, A. L., and McNamara, T. P. 2001. Systems of spatial reference in human memory. *Cognitive Psychology* 43: 274–310.

Shepard, R. N., and Metzler, J. T. 1971. Mental rotation of three dimensional objects. *Science* 171: 701–703.

Strack, F., Martin, L. L., and Stepper, S. 1988. Inhibiting and facilitating conditions of the human smile: A nonobtrusive test of the facial feedback hypothesis. *Journal of Personality and Social Psychology* 54: 768–777.

Thelen, E., and Smith, L. B. 1996. *A Dynamic Systems Approach to the Development of Cognition and Action.* MIT Press.

Wexler, M., Kosslyn, S. M., and Berthoz, A. 1998. Motor processes in mental rotation. *Cognition* 68: 77–94.

Wohlschlaeger, A., and Wohlschlaeger, A. 1998. Mental and manual rotation. *Journal of Experimental Psychology. Human Perception and Performance* 24: 397–412.

8 Enhancement of Spatial Processing in Sign-Language Users

Evie Malaia and Ronnie B. Wilbur

Discussion of human use and conceptualization of space is incomplete without understanding the spatial abilities of a large group of people whose primary medium of communication is visuospatial—users of sign language. Multiple studies indicate that users of sign language are better than non-signers at processing and manipulating spatial information (Colmenero et al. 2004; Springford 2006), owing to experience with the inherently present spatial component in signed languages. In this chapter, we provide a summary of what is currently known about space use, processing, and conceptualization by signers. In the first section, we explain how the use of space pervasively defines the linguistic system of sign languages at every scale of analysis, from formational parameters to discourse level. In the second section, we demonstrate how information processing based on the use of space affects perceptual, memory, and language networks. In the third section, we explore implications of sign-language learning for enhancement of visual perception, memory, and space representation in non-native[1] signers.

How Visual Languages Use Space

The acquisition of the rules of any sign language results in a major shift in how one looks at the world. In a room full of people or on a busy street, instead of a relatively passive view of the spatial scene, a signer actively (and peripherally) monitors the environment for eye gazes and hand movements that might signal active communication—either ongoing conversation or an attempt to gain attention. If eye gaze is detected, instead of briefly making eye contact and looking away, a signer will lock eye gaze to signal a readiness for receiving communication (Wilbur 2006; Wilbur and Petitto 1983). In order for a hand movement to be communicative, the hand must be at a certain height with respect to the body in order to be in standard signing space, and the movement must fall within a distinctive range of velocities, the upper and lower limits of which are still under experimental determination (Malaia, Borneman, and Wilbur 2013; Malaia and Wilbur 2012a; Malaia, Wilbur, and Milković 2013). In short, the signer is watching for specific pieces of sign formation the way that a listener tracks an auditory signal for sequences of consonants and vowels that constitute portions of syllables that make up allowable words in the language being listened to. In this sense, the signer is watching for phonemes,[2] the distinctions that not only separate signing from gestures and pantomime but also separate one sign from another (Brentari 1998).

Sign formation is generally viewed as consisting of four manual (hand) parameters (hand shape, location, movement, orientation) and possibly one non-manual (face/head/body) parameter (Brentari 1998). In contrast with sequences of consonants and vowels in spoken languages, in sign languages these distinctive parameters are simultaneously processed—that is, the hand shape, orientation, place of articulation, and the movement are processed at the same time, although of course, the movement unfolds over time. In American Sign Language (ASL), the signs for 'summer', 'ugly', and 'dry' are made with the same hand shape, movement, and palm orientation, but differ in location where they are articulated—at the forehead, at the nose, and at the chin, respectively (Klima and Bellugi 1979). These three signs take advantage of features on the face to distinctively locate different meanings. That is, location has been made discrete/categorical and lexicalized into words. When signs are made in the space in front of the chest (without chest contact), generally the height of the sign with respect to the rest of the signing space is not distinctive in this way; however, the ipsilateral/ and contralateral location and direction of movement between them, as well as between signer and addressee, may be used grammatically (Mathur and Rathmann 2012; Perniss 2012). For example, it is standard to introduce an individual (let's say someone named Taylor) into the discourse by providing a locus in space that can be used for future reference to Taylor. The locus, usually on the ipsilateral side of the signer at the lower-trunk or the mid-trunk level, can be established in one of several ways: signing the name at that location; signing the name in the center and pointing to the ipsilateral location; or signing the name and using eye gaze, head tilt/turn, or shoulder movement toward the location. A second individual (say, Kim) would be established similarly on the contralateral side. Sign languages have several elaborated mechanisms for establishing subsequent individuals as needed. Suppose, then, that the signer wishes to ask the addressee if the addressee knows whether Taylor will be coming to meet them. The question is addressed on a straight line between signer and addressee (this line is considered to be reserved for first-person and second-person reference), and can be constructed with only two signs ('know' and 'come') if the additional appropriate grammatical mechanisms are used. To ask a yes/no question, the signer looks at the addressee, raises his or her eyebrows, makes the sign 'know', moves one hand to the locus previously established for Taylor, and makes the sign 'come', starting at that locus and moving toward the signer. This sequence would be written as follows, with capital letters used for the names of signs, a line above the sign(s) to show when the non-manual marking (in this case, an eyebrow raise, indicated by 'br') starts and ends, and subscript letters used to show the locus for Taylor and the start of the movement for the verb, which ends at the location of the signer:

$$\overline{\qquad\qquad\text{br}\qquad\qquad}$$

(1) TAYLOR$_a$ KNOW $_a$COME   'Do you know if Taylor is coming here?'

Non-signers are not attuned to the face marking with the brows, or the appropriate head forward position and eye gaze (not marked in example (1)) that signals that the question is being asked to the addressee, nor do they realize that the starting location of the sign COME is significant—if there were two people established on the ipsilateral side, the one introduced after Taylor would be further forward than where Taylor is established. What might amount to an actual difference of maybe two inches would in fact be categorically and grammatically distinctive so that it would be clear that the signer is asking about Taylor coming and not the other person, and not Taylor AND the other person.

This discretization of space introduces both categories and variables into the signer's use of space. The normal signing space extends in front of the signer from the top of the head to about the level of the waist and out to both sides the width of slightly bent arms. (It can be enlarged for the equivalent of shouting and shrunk for the equivalent of whispering.) The system is overlaid on the space in such a structured way that when signers are whispering to each other so no one else can see, the signs need not actually go anywhere near their target locations (especially not up to the face), and the distinctions are sufficiently categorical that the message is completely comprehensible to fluent signers. From this discrete structure, sign languages have developed systematic uses to convey meaningful differences between signs (phonemic distinctions) and to show verb agreement when needed with subject and/or object (as marked on COME). Because the speed and the size of signs are not distinctive in this sense, they are available for prosodic purposes, showing the rhythmic modifications that may arise from changing signing rate, increased stress on an item (Wilbur 1999, 2009), and larger formation for shouting in addition to smaller formation for whispering, as mentioned above. It is quite likely that signers must make and detect distinctions in these dimensions in ways that non-signers are perfectly capable of doing but may never actually have to do. Signers are more actively attuned to the presence of such differences in their visual environment.

Under normal circumstances, space is symmetrical around the center of the signer, so it makes no difference if the signer is right-hand dominant or left-hand dominant. In the example above, a right-handed signer would normally put Taylor on the right side (the ipsilateral side) and a left-handed signer would use the left (also the ipsilateral side). But neither of these generalizations are fixed. A left-handed signer who is driving might hold the steering wheel with the left hand and sign with the right; a right-handed signer might hold a baby on the right and sign with the left. What is critical about this use of space is that it is being used grammatically, not as locations meaning 'on my right' or 'on my left', both of which require a different construction to express. When space is grammaticalized, the participants in an event (e.g., Taylor and Kim) are introduced and the viewer is expected to keep track of who is where. In English, 'Kim told me that Taylor is coming' and 'Taylor told me that Kim is coming' are crucially different with respect to the order, the person who is telling comes before the verb 'told', and the person who is coming precedes the verb 'is coming'.

In ASL, the subject of 'told' and 'is coming' are expressed through the use of space. Thus we have the following sentences, where (2) follows naturally as an answer to (1) whereas (3) leaves the specific question in (1) unanswered:

(2) $_b$TELL$_1$ $_a$COME 'Kim told me that Taylor is coming'
(3) $_a$TELL$_1$ $_b$COME 'Taylor told me that Kim is coming'

Note also that the verb TELL ends at the signer. (The subscript 1 means first person.) These examples have the verbs explicitly signed with the verb arguments (participants) affixed to the beginning or end of the sign to show who is doing what. With the verb 'give', the initial location is the subject and giver, whereas the final location is the object and recipient. However, not all verbs behave this way. Some verbs (called *plain verbs*, an example in ASL being LOVE) do not allow this type of agreement at all, and some verbs (called *backward verbs*, an example in ASL being INVITE) are constructed so that the arguments are reversed. In addition, a verb might be plain in some sign languages and agreeing in others; for example, in Italian Sign Language (LIS) the sign for LOVE is an agreeing verb.

For the vast majority of verbs, even if they are made with movement in space, their meaning is not referring to actual space (Wilbur 2003, 2008, 2010). The verb TELL starts at (or near) the locus of the teller and moves to the person told, within certain constraints. For both 'Kim told me' and 'I told Kim' this statement is true and unproblematic. But for 'Kim told Taylor' or 'Taylor told you', the sign TELL will start at the signer's chin, and the signer will either shift toward the locus of Kim or toward that of Taylor before moving the hand toward the (locus of the) person being told. Critically, in none of these situations is it asserted that the person doing the telling moves to the location of the person being told, even though that is where the hand stops. Thus, the hand movement is not indicating person movement.

For a special subset of verbs, appropriately called *spatial verbs*, the movement of the hand does in fact mean movement of the subject from the starting (source) location to the ending (goal) location. This use of space as space must be learned for each such verb as an exception to the general rule that use of space is grammatical, not literally spatial. As full natural languages, sign languages are expected to be able to express anything that a human wishes to convey. Non-signers who search for reasons why a sign is made the way it is (iconicity) are looking for this use of space; the fact that space has been grammaticalized means that what might be expected from gesture is not what is actually present, because languages need to be able to express situations that are not here and now, not real, but also hypothetical, counterfactual, or simply abstract. Grounding the use of space to mean only literal spatiality would eliminate these possibilities from sign languages and would severely limit what could be talked about.

Impact of Sign-Language Use on Visual Perception, Cognition, and Neural Processing of Spatial Information by Signers

From the standpoint of perception and information processing, sign languages are, essentially, a means of transmitting information from one user (the signer) to another (the signee). The signer produces visually observable linguistic code, which is then perceived and decoded by the signee in order to understand the content of the signer's message. Every step of this process uses spatially encoded information; here, we discuss each component of message transmission in sign languages and what effect it has on the signee's perceptual, cognitive, and neural systems.

Perceptual adaptation of the visual system

The experience of communicating using sign language alters signers' perceptual abilities independent of their hearing status. The reason is simply the exposure to an environment with altered spatiotemporal parameters, compared to the everyday surroundings of non-signers. Comparative analysis of photos of signers signing, and natural landscapes, demonstrated that the spatial frequencies of visual communication by signers are significantly more fractal; that is, they contain increased information content at different frequency bands (Bosworth et al. 2006). Similar work is underway for the temporal properties of signing (Malaia, Borneman, and Wilbur 2013). Over time, signers tune their perceptual systems to adapt to the properties of the main information channel.

One of the earliest observed adaptations in signers was their increased ability to notice object motion in their peripheral field of view (outside the foveal focus). The periphery of signers' visual fields is more sensitive to motion, and the attended visual field is larger and better regulated by selective attention (Bavelier et al. 2001; Bosworth and Dobkins 1999). Additionally, signers (both deaf and hearing) demonstrate strong right-visual-field advantage in visual perception, including smaller thresholds to detection of changes in motion in that visual field (Bosworth and Dobkins 2002; Brozinsky and Bavelier 2004). As neural processing is contralateral to the perceptual fields, this probably is due to recruitment of the left hemisphere for sign-language processing, especially since motion parameters, such as velocity and acceleration, play distinctive linguistic roles in several sign languages, including ASL and Croatian Sign Language (HZJ) (Malaia, Borneman, and Wilbur 2013; Malaia and Wilbur 2012a,b). The multi-channel property of information transfer in sign languages also appears to lead to qualitative changes in visual perception, in that signers are more sensitive to simultaneous information in the signal overall (Brentari et al. 2011).

Though it is not yet clear whether signers have a higher temporal resolution of attention, they clearly use the information they extract from the temporal dimension of visual stimuli differently from non-signers (Malaia and Wilbur 2008; Malaia and Wilbur 2010b). An investigation of visual perception using moving point-light "writing" of pseudo-hieroglyphs (Klima et al. 1999) found that signers looking at the stimuli were able to identify underlying targets—discrete structural elements of the stimuli—

based solely on the differences in motion. Non-signers (even those familiar with hieroglyphic systems, such as a Chinese group in the study) could not reproduce pseudo-hieroglyphic targets: They simply saw chaotic motion of a light on the screen. Both ASL signers and Chinese Sign Language signers, on the other hand, identified transitions between structural elements, indicating that they were able to use some characteristics of biological motion to infer the underlying structure of the stimuli. Such abilities can, of course, stem in equal measure from perceptual adaptations as well as adaptations to processing of visuospatial information.

Finally, signers are able to use the higher dimensionality of the visual communication channel in production and comprehension (Wilbur et al. 2012). Signers consistently produce several pieces of meaning simultaneously using the same articulator, such as using articulators on the face to indicate emotional content of the message and to modify verb semantics, and indicate perspective and verb agreement using hand location (Emmorey et al. 2000; Thompson et al. 2006). The adaptations underlying the combined processing of non-linguistic and multiple layers of linguistic meaning are not yet clear.

Cognitive benefits of sign-language use

Since sign discourse requires frequent shifts of perspective from one signer to another, an aspect of cognitive processing that has been researched is mental rotation. Emmorey et al. (1998) investigated both linguistic and non-linguistic-based mental rotation using narrative and spatial scene description and found that ASL signers performed significantly better than hearing non-signers under rotation in both types of task.

Another aspect of cognitive processing that has received particular attention in signers is working-memory ability. Although one specific aspect of working-memory functionality—serial recall—appears impaired when working-memory representations are based upon a spatio-temporal code, with speakers averaging 7 ± 2 items, vs. 5 ± 1 items for signers in serial recall tasks, the overall communicative ability (i.e., production and retention of complex information) of signers and non-signers is similar, regardless of the modality. Boutla et al. (2004) demonstrated that in complex sentence- or discourse-based tasks that require processing of multiple competing representations in working memory, signers and speakers perform identically, indicating that the capacity of working memory is comparable in speakers and signers; the seemingly larger short-term memory capacity of speakers is the result of their using a temporal rehearsal strategy (phonological loop) in spoken languages. However, recent work (Saito et al.

2008; van Dijck et al. 2013) indicates that the use of phonological loop competes with spatial attention even in speakers. The likely reason is that the temporal rehearsal uses the same neural substrate as the dorsal location-processing stream in visual cortex (Bavelier, Newport, Hall, Supalla, and Boutla 2008, indicating that inferior parietal cortex is used by speakers in encoding and rehearsal, but by signers during recall).

Neural processing adaptations to visuospatial communication

Processing adaptations of signers can be generally divided into quantitative and qualitative changes in the function of brain regions—the efficient, "professionalized" use of neural resources for visuospatial domains (Malaia, Borneman, and Wilbur 2008; Malaia, Ranaweera, Tamer, Wilbur, and Talavage 2009; Malaia, Ranaweera, Wilbur, and Talavage 2012; Malaia and Wilbur 2008, 2010a, 2012c). Although sometimes it is difficult to distinguish whether a specific change is brought about by deafness or signing experience, research on bimodal bilinguals has identified several modality-specific adaptations that clearly are attributable to communication in the visual modality.

One adaptive route involves neural representations of topographic, spatial information conveyed by sign languages using linguistic encoding. In a study of deaf and hearing native signers of British Sign Language (BSL), MacSweeney et al. (2002) found enhanced activation of the left inferior and superior parietal lobes during processing of topographic BSL sentences, indicating that precise configuration and location of hands in space to represent objects, agents, and actions were processed as linguistic signals. The observation that processing of motion in sign language is also reliant on left hemispheric brain region MT-MST (Bavelier et al. 2001) suggests that perceptual differences in motion processing between signers and non-signers are also due to pre-linguistic processing of visual motion.

At the same time, communication of spatial, topographic information (e.g., a route on a map) in sign language automatically engages neural regions responsible for visual working memory. A study in hearing bilingual signers of French Sign Language (LSF) showed that the comprehension of signed topographic discourse is supported by the additional recruitment of right superior parietal lobule and superior frontal sulcus. Activation of this spatial working-memory network suggested that sign-language discourse and mental representations of complex real environments share a common neural substrate (Courtin et al. 2010). A similar effect was found in studies of deaf and hearing ASL signers—that naming of spatial relations using ASL signs with prepositional meaning, as compared to naming objects, differentially activated right supramarginal gyrus (Emmorey et al. 2002, 2004).

Thus, using sign language appears to enhance several aspects of visuo-spatial processing: It leads to recruitment of linguistic regions for processing of phonological and lexical spatial information, and engages right-hemisphere spatial representation networks during topographic and metaphoric discourse, leading to overall increased inter-hemispheric activation.

Relevance of Sign-Language Learning to Development of Visuo-Spatial Skills

Visual-spatial thinking is a topic currently overlooked in school curriculum (Mathewson 1999; National Research Council 2006), despite clear evidence that early development of spatial skill is crucial to creative achievement in adulthood, especially in STEM fields (Greenfield 2009; Kell et al. 2013). Because sign languages are visually based, they can represent information in ways that spoken languages do not allow. Something as simple as the height of a very tall or very short addressee, if not properly encoded in the signed version of 'he asks a very tall/short person ...' can lead to ungrammaticality in ASL (Schlenker 2011). Sign languages do this because they can. Similarly, if one is describing a car trip from New York to Los Angeles by way of Toronto and Dallas in ASL, a straight-line movement from the location of New York to the location of Los Angeles is unacceptable, because Toronto and Dallas do not lie on a straight line between New York and Los Angeles (Bradley 2013). Instead, the signer must use encyclopedic knowledge of the geographical layout of these cities to properly construct the sentence that conveys the general layout of the trip. (Note that this is not the actual roadmap, only the general geography with respect to east, west, north and south.) This ability to project from geography to visual structure in ASL suggests that signing in a similar style (or even gesturing, which is less systematic) might provide several benefits to young learners. First, an error would be immediately obvious, so there might be greater motivation to pay attention to the details of geography. Second, the tracing of the path layout in such an exercise might contribute to better storage and recall of the relevant geographical facts. Third, games of various sorts can be constructed for group play—given a starting location, one student could trace a long or short path in some direction in space, and the group might try to guess where the car stopped at the end of that path. The next student could take the journey one leg further, and so on. Beyond geography, there is possibility in the domains of relative distances/widths/heights. Indeed, there is already some evidence that gesture use can be helpful in math instruction with hearing children (Broaders, Cook, Mitchell, and Goldin-Meadow 2007; Goldin-Meadow, Cook, and Mitchell 2009; Singer and Goldin-Meadow 2005). Multiple studies also indicate that sign language confers clear executive processing advantages for attentional modulation (attention-switching and intrusion resistance), orienting, and manipulation of visual content in spatial tasks (Brozinsky and Bavelier 2004; Finney and Dobkins 2001; Pavani and Bottari 2012).

Although most of the neurolinguistic and psycholinguistic studies of brain function and sign-language acquisition have been aimed at issues related to early remediation of young deaf children's communication needs, there is some evidence that indicates that even late learners of sign languages benefit in the spatial domain. For example, Mayberry and Witcher (2005) have shown that in a primed lexical decision task (to determine if the presence of a stimulus item results in faster/better processing of a subsequent target item) phonological priming by a sign's place of articulation is observed in native ASL signers (both deaf and hearing), as well as in hearing early acquirers of spoken English who learned ASL as a second language later in life. Insofar as learning of sign language (even late—i.e., in school or college) can lead to improved perception and conceptualization of space, use of sign language in a curriculum can enrich students' spatial representation.

Notes

1. Signers are considered native when they learn sign language within the critical period—most often before the age of 5 (Mayberry and Witcher 2005; Malaia and Wilbur 2010a,b).

2. A phoneme in sign language is the minimal distinctive unit that makes a difference between two meaningful signs. For example, the '5' hand shape (a flat palm with extended fingers) held perpendicularly to the face in ASL can mean "mother" or "father," depending on whether the sign is made at the level of the chin or that of the forehead. In this case, the place of articulation is the minimal distinctive unit between the two signs, or phoneme.

References

Bavelier, D., Brozinsky, C., Tomann, A., Mitchell, T., Neville, H., and Liu, G. 2001. Impact of early deafness and early exposure to sign language on the cerebral organization for motion processing. *Journal of Neuroscience* 21: 8931–8942.

Bavelier, D., Newport, E. L., Hall, M., Supalla, T., and Boutla, M. 2008. Ordered short-term memory differs in signers and speakers: Implications for models of short-term memory. *Cognition* 107: 433–459.

Bosworth, R. G., and Dobkins, K. R. 1999. Left-hemisphere dominance for motion processing in deaf signers. *Psychological Science* 10: 256.

Bosworth, R. G., Bartlett, M. S., and Dobkins, K. R. 2006. Image statistics of American Sign Language: Comparison with faces and natural scenes. *Journal of the Optical Society of America* 23: 2085–2096.

Bosworth, R. G., and Dobkins, K. R. 2002. Visual field asymmetries for motion processing in deaf and hearing signers. *Brain and Cognition* 49: 170–181.

Boutla, M., Supalla, T., Newport, E. L., and Bavelier, D. 2004. Short-term memory span: insights from sign language. *Nature Neuroscience* 7: 997–1002.

Bradley, C. 2013. Motion Events and Event Segmentation in American Sign Language. Master's thesis, Purdue University.

Brentari, D. 1998. *A Prosodic Model of Sign Language Phonology*. MIT Press.

Brentari, D., González, C., Seidl, A., and Wilbur, R. 2011. Sensitivity to visual prosodic cues in signers and nonsigners. *Language and Speech* 54: 49–72.

Broaders, S., Cook, S. W., Mitchell, Z., and Goldin-Meadow, S. 2007. Making children gesture brings out implicit knowledge and leads to learning. *Journal of Experimental Psychology. General* 136: 539–550.

Brozinsky, C. J., and Bavelier, D. 2004. Motion velocity thresholds in deaf signers: change in lateralization but not overall sensitivity. *Brain Research. Cognitive Brain Research* 21: 1–10.

Colmenero, J. M., Catena, A., Fuentes, L. J., and Ramos, M. M. 2004. Mechanisms of visuospatial orienting in deafness. *European Journal of Cognitive Psychology* 16: 791–805.

Corina, D., Chiu, Y. S., Knapp, H., Greenwald, R., San Jose-Robertson, L., and Braun, A. 2007. Neural correlates of human action observation in hearing and deaf subjects. *Brain Research* 1152: 111–129.

Courtin, C., Hervé, P. Y., Petit, L., Zago, L., Vigneau, M., Beaucousin, V., et al. 2010. The neural correlates of highly iconic structures and topographic discourse in French Sign Language as observed in six hearing native signers. *Brain and Language* 114: 180–192.

Emmorey, K., Damasio, H., McCullough, S., Grabowski, T., Ponto, L. L., Hichwa, R. D., and Bellugi, U. 2002. Neural systems underlying spatial language in American Sign Language. *NeuroImage* 17: 812–824.

Emmorey, K., Grabowski, T., McCullough, S., Damasio, H., Ponto, L., Hichwa, R., and Bellugi, U. 2004. Motor-iconicity of sign language does not alter the neural systems underlying tool and action naming. *Brain and Language* 89, 27–37.

Emmorey, K., Klima, E., and Hickok, G. 1998. Mental rotation within linguistic and non-linguistic domains in users of American sign language. *Cognition* 68: 221–246.

Emmorey, K., Tversky, B., and Taylor, H. A. 2000. Using space to describe space: Perspective in speech, sign, and gesture. *Spatial Cognition and Computation* 2: 157–180.

Finney, E. M., and Dobkins, K. R. 2001. Visual contrast sensitivity in deaf versus hearing populations: exploring the perceptual consequences of auditory deprivation and experience with a visual language. *Brain Research. Cognitive Brain Research* 11: 171–183.

Greenfield, P. M. 2009. Technology and informal education: What is taught, what is learned. *Science* 323 (5910): 69–71.

Goldin-Meadow, S., Cook, S. W., and Mitchell, Z. A. 2009. Gesturing gives children new ideas about math. *Psychological Science* 20: 267–272.

Kell, H. J., Lubinski, D., Benbow, C. P., and Steiger, J. H. 2013. Creativity and technical innovation: Spatial ability's unique role. *Psychological Science* 24: 1831–1836.

Klima, E. S., and Bellugi, U. 1979. *The Signs of Language*. Harvard University Press.

Klima, E. S., Tzeng, O., Fok, A., Bellugi, U., Corina, D., and Bettger, J. G. 1999. From sign to script: Effects of linguistic experience on perceptual categorization. *Journal of Chinese Linguistics* 13: 96–129.

MacSweeney, M., Woll, B., Campbell, R., Calvert, G. A., McGuire, P. K., David, A. S., et al. 2002. Neural correlates of British Sign Language comprehension: Spatial processing demands of topographic language. *Journal of Cognitive Neuroscience* 14: 1064–1075.

Malaia, E., Borneman, J., and Wilbur, R. B. 2008. Analysis of ASL motion capture data towards identification of verb type. In *Semantics in Text Processing*, ed. J. Bos and R. Delmonte. College Publications.

Malaia, E., Borneman, J., and Wilbur, R. B. 2013. Bioinformatic properties of sign language motion: Fractal complexity of optical flow. Presented at Advances in Biolinguistics conference, Geneva.

Malaia, E., Ranaweera, R., Tamer, G., Wilbur, R. B., and Talavage, T. M. 2009. Cortical representation of predicate processing in American Sign Language. *NeuroImage* 47: S164.

Malaia, E., Ranaweera, R., Wilbur, R. B., and Talavage, T. M. 2012. Event segmentation in a visual language: Neural bases of processing American Sign Language predicates. *NeuroImage* 59: 4094–4101.

Malaia, E., and Wilbur, R. B. 2008. The biological bases of syntax-semantics interface in natural languages: Cognitive modeling and empirical evidence. In *Biologically Inspired Cognitive Architectures: Papers from the AAAI Fall Symposium*, ed. A. V. Samsonovich. AAAI Press.

Malaia, E., and Wilbur, R. B. 2010a. Early acquisition of sign language: What neuroimaging data tell us. *Sign Language and Linguistics* 13: 189–193.

Malaia, E., and Wilbur, R. B. 2010b. Representation of verbal event structure in sign languages. In Proceedings of the Interdisciplinary workshop on verbs: The Identification and representation of verb features, Pisa.

Malaia, E., and Wilbur, R. B. 2012a. Motion capture signatures of telic and atelic events in ASL predicates. *Language and Speech* 55: 407–421.

Malaia, E., and Wilbur, R. B. 2012b. Telicity expression in visual modality. In *Telicity, Change, and State: A Cross-Categorical View of Event Structure*, ed. L. McNally and V. Delmonte. Oxford University Press.

Malaia, E., and Wilbur, R. B. 2012c. What sign languages show: Neurobiological bases of visual phonology. In *Towards a Bilinguistic Understanding of Grammar: Essays on Interfaces*, ed. A. M. Di Sciullo. John Benjamins.

Malaia, E., Wilbur, R. B., and Milkovič, M. 2013. Kinematic parameters of signed verbs at morpho-phonology interface. *Journal of Speech, Language, and Hearing Research* 56: 1677–1688.

Mathewson, J. H. 1999. Visual-spatial thinking: An aspect of science overlooked by educators. *Science Education* 83: 33–54.

Mathur, G., and Rathmann, C. 2012. Verb agreement. In *Sign Language: An International Handbook*, ed. R. Pfau, M. Steinbach, and B. Woll. Mouton De Gruyter.

Mayberry, R. I., and Witcher, P. 2005. Age of acquisition effects on lexical access in ASL: Evidence for the psychological reality of phonological processing in sign language. Presented at 30th Boston University Conference on Language Development.

National Research Council. 2006. *Learning to Think Spatially: GIS as a Support System in the K–12 Curriculum*. National Academies Press.

Pavani, F., and Bottari, D. 2012. Visual abilities in individuals with profound deafness: A critical review. In *The Neural Bases of Multisensory Processes*, ed. M. M. Murray and M. T. Wallace. CRC Press.

Perniss, P. 2012. Use of sign space. In *Sign Language: An International Handbook*, ed. R. Pfau, M. Steinbach, and B. Woll. Mouton De Gruyter.

Saito, S., Logic, R. H., Morita, A., and Law, A. 2008. Visual and phonological similarity effects in verbal immediate serial recall: A test with kanji materials. *Journal of Memory and Language* 59: 1–17.

Schlenker, P. 2011. Iconic agreement. *Theoretical Linguistics* 37 (3/4): 223–234.

Singer, M. A., and Goldin-Meadow, S. 2005. Children learn when their teachers' gestures and speech differ. *Psychological Science* 16: 85–89.

Springford, J. A. 2006. Signs of enhancement? A comparison of Visual Spatial Skills in Signers and Non-Signers. Doctoral dissertation, University of British Columbia.

Thompson, R., Emmorey, K., and Kluender, R. 2006. The relationship between eye gaze and verb agreement in American Sign Language: An eye-tracking study. *Natural Language and Linguistic Theory* 24: 571–604.

van Dijck, J. P., Abrahamse, E. L., Majerus, S., and Fias, W. 2013. Spatial attention interacts with serial order retrieval from verbal working memory. *Psychological Science* 24: 1854–1859.

Wilbur, R. B. 1999. Stress in ASL: Empirical evidence and linguistic issues. *Language and Speech* 42: 229–250.

Wilbur, R. B. 2003. Representations of telicity in ASL. *CLS* 39: 354–368.

Wilbur, R. B. 2006. Discourse and pragmatics in sign language. In *The Encyclopedia of Language and Linguistics*, second edition. Elsevier.

Wilbur, R. B. 2008. Complex predicates involving events, time and aspect: Is this why sign languages look so similar? In *Signs of the Time: Selected Papers from TISLR 2004*, ed. J. Quer. Signum.

Wilbur, R. B. 2009. Effects of varying rate of signing on ASL manual signs and non-manual markers. *Language and Speech* 52: 245–285.

Wilbur, R. B. 2010. The semantics-phonology interface. In *Cambridge Language Surveys: Sign Languages*, ed. D. Brentari. Cambridge University Press.

Wilbur, R. B., and Petitto, L. A. 1983. Discourse structure in American Sign Language conversations (or, how to know a conversation when you see one). *Discourse Processes* 6: 225–228.

Wilbur, R. B., Malaia, E., and Shay, R. 2012. Degree modification and intensification in American Sign Language adjectives. In *Logic, Language and Meaning*, ed. M. Aloni, V. Kimmelman, and F. Roelofsen. Springer.

9 What Do a Geologist's Hands Tell You? A Framework for Classifying Spatial Gestures in Science Education

Kinnari Atit, Thomas F. Shipley, and Basil Tikoff[1]

Geology is an intensively spatial discipline, and spatial gestures are widely used by geologists for communication. In this chapter we attempt to summarize progress made by a group of cognitive psychologists and geologists working together to understand how spatial relations are communicated in the context of the geological sciences. We propose a framework, based on the work of Chatterjee (2008), that captures well how geologists use and convey spatial information by gesturing.

Before we begin our formal discussion of spatial gestures, let us use a brief narrative to illustrate how spatial gestures are employed in geoscience education:

A geologist and her student are looking at an outcrop of a syncline (a concave-up fold). The expert readily identifies the separate bedding layers and sees the overall structure of the fold. In contrast, the student struggles to see the geological structure, even after being told "There is a fold here." The student is likely to be attending to the salient properties of the outcrop (e.g., the color and surface shape) that are not related to the form. To help the student see the structure and understand the relationship between what can be seen at this outcrop and the geometry of the rocks under the surface, the expert guides the student with gestures.

Initially, the student needs to see the fold, so the expert may trace one of the curved layers with a pointed finger while saying "there is one of the bedding layers." She then may cup both her hands into upward-facing c's, place one hand on top of the other, and explain that "one curved layer is stacked on top of another curved layer." Once the expert is sure that the student sees the form of the fold, she turns to a discussion of what is below the surface. Pointing out the banded pattern on the rock surface, she says "The pattern visible on the face actually extends into the structure." She configures her right hand to match the curves in the bedding planes and places it on the outcrop. To illustrate how the curved surface used to extend into the space in which they are currently standing, she might sweep her curved hand out from the outcrop and then back toward the surface while explaining that the curved pattern continues into the rock.

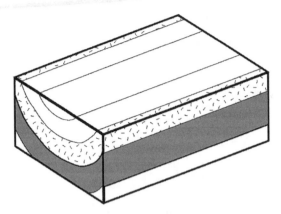

Figure 9.1
Block diagram of a syncline, or a concave-up fold. Image developed by Ormand,
Manduca, Shipley, and Tikoff (2013).

Once the instructor is confident that the student has made the proper inference
about the three-dimensional shape of the fold, she may turn to a discussion of what
can be inferred about local and regional geological history. To show the student
that deformation led to the present structure, the expert points to layers in the
fold and says "The rocks in these layers are all sedimentary, so they were once horizontal and must have tilted up in space to their current position." She then moves
a flat palm from a horizontal to a diagonal position to demonstrate the movement
of a part of the fold. She then explains the same is true for the other half of the
fold, now moving both hands from horizontal to tilted.

In the final step of the inferential sequence, the expert explains that the curved
shape in the rock indicates that the originally horizontal layers were shortened in
this particular direction. She flattens both hands and brings her two palms close
together. "The shortening," she explains, "would have caused the flat layers of rock
to fold up, resulting in the structure we see today," as she takes a flat palm and folds
it up, showing how the layers were transformed in space.

This scenario illustrates the sort of interactions that occur between an expert
and novice on a geology field trip. The expert uses gesture and speech to
guide the student to an understanding of the geological structure and
history of a region. Spatial gestures are commonly seen in geosciences field
classes for three reasons: (1) Students' understanding of domain specific
terms of art is tenuous and spatial gestures can scaffold their understanding
by providing a visual representation of the critical spatial relations (e.g.,
cupping hand for the word "syncline"). (2) Gestures can illustrate complex
spatial relations and thus support spatial inferences (e.g., using the two-
dimensional face to reason about the three-dimensional shape of the fold).

Figure 9.2
Similar to the expert in our narrative, the expert structural geologist in this image is using gesture to highlight the geometry of the rocks in the outcrop for a group of novices.

(3) Gestures can illustrate motion and change and thus support historical inferences (e.g., showing the folding and the direction of the regional shortening). Our initial work on developing a classification of spatial gestures is grounded in the geosciences, but we draw from cognitive science work on spatial thinking to develop a spatial gesture typology that can be broadly applied across scientific domains that require spatial thinking.

Gesturing to Communicate

Spatial information is expressed in gesture both for communicating with others and for individual problem solving (Alibali 2005). Common spatial activities, such as giving directions, often include gesture (Lavergne and Kimura 1987), and in domains of science (e.g., geology) that require communicating complex spatial ideas, experts and novices often gesture (Liben, Christensen, and Kastens 2010). Communicating three-dimensional spatial relationships by using only language is difficult because most spatial words are qualitative and do not convey metric information (Tversky and Lee 1998). Gesture allows one to communicate thoughts that do not easily fit into the categorical system that language offers (Goldin-Meadow 1999).

Scientists are often faced with the limitations of lay language. To overcome these limitations, experts have developed discipline-specific vocabulary to represent complex spatial relations. As one measure of the spatial demands in the sciences, science textbooks often present more new vocabulary than the load recommended for introductory foreign language courses (Groves 1995; Yager 1983). Indeed, the vocabulary in geosciences textbooks is substantial, and a recent analysis found that the vocabulary varies between books, making it difficult for students to learn a common language (Kortz 2011). For the students who are struggling to learn the new vocabulary, experts can use gestures to supplement discourse and scaffold understanding. Previous research indicates that implementing gestures in the classroom may be beneficial for novices' acquisition of scientific terminology (Crowder 1996; Roth 2000). Roth and Lawless (2002) suggest that gesturing helps students obtain the appropriate vocabulary during the transition from "muddled" talk to mature scientific discourse. Therefore, it is important to investigate the types of information experts and novices convey in language and in gesture to fully understand how spatial concepts are taught in the classroom.

Background

Representational gestures, the focus of this chapter, are defined as gestures that convey semantic content by virtue of the shape, placement, or movement of the hands (e.g., pointing to the right to mean "right") (Alibali 2005). Within representational gestures, most authors distinguish between *iconic* and *deictic* gestures as originally defined by McNeill (1992) (see, e.g., Goldin-Meadow 1999; Hostetter and Alibali 2008; Roth and Lawless 2002). Iconic gestures are those that "bear a close formal relationship to the semantic content of speech" (McNeill 1992, p. 12). An example from our narrative is the hand folding to imitate the folding of the rocks. Deictic gestures, in contrast, are used to identify a referent in the space of the conversation (McNeill 1992). One example would be a geologist pointing to a specific sedimentary layer in a rock outcrop to draw attention to that specific location.

Although there is broad agreement about the different basic types of gestures, no one has considered whether it is useful to make further

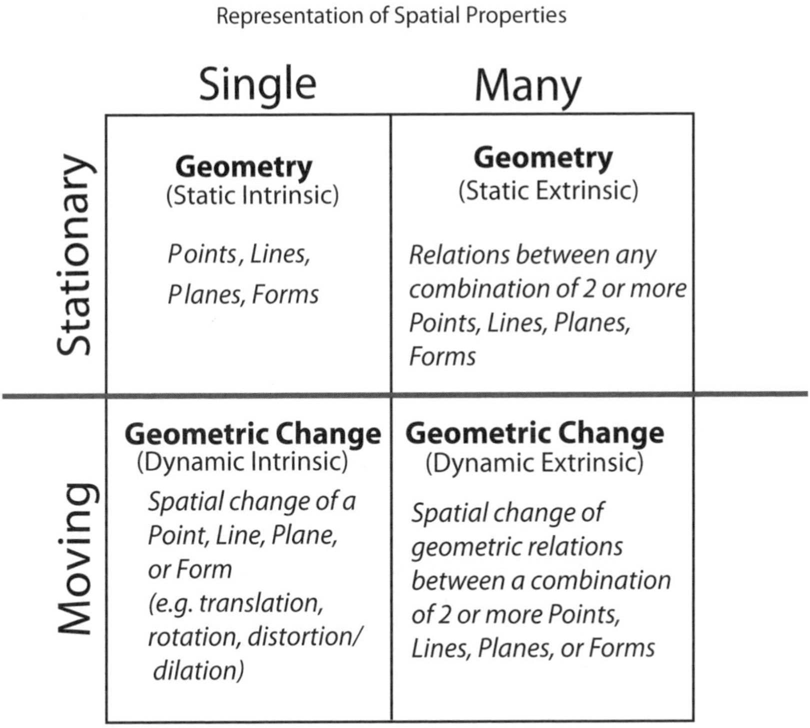

Representation of Spatial Properties

	Single	Many
Stationary	**Geometry** (Static Intrinsic) *Points, Lines,* *Planes, Forms*	**Geometry** (Static Extrinsic) *Relations between any* *combination of 2 or more* *Points, Lines, Planes,* *Forms*
Moving	**Geometric Change** (Dynamic Intrinsic) *Spatial change of a* *Point, Line, Plane,* *or Form* *(e.g. translation,* *rotation, distortion/* *dilation)*	**Geometric Change** (Dynamic Extrinsic) *Spatial change of* *geometric relations* *between a combination* *of 2 or more Points,* *Lines, Planes, or Forms*

Figure 9.3
Schematic of the four categories used to classify spatial relations. Spatial thinking and communicating can be divided into four distinct categories using two dichotomous properties: geometric relations within a single object (intrinsic) versus geometrical relations among many objects (extrinsic) and stationary geometrical relations (static) versus moving geometrical relations (dynamic).

divisions within the category of representational gestures. Research on spatial thinking and communicating spatial relations has found it useful to distinguish among different classes of spatial information. The focus of research on communicating spatial information has been on speech (e.g., Hayward and Tarr 1995; Landau and Jackendoff 1993). However, Trafton, Trickett, Stitzlein, Schunn, and Kirschenbaum (2006) examined the use of spatial gestures by scientists—specifically, whether expert and journeyman neuroscientists and meteorologists gestured about location/relation (characteristics of one object or spatial relations between multiple objects), magnitude (the size or amount of a spatial entity), and time (object-change or spatial transformation)—and found that iconic gestures were most prevalent when scientists were discussing time, less prevalent when scientists were discussing location/relation, and far less likely when scientists were discussing magnitude.

In working with geologists, we have noticed a variety of gestures that argues for an approach to gesture classification that offers more structured categories than those provided by Trafton et al. (2006). Here, we offer a framework for thinking about the breadth of spatial gestures and propose a theoretically grounded spatial gesture typology. We propose a categorization of spatial gestures that is based on what is known about communicating spatial relations in language. We start from a framework for organizing how spatial information is communicated in spoken discourse proposed by Chatterjee (2008). Our proposed framework separates object properties with two dichotomies, intrinsic versus extrinsic, and static versus dynamic. Crossing the two dichotomies yields four broad categories of spatial relations (static intrinsic, static extrinsic, dynamic intrinsic, and dynamic extrinsic). Research in neuroscience indicates that distinct areas of the brain are active when processing the four different types of spatial information. Furthermore, in linguistics, each spatial category requires a different structure in the English language (static nouns versus prepositions, motion path verbs versus manner verbs) (Chatterjee 2008). We draw on field observations to illustrate how this new typology of spatial gestures can help organize research on spatial thinking (see Shipley, Tikoff, Manduca, and Ormand 2013 for application of the typology to geological skills).

A Framework for the Representation of Spatial Relations in Gesture

Based on Chatterjee's (2008) framework for studying spatial semantics in speech, and on observations made about how gesture is used to convey spatial information in structural geology, our framework divides gestures based on two spatial dichotomies. (See figure 9.3.) Gestures can convey spatial relations involving static relations (stationary objects) or dynamic relations (moving objects). When one is discussing stationary or moving objects, gestures can convey intrinsic spatial relations (within one object) or extrinsic spatial relations (between objects).

Gestures that convey stationary properties
Gestures that represent the geometry of one object
One goal for geologists is to understand the history of the geological structures they see in the environment. In order to understand the geological relations of a region, such as understanding of what one outcrop reveals

about an area's topography and history, geologists often have to focus on individual objects. Focusing on one object entails reasoning about its spatial properties. Understanding the geometry of an object requires thinking about its location, orientation, and shape (visualizing an object in three-dimensional space).

When a geologist thinks about the geometry of a single object in three-dimensional space, that object may be anything from a volcano to an individual mineral crystal. For example, the geologist in our narrative uses gesture to convey the spatial properties of a single object when she makes an upward c-shape with her hand, configuring her whole hand to reflect the fold she saw in the outcrop. It is likely that both the types of geologically relevant objects present in the environment and the limits on the types of gestures one can make with hands influence the nature of the gestures structural geologists employ; nevertheless, we have observed gestures with a range of geometric properties. To broadly categorize different types of gestures for each cell in the framework, we consider the dimensionality of the gesture, as it can practically range from zero dimensions (a point) through one dimension (a line) and two dimensions (a plane) to three dimensions (a form). In the case of a static object, the dimensionality refers to the object being gestured. One thing to note before elaborating on how this information can structure a gesture: Although a zero-dimensional referent cannot have any intrinsic relations, such entities can have extrinsic relations, and thus they are included in all four cells of the framework for completeness.

Gestures used to indicate a specific location or point in space are common; for example, one points to a spot on a map to indicate a current position or a destination. Gestures used to indicate a line in three-dimensional space include tracing a line with the tip of a finger and using the orientation of an extended finger. A geologist often uses a finger or a pencil to indicate the orientation of a line running along the top (crest) or bottom (trough) of a fold, the direction of crystal growth, or the direction of a linear structural feature within a rock (e.g., mineral lineation). Unlike zero-dimensional gestures, one-dimensional gestures can have internal relations defined by a location along a line. Magnitude would be another example of a one-dimensional property. Although some magnitudes are spatial, not all of them are spatial. For example, the description of the length of a mineral crystal is spatial, but a description of a length of time is not spatial. Yet gestures can spatialize the quantity of magnitudes that are not inherently spatial, such as indicating the length of a time period by the relative distance of two hands. Thus, this framework categorizes the magnitude gestures reported by Trafton et al. (2006) as one-dimensional object gestures.

We would expect higher order mathematical properties might also be spatialized—to indicate, for example, a hyperplane or three-dimensional manifold in a high-dimensional space.

Predicting the use of the different functional types of gestures highlights the value of this new framework. To indicate a plane, such as when showing the angle of a fault surface, geologists use a flat palm (or field book) to indicate its orientation (Kastens, Ishikawa, and Liben 2006; Liben, Christensen, and Kastens 2010). To indicate a form (an object whose shape does not fit into the previously stated categories), such as a fold or a dome, one may configure a hand to match the object's shape. Alternatively, for complex forms, a hand may be used to sculpt space, tracing out the form of the object over time. (For a fuller discussion on the depictive use of gestures, see Streeck 2008.) Distinguishing between motions of the hand to indicate extended space, and motion to indicate movement, might be accomplished with speech to disambiguate the two cases. However, anecdotal inspection of expert geologists' gestures suggests an alternative—that the two types of gestures have different kinematics. The difference is captured in the formal Laban classification (Laban 1963; Laban and Lawrence 1974) as differing in *weight*—sculpting gestures are light (e.g., representing a dome by gently outlining the shape with one's hands) and moving object gestures have greater weight (e.g., representing an intrusion by moving one's hand up with some rigidity and overt bodily effort—see Runeson and Frykholm (1981, 1983) on the ability to perceive intended physical qualities in gestures). This observation will require confirmation with broader sampling. Eventually a careful kinematic analysis may reveal a simple description of bodily motion (biomechanics) that distinguishes the two cases.

There are a handful of studies that report gestures used to represent the geometry of a single object in STEM (science technology, engineering, and mathematics) practice (Becvar, Hollan, and Hutchins 2005; Valenzeno, Alibali, and Klatzky 2003). Valenzeno, Alibali, and Klatzky (ibid.) conducted a study to see if teachers' gestures influence students' learning of the concept of symmetry. During the lesson, the teacher explained the concept with respect to five shapes, and incorporated tracing gestures representing the geometry of individual objects. Students whose lessons incorporated gestures scored higher on the test of the concepts than those who only heard speech.

Gestures that represent the geometric relations of objects

The second broad class of static spatial relations is extrinsic spatial relations, those that relate two or more objects. Understanding a geological structure and its history requires understanding how local observations fit together and relate to other structures in the region. Explanations of why a rock or a structure is in its present state requires a discussion of the location, orientation, and shape of one object in relation to at least one more object (visualizing relations between two or more objects in three-dimensional space). For example, in our narrative, the expert geologist thinks about how the individual layers of rock within the fold are positioned in relation to each other. The practical limitation imposed by having only two hands available to gesture means that our initial focus is on two-handed gestures in which each hand may gesture a zero-dimensional to three-dimensional property of an object. Simple combinations define the small set of such relations, those between: two points, a point and a line, a point and a plane, a point and a form, two lines, a line and a plane, a line and a form, two planes, a plane and a form, and two forms. On occasion, a sequence of one-handed gestures may be used to communicate more than two locations of objects in a scene.

The gestures used for all of these instances are the same as the ones mentioned for the individual objects above, except that typically both hands are used. One object is represented by one hand and the other object by the other hand. In our narrative, the expert uses gesture when discussing the relations between two objects when she takes one c-shaped hand and places it on top of the other c-shaped hand, showing the relations between two layers of rocks in the fold. Extrinsic gestures were reported by Emmorey, Tversky, and Taylor (2000), who asked participants to describe a previously seen map. In their descriptions, participants used both hands to represent the locations of different objects within the space. It is not always the case that the whole hand represents a single location; Becvar, Hollan, and Hutchins (2005) reported that expert biochemists used individual fingers of one hand to represent the relative locations of loops of amino acids in a protein molecule.

Gestures are considered powerful means for representing complex spatial relations. They can represent relations in three-dimensions (Pozzer-Ardenghi and Roth 2006; Roth 2000), and thus they are well suited to portray shape, form, space, and position—all aspects of space for which there is a limited vocabulary, and for which metric properties are important but hard to convey in speech. There are studies that show that students especially use gestures when they are uncertain of the technical term for an object (Crowder and Newman 1993; Roth and Lawless 2002). Gestures also allow one to convey several spatial attributes at the same time. When explaining how the fold is composed of multiple layers of rock, the expert was concurrently able to show the *shape* of the layers and their relative *locations*.

Gestures that convey moving properties

A fundamental division in spatial thinking separates static and moving objects. Different areas of the brain process static and moving things (e.g., Beauchamp, Cox, and DeYoe 1997; Benton 1985; Watson et al. 1993). The dichotomy may be based in part on the potential actions associated with static things (for which the evolutionarily critical concern is often "Is that thing safe to eat?") and moving things (for which the evolutionarily critical concern is often "Is that thing going to try to eat me?"). Humans represent the movement of objects, and more generally events, as verbs in speech. Analogously events are represented in gesture with movement, where the spatiotemporal pattern in the gesture corresponds to a spatiotemporal pattern in the world (Emmorey and Casey 2002).

Here we argue that an isomorphism exists between spatial gestures and their referents that allows ready recognition of the meaning of a gesture, allows coordination with speech, and allows production of novel gestures. The important idea here is that there is a mathematically describable pattern that is present in every event and gesture that represents that event. The term Pittenger and Shaw (1975) use for this idea is *transformational invariant*. A transformational invariant is a spatiotemporal pattern that is present in all instances of the transformation and is independent of the specific object or objects involved in the transformation. The prototypical example is aging, in which the characteristic changes in the proportions of the head allow people to recognize a person's age. We suggest that gestures, such as bending a hand when illustrating folding, share a mathematical relationship with the event of folding rocks.

The field of geology requires experts to reason about and communicate an object's movement because geological structures observed today have moved in the past, and their geometries allow inferences to be made regarding the cause of events in a region. That the structures have changed (and, in the cases of active mountain building, are still changing) is fundamental to the nature of the science. Geologists can characterize how objects move in space and typically break down the deformation into three component parts: translation, rotation, and strain. When it comes to discussing their findings, conveying movement is more easily accomplished in gesture than in speech (Roth and Lawless 2002). Thus, consistent with the finding by Trafton et al. (2006) that experts use more iconic gestures when speaking about spatial transformations, we expect to see gestures employed in conversations about geologic events specifically, and more generally, whenever the spatial or spatiotemporal details of an event are important.

Gestures can describe the movement of one or more objects because they show movement in real time. The movement of a particle, for example, that is both varying in speed and direction, is easy to gesture but very difficult to verbally describe. The sequential nature of speech is a major problem for conveying multiple properties of a moving object because speech is inherently segmented and constrained to limited sequences (Roth and Lawless 2002). Since the details of motion are not easily communicated in language, gesture is a natural way to communicate these aspects of the world (Emmorey and Casey 2002). Expert geologists use gesture to convey geometric changes that occur both within and between objects.

Gestures that represent the geometric change of one object

The changes that are intrinsic to a single object are often expressed as verbs in English (e.g., walk, bend, and break). As with the single static object category, we distinguish among changes of zero-dimensional, one-dimensional, two-dimensional, and three-dimensional qualities (where the referent is either a changing physical quality or a changing spatialized quality, such as increasing temperature). A change of a zero-dimensional object would be using the tip of the finger to trace the path of motion of an object. As the dimensionality of the object increases, there is an increase in the spatial relations that can change. For a one-dimensional object, the change could involve either a change in location, orientation, or scale (e.g., moving a finger representing a force vector as a magnetic field changes). In principle, there is also the potential for the change to involve a change in dimensionality. In practice, we have only observed a change from a two-dimensional plane to a curved surface as would occur when horizontal sedimentary beds deform to accommodate regional strain.

In the literature on gestures, there are a number of studies that document gestures used to represent geometric changes of one object (e.g., Chu and Kita 2008; Garber and Goldin-Meadow 2002; Kita and Ozyurek 2003). For example, participants asked to explain a cartoon of a cat swinging between two buildings, or of a cat rolling down a hill, gesture both the manner and the trajectory of the cat in their stories (Kita and Ozyurek 2003). Participants asked to complete a mental-rotation task gesture the object motion and how a hand might rotate the object (Chu and Kita 2008 2011; Göksun et al. 2013; Hostetter, Alibali, and Bartholomew 2011). When asked to explain how they solved a Tower of Hanoi task, participants gesture the movement of the individual disks (Beilock and Goldin-Meadow 2010; Cook and Tanenhaus 2009; Garber and Goldin-Meadow 2002). Participants asked to describe where to place a group of blocks to complete a puzzle grid gestured the rotation direction of the individual blocks (Emmorey and Casey 2002). In sum, direction and orientation of movement are features of geometric change that are clearly conveyed in gesture, probably reflecting gesture's superiority to speech for conveying this information. Less work has focused on plastic (flow) and brittle (fracture) changes, which are particularly important classes of transformations in the geosciences (Atit, Shipley, and Tikoff 2013).

Gestures that represent the geometric changes of multiple objects

Communication about extrinsic spatial changes requires relating the movement of one or more objects relative to other moving or stationary objects. This type of communication is most often required when providing information for wayfinding—information such as where you are and how you should move relative to landmarks and your destination (Newcombe and Shipley 2014). However, such relations are also important in other contexts. As geoscientists' understanding of regional history is developing and before they achieve a unified representation that ties all the pieces together, they may have a collection of inferences about local motions. The geoscientist then needs to think about these extrinsic relations and describe them to other scientists. As in the case of static extrinsic relations, this category contains all combinations of relations among zero-dimensional and higher-dimensional objects.

A number of studies describe how gestures are used to represent geometric changes involving multiple objects (e.g., Ehrlich, Levine, and Goldin-Meadow 2006; Roth and Lawless 2002). For example, while completing a high school physics experiment on electrostatic induction, students gesture to show the movement of electrons being repelled from the source of charge (Roth and Lawless 2002). When asked to explain how they solved mental rotation and translation problems in a spatial transformation task, many five-year-olds gesture the movement of the individual pieces of the stimuli (Ehrlich, Levine, and Goldin-Meadow 2006). Participants asked to predict the movements of gears represented in a diagram gesture the gears' relative movements (Alibali, Spencer, Knox, and Kita 2011; Hegarty, Mayer, Kriz, and Keehner 2005). In the domain of geology, sixth graders studying plate tectonics used gesture to show how plates move relative to each other (i.e., rifting and subduction) (Singer, Radinsky, and Goldman 2008).

How Gestures Are Used for Spatial Tasks

We know that in math and science education instructors and students use hand and arm movements to convey the geometry and geometric change of one or more objects (e.g., Emmorey et al. 2000; Garber and Goldin-Meadow 2002; Hegarty et al. 2005). Because student gesturing has been connected to the successful acquisition of scientific concepts and use of the appropriate vocabulary, it is important to investigate the types of information experts and novices convey in gesture to inform science education in the classroom (Crowder 1996; Roth 2000; Roth and Lawless 2002). The power of gesture to illustrate multidimensional spatiotemporal information (Pozzer-Ardenghi and Roth 2006; Roth 2000) makes it a useful tool for scaffolding students' spatial thinking. Here, we focus our discussion of gesture for communicating and reasoning about static and dynamic aspects of the geosciences as manifested in three broad functional roles: highlighting, making spatial inferences, and making spatiotemporal inferences. We focus on a single domain to illustrate how spatial gestures classified within our framework are used to carryout these three tasks.

Highlighting

When a geologist guides a student at an outcrop in an unfamiliar region, the expert employs gestures that represent the geometry of one or more objects to draw the student's attention to important aspects of the outcrop. For example, in our narrative, the expert cups her hand into the shape of the fold to highlight the structure for the student. This separation of a set of qualities to consider for further cognitive processing is referred to as *selective attention* in cognitive science and *disembedding* by geologists. There are individual differences in this skill, and students who are good at disembedding are likely to succeed in the sciences (Heiser, Tversky, and Silverman 2004; Witkin, Moore, Goodenough, and Cox 1977).

Gestures are useful in separating relevant from irrelevant information (Roth 2000), and the simplest gesture to aid in disembedding is pointing at the object the speaker wishes to be the focus of common attention. In the literature on gestures, pointing would be classified as a deictic gesture, in contrast to an iconic gesture that resembles its referent. Here we use the term *highlighting* gesture because we have found that geologists often use complex spatial gestures, such as the curved shape of the fold (which might be classified as iconic), to draw a student's attention to a critical feature of an outcrop (Atit, Goksoun, Manduca, Ormand, Resnick, Shipley, and Tikoff

2013). (For further examples of the use of deictic gestures to direct joint attention, see Alibali and Kita 2010 and Roth 2000.)

Gestures may also help the speaker to focus his or her own attention. Gestures may highlight perceptually present information, helping the gesturer decide what to say. When prohibited from gesturing, children five to seven years old provided poor explanations for their solutions to a Piagetian conservation task and did not mention important properties of the displays (Alibali and Kita 2010). The children's explanations improved when they were allowed to gesture, which suggests that in the case of this cognitively demanding task the gestures helped the children focus their attention on critical information present in the stimuli. The influence of gesture on information processing could shape the types of strategies used for cognitively demanding processes such as problem solving (e.g., Alibali et al. 2011). The potential use of gesture to highlight important information for complex problem solving raises an important question for future research: Could teaching students to gesture improve their understanding of field instruction by providing them a way to focus on the information the teacher is trying to convey?

Spatial inference

From their observations, experts may make a variety of spatial inferences about objects in the region—for example, inferences about their three-dimensional form. When making spatial inferences, experts may incorporate gestures representing the geometry of one or more objects. For example, in our narrative the expert configures her hand to match the curves of a bedding surface and places her hand on the rock surface to indicate that the pattern extends back into the structure—a type of spatial inference called *penetrative thinking* (Kali and Orion 1996).

We note three broad categories of inferences: extrapolation, interpolation, and statistical inference. Extrapolation entails extending known information to a new area, such as projecting what is seen at an outcrop down into the earth (e.g., penetrative thinking). Interpolation entails inferring properties based on surrounding information, such as inferring the shape of a fold that has been eroded from the two remaining limbs. By statistical inference we mean cases where previous experience of a correlation between two properties allows the inference that if one property is observed, the other property is likely to be present.

Geologists have to infer aspects of a structure or a region that is no longer present (e.g., as a result of erosion) or that is not visible (e.g., as a result of being covered by younger rocks). This inferential process may be supported by gestures. For example, a student may use his hands to represent the orientations of the two limbs of a fold so as to better visualize the connection between the limbs. A gesture may also help construct the inferred shape.

In research by Kim Kastens and colleagues (Kastens, Agrawal, and Liben 2009; Kastens et al. 2006), artificial outcrops were positioned on a college campus and students were asked to reason about what the outcrops indicated about the shapes of the underlying structures. The students often used gestures to discuss filling in the missing connections between the outcrops. Alles and Riggs (2011) report a similar finding for penetrative thinking in an exercise in which students must interpolate surfaces in a block diagram where the corresponding regions are visible on two or three sides of a cube.

Spatiotemporal inference of geometric relationships

A goal for geologists is to understand the timing of the formation of various geological structures in a region. Geologists were able to sequence the order of events even before precise dating techniques were available. They used the spatial positions of rocks to infer the history of development; this is a space-for-time substitution that is common in all fields of natural history. Gestures can show the motions within and between objects, making gestures that represent geometric change a good tool to illustrate sequences of geological events and generally to support spatiotemporal inferences. In our narrative, the geologist uses the curved shape of the beds to reason that the beds once were flat and then were folded up, shown by a flat hand being curled (a gesture representing the geometric change of one object). The gesture may support inference by representing a spatial relationship of the present and illustrating the transformation back into the past, or forward from a hypothetical past configuration to the present. For example, in our narrative, the expert shows a transformation that occurred in the past and resulted in the present when she uses her hands to show the movement of previously flat layers to the tilted layers seen in the fold (a gesture representing the geometric change of many objects). Gestures showing spatiotemporal inferences could also support reasoning about potential future changes in the region.

Geology requires visualizing the movement of objects that are currently static and prototypically unchanging ("steady as a rock"). Inferring motion from a static form requires overcoming this bias. The transient nature of gesture may help by allowing the student to go back and forth between thinking about the static shape of the rocks and the motions that brought them there.

Conclusion

Gesture and speech make up a single integrated system for expressing meaning. They combine to construct a meaning that may not be fully present in one modality alone (McNeill 1992). Given the differences in the way spatial information is represented in language and gesture, a central problem in cognitive science is developing an understanding of how these two representational systems are combined. Furthermore, gesturing improves communication and learning, but the mechanisms underlying the use of this modality are not well understood.

Geologists use gestures when communicating with others. Gestures could have the following benefits: An expert's gestures may aid a student by helping them attend to and construct mental representations of important features. An expert's gestures may encourage a student to gesture, which could lighten the student's cognitive load (e.g., Wagner, Nusbaum, and Goldin-Meadow 2004), helping her to work on solving a spatial problem. An expert's gestures may help a student visualize moving spatial properties, facilitating spatial and spatiotemporal inferences.

We hope future investigations will explore this typology of spatial gestures from the perspectives of other scientific disciplines. For example, do physicists and chemists also convey geometric properties of and between objects using gestures? Extension of this framework to other STEM domains could provide a basis for comparison of the types of information conveyed in gesture in these different fields. Information about differences in gesture (e.g., geologists may gesture more about the geometry of single objects, whereas physicists may focus on the geometric change between objects) may guide targeted training of different types of spatial thinking skills (Newcombe and Shipley 2014).

The theoretically motivated typology that we offer should encompass most aspects of spatial gestures. It should help to organize research on differences between novices and experts, it should help to organize the development of scaffolds for learning to think spatially, and it may help to organize gesture research on measures of understanding or readiness to learn (Church and Goldin-Meadow 1986; Goldin-Meadow, Alibali, and Church 1993). This framework may not provide a complete description of all aspects of gesture that are important for spatial thinking. Nevertheless, we believe it provides a strong foundation for understanding gestures in spatial thinking, which is critical for science education.

Acknowledgment

The research was supported by a grant to the Spatial Intelligence and Learning Center, funded by the National Science Foundation (SBE-0541957 and SBE-1041707).

Note

1. The order of the authors' names is alphabetical.

References

Alibali, M. W. 2005. Gesture in spatial cognition: Expressing, thinking, and communicating about spatial information. *Spatial Cognition and Computation* 5: 307–331.

Alibali, M. W., and Kita, S. 2010. Gesture highlights perceptually present information for speakers. *Gesture* 10: 3–28.

Alibali, M. W., Spencer, R. C., Knox, L., and Kita, S. 2011. Spontaneous gestures influence strategy choices in problem solving. *Psychological Science* 22: 1138–1144.

Alles, M., and Riggs, E. M. 2011. Developing a process model for visual penetrative ability. In *Qualitative Inquiry in Geoscience Education Research*, ed. A. D. Feig and A. Stokes. Geological Society of America.

Atit, K., Goksoun, T., Manduca, C. A., Ormand, C. J., Resnick, I., Shipley, T. F., et al. 2013. Spatial gestures point the way: A broader understanding of the gestural referent. In *Proceedings of the 35th Annual Conference of the Cognitive Science Society*, ed. M. Knauff, M. Pauen, N. Sebanz, and I. Wachsmuth. Cognitive Science Society.

Atit, K., Shipley, T. F., and Tikoff, B. 2013. Twisting space: Are rigid and non-rigid mental transformations separate spatial skills? *Cognitive Processing* 14: 163–173.

Beauchamp, M. S., Cox, R. W., and DeYoe, E. A. 1997. Graded effects of spatial and featural attention on human area MT and associated motion processing areas. *Journal of Neurophysiology* 78: 516–520.

Becvar, L. A., Hollan, J., and Hutchins, E. 2005. Hands as molecules: Representational gestures used for developing theory in a scientific laboratory. *Semiotica* 156: 89–112.

Beilock, S. L., and Goldin-Meadow, S. 2010. Gestures changes thought by grounding it in action. *Psychological Science* 21: 1605–1610.

Benton, A. 1985. Visuoperceptive, visuospatial, and visuoconstructive disorders. In *Clinical Neuropsychology*, ed. K. Heilman and E. Valenstein. Oxford University Press.

Chatterjee, A. 2008. The neural organization of spatial thought and language. *Seminars in Speech and Language* 29: 226–238.

Chu, M., and Kita, S. 2008. Spontaneous gestures during mental rotation tasks: Insights into the microdevelopment of the motor strategy. *Journal of Experimental Psychology* 137: 706–723.

Chu, M., and Kita, S. 2011. The nature of gestures' beneficial role in spatial problem solving. *Journal of Experimental Psychology. General* 140: 102–116.

Church, R. B., and Goldin-Meadow. 1986. The mismatch between gesture and speech as an index of transitional knowledge. *Cognition* 23: 43–71.

Cook, S. W., and Tanenhaus, M. K. 2009. Embodied communication: Speakers' gestures affect listeners' actions. *Cognition* 113: 98–104.

Crowder, E. M. 1996. Gestures at work in sense-making science talk. *Journal of the Learning Sciences* 5, 173–208.

Crowder, E. M., and Newman, D. 1993. Telling what they know: The role of gesture and language in children's science explanations. *Pragmatics and Cognition* 1: 341–376.

Ehrlich, S. B., Levine, S. C., and Goldin-Meadow, S. 2006. The importance of gesture in children's spatial reasoning. *Developmental Psychology* 42: 1259–1268.

Emmorey, K., and Casey, S. 2002. Gesture, thought, and spatial language. In *Spatial Language: Cognitive and Computational Perspectives*, ed. K. R. Coventry and P. Olivier. Kluwer.

Emmorey, K., Tversky, B., and Taylor, H. A. 2000. Using space to describe space: Perspectives in speech, sign, and gesture. *Spatial Cognition and Computation* 2: 157–180.

Garber, P., and Goldin-Meadow, S. 2002. Gestures offers insight into problem solving in adults and children. *Cognitive Science* 26: 817–831.

Göksun, T., Goldin-Meadow, S., Newcombe, N., and Shipley, T. 2013. Individual differences in mental rotation: What does gesture tell us? *Cognitive Processing* 14: 153–162.

Goldin-Meadow, S. 1999. The role of gesture in communication and thinking. *Trends in Cognitive Sciences* 3: 419–429.

Goldin-Meadow, S., Alibali, M. W., and Church, R. B. 1993. Transitions to concept acquisition: Using the hand to read the mind. *Psychological Review* 100: 279–297.

Groves, F. H. 1995. Science vocabulary load of selected secondary science textbooks. *Science Vocabulary* 95 (5): 231–235.

Hayward, W. G., and Tarr, M. J. 1995. Spatial language and spatial representation. *Cognition* 55: 39–84.

Hegarty, M., Mayer, S., Kriz, S., and Keehner, M. 2005. The role of gestures in mental animation. *Spatial Cognition and Computation* 5: 333–356.

Heiser, J., Tversky, B., and Silverman, M. 2004. Sketches for and from collaboration. In, *Visual and Spatial Reasoning in Design III*, ed. J. S. Gero, B. Tversky, and T. Knight. Key Centre for Design Research.

Hostetter, A. B., and Alibali, M. W. 2008. Visible embodiment: Gestures as simulated action. *Psychonomic Bulletin and Review* 15: 495–514.

Hostetter, A. B., Alibali, M. W., and Bartholomew, A. 2011. Gesture during mental rotation. Paper presented at Annual Meeting of Cognitive Science Society, Boston.

Kali, Y., and Orion, N. 1996. Spatial abilities of high-school students in the perception of geologic structures. *Journal of Research in Science Teaching* 33: 369–391.

Kastens, K. A., Agrawal, S., and Liben, L. S. 2009. How students and field geologists reason in integrating spatial observations from outcrops to visualize a 3-D geological structure. *International Journal of Science Education* 31: 365–393.

Kastens, K. A., Ishikawa, T., and Liben, L. S. 2006. Visualizing a 3-D geologic structure from outcrop observations: Strategies used by geoscience experts, students, and novices. Paper presented at annual meeting of Geological Society of America, Philadelphia.

Kita, S., and Ozyurek, A. 2003. What does cross-linguistic variation in semantic coordination of speech and gesture reveal?: Evidence for an interface representation of spatial thinking and speaking. *Journal of Memory and Language* 48: 16–32.

Kortz, K. M. 2011. Geology as a foreign language: The case of language versus conceptual understanding. Paper presented at annual meeting of Geological Society of America, Minneapolis.

Laban, R. V. 1963. *Modern Educational Dance*. Macdonald and Evans.

Laban, R. V., and Lawrence, F. C. 1974. *Effort: Economy in Body Movement*. Plays, inc.

Landau, B., and Jackendoff, R. 1993. "What" and "where" in spatial language and cognition. *Behavioral and Brain Sciences* 16: 217–265.

Lavergne, J., and Kimura, D. 1987. Hand movement asymmetry during speech: No effect of speaking topic. *Neuropsychologia* 25: 689–693.

Liben, L. S., Christensen, A. E., and Kastens, K. A. 2010. Gestures in geology: The roles of spatial skills, expertise, and communicative context. In *Spatial Cognition VII*, ed. C. Hoelscher, T. F. Shipley, M. O. Belardinelli, J. A. Bateman, and N. S. Newcombe. Springer.

McNeill, D. 1992. *Hand and Mind: What Gestures Reveal about Thought*. University of Chicago Press.

Newcombe, N., and Shipley, T. F. 2014. Thinking about spatial thinking: New typology, new assessments. In *Studying Visual and Spatial Reasoning for Design Creativity*, ed. J. S. Gero. Springer.

Ormand, C. J., Manduca, C. A., Shipley, T. F., and Tikoff, B. 2013. Developing and testing materials to improve spatial skills in upper division geoscience courses. Paper presented at TUES/CCLI PI Conference, Washington.

Pittenger, J. B., and Shaw, R. E. 1975. Aging faces as viscal-elastic events: Implications for a theory of nonrigid shape perception. *Journal of Experimental Psychology. Human Perception and Performance* 1: 374–382.

Pozzer-Ardenghi, L., and Roth, W.-M. 2006. On performing concepts during science lectures. *Science Education* 91: 96–113.

Roth, W.-M. 2000. From gesture to scientific language. *Journal of Pragmatics* 32: 1683–1714.

Roth, W.-M., and Lawless, D. 2002. Science, culture, and the emergence of language. *Science Education* 86: 368–385.

Runeson, S., and Frykholm, G. 1981. Visual perception of lifted weight. *Journal of Experimental Psychology. Human Perception and Performance* 7 (4): 733–740.

Runeson, S., and Frykholm, G. 1983. Kinematic specification of dynamics as an informational basis for person-and-action perception: Expectation, gender recognition, and deceptive intention. *Journal of Experimental Psychology. General* 112 (4): 585–615.

Shipley, T., Tikoff, B., Manduca, C., and Ormand, C. J. 2013. Structural geology practice and learning, from the perspective of cognitive science. *Journal of Structural Geology* 54: 72–84.

Singer, M., Radinsky, J., and Goldman, S. R. 2008. The role of gesture in meaning construction. *Discourse Processes* 45: 365–386.

Streeck, J. 2008. Depicting by gesture. *Gesture* 8: 285–301.

Trafton, J. G., Trickett, S. B., Stitzlein, C. A., Saner, L., Schunn, and Kirschenbaum, S. S. 2006. The relationship between spatial transformations and iconic gestures. *Spatial Cognition and Computation* 6: 1–29.

Tversky, B., and Lee, P. 1998. How space structures language. In *Spatial Cognition: An Interdisciplinary Approach to Representing and Processing Knowledge*, ed. C. Freksa, C. Habel, and K. F. Wender. Springer.

Valenzeno, L., Alibali, M. W., and Klatzky, R. 2003. Teachers' gestures facilitate students' learning: A lesson of symmetry. *Contemporary Educational Psychology* 28: 187–204.

Wagner, S., Nusbaum, H., and Goldin-Meadow, S. 2004. Probing the mental representation of gesture: Is handwaving spatial? *Journal of Memory and Language* 50: 395–407.

Watson, J. D. G., Myers, R., Frackowiak, R. S. J., Hajnal, J. V., Woods, R. P., Mazziotta, J. C., et al. 1993. Area V5 of the human brain: Evidence from a combined study using positron emission tomography and magnetic resonance imaging. *Cerebral Cortex* 3: 79–94.

Witkin, H. A., Moore, C. A., Goodenough, D. R., and Cox, P. W. 1977. Field-dependent and field-independent cognitive styles and their educational implications. *Review of Educational Research* 47: 1–64.

Yager, R. E. 1983. The importance of terminology in teaching K–23 science. *Journal of Research in Science Teaching* 20: 577–588.

10 Using Spatial Strategies to Facilitate Skillful Wayfinding and Spatial Problem Solving: Implications for Education

Alycia M. Hund

Thinking spatially is important for everyday functioning. For example, children and adults rely on spatial skills to create and interpret charts and graphs, to understand details portrayed in diagrams and maps, to solve complex mathematics and scientific problems, and to find their way from place to place. Researchers have used a variety of taxonomies to explain spatial thinking, describing performance depending on spatial scales (Hegarty et al. 2006), spatial domains (i.e., perception, visualization, mental rotation; Linn and Petersen 1985), and spatial strategies (Taylor and Tversky 1996). This chapter focuses on spatial strategies, or perspectives, and their consequences for skillful wayfinding and spatial problem solving. One goal is to synthesize what is known about how survey and route perspectives are involved in wayfinding and spatial problem solving. A second goal is to describe implications for education in formal and informal settings. In particular, supporting flexibility and adaptability in spatial strategy use can improve spatial performance in a variety of contexts, including wayfinding and spatial problem solving.

Spatial Strategies for Wayfinding

People rely on survey and route strategies, or perspectives, when finding their way from place to place and when thinking about space more generally (Taylor and Tversky 1996). A route perspective involves adopting a first-person spatial perspective (e.g., assuming the perspective of the traveler) as the frame of reference. Route directions are like mental tours that include references to segments of the route, one at a time, as a traveler would experience them during locomotion. In particular, they include left and right turns and landmark descriptions that provide a set of procedures for navigating through the environment (e.g., "Go left on Main, you'll see the park on your right"). In contrast, a survey perspective involves adopting a third-person spatial perspective akin to seeing the entire environment at once (e.g., an aerial view or a map). Survey directions provide an overview of the environmental layout, where the frame of reference is global in nature (e.g., the sun, a mountain range). When describing how to get somewhere, the most common survey reference frame involves cardinal directions (i.e., north, south, east, and west) and precise distances (i.e., blocks, miles; Shelton and Gabrieli 2002; Taylor and Tversky 1996). These differences between survey and route perspectives have received much research attention (e.g., Golledge 1999; Hirtle and Hudson 1991; Hund and Padgitt 2010; Shelton and McNamara 2004) and parallel the theoretical distinction between configural (also known as orientation or survey) knowledge and route knowledge often discussed in the literature (e.g., Siegel and White 1975; Taylor and Tversky 1996).

How might perspective affect direction giving in the service of wayfinding? Previous findings indicate that people tend to use route descriptors more often than survey descriptors when asked to describe environments for listeners (e.g., Taylor and Tversky 1996). For example, in one classic study, when asked to describe their apartments, 97 percent of participants provided a walking tour starting at the front door, whereas only 3 percent of participants provided a survey-like description of the overall layout (Linde and Labov 1975). Similarly, when asked to give directions from their current location to a nearby shopping area, residents in Buffalo, Vancouver, Santa Barbara, and Valencia included many landmarks, turns, left-right descriptions, and street names and very few cardinal directions or distances (Mark and Gould 1995). Older children are more likely to organize their descriptions using a mental tour than are younger children, highlighting the importance of experience (Gauvain and Rogoff 1989). This preference for route strategies may be stronger in the United States than in other parts of the world, such as Hungary (Lawton and Kallai 2002).

We know that people are sensitive to recipients' needs when providing directions, and that they adapt their directions accordingly. For example, Hund, Haney, and Seanor (2008) examined how recipient perspective affects direction giving in the service of wayfinding. In experiment 1, participants provided directions from starting locations to destinations for fictional recipients driving through a town (route perspective) or looking at a map of the town (survey perspective). As expected, participants mentioned left and right and landmarks more frequently when addressing a person driving in the town and cardinal descriptors more frequently when addressing a person looking at a map. In experiment 2, participants rated the effectiveness of directions. Effective directions contained significantly more left-right references than did less effective directions, highlighting people's preference for route descriptors. In the final experiment, participants gave wayfinding directions to destinations in a familiar town. Again, direction features depended on recipient perspective, highlighting the dynamic nature of wayfinding processes. These results confirm that people provide wayfinding directions appropriate for their recipients, adjusting the cues provided according to listener perspective. It is possible that these changes result from a combination of shifts in direction-giver perspective (Golledge 1999; Shelton and McNamara 2004; Siegel and White 1975; Taylor and Tversky 1996) and pragmatic considerations, particularly communicative conventions for providing directions in diverse contexts (Allen 2000; Golding, Graesser, and Hauselt 1996; Lloyd 1991; Ward, Newcombe, and Overton 1986). These findings suggest not only fine tuning to listener perspective, but also adaptive flexibility in providing wayfinding directions containing a variety of perspective cues.

Perspective also affects wayfinding performance and spatial understanding. Although both survey and route perspectives can be effective for wayfinding, people using a route perspective may find it difficult to deviate from the designated route and, thus, are more likely to become disoriented or lost. In contrast, people using an integrated, survey perspective evince more flexible coding, so they can deviate from a path, find effective shortcuts or detours, and retrace a route in reverse (Brunyé, Rapp, and Taylor 2008; Lawton 2001; Saucier et al. 2002; Siegel and White 1975).

In one classic study, Lawton (1996) assessed the relation between wayfinding strategies and spatial performance. Participants learned a route through one floor of an academic building, then were asked to point to the four landmarks from an unfamiliar location on the floor. The landmarks were not visible from this location, so participants had to rely on their memory of the locations. Participants also completed a self-report measure of wayfinding strategies. Survey/Orientation strategies involve maintaining a sense of one's own position in relation to a given a point (e.g., "I keep track of the direction [north, south, east, or west] in which I am going."). Route strategies involve using a particular route to get from place to place (e.g., "I ask for directions telling me whether to turn right or left at particular landmarks."). As reliance on survey strategies increased, pointing accuracy to unseen locations also increased, presumably owing to reliance on global perspective. In contrast, reported use of route strategies was unrelated to pointing error. These findings support the claim that survey strategies are related to spatial performance involving global perspectives.

In a related study, Lawton and Kallai (2002) examined individual differences in wayfinding strategies. Men reported using survey strategies more than women did, whereas women reported using route strategies more than men did. Similar gender differences were evident in another classic study by Ward et al. (1986). They asked participants to learn a map containing many landmarks and roads and then to give directions from a starting location to a destination. Men provided more cardinal descriptors and mileage information than women did, again indicating a preference for survey details. In a similar study, MacFadden, Elias, and Saucier (2003) asked participants to study a set of routes on a map. Participants then wrote a set of directions to help someone navigate from the starting location to the destination. Men included cardinal descriptors and distance more frequently than women did. Women included landmarks and left and right turns more often than men did. These findings suggest that there are interesting gender differences in wayfinding strategies. (For a recent review, see Lawton 2010.)

Using a variety of survey and route cues, Saucier et al. (2002) extended the investigation of direction following. In particular, they examined the efficiency with which men and women navigated using directions involving landmarks or survey descriptors (e.g., cardinal directions and distances). In experiment 1, participants navigated to unknown destinations on campus by reading directions one segment at a time. Women and men who followed directions containing landmark descriptors navigated more quickly than women who followed directions containing survey descriptors. In experiment 2, the task was to navigate in a small-scale matrix. Men were faster and more accurate in the survey condition than in the landmark condition; women were faster and more accurate in the landmark condition than in the survey condition. These findings reveal interesting gender differences in wayfinding and spatial problem solving based on directions containing survey and route cues.

Hund and Minarik (2006) investigated how wayfinding strategies relate to wayfinding performance. Participants navigated through a model town using landmark or cardinal directions. In general, as reliance on survey strategies increased, overall wayfinding efficiency and efficiency using cardinal directions increased. As reliance on route strategies increased, wayfinding efficiency using landmark directions increased, though the magnitude of this effect was only marginally significant. Together, these findings suggest that wayfinding strategies are related to performance.

Padgitt and Hund's (2012) goal was to specify the effectiveness of way-finding directions in a complex indoor environment. Direction quality was assessed via effectiveness ratings and behavioral indices. In study 1, participants provided effectiveness ratings for seven combinations of wayfinding descriptions. In general, ratings were higher for directions containing route cues than for directions containing survey cues, and ratings increased as the number of features increased. Moreover, people with a keen sense of direction gave higher ratings to survey descriptions relative to those with a poor sense of direction. In study 2, participants provided effectiveness ratings for directions containing route and survey cues before and after wayfinding using these directions. Route directions resulted in fewer wayfinding errors and higher effectiveness ratings than did survey directions. Together, these findings show not only a preference for descriptions from a route perspective but also better wayfinding efficiency following those descriptions. (See also Denis, Pazzaglia, Cornoldi, and Bertolo 1999.)

Neural Mechanisms Underlying Spatial Strategies

Shelton and Gabrieli (2002) examined the neural mechanisms underlying survey and route perspectives. As expected, they found that the two perspectives were associated with different areas of neural activation. (See also Shelton 2004.) Areas in the medial temporal lobe, anterior superior parietal cortex, and postcentral gyrus showed greater activation when participants were using a route perspective. In contrast, areas in the inferior temporal lobe and posterior superior parietal cortex exhibited greater activation when participants were using a survey perspective. These neural findings offer additional support for the distinction between survey and route perspectives.

Moffat, Elkins, and Resnick (2006) specified the neural mechanisms of wayfinding using functional magnetic resonance imaging (fMRI). Healthy younger and older adults completed a navigation task in a virtual environment, as well as a control task with similar perceptual-motor demands but without navigation demands. Overall, older adults showed less activation in the posterior hippocampus, the parahippocampal gyrus, and the retro-splenial cortex relative to younger adults. In addition, activation in the hippocampus and parahippocampal gyrus was associated with wayfinding accuracy. These findings indicate that decreased hippocampal/parahippo-campal activation may underlie age-related declines in wayfinding. (See also Driscoll et al. 2003; Head and Isom 2010; Wolbers and Hegarty 2010.)

These areas have long been associated with cognitive mapping, especially survey strategies (O'Keefe and Nadel 1978). Additional research is needed to clarify the contributions of prefrontal networks involved in executive and strategic processing (Moffat 2009; Raz, Briggs, Marks, and Acker 1999) and striatal networks (including the caudate nucleus) involved in procedural aspects of responding (Head and Isom 2010; Iaria, Petrides, Dagher, Pike, and Bohbot 2003; Moffat et al. 2006).

Gender Differences in Spatial Strategies

Gender differences in spatial strategies are well documented. For example, numerous studies have shown that men prefer survey perspectives more than women do, whereas women prefer route perspectives more than men do (Lawton 2010). Interestingly, similar gender differences emerge both when giving and following wayfinding directions (Galea and Kimura 1993; Lawton 1994; Moffat, Hampson, and Hatzipantelis 1998; Prestopnik and Roskos-Ewoldsen 2000; Sholl, Acacio, Makar, and Leon 2000; Ward et al. 1986). For example, Lawton (2001) asked participants to provide directions to help a friend reach a desired destination. Men included significantly more cardinal directions than women did, whereas women included significantly more left and right turns and landmarks than men did. These findings reveal robust gender differences in wayfinding strategies and spatial performance (for reviews, see Lawton 2010; Linn and Petersen 1985; Montello, Lovelace, Golledge, and Self 1999; Voyer, Voyer, and Bryden 1995). Nonetheless, questions remain regarding the locus of such differences.

Task Demands Influence Spatial Strategies

Similarly, the nature of learning and testing experiences affects spatial performance. That is, wayfinding differs when participants learn via direct travel through a space versus via a map of a space (Pazzaglia and De Beni 2001) and when their goals involve learning a route versus learning the overall layout (Magliano, Cohen, Allen, and Rodrigue 1995; Taylor and Naylor 2002). For example, many studies have probed the extent to which spatial knowledge gained from maps is orientation-specific, whereas knowledge gained from direct travel is orientation-independent (Montello, Hegarty, Richardson, and Waller 2004; Presson, DeLange, and Hazelrigg 1989; Richardson, Montello, and Hegarty 1999; for contradictory findings, see Roskos-Ewoldsen, McNamara, Shelton, and Carr 1998). The nature of the wayfinding task faced by direction givers and followers affects their interactions. For instance, Plumert, Carswell, DeVet, and Ihrig (1995) demonstrated that participants organize their descriptions differently when describing a space than when giving directions to a traveler. (See also Golding et al. 1996.) When describing the location of a coffee cup, for instance, people note that it is on the desk, in the office, on the fourth floor of the psychology building. In contrast, when giving directions for locating the same cup, they note that it is in the psychology building, on the fourth floor, in the office, on the desk. To avoid confusion, direction givers and followers must coordinate their efforts by selecting an appropriate perspective or frame of reference, assessing the familiarity of the environment, and understanding their individual skills and preferences, as well as cultural conventions for communication (Allen 2000; Carlson-Radvansky and Radvansky 1996; Devlin 2003; Hölscher et al. 2011). For instance, Golding et al. (1996) found that when approached by a student requesting wayfinding directions, participants asked clarifying questions to be sure that they were describing the correct destination and to assess the requester's knowledge of the campus. This example demonstrates two ways direction givers and direction followers coordinate their efforts to facilitate successful wayfinding.

It is important to note the potential effect of reliance on memory versus external cues in determining wayfinding effectiveness. Several recent theoretical and empirical assertions focus on the importance of working memory for wayfinding (Davis, Therrien, and West 2009; Meilinger, Knauff, and Bülthoff 2008; Nori, Gandicelli, and Giusberti 2009; Padgitt and Hund 2012; Wen et al. 2011; see also Brunyé and Taylor 2008). For example, Meilinger et al. (2008) explored the importance of working memory in wayfinding using a dual task methodology. Participants learned two routes through a virtual environment while disrupted by a visual, spatial, verbal, or no secondary task. They were then asked to follow the routes again. All three secondary tasks interfered with wayfinding, though the effects were strongest for verbal and spatial tasks. Meilinger et al. proposed that dual coding theory might explain these results. That is, both spatial and verbal processing are important while wayfinding because details are coded in both formats. In particular, Meilinger et al. assert that spatial details are coded also in verbal format. This additional verbal coding adds durability and flexibility. Meilinger et al. further concluded that verbal memory is most important during wayfinding at points where a decision needs to be made. In general, the memory demands of survey directions might be greater because one must keep track of global orientation and individual position, rather than utilizing step-by-step descriptions of route segments and vistas in route directions. (See also Nori et al. 2009.) However, lengthy route directions may tax working memory capacity in the absence of external supports. This constraint may underlie people's preference for complete yet concise wayfinding directions (Allen 2000; Devlin 2003; Lovelace, Hegarty, and Montello 1999; Vanetti and Allen 1988).

The structure of the physical environment also shapes wayfinding strategies and performance. For instance, people are more likely to provide route descriptions when the available landmarks are similar in size and an obvious path is available (Taylor and Tversky 1996). Similarly, environmental scale might affect efficiency. In an indoor environment where navigation is dependent on finding appropriate hallways and knowing which direction to turn down these hallways, perhaps it is more beneficial to know particular routes than to know what cardinal direction to travel next (Lawton et al. 1996). As a result, following descriptions via a route perspective may be more critical in large indoor environments than in other environments, such as outdoors where more external cues are present to maintain orientation or in a small-scale space where an extrinsic point of view is predominant.

Cultural and Regional Differences in Spatial Strategies

It is likely that culture influences the relation between perspective and wayfinding. That is, psychological, social, and physical aspects of communities and cultures affect wayfinding, particularly verbal descriptions to facilitate finding one's way. For instance, Evans (1980) highlighted the importance of daily activity patterns for spatial cognition, including wayfinding. In particular, it is critical to consider the ways in which topography, landmarks, and the layout of property boundaries and road patterns interact to shape people's experiences with the environment, as well as their knowledge about and descriptions of their surroundings (Davies and Pederson 2001; Evans 1980; Lawton 2001; Wolbers and Hegarty 2010). For example, in one cross-cultural study, Davies and Pederson (2001) assessed differences in spatial knowledge for residents of Milton Keynes, England and Eugene, Oregon. Unlike many other cities in England, Milton Keynes was designed with a grid system of streets and relatively systematic patterns of street names and address numbering, which make it similar to Eugene in those respects. Nonetheless, the authors hypothesized that residents of Milton Keynes would be less familiar with the grid system, which would result in differences in sketch maps and pointing accuracy across cultural groups. As expected, Eugene residents evinced greater reliance on grid features than did Milton Keynes residents when drawing maps and when pointing to unseen locations.

In a related study, Lawton (2001) assessed regional differences in spatial strategies within the United States by asking adults to provide driving directions to locations in their home towns. As in many parts of Europe and elsewhere in the world, the patterns of property boundaries and roads in the northeastern and southern states of the US are irregular. In contrast, property boundaries and road systems are much more regular (e.g., often following a grid system) in the midwestern and western states, thanks in large part to the US Public Land Survey. Consistent with these environmental differences and resulting differences in patterns of daily activities, people from the midwest and the west provided cardinal directions more frequently than did people from the northeast and the south when giving driving directions for people finding their way through their communities. Moreover, preferences for cardinal directions increased with age, which suggests that experience plays an important role.

Recently, Hund, Schmettow, and Noordzij (2012) examined how culture and recipient perspective affect direction giving during wayfinding. Participants from the United States and the Netherlands provided directions from starting locations to destinations for fictional recipients driving through a town (route perspective) or looking at a map of the town (survey perspective). As predicted, participants provided cardinal descriptors, landmarks, left-right descriptors, and street names with varying frequencies depending on recipient perspective and culture. In particular, American participants exhibited a far stronger tendency to mention cardinal terms than did Dutch participants. They provided street names more frequently than did Dutch participants, whereas Dutch participants provided landmarks more frequently than did American participants. Moreover, American participants provided more cardinal descriptors when addressing listeners adopting a survey perspective relative to a route perspective but more landmarks and left-right descriptors when addressing listeners adopting a route perspective relative to a survey perspective. (See also Hund et al. 2008.) Participants from the Netherlands evinced a similar pattern with the important distinction that they mostly ignored cardinal terms, unless explicitly primed to do so and in a survey condition. In addition, this very low usage of cardinal terms seemed to be replaced by using more landmark descriptions. This study revealed remarkable flexibility in people's spatial descriptions but also stressed major differences in the use of spatial cues and strategies between American and Dutch participants.

Age Differences in Spatial Strategies

It is important to specify the emergence of spatial skills in the course of development (Newcombe, Uttal, and Sauter 2012). Toward that end, Allen (1999) examined the abilities of 8-year-olds and 10-year-olds to remember and infer spatial information from descriptions of spatial layouts. Participants heard descriptions of three spatial layouts. Each was described using a different perspective. In one description, a survey perspective was used (i.e., one perspective was described via cardinal directions); in another, a route perspective (i.e., a route through the space) was described; in another, a vantage-point perspective was used (i.e., one perspective was described in terms of left and right details). After learning, participants verified the truth of statements regarding the space. Children were most accurate after learning based on vantage-point descriptions. In a similar set of studies, Ondracek and Allen (2000) presented verbal descriptions of three spaces to 6-year-olds and 8-year-olds and asked them to verify statements about the spaces. In addition, the children were asked to place tokens of the objects on a map of the space. The 8-year-olds were more accurate than the 6-year-olds in verifying statements and in placing the tokens on a map. As in the previous study, the older children were most accurate after learning based on vantage-point descriptions. The younger children were most accurate after learning based on route perspective descriptions, which suggests that reliance on route directions may emerge earlier than reliance on cardinal and vantage-point directions. In a second experiment, Ondracek and Allen tested the efficacy of an intervention designed to improve children's understanding of directional terms. Children first heard one description. Then, half of the children viewed a map (which included labels of north, left, and right) while listening to a description. Finally, all the children heard another description and completed the verification and token-placement tasks. The children who viewed the labeled map during the second description were more accurate than the children who did not view the labeled map. In general, maps have been shown to improve survey knowledge for children, especially when used in concert with verbal descriptions (Uttal, Fisher, and Taylor 2006).

We know that adults rely on survey and route strategies in a variety of contexts. Recent evidence suggests that strategies may differ as a function of sense of direction. That is, adults with poor sense of direction rely on landmarks and route strategies to learn about spatial layouts, focusing on verbal and visual details. In contrast, adults with good sense of direction rely on survey strategies, integrating spatial, verbal, and visual details to understand the overall layout. Spatial integration of landmark and route details appears to be particularly important for making sense of global details (Wen, Ishikawa, and Sato 2011).

Recent research has focused on specifying how spatial strategies differ as a function of aging, providing additional details about the processes involved. Anecdotally and empirically, it is well established that spatial thinking declines with aging, and that these declines affect everyday activities. For example, older adults show large deficits in mental rotation ability relative to younger adults (e.g., Armstrong and Cloud 1998; Briggs, Raz, and Marks 1999; Hertzog, Vernon, and Rypma 1993). Moreover, older adults report difficulties with wayfinding, especially in unfamiliar locations (Burns 1999). Older adults take longer than younger adults to learn details about novel environments, such as supermarkets and hospitals (Kirasic 1991; Wilkniss, Jones, Korol, Gold, and Manning 1997).

Why might spatial thinking decline with aging? It is possible that declines in working memory, especially in complex and unfamiliar tasks for which speed is important, may underlie declines in mental rotation and spatial processing (Raz et al. 1999; Sharps and Nunes 2002). In addition, declines in processing speed may hinder spatial performance (Dror and Kosslyn 1994), especially in effortful tasks involving mental imagery (Craik and Dirkx 1992). For instance, Hertzog et al. (1993) asked participants to complete a serial mental rotation task in which each aspect was completed in isolation, demonstrating age-related declines in encoding, rotation, and decision processes. Older adults may employ more conservative response criteria when solving spatial problems (Hertzog et al. 1993), valuing certainty and accuracy more than speed. Despite precipitous declines in cognitive processes, everyday spatial functioning may decline surprisingly little as a result of compensatory strategies. One possibility is to use verbal processing to augment spatial details (Clarkson-Smith and Halpern 1983; Moffat 2009).

Recent research suggests that differences in strategy preferences may explain age-related declines in spatial skills (Moffat 2009) such that modest preferences for survey strategies among younger adults give way to larger preferences for route strategies among older adults (Rodgers, Sindone, and Moffat 2012). Moreover, survey strategies are positively related to wayfinding success, which suggests one avenue for intervention. For example, self-reports indicate that survey strategies decline with age (Driscoll et al. 2005). Similarly, Rodgers et al. (2012) noted a large decline in survey strategy usage with age. Results from their study that involved a virtual Y maze revealed preferences for both survey and route strategies by younger adults but an overwhelming preference for route strategies by older adults. In particular, participants started at the same location on every trial and were trained to find the goal location in another arm of the Y maze. After training, the starting location was shifted to a new location in the arm that did not serve as the start or goal, and participants were asked to find the original goal location. Older adults primarily attempted to follow the same sequence as during training (i.e., turn right), highlighting their reliance on a route strategy/intrinsic cues. This strategy did not lead to the goal given the starting location had shifted. Reliance on a survey strategy/extrinsic cues, on the other hand, resulted in participants reaching the goal by relying on their overall sense of place. In a recent review, Moffat (2009) summarized substantial evidence indicating strong age-related declines in wayfinding, especially survey strategies and reliance on extrinsic cues.

Recent pilot results from our laboratory attempted to add clarity with regard to age-related differences in wayfinding strategies (Gill, Hatch, Frontera, and Hund 2012). Fifty-eight undergraduate students and 25 healthy adults at least 60 years old completed a battery of tasks including mental rotation, map sketching, rating the effectiveness of wayfinding directions using survey and route descriptors, and self-report measures of wayfinding strategies, spatial anxiety, and sense of direction. As expected, mental rotation accuracy declined significantly with age. Interestingly, older adults reported higher sense of direction and wayfinding strategy preferences than did younger adults, indicating that the older adults were spatially adept. Effectiveness ratings for route descriptors were significantly greater for younger than older women, but did not differ for younger and older men. Ratings for survey descriptors did not differ across age groups for either gender. Route and survey strategy preferences and performance evinced tight, yet divergent, correlations, providing support for this distinction. Overall, the findings confirm age-related differences in spatial thinking and point toward strategy preferences as a potential mechanism of change.

Implications for Education

We know that spatial skills are malleable (Uttal et al. 2013). Over time, cascading experience shapes spatial strategies and performance, inviting researchers and practitioners to think seriously about training and intervention options. For example, Lawton and Kallai (2002) found that wayfinding experiences during childhood and adulthood were related to individual differences in spatial skills. Interestingly, playing video games has been found to relate to spatial thinking abilities (Terlecki and Newcombe 2005). Moreover, Ward et al. (1986) suggested that driving experience, geography courses, and activities involving cardinality might account for gender differences in wayfinding. (See also Kozlowski and Bryant 1977.)

In a recent review, Newcombe et al. (2012) outlined normative development and individual differences in spatial thinking and called for increased research focused on how incorporating spatial skills in formal and informal learning contexts could improve spatial thinking and thereby improve science, technology, engineering, and mathematics (STEM) outcomes. One important issue to consider is training effectiveness across age groups, genders, and contexts. Another issue involves testing direct links between various spatial skills and improvements in STEM learning and career trajectories. (For supportive evidence see Shea, Lubinski, and Benbow 2001; Wai, Lubinski, and Benbow 2009.) It is important to note that training programs involving a wide array of components are effective in improving spatial outcomes (Uttal et al. 2013). Sometimes training involves adding explanations and exercises to pre-existing coursework that is spatially demanding, such as geoscience or engineering courses (Piburn et al. 2005; Sorby and Baartmans 2000). For example, Sorby and Baartmans (2000) developed a course to help beginning engineering students improve their visualization skills for three-dimensional objects, demonstrating improvement in retention in the major. Other training programs focus on improving students' spatial analysis by using geographic information systems (Baker and Bednarz 2003; Keiper 1999; Kerski 2003; Shin 2006) to facilitate problem solving. Still other work focuses on informal experiences, such as action video games, that lead to improvements in spatial performance (Basak et al. 2008; Feng, Spence, and Pratt 2007; Green and Bavelier 2007).

We know that training affects the wayfinding performance of adults. For instance, Hund and Nazarczuk (2009) found that participants who received training experience following survey or route directions to find destinations in a scale model evinced faster wayfinding when later tested in an analogous large-scale space than did participants in the control condition, especially when following directions involving cardinal descriptors. It is interesting to note that experience with a scale model enhanced wayfinding performance within the corresponding large-scale environment. These findings add to growing support for including maps when helping children and adults understand spatial relations (Uttal

2000; Uttal et al. 2006), adding support to claims that spatial skills should be included in school curricula (Heffron and Downs 2012; National Council for Social Studies 2010). Interestingly, the effects of training experience and sense of direction on wayfinding efficiency were most pronounced when participants used directions containing cardinal descriptors. This suggests that training experience is most beneficial in cases where performance is difficult (i.e., cases requiring finding the way using an integrated, survey perspective). Perhaps efforts to facilitate wayfinding and to intervene to improve wayfinding skills should focus on survey perspectives. This focus may be particularly important for children and older adults. Experience using well-designed signs and aligned you-are-here maps (in concert with reasonable layouts and numbering schemes) also are beneficial (Butler, Acquino, Hissong, and Scott 1993; Levine, Marchon, and Hanley 1984).

These findings have important implications for law enforcement, transportation, and other fields in which skillful wayfinding is required, for education aimed at fostering skillful wayfinding in schools and museums, and for everyday settings that require wayfinding (e.g., shopping centers and tourist sites). It is encouraging to know that people benefit from practicing their wayfinding skills, though the generalizability and temporal limits of such practice are not known. Moreover, the fact that practice involving a tabletop model was applicable to later wayfinding in the analogous large-scale environment increases the feasibility of such practice or training as one aspect of building survey knowledge (Hund and Nazarczuk 2009). Certainly, it is often more practicable to use small models, maps, or virtual representations to facilitate such training, as opposed to practicing finding the way through large environments. Importantly, we know that the benefits of spatial training transfer to other tasks when the training is intensive (Wright et al. 2008), though it is not clear to what extent training involving wayfinding strategies transfers to performance on other spatial tasks or vice versa. Additional basic and applied research is needed.

Facilitating flexibility and adaptability in spatial strategies is important as we strive to enhance wayfinding and spatial problem solving more generally. Children and adults benefit from access to survey cues that integrate spatial details (in addition to route details that rely on verbal and visual coding) both when finding their way through the environment and when solving spatial problems. These skills are important in their own right (National Research Council 2006) and also because they are critical for excellence in STEM domains (Uttal and Cohen 2012). Thus, we must work to facilitate skillful wayfinding and spatial problem solving, which may lead to greater success in STEM pursuits.

References

Allen, G. L. 1999. Children's control of reference systems in spatial tasks: Foundations of spatial cognitive skill? *Spatial Cognition and Computation* 1: 413–429.

Allen, G. L. 2000. Principles and practices for communicating route knowledge. *Applied Cognitive Psychology* 14: 333–359.

Armstrong, C. L., and Cloud, B. 1998. The emergence of spatial rotation deficits in dementia and normal aging. *Neuropsychology* 12: 208–217.

Baker, T. R., and Bednarz, S. W. 2003. Lessons learned from reviewing research in GIS education. *Journal of Geography* 102: 231–233.

Basak, C., Boot, W., Voss, M., and Kramer, A. 2008. Can training in a real-time strategy video game attenuate cognitive decline in older adults? *Psychology and Aging* 23: 765–777.

Briggs, S. D., Raz, N., and Marks, W. 1999. Age-related deficits in generation and manipulation of mental images: I. The role of sensorimotor speed and working memory. *Psychology and Aging* 14: 427–435.

Brunyé, T. T., Rapp, H. A., and Taylor, H. A. 2008. Representational flexibility and specificity following spatial descriptions of real-world environments. *Cognition* 108: 418–443.

Brunyé, T. T., and Taylor, H. A. 2008. Working memory in developing and applying mental models from spatial descriptions. *Journal of Memory and Language* 58: 708–729.

Burns, P. C. 1999. Navigation and the mobility of older drivers. *Journals of Gerontology. Series B, Psychological Sciences and Social Sciences* 54B: S49–S55.

Butler, D. L., Acquino, A. L., Hissong, A. A., and Scott, P. A. 1993. Wayfinding by newcomers in a complex building. *Human Factors* 35: 159–173.

Carlson-Radvansky, L. A., and Radvansky, G. A. 1996. The influence of functional relations on spatial term selection. *Psychological Science* 7: 56–60.

Clarkson-Smith, L., and Halpern, D. F. 1983. Can age-related deficits in spatial memory be attenuated through the use of verbal coding? *Experimental Aging Research* 9: 179–184.

Craik, F. I. M., and Dirkx, E. 1992. Age-related differences in three tests of visual imagery. *Psychology and Aging* 7: 661–665.

Davies, C., and Pederson, E. 2001. Grid patterns and cultural expectations in urban wayfinding. In *Spatial Information Theory: Foundations of Geographic Information Science*, ed. D. R. Montello. Springer.

Davis, R. L., Therrien, B. A., and West, B. T. 2009. Working memory, cues, and wayfinding in older women. *Journal of Applied Gerontology* 28: 743–767.

Denis, M., Pazzaglia, F., Cornoldi, C., and Bertolo, L. 1999. Spatial discourse and navigation: An analysis of route directions in the city of Venice. *Applied Cognitive Psychology* 13: 145–174.

Devlin, A. S. 2003. Giving directions: Gender and perceived quality. *Journal of Applied Social Psychology* 33: 1530–1551.

Driscoll, I., Hamilton, D. A., Petrepoulos, H., Yeo, R. A., Brooks, W. M., Baumgarten, R. M., et al. 2003. The aging hippocampus: Cognitive, biochemical, and structural findings. *Cerebral Cortex* 13: 1344–1351.

Driscoll, I., Hamilton, D. A., Yeo, R. A., Brooks, W. M., and Sutherland, R. J. 2005. Virtual navigation in humans: The impact of age, sex, and hormones on place learning. *Hormones and Behavior* 47: 326–335.

Dror, I. E., and Kosslyn, S. M. 1994. Mental imagery and aging. *Psychology and Aging* 9: 90–102.

Evans, G. W. 1980. Environmental cognition. *Psychological Bulletin* 88: 259–287.

Feng, J., Spence, I., and Pratt, J. 2007. Playing an action video game reduces gender differences in spatial cognition. *Psychological Science* 18: 850–855.

Galea, L. A. M., and Kimura, D. 1993. Sex differences in route-learning. *Personality and Individual Differences* 14: 53–65.

Gauvain, M., and Rogoff, B. 1989. Ways of speaking about space: The development of children's skill in communicating spatial knowledge. *Cognitive Development* 4: 295–307.

Gill, D., Hatch, C., Frontera, C., and Hund, A. M. 2012. Using survey and route strategies: Analyzing spatial skills across adulthood. Poster presentation at annual conference of Midwestern Psychological Association, Chicago.

Golding, J. M., Graesser, A. C., and Hauselt, J. 1996. The process of answering direction-giving questions when someone is lost on a university campus: The role of pragmatics. *Applied Cognitive Psychology* 10: 23–39.

Golledge, R. G. 1999. Human wayfinding and cognitive maps. In *Wayfinding Behavior: Cognitive Mapping and Other Spatial Processes*, ed. R. G. Golledge. Johns Hopkins University Press.

Green, C. S., and Bavelier, D. 2007. Action-video-game experience alters the resolution of vision. *Psychological Science* 18: 88–94.

Head, D., and Isom, M. 2010. Age effects on wayfinding and route learning skills. *Behavioural Brain Research* 209: 49–58.

Heffron, S., and Downs, R. 2012. *Geography for Life: National Geography Standards*, second edition. National Geographic Society.

Hegarty, M., Montello, D. R., Richardson, A. E., Ishikawa, T., and Lovelace, K. 2006. Spatial abilities at different scales: Individual differences in aptitude-test performance and spatial-layout learning. *Intelligence* 34: 151–176.

Hertzog, C., Vernon, M. C., and Rypma, B. 1993. Age differences in mental rotation task performance: The influence of speed/accuracy tradeoffs. *Journals of Gerontology. Series B, Psychological Sciences and Social Sciences* 48: 150–156.

Hirtle, S. C., and Hudson, J. 1991. Acquisition of spatial knowledge for routes. *Journal of Environmental Psychology* 11: 335–345.

Hölscher, C., Tenbrink, T., and Wiener, J. M. 2011. Would you follow your own route description? Cognitive strategies in urban route planning. *Cognition* 121: 228–247.

Hund, A. M., Haney, K. H., and Seanor, B. D. 2008. The role of recipient perspective in giving and following wayfinding directions. *Applied Cognitive Psychology* 22: 896–916.

Hund, A. M., and Minarik, J. L. 2006. Getting from here to there: Spatial anxiety, wayfinding strategies, direction type, and wayfinding efficiency. *Spatial Cognition and Computation* 6: 179–201.

Hund, A. M., and Nazarczuk, S. N. 2009. The effects of sense of direction and training experience on wayfinding efficiency. *Journal of Environmental Psychology* 29: 151–159.

Hund, A. M., and Padgitt, A. J. 2010. Direction giving and following in the service of wayfinding in a complex indoor environment. *Journal of Environmental Psychology* 30: 553–564.

Hund, A. M., Schmettow, M., and Noordzij, M. L. 2012. The impact of culture and recipient perspective on direction giving in the service of wayfinding. *Journal of Environmental Psychology* 32: 327–336.

Iaria, G., Petrides, M., Dagher, A., Pike, B., and Bohbot, V. D. 2003. Cognitive strategies dependent on the hippocampus and caudate nucleus in human navigation: Variability and change with practice. *Journal of Neuroscience* 23, 5945–5952.

Keiper, T. A. 1999. GIS for elementary students: An inquiry into a new approach to learning geography. *Journal of Geography* 98: 47–59.

Kerski, J. J. 2003. The implementation and effectiveness of geographic information systems technology and methods in secondary education. *Journal of Geography* 102: 128–137.

Kirasic, K. C. 1991. Spatial cognition and behavior in young and elderly adults: Implications for learning new environments. *Psychology and Aging* 6: 10–18.

Kozlowski, L. T., and Bryant, K. J. 1977. Sense of direction, spatial orientation, and cognitive maps. *Journal of Experimental Psychology. Human Perception and Performance* 3: 590–598.

Lawton, C. A. 1994. Gender differences in way-finding strategies: Relationship to spatial ability and spatial anxiety. *Sex Roles* 30: 765–779.

Lawton, C. A. 1996. Strategies for indoor wayfinding: The role of orientation. *Journal of Environmental Psychology* 16: 137–145.

Lawton, C. A. 2001. Gender and regional differences in spatial referents used in direction giving. *Sex Roles* 44: 321–336.

Lawton, C. A. 2010. Gender, spatial abilities, and wayfinding. In *Handbook of Gender Research in Psychology*, ed. J. C. Chrisler and D. R. McCreary. Springer.

Lawton, C. A., Charleston, S. I., and Zieles, A. S. 1996. Individual- and gender-related differences in indoor wayfinding. *Environment and Behavior* 28: 204–219.

Lawton, C. A., and Kallai, J. 2002. Gender differences in wayfinding strategies and anxiety about wayfinding: A cross-cultural comparison. *Sex Roles* 47: 389–401.

Levine, M., Marchon, I., and Hanley, G. 1984. The placement and misplacement of you-are-here maps. *Environment and Behavior* 16: 139–157.

Linde, C., and Labov, W. 1975. Spatial structures as a site for the study of language and thought. *Language* 51: 924–939.

Linn, M. C., and Petersen, A. C. 1985. Emergence and characterization of sex differences in spatial ability: A meta-analysis. *Child Development* 56: 1479–1498.

Lloyd, P. 1991. Strategies used to communicate route direction by telephone: A comparison of the performance of 7-year-olds, 10-year-olds, and adults. *Child Language* 18: 171–189.

Lovelace, K. L., Hegarty, M., and Montello, D. R. 1999. Elements of good route directions in familiar and unfamiliar environments. In *Spatial Information Theory: Cognition and Computational Foundations of Geographic Information Science*, ed. C. Freksa and D. M. Mark. Springer.

MacFadden, A., Elias, L., and Saucier, D. 2003. Males and females scan maps similarly, but give directions differently. *Brain and Cognition* 53: 297–300.

Magliano, J. P., Cohen, R., Allen, G. L., and Rodrigue, J. R. 1995. The impact of a wayfinder's goal on learning a new environment: Different types of spatial knowledge as goals. *Journal of Environmental Psychology* 15: 65–75.

Mark, D. M., and Gould, M. D. 1995. Wayfinding directions as discourse: Verbal directions in English and Spanish. In *Deixis in Narrative: A Cognitive Science Perspective*, ed. J. F. Duchan, G. A. Bruder, and L. E. Hewitt. Erlbaum.

Meilinger, T., Knauff, M., and Bülthoff, H. H. 2008. Working memory in wayfinding—A dual task experiment in a virtual city. *Cognitive Science* 32: 755–770.

Moffat, S. D. 2009. Aging and spatial navigation: What do we know and where do we go? *Neuropsychology Review* 19: 478–489.

Moffat, S. D., Elkins, W., and Resnick, S. M. 2006. Age differences in the neural systems supporting human allocentric spatial navigation. *Neurobiology of Aging* 22: 787–796.

Moffat, S. D., Hampson, E., and Hatzipantelis, M. 1998. Navigation in a "virtual" maze: Sex differences and correlation with psychometric measures of spatial ability in humans. *Evolution and Human Behavior* 19: 73–87.

Montello, D. R., Hegarty, M., Richardson, A. E., and Waller, D. 2004. Spatial memory of real environments, virtual environments, and maps. In *Human Spatial Memory: Remembering Where*, ed. G. L. Allen. Erlbaum.

Montello, D. R., Lovelace, K. L., Golledge, R. G., and Self, C. M. 1999. Sex-related differences and similarities in geographic and environmental spatial abilities. *Annals of the Association of American Geographers* 89: 515–534.

National Council for Social Studies. 2010. *National Curriculum Standards for Social Studies: A Framework for Teaching, Learning, and Assessment.*

National Research Council. 2006. *Learning to Think Spatially.* National Academies Press.

Newcombe, N. S., Uttal, D. H., and Sauter, M. 2012. Spatial development. In *Oxford Handbook of Developmental Psychology*, ed. P. Zelazo. Oxford University Press.

Nori, R., Gandicelli, S., and Giusberti, F. 2009. Individual differences in visuo-spatial working memory and real-world wayfinding. *Swiss Journal of Psychology* 68: 7–16.

O'Keefe, J., and Nadel, L. 1978. *The Hippocampus as a Cognitive Map.* Oxford University Press.

Ondracek, P. J., and Allen, G. L. 2000. Children's acquisition of spatial knowledge from verbal descriptions. *Spatial Cognition and Computation* 2: 1–30.

Padgitt, A. J., and Hund, A. M. 2012. How good are these directions? Determining direction quality and wayfinding efficiency. *Journal of Environmental Psychology* 32: 164–172.

Pazzaglia, F., and De Beni, R. 2001. Strategies of processing spatial information in survey and landmark-centered individuals. *European Journal of Cognitive Psychology* 13: 493–508.

Piburn, M. D., Reynolds, S. J., McAuliffe, C., Leedy, D. E., Birk, J. P., and Johnson, J. K. 2005. The role of visualization in learning from computer-based images. *International Journal of Science Education* 27: 513–520.

Plumert, J. M., Carswell, C., DeVet, K., and Ihrig, D. 1995. The content and organization of communication about object locations. *Journal of Memory and Language* 34: 477–498.

Presson, C. C., DeLange, N., and Hazelrigg, M. D. 1989. Orientation specificity in spatial memory: What makes a path different from a map of the path? *Journal of Experimental Psychology. Learning, Memory, and Cognition* 15: 887–897.

Prestopnik, J. L., and Roskos-Ewoldsen, B. 2000. The relations among wayfinding strategy use, sense of direction, sex, familiarity, and wayfinding ability. *Journal of Environmental Psychology* 20: 177–191.

Raz, N., Briggs, S. D., Marks, W., and Acker, J. D. 1999. Age-related deficits in generation and manipulation of mental images: II. The role of dorsolateral prefrontal cortex. *Psychology and Aging* 14: 436–444.

Richardson, A. E., Montello, D. R., and Hegarty, M. 1999. Spatial knowledge acquisition from maps and from navigation in real and virtual environments. *Memory and Cognition* 27: 741–750.

Rodgers, M. K., Sindone, J. A., III, and Moffat, S. D. 2012. Effects of age on navigation strategy. *Neurobiology of Aging* 33: e15–e22.

Roskos-Ewoldsen, B., McNamara, T. P., Shelton, A. L., and Carr, W. 1998. Mental representations of large and small spatial layouts are orientation dependent. *Journal of Experimental Psychology. Learning, Memory, and Cognition* 24 (1): 215–226.

Saucier, D. M., Green, S. M., Leason, J., MacFadden, A., Bell, S., and Elias, L. J. 2002. Are sex differences in navigation caused by sexually dimorphic strategies or by differences in the ability to use the strategies? *Behavioral Neuroscience* 116: 403–410.

Sharps, M. J., and Nunes, M. A. 2002. Gestalt and feature-intensive processing: Toward a unified model of human information processing. *Current Psychology* 21: 68–84.

Shea, D. L., Lubinski, D., and Benbow, C. P. 2001. Importance of assessing spatial ability in intellectually talented young adolescents: A 20-year longitudinal study. *Journal of Educational Psychology* 93: 604–614.

Shelton, A. L. 2004. Putting spatial memories into perspective: Brain and behavioral evidence for representational differences. In, *Human Spatial Memory: Remembering Where* ed. G. L. Allen. Erlbaum.

Shelton, A. L., and Gabrieli, J. D. E. 2002. Neural correlates of encoding space from route and survey perspectives. *Journal of Neuroscience* 22: 2711–2717.

Shelton, A. L., and McNamara, T. P. 2004. Orientation and perspective dependence in route and survey learning. *Journal of Experimental Psychology. Learning, Memory, and Cognition* 30: 158–170.

Shin, E. K. 2006. Using geographic information systems (GIS) to improve fourth graders' geographic content knowledge and map skills. *Journal of Geography* 105: 109–120.

Sholl, M. J., Acacio, J. C., Makar, R. O., and Leon, C. 2000. The relation of sex and sense of direction to spatial orientation in an unfamiliar environment. *Journal of Environmental Psychology* 20: 17–28.

Siegel, A. W., and White, S. H. 1975. The development of spatial representations of large-scale environments. In *Advances in Child Development and Behavior*, ed. H. W. Reese. Academic Press.

Sorby, S. A., and Baartmans, B. J. 2000. The development and assessment of a course for enhancing the 3-D spatial visualization skills of first year engineering students. *Journal of Engineering Education* 89: 301–307.

Taylor, H. A., and Naylor, S. J. 2002. Goal-directed effects on processing a spatial environment. In *Spatial Language*, ed. K. R. Coventry and P. Olivier. Kluwer.

Taylor, H. A., and Tversky, B. 1996. Perspective in spatial descriptions. *Journal of Memory and Language* 35: 371–391.

Terlecki, M. S., and Newcombe, N. S. 2005. How important is the digital divide? The relation of computer and videogame usage to gender differences in mental rotation ability. *Sex Roles* 53: 433–441.

Uttal, D. H. 2000. Maps and spatial thinking: A two-way street. *Developmental Science* 3: 283–286.

Uttal, D. H., and Cohen, C. A. 2012. Spatial thinking and STEM education: When, why, and how? *Psychology of Learning and Motivation* 57: 147–181.

Uttal, D. H., Fisher, J. A., and Taylor, H. A. 2006. Words and maps: Developmental changes in mental models of spatial information acquired from descriptions and depictions. *Developmental Science* 9: 221–235.

Uttal, D. H., Meadow, N. G., Tipton, E., Hand, L. L., Alden, A. R., Warren, C., and Newcombe, N. S. 2013. The malleability of spatial skills: A meta-analysis of training studies. *Psychological Bulletin* 139: 352–402.

Vanetti, E. J., and Allen, G. L. 1988. Communicating environmental knowledge: The impact of verbal and spatial abilities on the production and comprehension of route directions. *Environment and Behavior* 20: 667–682.

Voyer, D., Voyer, S., and Bryden, M. P. 1995. Magnitude of sex differences in spatial abilities: A meta-analysis and consideration of critical variables. *Psychological Bulletin* 117: 250–270.

Wai, J., Lubinski, D., and Benbow, C. P. 2009. Spatial ability for STEM domains: Aligning over 50 years of cumulative psychological knowledge solidifies its importance. *Journal of Educational Psychology* 101: 817–835.

Ward, S. L., Newcombe, N., and Overton, W. F. 1986. Turn left at the church, or three miles north: A study of direction giving and sex differences. *Environment and Behavior* 18: 192–213.

Wen, W., Ishikawa, T., and Sato, T. 2011. Working memory in spatial knowledge acquisition: Differences in encoding processes and sense of direction. *Applied Cognitive Psychology* 25: 654–662.

Wilkniss, S. M., Jones, M. G., Korol, D. L., Gold, P. E., and Manning, C. A. 1997. Age-related differences in an ecologically based study of route learning. *Psychology and Aging* 12: 372–375.

Wolbers, T., and Hegarty, M. 2010. What determines our navigational abilities? *Trends in Cognitive Sciences* 14: 138–146.

Wright, R., Thompson, W. L., Ganis, G., Newcombe, N. S., and Kosslyn, S. M. 2008. Training generalized spatial skills. *Psychonomic Bulletin and Review* 14: 763–771.

IV Spatial Thinking and Education

11   Spatial Learning in Higher Education

Diana S. Sinton

Learning that is based on spatial approaches, spatial constructs, and spatial principles takes place in many arenas of higher education. (See the chapter by Grossner and Janelle in this volume.) Anyone studying engineering, art, physics, geography, computer science, planning, or geology regularly uses spatial understanding to reason through the discipline's topics or ideas. One may study where a phenomenon or an object is located, figure out how it fits or is placed relative to other objects, measure or study its movement over time, or model the effects of its changes on other phenomena or objects. However, the role of space and the application of spatial thinking are most often implicit or tacit in these actions and decisions. Rarely is direct and explicit attention given to the ways in which spatial thinking underlies and supports learning.

Recognition that this mode of thinking exists, and that it can be measured, dates back more than 100 years (Eliot and Smith 1983). Early in the twentieth century, the intelligence tests used on Ellis Island to assess the suitability of immigrants for admission to the United States were largely spatial and visual ones, not because the government was prioritizing such skills but because it wanted to have some methods of evaluation that did not rely on oral or written language (Murdoch 2007; Richardson 2011). Many other non-verbal tests were developed during and after World War I, when the links between general intelligence and language were being explored (Eliot and Smith 1983). Eventually, a recognition of spatial abilities emerged from the portions of such tests concerned with mechanical and abstract reasoning. Since the 1950s, differential aptitude tests that evaluate spatial abilities and skills have continued to guide youth toward different career paths on the basis of measures of their spatial prowess (Bennett, Seashore, and Wesman 1956; Berdie 1951). By the 1980s, when the educational psychologist Howard Gardner singled out spatial thinking as one of the multiple intelligences that people possess, it was well established that such a collection of cognitive abilities existed, and that it was differentially represented among people (Gardner 2011).

Yet scholars interested in the domain of spatial thinking have claimed this topic cannot be taught or learned on its own, apart from any specific context (National Research Council 2006). Surgeons, auto mechanics, and dentists are all thinking spatially within their own domains, reasoning about the internal structure of complex things they can see only partially. Yet all those experts developed their professional skills through domain-specific practice, and that form of spatial thinking remains distinct from the skills involved in parallel parking a car or designing a website. Moreover, according to the National Research Council (2006, p. 232) "spatial thinking is not a content-based discipline in the way that physics, biology, or economics are disciplines: it is not a stand-alone subject in its own right. Spatial thinking is a way of thinking that permeates those disciplines and … virtually all other subject matter disciplines. Instruction in spatial thinking should play an equivalent role to that of the 'writing across the curriculum' approach."

It is undeniable that spatial approaches to thinking are becoming a topic of interest in higher education and academia. Among the relatively new journals publishing research on spatial approaches are *Spatial Cognition and Computation* (launched in 1999), the *European Journal of Spatial Development* (2003), the *Journal of New Frontiers in Spatial Concepts* (2009), and the *Journal of Spatial Information Science* (2010). In 2009, the University of Toledo, in Ohio, established a doctoral degree program in Spatially Integrated Social Science (Alam, Eckert, and Lindquist 2012). In late 2012, academics and scholars gathered at a multi-disciplinary conference on Spatial Thinking across the College Curriculum (UCSB Center for Spatial Studies 2012). What do these trends mean?

To begin, we must acknowledge that multiple and diverse definitions of 'spatial' exist and vary within and between disciplines. Many geographers or geoscientists would argue that they rely on spatial thinking as much as an engineer, architect, or physicist would, but they are referring to different meanings, applications, and connotations of spatial thinking. Within human psychology, too, multiple scales and ways of interacting with space mean that "space is not space is not space" (Montello 1993, p. 313). Often these disciplinary distinctions are on the basis of scale (Downs and Stea 1977; Freundschuh and Egenhofer 1997; Jones, Gardner, Taylor, Wiebe, and Forrester 2010; Montello 1993; National Research Council 2006), but scale is just one of many ways to differentiate among interpretations of space (Hirtle 2011), and only one of the reasons why space is a topic of interest.

We are thus faced with numerous senses of spatiality and numerous terms associated with the mental or intellectual activity under discussion. The words 'thinking', 'reasoning', and 'cognition' are often used interchangeably, and many distinctions are nuanced ones of semantics. Is the activity automatic, or deliberate? Is the individual being responsive and reactive, or forward thinking and speculative? Is the individual using internal spatial representations, or external ones, such as maps? Does the activity involve the acquisition of new knowledge, or the application and transfer of old knowledge? Though these distinctions are critically important when scholars are communicating among themselves, and when they are designing experiments to be evaluated empirically, they are beyond what most people outside the research realm ever consider.

One way in which spatial thinking has been defined is as an "amalgam of spatial concepts, tools for representations, and processes of reasoning" (National Research Council 2006). According to the Science Education Research Center (n.d.), spatial thinking is "thinking that finds meaning in the shape, size, orientation, location, direction or trajectory, of objects, processes or phenomena, or the relative positions in space of multiple objects, processes or phenomena." Another recent geographically based definition states that spatial thinking consists of "identifying, analyzing, and understanding the location, scale, patterns, and trends of the geographic and temporal relationships among data, phenomena, and issues" (Kerski 2013). My own working definition is that spatial thinking is the ability to visualize and interpret location, position, distance, direction, movement, change, and relationships over space (Sinton 2011). This definition has proved to be resilient and robust over time, and able to encompass many situations while being clear enough to be easily understood by non-experts. Defining complex and nuanced ideas requires a straightforward approach, especially for non-specialized audiences, and using words such as 'amalgam' can further confuse.

These diverse definitions of spatial thinking partially overlap, and it may be largely an academic concern that multi-disciplinary consensus among interested parties is unlikely. Apart from accepting the most general and circular of definitions (such as that spatial thinking is a form of thinking within or pertaining to space), it may be a futile effort for people from different disciplines to try to reach a consensus on a singular, common definition. Instead, research and educational inquiries will continue to define tasks, knowledge, and practices as they are needed. Multiple and competing definitions may be confusing for panels of reviewers considering grant proposals, but few outside that group are bothered by the lack of a single consensual definition.

More important, what we must begin to differentiate within and among these spatially based programmatic areas are their intentions and their outcomes. They may all fall under the heading of education, but they vary significantly with regard to "of what," "to whom," "how," and "why."

Existing Models of Explicitly Spatially Focused Curricula

In this section, I will share an overview of several different higher education or general adult classes that are designed explicitly with spatial thinking or reasoning in mind. I would like to claim that these are representatives from a larger group, but in reality the overall known population of courses choosing to identify themselves as "spatial thinking" courses is very small. The courses have been grouped into three categories on the basis of the most salient properties and characteristics: those that focus directly on spatial skills, those that are grounded in geography and mapping, and those that take a broader and more inclusive approach to spatial thinking. I have used a course's syllabus, its website, conversations with the course instructor, and/or my own direct experience with a class (as its author or as a former student in the class) as the bases for grouping and differentiating among these courses.

Curricula based on spatial skills

One of the most discrete and well-defined curricula having to do with spatial thinking is one that was first designed for an engineering audience (Sorby 2001; Sorby and Baartmans 2000). The expected outcome is very specific: to improve a person's ability to perform tasks of mental rotation, three-dimensional visualization, and related activities. Such skills have long been recognized as necessary for success in engineering and related fields (Hsi, Linn, and Bell 1997; Rudy and Hauck 2008). The curriculum under discussion here has been adopted by and adapted for a number of engineering programs (Hamlin, Veurink, and Sorby 2009; Martín-Dorta, Saorin, and Contero 2008).

The "how" and the "why" of this curriculum are straightforward. Simple and repetitive exercises are supported by a workbook and by software. (Figure 11.1 shows a sample page from the workbook.). Students work through these training activities independently, dedicated to an unambiguous "why": to increase the likelihood that they will be successful in their professional lives as engineers. Correlations between these particular spatial

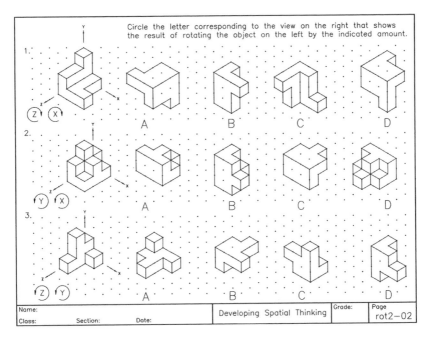

Figure 11.1
A sample page from *Developing Spatial Thinking*, a workbook by Sheryl Sorby (Delmar Cengage Learning, 2011).

skills and success in engineering and other spatially based disciplines are strongly positive (Martín-Dorta et al. 2008). Though to some people progressing through a workbook of this sort may be a mind-numbing experience, there are immediate benefits when one's profession expects competence with the skills this workbook demands.

Measured outcomes from a curriculum of this type can be immediate. How does one know when the curriculum has been successful? In the short run, students will be able to perform the psychometric exercises more quickly and more accurately, and will perform more strongly in their ongoing studies of engineering than they might have otherwise. In the long run, students are expected to be able to transfer and apply their improved abilities on the simple tasks in the curriculum to their jobs, fluently using spatial skills to address and solve the diverse problems and situations they encounter. Such would be a characteristic of a *successful* engineer, architect, designer, or dentist.

By design, this type of spatial course is intended to be undertaken by students working individually and then only by certain groups of students.

Not only is there no obvious or direct pedagogical benefit gained for those individuals from having the exercises conducted in a group setting; there is little need to market this curriculum to anyone outside of those in the aforementioned disciplines. Mental rotation and three-dimensional visualization may be generic tasks of spatial cognition in that they are used by humans in their context of daily life, such as in the use of You-Are-Here maps and the assembling of furniture. But realistically, this particular type and format of spatial learning, characterized by structured practice with abstract shapes and blocks in a workbook, is goal-oriented education for certain groups and individuals (Montello and Raubal 2012). Arguably, this course is more training than education.

Curricula based on geography

Geography has to do with the patterns and processes of interactions between people and their environments, most often on the surface of the earth. These interactions are directly affected by the location of the entities or phenomena, as well as the distances, directions, gradients, hierarchies, transitions, and a host of other spatial relationships. Many geographers use maps to help them understand these patterns and relationships and communicate about them. Of course geographers also use non-spatial information in the questions they ask and in their research.

Geographers have long defined their particular approach to understanding the world by its application of a geographical "lens," or by calling out the geographical "advantage" that this discipline's perspective provides (Cutter, Golledge, and Graf 2002; Golledge 2002; Hanson 2004; Taaffe 1974). The lens or advantage goes beyond the simple notion of where things are to the more substantial issues of location, such as the relationships between entities or phenomena based on spatial properties and concepts such as distance, networks, and hierarchies. Insofar as these are spatial relationships, the geographical lens applies spatial thinking practices, most often at the scale at which most human interactions take place. This mesoscale has also been referred to as *environmental* or *geographical* space (Montello 1993).

However, geographers are inconsistent about identifying themselves as promoting or applying spatial thinking in their practice. It was noted in 1964 that the "spatial tradition of thoughts had made a deep penetration (of American professional geography) from the very beginning" (Pattison 1964, p. 212). Yet the word 'spatial" did not appear in the title of an article in the *Annals of the Association of American Geographer*—the discipline's flagship journal, established in 1911—until 1957. Since that time, there

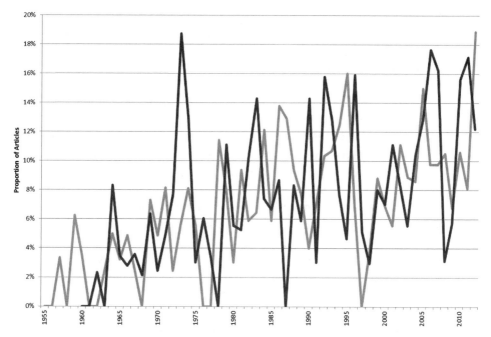

Figure 11.2
Presence of the word 'spatial' in the title of articles published in *Annals of the Association of American Geographers* and *The Professional Geographer*, two publications of the Association of American Geographers. Only original, research, and special focus articles were counted. *Annals* was first published in 1911, but the word 'spatial' first appeared in a title in 1957. *The Professional Geographer* was launched in 1949, but only began to publish articles in 1960. The counts themselves were summed over each years' total number of issues, and ranged from 0 to 17 (*Annals*) and from 0 to 7 (*PG*) articles.

has been a slow but steady increase in the use of the word by geography academics, both in publications and in practice. (See figure 11.2.) In 2008, the National Science Foundation's Geography and Regional Sciences Program changed its name to Geography and Spatial Sciences, stating its intention to "extend beyond the boundaries associated with its historic name" (National Science Foundation 2008). Still, students graduating with an undergraduate degree in geography use the word 'spatial' infrequently when asked to describe what is distinctive about how geographers approach knowledge or how they understand problems and situations (Sinton, unpublished data).

Such trends also can be found within primary and secondary education. The first standard of the K–12 National Geography Standards (first published in 1994) states that a geographically informed person knows "how to use maps and other geographic representations, tools, and technologies to acquire, process, and report information" (Geography Education National Implementation Project 1994). In the revised second edition, that phrase was changed to "how to use maps and other geographic representations, geospatial technologies, *and spatial thinking* to understand and communicate information" (Geography Education National Implementation Project 2012; emphasis added). The glossary to the 2012 standards includes a definition of 'spatial' ("pertaining to space on Earth's surface"), but there is no entry for spatial thinking.

The uneven use of 'spatial' among the geography community is the result of multiple push and pull factors operating concurrently, including the interaction of geographers with other researchers and educators who are using 'spatial', the need for geographers to be able to describe their practices with a word that is increasingly familiar to external audiences, a perceived need by some geographers to distance themselves from the term 'geography' and its K–12 school connotations of memorizing place names, and the satisfying appeal of a single term that encompasses a diverse range of place-based relationships. Within this background context, we find a few classes, some taught by members of geography departments and some by people not affiliated with geography departments, that aim to introduce students to "spatial thinking" from an unambiguously geographic perspective. Classes in this category often focus on maps and mapping, tapping into the familiarity of Web-based maps and location-based services that students may be encountering via their cell phones. This "hook" allows instructors to demonstrate the modern relevance of geography and contemporary applications, such as those associated with the neo-geography movement (Haklay, Singleton, and Parker 2008; Hudson-Smith and Crooks 2008; Rana and Joliveau 2009).

The degree to which these types of courses, labeled and marketed as emphasizing "spatial thinking," are explicit about their approach to spatial thinking, or differ from what would otherwise be an introductory class on maps or geography, is unclear and varies. As no guidelines or standards exist for what constitutes "spatial thinking," instructors are free to interpret and design as they choose. For example, an educational network in Colorado offers two low-cost online classes, Isn't That Spatial? Analyzing Our World Using Digital Maps and Spatial Thinking (e-NET Colorado 2012) and its follow-up, Investigations in Spatial Thinking (e-NET Colorado 2013). Each is taught by Joseph Kerski, a geographer who works in the commercial geographic information systems (GIS) industry, and both classes are structured around the use of GIS and digital geospatial technologies. Critical thinking *through* maps is the basis for spatial thinking in these curricula. Students are guided to consider questions about scale of maps and data; levels of spatial data aggregation; and spatial relationships based on proximity, hierarchies, etc.

Another example is Maps and Spatial Reasoning: An Introduction to the Science of Cartography, an online geography class currently offered by the University of California at Santa Barbara (Clarke 2011). Its topics include traditional topics such as projections, coordinate systems, and map interpretation. Specific attention to "spatial" properties includes the explicit use of distance and direction in describing personal navigation and how GPS and other technologies support it. One lecture is devoted to shape, patterns, and distributions within the context of measurement and map interpretation.

A third example is Geographic Information Science and Spatial Reasoning, a course offered by the Geographic Information Science and Technology Program at Southwestern College in Chula Vista, California (Southwestern College, n.d.). This course explores the use of geospatial technologies and provides an overview of map basics, spatial data models, spatial analysis, and introductory remote sensing.

These geography-based classes emphasize the ways in which the production and the interpretation of maps require people to think through how geographic data are collected, analyzed, and represented. By asking students to consider questions of scale, location, distance, densities, and relationships within and across data sets, approaches to spatial reasoning are modeled. The class at Santa Barbara is required of students pursuing an academic minor with a concentration in Spatial Thinking, Spatial Science, or Place and Space (UCSB Center for Spatial Studies 2013). Across the three distinct "focuses" within the minor, the Maps and Spatial Reasoning course is the sole common requirement; students then select from a wide range of courses (including courses in art, psychology, biology, physics, music, and architecture) having "spatial" content.

Southwestern's Geographic Information Science and Spatial Reasoning class satisfies two different general education requirements: Computer Literacy and Analytical Thinking. Having courses satisfy such requirements is a popular and effective strategy for ensuring enrollment and recruiting majors into a program. This is especially true of classes in geography or geospatial technologies, topics that are likely to be unfamiliar and therefore less initially appealing to students. Showing an increased demand for classes may be the most powerful collateral that a group of faculty members can use to obtain more resources from the administration.

The courses profiled above also highlight the ubiquity of maps in our visual-media-filled world, and the use of location-based services. This tactic creates relevancy for new or current geography students, as the students are encouraged to appreciate how much geography and mapping they already encounter in their everyday lives. The role of "location" is a common element within their use of social media, but probably not one that they have ever considered explicitly. Unlike a spatial skills curriculum targeted toward groups (of engineers, or architects, etc.) or individuals (people who are setting out to improve specific spatial skills), the spatial cognition achieved in these courses is "generic" and designed for all (Montello and Raubal 2012).

Since these classes in spatial reasoning are all associated with programs in geography or geographic information systems, or offered by a GIS professional, it is not surprising that they link spatial reasoning with the use of maps, and maps specifically produced by means of digital geotechnologies. GIS becomes the platform on which the added value of spatial reasoning is modeled and enabled. GIS itself may or may not be an explicit component of the published learning outcomes of these classes, most of which involve map making and map interpretation.

General and multi-disciplinary curricula

A third category of spatially based curricula includes classes and programs that give insight into spatial thinking as a broad idea. Instead of pursuing spatial cognition or reasoning as it is relevant to one discipline or one type of outcome, these curricula recognize—from the outset—that the very nature of spatial thinking's breadth can serve to structure the course itself. Thus the course aims to be multi-disciplinary and inclusive in its definitions and boundaries of spatial thinking. The intent is to build awareness and curiosity. Every student in the class finds one or more elements of the content that is relevant to his or her experiences in social, academic, or professional life. Spatial thinking becomes the common denominator for life's experiences and for how one can learn.

Such a class has been taught to several different audiences at the University of Redlands in Redlands, California. It began as a first-year seminar, in part because such seminars are designed to address broad topics and appeal to students with diverse interests. It was structured as a "sampler" of topics related to spatial thinking, including the use of spatial metaphors, the spatial skills necessary to play different games, and the cognitive spatial processes behind map interpretation. It approached spatial thinking from many scales and perspectives, and addressed both the spatial skills of engineers and the geospatial practices of geographers. The course is now based within the School of Education. Titled Foundations of Spatial Thinking, it is the first of four courses that lead to an online Graduate Certificate in Spatial Literacy for Educators (University of Redlands 2013). The sampler format continues, but its topics are linked together through an educationally grounded common thread. (For an overview of the course's contents, see figure 11.3.) Many of the students have been in-service K–12 teachers, few of them with any background in either psychology or geography. Making connections with their ongoing geographically based activities gives the curriculum a wide and general appeal. Topics that are more foreign to the students, such as the role of mental rotation or three-dimensional visualization as part of spatial cognition, take on new relevancy when they are linked to the activities in which they or their students may engage, such as playing video games.

The course at the University of Redlands exists in this form and for these students mostly as a result of the linkages between spatial thinking and learning in general that were established there. The class was designed around the tenet that learning to think spatially is a form of learning how to learn (National Research Council 2006). Spatially based learning often involves the use of internal or external representations, such as maps in various forms. Learning through maps requires skills of visual critical thinking, so this course also incorporates the ideas of *graphicacy*, the ability to design, organize, and interpret information that is represented in non-text forms, including graphs, charts, figures, and maps (Aldrich and Sheppard 2000; Anning 1997; Wilmot 1999). The K–12 educational audience is well familiar with contemporary needs for information and media literacy, and graphicacy adds viewing skills to a students' knowledge base. Applying spatial thinking to graphicacy can mean critical and informed map reading, but it can also go well beyond that. To design, organize, and interpret a graph, a chart, or a figure also requires fundamental spatial thinking skills. The spatial constructs of position, direction, distance, and relationships among data are involved in the learning process itself. We interpret a graph or chart by considering the spatial arrangement of its elements. That arrangement itself embodies meaning that becomes familiar, quickly, and intuitively: we know something about the relationship between people by considering their position within an organizational chart or a family tree; we know how ideas are related to one another

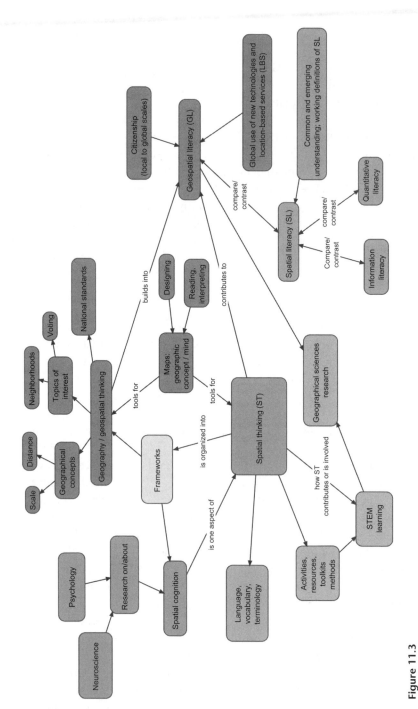

Figure 11.3

The course content of Foundations of Spatial Thinking, a graduate-level course (EDUC 616) taught in the School of Education at the University of Redlands. This figure represents the course syllabus for a fall 2012 section of the class.

through concept maps; we understand temporal dependencies by the sequence of steps on a work-flow chart. This power of space to communicate knowledge is also an important piece of the courses in spatial thinking at Redlands, especially because they are designed specifically for K–12 educators.

A version of the graduate-level education class is now being designed for undergraduate students in the College of Arts and Sciences at Redlands. Along with an introductory course in GIS, it will be one of the required classes in a new academic minor in spatial studies that will be very similar to the one at Santa Barbara. This will be the third known academic minor of its kind. (The University of Southern California has recently launched one.) These minors are characterized by having one or more required classes that are based either on spatial thinking or on mapping, followed by a wide set of courses from which to choose, all of which have somehow been filtered and selected for their spatial content or approach. What remains to be seen is whether, or how, a student's experience through these five or six different college classes will be woven together to generate an overall understanding of spatial thinking and learning. As is the case with most multi- and inter-disciplinary minors, students are rarely asked to reflect on how their particular collection of courses relates to one another, and to share that synthesized knowledge back to their peers and instructors.

A course with such a substantial commitment to broad forms of spatial learning must necessarily have longer-term and broader goals, differentiating this multi-disciplinary course from the ones profiled in the other categories of spatial thinking courses. For example, having the "habit of mind of thinking spatially" is a quality of a spatially literate student (National Research Council 2006, p. 20). Yet there is no known formulaic way of reaching that goal, and no widespread method for assessing when or whether it has been reached. Currently there are no psychometric tests that could be aligned with having such a habit. As a first foray into this area, Kim and Bednarz (2013) recently developed a "spatial habit of mind inventory" (SHOMI) for self-assessment. The test items included dimensions of pattern recognition, spatial descriptions, visualization, spatial concept use, and spatial tool use. The design of such instruments is an important development for educational researchers interested in the field of spatial thinking. Even though Kim and Bednarz found that GIS use had a positive effect on students' SHOMI scores, the development of spatial habits of mind, or spatial literacy, is unlikely to be the outcome of a single learning experience.

Is It Important to Make the Spatial Explicit?

At what level is it important for the students to know, explicitly, that they are employing a spatial approach to help themselves learn, or that a spatial teaching strategy is being used by their professors? How deliberate does an instructor need to be when designing a spatially based learning experience? In math classes, do he instructors stop and say "Today we're going to use numbers to reach a solution to a problem?" No, they just use them. I began this chapter by noting that engineering, art, geology, physics, planning, computer science, and geography are inherently spatial and frequently require the application of spatial thinking. Yet one can major in any of those subjects, quite successfully, without ever taking a class with the word 'spatial' in its title.

If the spatial nature or approach or content of a class is obvious and explicit, spatial thinking becomes a *meta-learning* or *meta-cognitive* outcome. For an instructor, given the problematic *deceptive obviousness* of spatial thinking, having the approach be explicit can enable and facilitate Socratic teaching activities. When spatial thinking is raised to the forefront, students and instructors grant a level of awareness to a process that otherwise often takes place in the background.

For example, while people are playing video games, their brains are naturally and automatically employing spatial strategies to achieve their goals. They must gauge distances and angles to shoot at targets, or estimate proximities between neighboring playing pieces, or group pieces by size and shape, or fit pieces into fixed arrangements. To achieve a meta-cognitive educational goal about how such strategies help a person reach solutions, students must first learn the vocabulary and expression of such strategies. Then they are able to self-identify which different strategies they use in different situations. As a simple example, students in one class activity are charged with playing a wide range of games, digital and otherwise, but only for five minutes at a time. After five minutes (or having concluded the game, whichever comes first), they must stop playing and make note of all spatial strategies they had been using, including whether there were necessary sequences of strategies or dependencies between strategies.

The game activity models for students what steps might be necessary to structure the solving of a spatial problem at a much larger scale, and *the ability to scale a problem* is itself a learning outcome of the activity. Here are some other examples of when the pedagogy should involve explicit spatial instruction or spatial approaches:

• In the practice of teacher education or professional development, building spatial thinking vocabulary and approaches into a "methods" course may be necessary, and may require beginning with the very basics. In one such program, researchers found that during high school geography classroom activities in which students were to identify patterns from aerial imagery, both the teachers and the students lacked the spatial language necessary to describe geographical patterns (Jo, Bednarz, and Metoyer 2010). All participants required explicit and deliberate instruction in how to use those seemingly simple English words (e.g., 'smooth', 'rough', 'edge') as applied to geographical contexts and aerial imagery.

• When a phenomenon is inherently and thoroughly spatial, such as the earth-sun relationship that contributes to seasons or the pattern of orbiting planets, its description may mandate a visuo-spatial explanatory approach. For example, astronomy students do poorly when their instructors fail to effectively use spatial language, spatial representations, and spatial animations during their teaching, and this further propagates misperceptions and incorrect knowledge (Slater 2012). Text-based descriptions of spatial processes are inadequate, inefficient, and ineffective at communicating, and may further obfuscate, spread misperceptions, or delay comprehension (Arnheim 1969; Yau 2011). Spatial representations are essential formats and expressions for spatial phenomena (Hallisey 2005).

Thoughts for Developing the Next Generation of Spatially Informed Curricula

Having been involved for many years in developing curricular programming related to spatial thinking and spatial literacy, and regularly offering a class in spatial thinking, I have had opportunities to think deeply about how we teach and learn spatial thinking. I offer these observations from that perspective, and as a geographer who appreciates and respects the perspectives from other spatially focused disciplines as well.

• *Recognize that different definitions, objectives, and audiences exist and are not mutually exclusive.* By its nature, spatial thinking involves concepts and processes that will always be of interest to people from many disciplinary backgrounds and with very different intentions. Forced reconciliations are unlikely to be productive. Natural overlaps do exist and will continue to occur, but even though that happens, there is little need to force this issue. In fact, forcing a multi-disciplinary merging may be counterproductive. The most fruitful outcomes may emerge when the diverse groups are able to have non-contentious conversations, listen to each other, appreciate and come to understand the different perspectives, and have that enrich and inform, but not subsume, their own work.

• *Develop, evaluate, and widely distribute instructional materials, assessment tools, and support systems for all of the approaches.* For many decades, the vast majority of published research around spatial thinking has focused on spatial skills and abilities, those which can most readily be measured with psychometric tests of mental rotation and spatial orientation (Carroll 1993). More recently, several new instruments have been designed to measure other facets of spatial thinking, including those that affect our activities of daily life (Eliot and Czarnolewski 2007; Kim and Bednarz 2013) and our ability to interpret geographical patterns and geospatial processes (Lee and Bednarz 2009 2012). Moreover, researchers are beginning to ask questions about the cognitive processes that cross these areas of traditional spatial and geospatial thinking. Ishikawa (2013) found that even expert geoscientists, long thought to have exemplary spatial thinking skills, struggle with some forms of spatial tasks. This emerging knowledge can inform the next generation of educational materials and assessments. If having a "spatial habit of mind" is a goal, we should have a way of documenting when such a goal is achieved.

• *Be clever, resourceful, and strategic about the incentives that drive educational decisions and consumer choices.* The designing of new curricula simply cannot take place within an academic vacuum any longer. Traditionally, many institutions of higher education granted individual departments extensive discretion over what content formed a "major," or how a particular class achieved and measured its learning outcomes, or great flexibility and accepting attitudes about taking an elective class. Today, a stronger consumer mentality affects student decisions and a stronger accountability mentality affects programs, departments, and institutions. Thus, new curricula focused on spatial thinking and learning must be aligned and connected with existing academic activities and incentives. Having a class contribute to a required General Education category is one such tactic at the undergraduate level. For pre-service and in-service educators, making a connection with the Continuing Education units that they must regularly seek, or specific academic credits that support a teacher's movement up a restricted pay scale, is a strategic curricular design choice. At the same time, new course content that is targeted toward the K–12 public schools should leverage the national commitment to new Common Core State Standards and a parallel pledge to STEM growth. In the licensed, professional arena of the spatial fields of dentistry, engineering, architecture and landscape architecture, etc., courses should be prepared to improve performances in applied tasks as necessary for professional development.

• *Continue to address the research/practice divide.* Though we can describe to people that spatial thinking is actually something with which they are engaged throughout their waking moments and their daily lives (National Research Council 2006; Sinton, Bednarz, Gersmehl, Kolvoord, and Uttal 2013), overall the topic of spatial thinking is still largely one of interest to narrow sector of academics. Because we share a strong conviction that spatial thinking enables people around the world to structure problems, find answers, and express and communicate solutions (National Research Council 2006), it behooves us to raise awareness of spatial thinking to educators, policy makers, and the general public. Families with young children, and the educators who engage with them in different formal and informal learning environments, have a significant opportunity to build spatial literacy among our youth, but this will require a translation of research-based understanding into the practice of learning and living. This is a rich area for applied research and public funding.

References

Alam, B. M., Eckert, J., and Lindquist, P. S. 2012. A reflection on the Ph.D. program in spatially integrated social science at the University of Toledo. *International Journal of Applied Geospatial Research* 3: 72–77.

Aldrich, F., and Sheppard, L. 2000. 'Graphicacy': The fourth 'R'? *Primary Science Review* 64: 8–11.

Anning, A. 1997. Drawing out ideas: Graphicacy and young children. *International Journal of Technology and Design Education* 7: 219–239.

Arnheim, R. 1969. *Visual Thinking.* University of California Press.

Bennett, G. K., Seashore, H. G., and Wesman, A. G. 1956. The differential aptitude tests: An overview. *Personnel and Guidance Journal* 35: 81–91.

Berdie, R. F. 1951. The Differential Aptitude Tests as predictors in engineering training. *Journal of Educational Psychology* 42: 114–123.

Carroll, J. B. 1993. *Human Cognitive Abilities: A Survey of Factor Analytic Studies.* Cambridge University Press.

Clarke, K. 2011. Geography 12, Maps and Spatial Reasoning. Retrieved from http://www.geog.ucsb.edu.

Cutter, S. L., Golledge, R., and Graf, W. L. 2002. The big questions in geography. *Professional Geographer* 54: 305–317.

Downs, R. M., and Stea, D. 1977. *Maps in Minds: Reflections on Cognitive Mapping.* Harper and Row.

Eliot, J., and Czarnolewski, M. 2007. Development of an everyday spatial behavioral questionnaire. *Journal of General Psychology* 134: 361–381.

Eliot, J., and Smith, I. M. 1983. *An International Directory of Spatial Tests.* NFER-Nelson.

e-NET Colorado. 2012. Isn't That Spatial? Analyzing Our World Using Digital Maps and Spatial Thinking. Retrieved from http://onlinelearning.enetcolorado.org.

e-NET Colorado. 2013. Investigations in Spatial Thinking. Retrieved from http://onlinelearning.enetcolorado.org.

Freundschuh, S. M., and Egenhofer, M. J. 1997. Human conceptions of spaces: Implications for geographic information systems. *Transactions in GIS* 2: 361–375.

Gardner, H. 2011. *Frames of Mind: The Theory of Multiple Intelligences*, third edition. Basic Books.

Geography Education National Implementation Project. 1994. *Geography for Life: National Geography Standards*, first edition. National Council for Geographic Education.

Geography Education National Implementation Project. 2012. *Geography for Life: National Geography Standards*, second edition. National Council for Geographic Education.

Golledge, R. G. 2002. The nature of geographic knowledge. *Annals of the Association of American Geographers* 92: 1–14.

Haklay, M., Singleton, A., and Parker, C. 2008. Web mapping 2.0: The neogeography of the GeoWeb. *Geography Compass* 2: 2011–2039.

Hallisey, E. J. 2005. Cartographic visualization: An assessment and epistemological review. *Professional Geographer* 57: 350–364.

Hamlin, A. J., Veurink, N. L., and Sorby, S. A. 2009. Enhancing Visualization Skills-Improving Options aNd Success (EnViSIONS): An overview. In proceedings of 63rd Annual American Society for Engineering Education (ASEE) / Engineering Design Graphics Division (EDGE) Mid-Year Conference, Berkeley.

Hanson, S. 2004. Who are "we"? An important question for geography's future. *Annals of the Association of American Geographers* 94: 715–722.

Hirtle, S. C. 2011. *Geographical Design: Spatial Cognition and Geographical Information Science.* Morgan and Claypool.

Hsi, S., Linn, M. C., and Bell, J. E. 1997. The role of spatial reasoning in engineering and the design of spatial instruction. *Journal of Engineering Education* 86: 151–158.

Hudson-Smith, A., and Crooks, A. 2008. The renaissance of geographic information: Neogeography, gaming and second life. Working paper 142, Centre for Advanced Spatial Analysis, University College London.

Ishikawa, T. 2013. Geospatial thinking and spatial ability: An empirical examination of knowledge and reasoning in geographical science. *Professional Geographer* 65: 636–646.

Jo, I., Bednarz, S. W., and Metoyer, S. 2010. Selecting and designing questions to facilitate spatial thinking. *Geography Teacher* 7: 49–55.

Jones, M. G., Gardner, G., Taylor, A. R., Wiebe, E., and Forrester, J. 2010. Conceptualizing magnification and scale: The roles of spatial visualization and logical thinking. *Research in Science Education* 41: 357–368.

Kerski, J. 2013. A Working Definition of Spatial Thinking. Retrieved from http://blogs.esri.com.

Kim, M., and Bednarz, R. 2013. Effects of a GIS course on self-assessment of spatial habits of mind (SHOM). *Journal of Geography* 112: 165–177.

Lee, J., and Bednarz, R. 2009. Effect of GIS learning on spatial thinking. *Journal of Geography in Higher Education* 33: 183–198.

Lee, J., and Bednarz, R. 2012. Components of spatial thinking: Evidence from a spatial thinking ability test. *Journal of Geography* 111: 15–26.

Martín-Dorta, N., Saorin, J. L., and Contero, M. 2008. Development of a fast remedial course to improve the spatial abilities of engineering students. *Journal of Engineering Education* 97: 505–513.

Montello, D. R. 1993. Scale and multiple psychologies of space. In *Spatial Information Theory: A Theoretical Basis for GIS*, ed. A. U. Frank and I. Campari. Springer.

Montello, D. R., and Raubal, M. 2012. Functions and applications of spatial cognition. In *The APA Handbook of Spatial Cognition*, ed. D. Waller and L. Nadel. American Psychological Association.

Murdoch, S. 2007. *IQ: A Short History of a Failed Idea*. Wiley.

National Research Council. 2006. *Learning to Think Spatially: GIS as a Support System in the K–12 Curriculum*. National Academies Press.

National Science Foundation. n.d. Strategic Plan 2008–2012. Retrieved from http://www.nsf.gov.

Pattison, W. D. 1964. The four traditions of geography. *Journal of Geography* 63: 211–216.

Rana, S., and Joliveau, T. 2009. NeoGeography: An extension of mainstream geography for everyone made by everyone? *Journal of Location Based Services* 3: 75–81.

Richardson, J. T. E. 2011. *Howard Andrew Knox: Pioneer of Intelligence Testing at Ellis Island*. Columbia University Press.

Rudy, M., and Hauck, R. 2008. Spatial cognition support for exploring the design mechanics of building structures. *Journal of Interactive Learning Research* 19: 509–530.

Science Education Research Center. n.d. Spatial Thinking in Geosciences. Retrieved from http://serc.carleton.edu.

Sinton, D. S. 2011. Spatial thinking. In *21st Century Geography: A Reference Handbook*, ed. J. Stoltman. SAGE.

Sinton, D. S., Bednarz, S., Gersmehl, P., Kolvoord, R., and Uttal, D. 2013. *The People's Guide to Spatial Thinking*. National Council for Geographic Education.

Slater, S. J. 2012. Invasion of the cognitive scientists: subverting college astronomy. Paper presented at meeting on Spatial Thinking Across the College Curriculum, Santa Barbara.

Sorby, S. A. 2001. A course in spatial visualization and its impact on the retention of female engineering students. *Journal of Women and Minorities in Science and Engineering* 7: 153–172.

Sorby, S. A. 2011. *Developing Spatial Thinking*. Delmar Cengage Learning.

Sorby, S. A., and Baartmans, B. J. 2000. The development and assessment of a course for enhancing the 3-d spatial visualization skills of first year engineering students. *Journal of Engineering Education* 89: 301–307.

Southwestern College. n.d. Geography 150, Geographic Information Science and Spatial Reasoning. Geography Program. Retrieved from http://www.swccd.edu.

Taaffe, E. J. 1974. The spatial view in context. *Annals of the Association of American Geographers* 64: 1–16.

UCSB Center for Spatial Studies. 2012. Spatial Thinking Across the College Curriculum. Retrieved from http://www.spatial.ucsb.edu.

UCSB Center for Spatial Studies. 2013. Academic Minor in Spatial Studies. Retrieved from http://spatial.ucsb.edu.

University of Redlands. 2013. Spatial Literacy Program. Retrieved from http://www.redlands.edu.

Wilmot, P. D. 1999. Graphicacy as a form of communication. *South African Geographical Journal* 81: 91–95.

Yau, N. 2011. *Visualize This: The Flowing Data Guide to Design, Visualization, and Statistics*. Wiley.

12 Concepts and Principles for Spatial Literacy

Karl Grossner and Donald G. Janelle

Spatial thinking capability is strongly correlated with educational and professional performance in science, technology, engineering, and mathematics (STEM) fields (Shea, Lubinski, and Benbow 2001; Uttal and Cohen 2012; Wai, Lubinski, and Benbow 2009; Webb, Lubinski, and Benbow 2007), but the systematic and integrative instruction of spatial concepts, principles, and reasoning skills is not an explicit goal in K–12 or college curricula. Spatiality also is ubiquitous in many humanities fields, including history and fine arts. Although educators do set standards for verbal literacy, numeracy, and analytical reasoning, there has been no comparable articulation of what it means to be spatially literate. That said, the 2006 National Research Council report *Learning to Think Spatially* did outline high-level "components of spatial literacy" (NRC 2006, pp. 16–20) that are a useful starting point. To paraphrase: A spatially literate person has (1) good knowledge of fundamental spatial concepts, (2) "spatial ways of thinking and acting"—that is, the "habit of mind" to think spatially and to apply spatial methodologies to solve problems, and (3) proficiency in the use of spatial tools and technologies. From this we derive a concise working definition of spatial literacy for this chapter: an understanding of fundamental spatial concepts and principles and the capability to recognize their appropriate application in answering scientific, engineering, and humanistic questions, aided by spatial technologies.

This chapter primarily addresses spatial conceptual knowledge. After summarizing our recent efforts to enumerate spatial concepts, we outline a prospective college-level course that entails applications of spatial concepts and related principles. Although many spatial concepts and principles are highly general, they are typically specialized distinctively in individual disciplines. Important complementary studies of such specializations are being undertaken by cognitive psychologists and education researchers working with interested professionals from several fields—most notably the geosciences, geography, and chemistry (Hegarty, Stieff, and Dixon 2013; Jo and Bednarz 2009; Manduca and Kastens 2012)—a practice we term *discipline-diving*. In this chapter, drawing on discipline-specific concepts and principles (the likely pragmatic source for defining spatial learning objectives for course modules and lesson plans), we frame an initial course outline to enhance spatial literacy across the undergraduate curriculum.

Given the reality of finite "curricular space," we recognize the difficulties of introducing a new course at any educational level. Correspondingly, the proposed course and related discussion are intended to raise awareness of spatial literacy among educators; it is a thought experiment that presents an answer to the question "What should a spatially literate person know?" In instances where an entirely new course or course module is not feasible, the outline may suggest the insertion of simple examples that expand on concepts and on the articulation of problems to contribute spatial perspectives that enhance parts of existing courses. (See Hegarty et al. 2013.)

Perhaps it is the ubiquity of spatiality that prevents us from viewing spatial reasoning as a distinct practice, as we do mathematics, reading, and writing. Yet the 2006 NRC report presents the case for regarding spatial thinking as a distinct complement to the three Rs. (See Hegarty 2010 for a discussion of "spatial intelligence.") The report documents how we think *in* space, *about* space, and *with* space. We think *in* space as we navigate through buildings and cityscapes, play sports, dance, or organize storage shelves. We think *about* space when analyzing the structure, function, motion, and distribution of things in the world, at scales from nano to cosmic—whether seeking scientific explanations for natural phenomena or designing a tool, a building, or a dam. We think *with* space when we create or interpret diagrams and maps, or reason by spatial metaphor—a powerful and commonplace cognitive strategy (Lakoff and Johnson 1980).

Thinking in, thinking about, and thinking with space are expressed differently depending on the conceptual foundations and methodologies associated with disciplines and professional pursuits. General spatial literacy does not entail the specialized spatial approaches and levels of expertise required for careers as surgeons, geologists, architects, or fighter pilots. We are not all gifted writers or mathematicians, but nearly everyone can become sufficiently proficient at reading, writing, and manipulating numbers to be an informed and fulfilled citizen. Similarly, we maintain that general spatial literacy is within reach of nearly everyone, will enhance skills for problem solving in careers and in daily life, and should be a goal of basic education.

Locating Spatial Concepts

One of the foundations of spatial literacy is the ability to reason with and to apply spatial concepts. Our efforts in nurturing such capabilities have focused on the support of spatial teaching and learning at the college level. In the sections that follow, we first describe research initiatives to identify the spatial concepts used in different fields (Grossner 2012), then present a preliminary framework for organizing those concepts, and finally describe the development of a semi-automated mapping of concepts to enable the discovery of teaching resources cataloged in the National Science Digital Library.

Mining existing spatial taxonomies

We examined twenty articles and books in which authors from eight disciplines discuss the centrality of spatial thinking in their fields and attempt to delineate fundamental spatial concepts (table 12.1). Some of these include an explicit taxonomy or schema of spatial concepts. For other authors and disciplines, important spatial concepts and concept relationships are extracted through content analysis of the text and section headings. The dominance of geography and psychology in the listing reflects disciplinary interests in, respectively, space as a primary dimension of analysis, and concepts, thinking and learning more generally. Although far less attention is paid to the role of spatial thinking in the literature of other

Table 12.1
Source documents on spatial concepts used in various disciplines.

Discipline	Source documents
Architecture and urban planning	Alexander 2004; Lynch 1984
Earth science	Kastens and Ishikawa 2006
Geography	DiBiase et al. 2008; Gersmehl 2005; Gersmehl and Gersmehl 2007; Golledge 1995; Golledge et al. 2008; Kaufman 2004; Marsh et al. 2007; de Smith et al. 2008; Nystuen 1963; O'Sullivan and Unwin 2002
Mathematics	Battista 2007
Linguistics	Johnson 1987
Psychology	Newcombe and Huttenlocher 2000; Piaget and Inhelder 1967; Tversky 2005
Science education	Mathewson 2005
Social science	Janelle and Goodchild 2011

Table 12.2
Categorized spatial concepts in TeachSpatial lexicon.

Category	Spatial concepts
Spatial structures	object, field, surface, network, region, area, place, neighborhood, landscape, zone, landmark, atom, cell, molecule, nucleus, conduit, coil
Spatial properties	composition, structure, size, shape, texture, mass, boundary, part, feature, center, layer, stratum
Space-time Context	space, space-time, location, environment, setting, site, situation, global, local, reference frame
Position	position, distance, direction, orientation
Spatial dynamics	motion, movement, dispersion, diffusion, transfer, transport, migration, explore, formation, destruction, grow, expand, diminish, merge, split, trajectory, wave, route, cycle, force, attract, repel, gravity, radiation, convection, absorb, release, erosion, eruption, flow, navigation, deformation
Spatial relations	adjacency, proximity, centrality, distribution, density, container, external, internal, spatial hierarchy, level, order, spatial organization, pattern, proportion, straight, symmetry, chirality, alignment, gradient
Spatial interaction	connection, link, bond, interaction, system, coordination, ecosystem
Spatial transformations	scale, rotation, projection, spatial integration, spatial interpolation
Representation	map, diagram, graph, cognitive map, representation, overlay, path, grid, coordinates, point, line, polygon, polyhedron, route perspective, survey perspective
Spatial principles	spatial autocorrelation, spatial heterogeneity, spatial association, distance decay, access, availability, isotropy, congruence

fields, this study (described more fully at teachspatial.org) seeks to make explicit their reliance on spatial principles and methodologies.

Although 185 concept terms were harvested from the sources listed in table 12.1, subsequent analysis pared the listing to 129 terms through removal of near-synonyms and redundancies. In turn, we grouped the terms into ten general categories (table 12.2). The 129 terms differ significantly with respect to complexity or level of abstraction and many have multiple definitions that often reflect disciplinary traditions. Furthermore, the positioning of terms within more general categories (although generally intuitively apparent) faces the inevitable ambiguity of terms that fit within multiple categories, leading to philosophical questions about the very nature of concepts. Two survey volumes on the topic (Margolis and

Laurence 1999; Murphy 2002) show that research has been almost universally limited to fairly simple exemplars—concepts as classes of things in the world, like birds and chairs—not especially helpful for more complex relationships associated with spatial concepts such as *neighborhood, connection,* and *structure.*

Measuring spatiality

We have adopted an extensional notion of what a concept is—mental constructs representing material and non-material entities, properties, and processes in the world, about which we communicate with language. Thus, concepts are comprised in part by the words and gestures used to communicate their intended meaning. For two perspectives on spatial gestures see the chapters by Malaia and Waller and the one by Atit, Shipley, and Tikoff.

In an experimental study, Grossner and Montello (2010) undertook to confirm whether the presence of spatial terms in scientific texts corresponded with human judgments of spatiality. First, they built a lexicon of 120 spatial terms from three sources: a distillation of the 185-term list mentioned above, salient terms in the topical headings of two spatial analysis textbooks, and a glossary of topological terms. They then assembled a corpus of 195,000 titles and abstracts of the National Science Foundation grant awards made by all NSF directorates and divisions between 1989 and 2009. A measure of "spatial-term density" for each award was generated using a computer program written to count occurrences of each term in each abstract document and, then, divide the sum of those counts by the number of words in the abstract. Per-document spatial-term-density values ranged from 0.00 to 0.61. For comparison with "'standard English,'" the same lexicon was used to rate the spatiality of other corpora, including 2,615 Wikipedia "featured" articles, the Academic subset of the Corpus of Contemporary American English (COCA), and course descriptions from seven schools within a major university (UNIV). The results are summarized in figure 12.1.

To help ground the spatial-term-density measure, Grossner and Montello conducted a survey that asked participants to rate the spatiality of twenty NSF abstracts, chosen to be representative of divisions across all eight directorates. The seventy respondents represented a sampling frame of (a) a university geography department's graduate students, faculty, and research staff, (b) individuals registered on the teachspatial.org website, and (c) members of the Spatial Intelligence and Learning Center's spatial network. This group is considered expert relative to the general population.

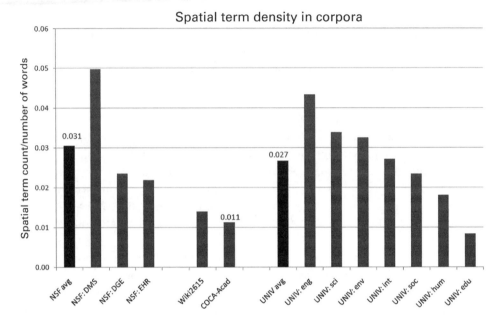

Figure 12.1
Spatial-term density in various corpora.

There was a rank correlation of 0.73 between the term-density measure and human judgments about the spatiality of the twenty abstracts. These results confirmed the value of using this method to search for spatiality in other texts, such as K–12 teaching standards and university course descriptions.

Locating spatial concepts in K–12 science standards

The next step in this investigation was to examine K–12 science teaching content standards to learn what spatial conceptual knowledge the average new college freshman might be expected to have. We convened a panel of eight "spatial experts" from the fields of science education, cognitive psychology, geography, and mathematics, and asked them to identify spatial concept terms present in each of the 150 National Science Education Standards for the subject areas of Physical, Life, and Earth and Space Sciences (NRC 1996), then subjectively rate each standard for its spatiality. We then rated the agreement among the eight spatial experts.

Each of the 150 NSES content standards was examined by four to six of the panel's experts and given a "spatiality rating" between 0 and 100. Averaged values indicated that Life Science was the least spatial of the three domains; that, although physics was seen as the most spatial, agreement among the experts varied more than for life and earth sciences; and that agreement among experts was greatest for standards judged as "very spatial" and "not very spatial."

In reading the NSES content standards, panelists highlighted all terms in the text that they judged to be spatial. Almost all of the spatial concept terms from table 12.2 were tagged when encountered, but many other terms were also deemed markers for spatial conceptual content in the standards—examples include 'earth', 'absorption', 'proportion', 'erosion', and 'coordination'. After rating and tagging standards, the group was asked what factors led to considering a standard as highly spatial. The following responses indicate the range of considerations. A standard can be considered highly spatial if

- spatial reasoning methods are essential to understanding it,
- it concerns relationships among objects either directly involving or bringing to mind distance, hierarchies, networks, structure (e.g., containment, or parts), or patterns,
- it concerns observable components for which we can develop either mental or physical (graphic) spatial imagery,
- entities involved have measurable extension (i.e., size, shape, or geometric characteristics),
- it involves changes of distance, or clumping vs. separation along a gradient,
- it concerns movement or motion (e.g., coming together, going/growing apart),
- it concerns attraction and force,

and

- it may be readily represented in terms of points, lines, areas, and trajectories.

The expert participants in this exercise noticed that certain highly spatial terms, such as 'region' and 'network', were missing. This prompted a similar search of the Geography for Life: National Geography Standards (Geography Education Standards Project 1994), in which region and network did appear, along with many other distinctive terms. All terms occurring in three or more standards were cross-referenced in a discipline interaction matrix (figure 12.2). Spatial terms (lexical concepts) unique to a single domain of science appear along the diagonal; terms found in multiple subject areas appear in the remaining upper cells, with counts in parentheses. The matrix should be instructive as we seek to find conceptual

B - Physical	C - Life	D - Earth and space	Geography
object (10), atom (7), bond (7), wave (7), nucleus (6), emission (5), direction (4), mass (4), path (4), line (3), measurement (3), order (3), proportion (3), straight (3), wavelength (3)	motion (17, 3), interaction (8, 7), composition (7, 5), size (7, 5), scale (6, 4), movement (5, 4), molecule (4, 7), structure (3, 8), absorption (3, 3)	motion (17, 13), interaction (8, 3), composition (7, 6), force (11, 5), transfer (6, 3), movement (5, 12), position (5, 3), gravity (3, 3)	interaction (8, 7), distance (7, 5), size (7, 4), structure (3, 9)
	behavior (5), cell (5), external (4), storage (4), availability (3), coordination (3), hierarchy (3), level (3), organization (3), release (3), synthesis (3), unit (3)	containment (7, 3), interaction (7, 3), internal (7, 3), growth (6, 3), formation (3, 8), motion (3, 13)	environment (19, 15), structure (8, 9), interaction (7, 7), ecosystem (7, 5), containment (7, 4), transport (3, 8)
		surface (8), cycle (6), plate (5), building (3), change (3), convection (3), earth (3), eruption (3), layer (3), matter (3), solid (3), system (3), volcano (3), weathering (3)	location (5, 14), containment (3, 4), erosion (3, 4), interaction (3, 7)
			region (29), area (20), pattern (13), place (12), map (11), migration (10), distribution (9), settlement (9), spatial organization (8), center (7), access (6), connection (6), density (6), feature (6), exploration (5), neighborhood (5), network (5), route (5), site (5), boundary (4), expansion (4), global (4), landscape (4), local (4), proximity (4), shape (4), space (4), zone (4)
B - Physical	**C - Life**	**D - Earth and space**	**Geography**

Figure 12.2

Spatial terms in science domains. Terms along the diagonal were tagged only in standards for that topic area. Terms in bold were tagged in standards for three of the four topic areas, with the exception of 'interaction' (the only term tagged in all four). Numbers in parentheses on axes are counts of standards having the tagged term. Only terms appearing in three or more standards are displayed.

threads between disciplines, but it also highlights the specialization of concepts distinct to specific subject areas.

Mapping concepts to teaching resources

A lexicon of spatial terms derived from the three studies referenced above aided the development of teaching resource collections for the National Science Digital Library, available within the NSDL master catalog at http://nsdl.org and published at the TeachSpatial website, http://teachspatial.org. For the annotations collection, a computer script ran 69 queries (sets of spatial terms from the 69 NSES grade 9–12 content standards) eight times each, once for each of the NSDL "pathway" subject domains (Chemistry, Geoscience, Life Science, Physics, Mathematics, Engineering, Social Sciences, and Space Science). The 3,000 distinct records returned were then culled to produce a new NSDL TeachSpatial collection of 2,476 teaching resources that align with one or more of the science content standards. We added 80 additional spatial learning resources from the Center for Spatial Studies at the University of California at Santa Barbara.

In the Resource Browser section of the TeachSpatial website, users can select any of the 129 terms in table 12.2 and get a list of links to free teaching resources relevant to that concept, in most cases from multiple science domains or disciplines. For example, a query for the term 'surface' returns four records with differing perspectives: those of earth science (ocean surface currents), mathematics (Archimedes' Law of Floating Bodies), biology (microbe behavior on surfaces), and physics (double curvature minimal surfaces in tensile structures). TeachSpatial provides a resource for instructors to add spatial content to existing courses in specific disciplines or, if so emboldened, to tap resources from several disciplines to highlight possible interdisciplinary transfer of spatial concepts in a more general course on spatial thinking.

Concept-Based Principles for a Course in Spatiality

All the work described thus far was originally motivated by the question "If there were a general course in spatial thinking at the undergraduate level, what would it cover?" To help answer this question, we identified the spatial concepts considered fundamental in a number of fields and found that most are meaningful in other, often disparate, fields. We then sought to learn which of the spatial concepts, principles, and skills appearing in K–12 curricula one could reasonably expect incoming college freshmen to be conversant with. However, while one can suggest that *scale* is a fundamental spatial concept for many fields, and should be well under-stood—*what is there about* scale that spatially literate people should know? Are there basic axioms or principles that concern scale? What scale-related tasks should they be able to perform? In addressing such questions, one can simultaneously invoke multiple concepts, joined through general spatial principles that span multiple fields. Thus, general concepts are building blocks for general principles and, in most cases, both principles and their component concepts have discipline-specific variation in meaning or perspective.

We find it most useful at this stage to organize fundamental spatial concepts and principles into several categories in a speculative course outline. We asked ourselves what conceptual content would lead to spatially literate students. This is a very different goal than achieving sufficient mastery in specialized spatial reasoning and computational methods to (for example) analyze landforms for their geological history, differentiate similar molecules from diagrams, or perform surgery. This high-level course would be foundational and motivational, diverse, even fun.

Such a course might best be co-taught—or at least co-designed—by a physicist, an astronomer, a biologist, a geologist, a geographer, a historian, a professor of literature, a cognitive psychologist, and an artist (or a similar combination). In lieu of such a committee, we will speculate on the contents of a course outline that such a group might produce. To do this, we will leap back and forth between spatial concepts such as those listed earlier and spatial principles—defined here as precepts, axioms, laws, or law-like statements underlying the practice of many diverse professions. As geographers, we admit to having only surface knowledge in most of these fields, along with a potential bias toward the geographic scales of phenomena. Nonetheless, we are intent on having the breadth of this imagined course span all fields for which "spatial is special" in some way.

A Course Outline: "Spatial Reasoning Across Disciplines"

Week 1: Space, time, and place
There are multiple ways to conceive, represent, and analyze space and spatiality.

Space and space-time
According to the online Oxford English Dictionary, the term 'space' implies "continuous, unbounded, or unlimited extent in every direction, without reference to any matter that may be present ... an attribute of the universe,

describable mathematically." This corresponds to the naive conception of three-dimensional space as the void containing objects in the universe, or some portion thereof. The concept of *space-time*, an important theoretical construct in physics, is more difficult: time and space fused in a four-dimensional continuum within which all worldly phenomena exist, in a sense, as events.

Space and place

Space and place are sometimes used interchangeably, but more often differentiated, with space as an abstract construct described geometrically and place as "experienced space"—a subjective mental construction, possibly shared, and exemplified by "sense of place," a common phrase of uncertain origin. (See Tuan 1977.) The distinction becomes clear if you ask residents of a city to describe it verbally or to draw a map of it. Representations will differ, often radically. The area bounding the physical city and the position of things within it are spatial—that is, they have spatial extension and can be described geometrically. Alternatively, the distinctive memories of human experience in such spaces constitute places, such as Hemingway's Havana or the neighborhood of one's youth.

Location and position

Location is absolute, but descriptions of location are necessarily relative. We cannot say where something is (its position) without referring either to some other thing or to an arbitrary reference grid of some kind. Earth locations are normally described with coordinate points related to an estimated earth center. We also use qualitative terms of connectedness and distance to describe location in relation to other things. Topological terms such as 'adjacent', 'contains', 'overlaps', 'above', and 'north of' are amenable to formal definition; terms for qualitative metrics, such as 'near' and 'far', are highly contextual and less so.

Week 2: The nature of spatial thinking

Humans think in space, about space, and with space. Cognitive scientists have studied spatial thinking from at least three perspectives, each relevant for one or more of those contexts: spatial ability, acquired spatial reasoning skills, and use of spatial metaphor. We think in space as we maneuver through the world of everyday tasks and wayfinding, and about space as we reason about and analyze spatial configurations of natural phenomena. In both cases we draw upon spatial abilities such as mental imagery and spatial memory for making mental representations and for reasoning about alternative perspectives, cross-sections through objects, and transformations of material and objects over time—often aided by external representations, like maps, diagrams, and animations. There are individual and gender differences in such abilities (Hegarty and Waller 2006), but research is showing that performance at any level can be improved through instruction and practice (Uttal and Cohen 2012).

Spatial metaphor has been shown to be an essential reasoning strategy for non-spatial phenomena (Lakoff and Johnson 1980), i.e., thinking *with* space. Two commonplace examples of such spatialization are the "distance-similarity metaphor" (Montello, Fabrikant, Ruocco, and Middleton 2003) and "magnitude as size," as seen in concept maps, other network or graph representations, and statistical charts.

Cognitive maps and mental models
The term 'cognitive map' has been used in several senses. As introduced by Tolman (1948), it refers to the mental representations of the environment that humans and other animals will create and maintain, and which are consulted routinely in navigating around the house (or a maze), or through the town (or cage) they live in. The concept has been extended considerably in spatial and non-spatial ways—e.g., by environmental geographers studying the role of various cognitive processes in humans' mental models of space and place (Downs and Stea 1977) and as spatialized mental models of relations between diverse concepts.

Week 3: Spatial is special
There are several interwoven spatial principles that are fundamental and far-reaching across many scientific, engineering, and design fields. Their generality lies at the heart of why "spatial is special." A spatially literate person is familiar with the conceptual content of the principles and the fact of their generality.

Pattern and process; form and function
Kim Kastens, one of the experts who rated the spatiality of NSES content standards in the study by Grossner and Montello (2010), identified what she referred to as "spatial principle zero":

A spatially literate person understands that the form, locations, and relative position of things in the universe contain meaning about the causes and consequences of their structure or arrangement, and should be able to provide examples from more than one field.

The spatial form of natural objects (their size, shape, structure, orientation, texture), at every scale, is strongly related to underlying processes of their creation and, particularly in the case of biological objects, to function. The form of earth features such as mountains, glaciers, and watersheds follow from processes we understand in large part by studying the spatial configuration and structure of their products. The composition and structure of organic and inorganic molecules are also functional, in that chemical processes both depend upon and produce them. The configuration of the solar system is the product of ongoing processes, but it seems a stretch to say they are functional. In a rather different sense, we say that cells, tree roots, thumbs, wings, and brains have any number of functions. Issues of purpose in these cases are often controversial, particularly outside scientific circles.

Human purpose plays an enormous role in the design of artifacts at all scales, from nano-scale robots to massive earthworks. With respect to chemical compounds, tools, vehicles, clothing, buildings, and cities, form largely follows function. Nevertheless, we like things that both work well and are pleasing to look at, so aesthetics of form can play an important role. Function is far less relevant to works of artistic expression, but aspects of spatiality are critical elements in the design of all artifacts, whether functional, purely artistic, or somewhere in between. Many associated concept terms hold meaning in other fields. For example, although *symmetry*, *perspective*, and *reference frames* are central to urban design, architecture, and most fine arts, symmetry and its close cousin *chirality* are also important for understanding molecular structure. *Perspective* and *reference frames* are central aspects of spatial cognition studied by cognitive psychologists.

Spatial context matters—at all scales, in all disciplines. Natural phenomena—things and happenings—are significantly affected by their surroundings (i.e., their environment or setting). This includes neighboring things and any networks or ecosystems they are part of.

What you can know depends upon where you or your sensors are and what you can perceive. Observations and analyses of phenomena occur within a reference frame. In very general terms this refers to situational and observational context: the spatial, temporal, and thematic bounds for what is being considered, along with associated measurement or classification systems. Reference frames can be global or local in absolute or relative terms, and resolution of representations can vary from fine to coarse (i.e., more or less generalized). As such, they are closely tied to concepts of *scale* and *granularity*. In physics, the motion of objects of interest and observers are essential determinants. In spatial analyses of social and natural phenomena at geographic scales, the bounds of a study area and areal divisions within it are critical factors influencing results and interpretations. Related concepts from the visual arts include *field of view* and *perspective*.

Near things tend to be more similar than distant things. Attributes of things that are near each other tend to be more similar than attributes of things that are far apart; such similarity leads to the identification of *clusters, regions,* and *neighborhoods*. This is a generalization of Tobler's First Law of Geography, which asserts this for scales associated with geographical space. Gravity models derived from Newton's Law have been applied in many fields (particularly in social science). Thus, the level of interaction between entities at two locations is a function of their mass (defined physically or otherwise) and declines in inverse proportion to some function of the distance between them.

The fallacy of independent observations

A spatially literate person will be aware that assumptions of independence for observational data in statistical studies are in many cases a fallacy. Whereas proximity is often an explanatory factor, many scientific models do not make location an explicit parameter. Hence, in cases where spatial association and dependence are factors but have not been modeled, statistical analyses may be flawed.

Spatial indexing aids knowledge discovery. To the extent that we georeference objects of interest in library and archive catalogs and in Web-accessible documents, adding spatial metadata, particularly for geographic locations, enables the discovery of spatial and spatial-temporal patterns that may be critical to understanding natural and social processes.

Week 4: Representation, part I—Size, scale, and error

Although every material thing has an absolute size in space, representations of its extent are relative to an ordered reference standard such as the metric scale of length. When something is seen as large or small, it is in relation to another thing or to a particular scale. A small elephant dwarfs the largest dog. On the scale of star size, our sun is small.

Graphic representations of things and designs are often made "to scale"—proportional to their actual size, faithfully rendering the relative sizes of their components. Representation scales are naturally related to the size of human beings. Representations can be at a smaller scale to visualize the entirety of something too large to see all at once, such as a house, a mountain, or a galaxy. Many realms of phenomena cannot be perceived directly without the use of tools and technology, such as microscopes, telescopes, and radiometers. In this case large-scale representations enable us to visualize things like the parts of a watch or a molecule with greater detail than is possible at their actual size.

Scientific and engineering disciplines are divided to some extent by scale. Although it is an oversimplification, we say the atomic and sub-atomic scales are the domain of physics; molecular scales the domain of chemistry, cosmic scales that of astronomy, and so on. The work of architects, planners, and environmental and social scientists involves scales associated with environmental and geographic space (Montello 1993).

Scale is an important consideration in art and in all design professions, and is linked to the concept of balance. Elements that are relatively large in one's field of view are said to have more weight, figuratively speaking, than smaller elements. Achieving a balance of graphical weight is often desirable, although deliberately unbalanced arrangements can be used to purposeful artistic effect too.

Many natural phenomena have a fractal nature (Mandelbrot 1983). That is, their structure is self-similar at any scale of observation. We see this when viewing higher and higher magnifications of crystals, for example. Clouds, river networks, and coastlines are said to have fractal qualities, though apparently this is only approximately true.

All representations are necessarily abstractions and tend to generalize away detail, making them the source not only of insight, but also error and uncertainty. This is true of internal representations (mental imagery, cognitive maps, and so forth) as well as graphical representations.

For graphical representations, greater resolution can mitigate that effect. The more pixels, points, or lines rendered per square centimeter of media (for screens, print, and film respectively), the higher the resolution and the greater the potential accuracy. For satellite imagery, a single point of data can represent an area of earth surface corresponding to anywhere between a few square centimeters and 1,000 square meters.

Week 5: Representation, part II—Objects and fields

Objects can be viewed as discretizations of material phenomena (e.g., storms, ancient figurines). Depending on the scales of observation, representation, and analysis, natural phenomena can be viewed variously as continuous fields, as discrete objects, or both. Fields represent values of some attribute for every point in a region of space-time, and are most useful for studying essentially continuous phenomena. For example, the atmosphere has (potentially) a different temperature at every point in space (or space-time). Representation choices are pragmatic, in part a function of desired resolution or granularity. For example, thunderstorms can be represented as continuous fields or as discrete objects having trajectories. But, at some scale, the boundary between storm and non-storm is difficult to discern. Viewed at larger scales, many continuous phenomena are composed of discrete objects (the water droplets and oxygen molecules of a storm), and we often discretize regions of continuous phenomena and material substances having similar attribute values as objects of study (thunderstorms). Some archeological finds are clumps of material whose identity as intentionally fabricated objects may be contestable.

Week 6: Spatial structure, part I—Clusters and regions

One goal of scientific analysis is the discovery of spatial structure—instances of identifiable patterns that can be classified as objects in their own right and compared. One such structure is the *cluster*, the identification of which can depend upon many factors: the original hypothesis, the scale of analysis and reference frame, theory-driven categorical attributes and threshold values for them, and the type and quality of measurement instruments, to name a few. We discover and study clusters of things of every conceivable scale, including nanoparticles, cell, diseases, people, and stars.

Another highly general spatial structure is the *region*. Like clusters, regions exist in nature, but their identification likewise depends upon subjective definitional criteria in many cases. Regions can be purely spatial (anterior, northern, central) or be defined as areas having similar values for one or more attributes (common activity, geology, belief, demographics, etc.). That is, they are human-created objects of analysis. The concept of region is primarily associated with geography and astrophysics, but a recent scan of the Corpus of Contemporary American English for terms completing the phrase "region of the ___" yielded 'gene', 'cell', 'sky', 'ship', 'neck', 'bat', 'brain', 'rotor', and 'amygdala' in addition to the expected 'country' and 'world'. This suggest that the term 'region' is often applied to approximate locations on or within something, with no precise boundary implied.

Week 7: Spatial structure, part II—Networks, connection, and interaction

Networks exist throughout nature (e.g., watersheds, circulatory systems, proteins, lightning, neurons), they are the essential structure of many human artifacts (e.g., transport, utilities infrastructure), and they are an invaluable method of representing connectivity and interaction of all

Figure 12.3
The globular star cluster Messier 69. Credit: NASA/STScI/WikiSky.

kinds. Network science is an increasingly important interdisciplinary field, with a formal mathematical foundation in graph theory. A spatially literate person will be familiar with the basic principles of networks and graphs, and will recognize network structures in science, engineering, and social behavior, and in the global spatial interactions of the highly connected twenty-first-century world. Networks are composed of nodes and the links between them. Nodes can be any material or non-material thing—a city, a person, a concept. They can be hierarchically ordered in multiple ways, according to a magnitude derived either from intrinsic properties or from network measures like connectedness (degree) or centrality. Links can be any material or non-material connection or association between nodes. They can be directed, undirected, or mixed, and have a magnitude (weight) derived from potential or actual flows or interaction on them. Graphs are the mathematical expressions of network structure, and many descriptive terms and measures are used interchangeably for both graphs and networks. Graphs can be represented as matrices of numbers and as node-link diagrams.

Week 8: Spatial dynamics

The processes that produce spatial patterns are dynamic; they occur over time whether or not analyses focus on or reflect that fact. A significant proportion of the phenomena we observe, measure, and analyze in seeking explanation concerns spatial change: change of position, form, orientation, and spatial identity (e.g., composition in parts, splitting, and merging). The same holds true for many forms of humanistic inquiry and expression, in history and the fine arts for example.

Concepts in spatial dynamics are relevant in many fields and at most scales. Most have precise meanings in physics and chemistry, and alternate but similar or metaphorical meanings in other fields. For example, in physics 'diffusion' refers to a random walk of particles in a heat exchange process where a high concentration of a finite number of particles spread throughout a solution. In other fields, diffusion can refer to the spread of a concept or practice from one or more locations to many more. Meanings of 'migration' are largely consistent between disciplines. In the sciences, 'flow' refers to the continuous movement of matter (normally fluids) in a stream-like fashion; it is also used metaphorically—and effectively—to refer to non-material things (such as ideas), and to non-fluids (such as currency in trade activity).

Week 9: Spatialization

Spatialization is the use of spatial concepts and their linguistic and graphical representations to reason and communicate about non-spatial concepts. Lakoff and Johnson (1980, p. 17) have demonstrated the pervasiveness of spatial metaphors in the English language, and assert that "most of our fundamental concepts are organized in terms of one or more spatialization metaphors." A few important examples include similarity as distance; time as distance; associations of any kind in topological terms (adjacent, overlapping, containment, connection); and magnitude of any type or by any measure, as size. A spatially literate person will recognize the practice of spatialization in information visualizations, including Venn diagrams, flow charts, concept maps, scatter plots, line and bar graphs, and network diagrams.

Week 10: Critical spatial thinking and analysis with representations

A spatially literate person is proficient at critically interpreting the most common forms of graphical representation of spatial data at all scales: maps, plans, and diagrams. They are also able to read and critically evaluate graphical spatializations of non-spatial information, from the scatter plots, line graphs, and bar charts used for visualizing statistical data, to the network diagrams describing the relationships between people or concepts, or the flow charts depicting dynamic procedures and processes. Critical interpretation is informed in both cases by many of the principles and concepts discussed earlier—particularly in Week 4—concerning scale, generalization, and accuracy. Interpretation must also be informed by an awareness of the subjective nature of data selection, the limitations of spatial tools, and the underlying assumptions of descriptive and predictive models.

A spatially literate person will also be able to understand and use spatial language for conveying relationships of proximity, connectivity, and containment.

Discussion and Conclusions

We have described a multi-year, multi-phase research effort motivated by a belief in the value of making both the importance and breadth of spatial concepts, reasoning, and skills more explicit at the lower-division college level. We identified spatial concepts and principles found in teaching standards, course content, and research investigations across a variety of fields within the physical and social sciences, design disciplines, and, to a lesser extent, the arts and humanities. Among the results of that work are the TeachSpatial Web portal for spatial teaching and learning resources (http://teachspatial.org) and the establishment of a minor in Spatial Studies at the University of California at Santa Barbara.

In this chapter, we identified sets of spatial concepts and principles that are both fundamental and trans-disciplinary. Recognizing that most spatial concepts and principles have discipline-specific applications and perspectives, we organized them within an outline for a prospective "course for spatial literacy." The course is aimed at college freshmen, although we anticipate that this work may also be useful for developers of K–12 curricula. By beginning the enumeration of a set of spatial concepts, principles, and skills that we should expect college freshmen to have some proficiency in, we hope to encourage incremental steps toward making a "spatial thread" within existing K–12 content standards more explicit, thereby reducing the need for spatial remediation at the college level. Spatial literacy offers a pathway to informed problem solving in a broad range of human endeavors; it is within reach of nearly everyone, and it should be a goal of basic education.

Acknowledgments

We thank Sarah Battersby, Bill Jacob, Kim Kastens, Nora Newcombe, Diana Sinton, and Lisa Weckbacher, who, along with us, participated as panelists in locating spatial concepts in K–12 science standards; Daniel Montello, who contributed with Karl Grossner to the measurement of spatiality in NSF award abstracts; Karen Doehner, Guylene Gadal, and Michael Goodchild, who supported the TeachSpatial project through the Center for Spatial Studies at UCSB; and the National Science Foundation (NSF DUE 1043777) for funding the NSDL Pathways small grant for "TeachSpatial: A Portal to Instructional Resources on Spatial Concepts for STEM Education."

References

Alexander, C. 2004. *The Nature of Order,* book 1: *The Phenomenon of Life.* Routledge.

Battista, M. T. 2007. The development of geometric and spatial thinking. In *Second Handbook of Research on Mathematics Teaching and Learning,* ed. F. K. Lester Jr. Information Age.

de Smith, M. J., Goodchild, M. F., and Longley, P. A. 2008. *Geospatial Analysis: A Comprehensive Guide to Principles, Techniques, and Software Tools,* second edition. Troubador.

DiBiase, D., DeMers, M., Johnson, A., Kemp, K., Luck, A. T., Plewe, B., et al., eds. 2008. *Geographic Information Science and Technology Body of Knowledge.* Association of American Geographers.

Downs, R. M., and Stea, D. 1977. *Maps in Minds: Reflections on Cognitive Mapping.* Harper and Row.

Geography Education Standards Project. 1994. *Geography for Life: National Geography Standards 1994.* National Geographic Research and Exploration.

Gersmehl, P. J. 2005. *Teaching Geography.* Guilford.

Gersmehl, P. J., and Gersmehl, C. A. 2007. Spatial thinking by young children: Neurologic evidence for early development and "educability." *Journal of Geography* 106: 181–191.

Golledge, R. G. 1995. Primitives of spatial knowledge. In *Cognitive Aspects of Human-Computer Interaction for Geographic Information Systems*, ed. T. L. Nyerges, D. M. Mark, R. Laurini, and M. J. Egenhofer. Kluwer.

Golledge, R. G., Marsh, M., and Battersby, S. E. 2008. Matching geographical concepts with geographic educational needs. *Geographical Research* 46: 85–98.

Grossner, K. 2012. Finding the spatial in order to teach it. In *Earth and Mind II: A Synthesis of Research on Thinking and Learning in the Geosciences*, ed. K. A. Kastens and C. A. Manduca. Volume 486, Geological Society of America Special Papers.

Grossner, K., and Montello, D. R. 2010. Locating and measuring spatial thinking in text corpora. Downloaded from http://kgeographer.com.

Hegarty, M. 2010. Components of spatial intelligence. In *The Psychology of Learning And Motivation*, volume 52, ed. B. H. Ross. Academic Press.

Hegarty, M., Newcombe, N. S., Goodchild, M. F., Janelle, D. G., Shipley, T. F., and Sinton, D. 2013. Spatial Thinking Across the College Curriculum: Specialist Meeting Final Report. Downloaded from http://www.spatial.ucsb.edu.

Hegarty, M., Stieff, M., and Dixon, B. L. 2013. Cognitive change in mental models with experience in the domain of organic chemistry. *Journal of Cognitive Psychology* 25: 220–228.

Hegarty, M., and Waller, D. 2006. Individual differences in spatial abilities. In *Handbook of Visuospatial Thinking*, ed. P. Shah and A. Miyake. Cambridge University Press.

Janelle, D. G., and Goodchild, M. F. 2011. Concepts, principles, tools, and challenges in spatially integrated social science. In *The SAGE Handbook of GIS and Society*, ed. T. L. Nyerges, R. McMaster, and H. Couclelis. SAGE.

Jo, I., and Bednarz, S. W. 2009. Evaluating geography textbook questions from a spatial perspective: Using concepts of space, tools of representation, and cognitive processes to evaluate spatiality. *Journal of Geography* 108: 4–13.

Johnson, M. 1987. *The Body in the Mind*. University of Chicago Press.

Kastens, K. A., and Ishikawa, T. 2006. Spatial thinking in the geosciences and cognitive sciences: A cross-disciplinary look at the intersection of the two fields. In *Earth and Mind: How Geologists Think and Learn about the Earth*, ed. C. A. Manduca and D. W. Mogk. Volume 413, Geological Society of America Special Papers.

Kaufman, M. M. 2004. Using spatial-temporal primitives to improve geographic skills for preservice teachers. *Journal of Geography* 103: 171–181.

Lakoff, G., and Johnson, M. 1980. *Metaphors We Live By*. University of Chicago Press.

Lynch, K. 1984. *Good City Form*. MIT Press.

Mandelbrot, B. 1983. *The Fractal Geometry of Nature*. Freeman.

Manduca, C., and Kastens, K. 2012. Mapping the domain of spatial thinking in the geosciences. In *Earth and Mind II: A Synthesis of Research on Thinking and Learning in the Geosciences*, ed. K. A. Kastens and C. A. Manduca. Volume 486, Geological Society of America Special Papers.

Margolis, E., and Laurence, S., eds. 1999. *Concepts: Core Readings*. MIT Press.

Marsh, M., Golledge, R. G., and Battersby, S. E. 2007. Geospatial concept understanding and recognition in G6–college students: A preliminary argument for minimal GIS. *Annals of the Association of American Geographers* 97: 696–712.

Mathewson, J. H. 2005. The visual core of science: Definition and applications to education. *International Journal of Science Education* 27: 529–548.

Montello, D. R. 1993. Scale and multiple psychologies of space. In *Spatial Information Theory: A Theoretical Basis for GIS*, ed. A. U. Frank and I. Campari. Springer.

Montello, D. R., Fabrikant, S. I., Ruocco, M., and Middleton, R. S. 2003. Testing the first law of cognitive geography on point-display spatializations. In *Spatial Information Theory: Foundations of Geographic Information Science*, ed. W. Kuhn, M. F. Worboys, and S. Timpf. Springer.

Murphy, G. L. 2002. *The Big Book of Concepts*. MIT Press.

Newcombe, N. S., and Huttenlocher, J. 2000. *Making Space*. MIT Press.

NRC. 1996. *National Science Education Standards*. National Academies Press.

NRC. 2006. *Learning to Think Spatially—GIS as a Support System in the K–12 Curriculum*. National Academies Press.

Nystuen, J. D. 1963. Identification of some fundamental spatial concepts. *Michigan Academy of Science, Arts, and Letters* 48: 373–384.

O'Sullivan, D., and Unwin, D. J. 2002. *Geographic Information Analysis*. Wiley.

Piaget, J., and Inhelder, B. [1948] 1967. *The Child's Conception of Space*. Norton.

Shea, D. L., Lubinski, D., and Benbow, C. P. 2001. Importance of assessing spatial ability in intellectually talented young adolescents: A 20-year longitudinal study. *Journal of Educational Psychology* 93: 604–614.

Tolman, E. C. 1948. Cognitive maps in rats and men. *Psychological Review* 55: 189–208.

Tuan, Y. F. 1977. *Space and Place: The Perspective of Experience*. University of Minnesota Press.

Tversky, B. 2005. Functional significance of visuospatial representations. In *Cambridge Handbook of Visuospatial Thinking*, ed. P. Shah and A. Miyake. Cambridge University Press.

Uttal, D. H., and Cohen, C. A. 2012. Spatial thinking and STEM education: When, why and how. *Psychology of Learning and Motivation* 57: 147–181.

Wai, J., Lubinski, D., and Benbow, C. P. 2009. Spatial ability for STEM domains: Aligning over fifty years of cumulative psychological knowledge solidifies its importance. *Journal of Educational Psychology* 101: 817–835.

Webb, R. M., Lubinski, D., and Benbow, C. P. 2007. Spatial ability: A neglected dimension in talent searches for intellectually precocious youth. *Journal of Educational Psychology* 99: 397–420.

13 Cognition and Communication in Architectural Design

Thora Tenbrink, Christoph Hölscher, Dido Tsigaridi, and
Ruth Conroy Dalton

What, do you think, is a corner, and what might it be important for? Your answer will depend on who you are and what is relevant for you in a given discourse context. Even in the restricted context of buildings, corners can be associated with multiple concepts. Perceived from the outside, corners are typically convex and define the overall form of a building. From the inside, they are often concave, and represent semi-enclosed spaces formed by intersecting wall-planes. In each case, different levels of function and perception are revealed.

As such, convexity and concavity establish the status of a phenomenon's entity—they define where objects and regions begin and end, and are perceived at a high level of abstraction (Wang 2011). Corners, in particular, play different roles for different people, depending on the level of granularity, vantage point, and context. Inside a building, a room's corner provides space to place furniture; a corner in a hallway may signal the existence of a turn, and thus obscure the view ahead. The interior of a corner can be used for shelter and provide a space for retreat, whereas the exterior of a corner might serve as an outlook point.

Architects typically determine a building's massing (its overall shape and size) on the basis of its outside bounding edges, captured by diagrams outlining the formal composition of the external convex shape. Sometimes these formal considerations are so heavily semantically loaded that they may lead to exceptional treatment of the building corners. Ludwig Mies van der Rohe, one of the most influential modern architects of the twentieth century, was obsessed with the detail of the corner; he offered design solutions on how to articulate this unique endpoint of the building so as to smooth the transition from one wall to the other. (One example of this is the Illinois Institute of Technology's Crown Hall.) In the Cooper Union's Foundation Building (2009), the architect, Thom Mayne, takes the symbolic function of the corner to a different level. He curves the corner of the entire building block by lifting it up—a gesture meant to invite the passers-by into the lobby.

Whereas architects are preoccupied with formal, aesthetic, symbolic and functional considerations, clients (the people commissioning the architects) may view buildings' corners quite differently. For a client, interior corners may be economically relevant, as they provide space to be used commercially. The act of "lifting" a corner of a building, for example, might be viewed by clients as a financial waste because of lost usable space and increased construction costs. And a user's perception and appropriation of a building's corner space may differ from those of the architect and those of the client. Users (the people who will ultimately inhabit/visit/work in a building) may appreciate the aesthetic appearance of corners and their effect on the functionality of the building, but they may also perceive a corner as relevant for their personal building use. Owing to these discrepancies, encountering the word 'corner' may lead to different associations, to the point of referring to completely discrepant concepts. Consequently, communication about corners may require substantial elaboration and negotiation.

This chapter aims to shed light on these issues more systematically by addressing the diversity of conceptual perspectives involved in architectural design, focusing on the individual roles of the architect, the user, and the client. The need to interact and communicate so as to enable design solutions favored by all parties pose major challenges for everybody involved, and this has clear educational implications.

As in our example, architectural design generally involves various expectations, functions, and purposes, depending on the perspective adopted toward the design task. This already poses challenges for architects dealing with diverse demands—even without the need to communicate. Then, in discussions of particular aspects of a building among various stakeholders, the diversity of concepts may lead to communication problems that may increase if the discrepancy remains undetected. Unfortunately, neither graphic nor verbal language reflects the fundamental differences in perspectives in directly observable ways. For example, a corner may always be referred to as corner, independent of the actual concept at stake. Though conceptual divergences between speakers may be subtle, and the language used may converge, people may still be talking at cross-purposes without necessarily being able to pinpoint any concrete discrepancies. They may not notice that they are engaging in diverging discourses, drawing on different background assumptions, and pursuing different goals.

Adrian Forty (2000) dedicated a voluminous book to the relation between language and modern architecture, providing insights into an impressive range of concepts at the heart of architectural thinking—using words that may be associated with different, perhaps less rich, concepts by non-architects. For instance, the concept of *flexibility* in architecture touches upon issues of redundancy (creating margins for flexible usage), technical means (enabling flexible usage by installing moveable partitions), and political strategies (disturbing established social order). Non-architects, even if centrally involved with building and construction, would not necessarily associate these phenomena with the term 'flexibility'; this conceptual leap involves a world of background knowledge and experience with a particular kind of discourse, or a particular way of thinking.

As in this example, architecture theory can provide a range of important insights into architects' perspectives and procedural knowledge. Other disciplines play further roles in understanding architectural phenomena and processes. Cognitive linguistics sheds light on words, associations, and communication issues. Design cognition addresses mental representations and cognitive strategies during the design process, and spatial cognition addresses wayfinding and comprehension problems of users of complex public buildings. Although our focus in this chapter is on the conceptual perspectives of individuals and the degree to which they can adopt other relevant perspectives and communicate successfully, the discourses employed by these disciplines and communities inform our understanding of the discrepancies we are aiming to capture.

Language and Thought

Communication, in a very basic sense, means conveying and exchanging thoughts between different minds, typically using language as a medium. Language, both graphic and verbal, serves as a tool to represent meanings selected from the broad spectrum of knowledge, opinions, perspectives, associations, and ideas that each communicator has available. Like any other tool, language can be used in flexible ways, depending on the users' individual needs in particular contexts. This can be easily demonstrated when considering the many different meanings of a simple word such as 'Okay'. This word can be uttered with various stress and intonation patterns, and it can refer to ideas as varied as acknowledgment of perceiving an utterance, agreement with its content, starting a new topic or discourse or task, and other things, depending on context. This flexibility does not necessarily lead to misunderstandings; typically, speakers manage to get their meanings across "sufficiently for current purposes" (Clark 1996), even though they may misinterpret subtle elements of the intended communication.

From a cognitive linguistic point of view, words do not actually transfer meaning in any deterministic way, but rather serve as access points to an intricate network of concepts within the speakers' minds (Evans 2009). Thus, although we use words (or, by analogy, drawings) to convey meanings, and we typically agree on one or more basic senses of meaning, words are flexible enough to activate different sets of concepts, depending on an individual's mindset and conceptual background. With a sufficient amount of shared common ground, this is not problematic. However, problems can arise if the same (seemingly unambiguous) expressions are used by people who draw on substantially different background knowledge, perspectives, and interests, without realizing the effect that these differences may have on understanding a concept.

Architecture is a domain in which people come together to communicate about a shared topic, yet diverge greatly with respect to expertise, experience, discourse, task goals, roles, responsibilities, and expectations. Communication in building design relies heavily on graphic language; the interaction architects have with their clients begins with verbal communication (clients use words to express their desires) and continues with graphic explorations (words are transformed into drawings and images). This process introduces substantial ambiguity (Cuff and Robertson 1982).

Consider a discussion about a staircase to be built. Architects may view this as a central element for circulation as well as aesthetic design. A staircase connects building levels, but it can also be highly visible to visitors if it presents an open space—with associated opportunities for architectural representation. Clients may be concerned with practical considerations and constraints, such as financial limitations, functional requirements concerning access to specific parts of the building, or meeting local fire regulations. Building users will appreciate a well-designed staircase, but they also want to reach their goal without getting lost. Staircases can support wayfinding and orientation; if visually prominent and placed centrally, they serve as visual landmarks and provide easy access to each part of the building, ideally allowing for suitable inferences about unencountered parts of the building. With repeated use, users of a building may gradually develop a sense of appropriation, which in the case of staircases may lead to a preference for a particular path—"their" staircase.

Similar observations could be made for many other parts of a building. Terms such as 'corner' and 'staircase' are not necessarily perceived as ambiguous. Even if they are, this may not be problematic, because the context will typically disambiguate basic senses of a polysemous term. The issue at stake is that these terms (and corresponding drawings) will inevitably activate access to different sets of concepts and associations in the minds of the people involved. Typically, the associated concepts and considerations are not made explicit. Architects considering a staircase may take it for granted that they understand it in terms of circulation, solid and void relationships, and aesthetics; their clients may be puzzled about some of these associations when they appear in the architect's communications.

Moreover, it is typically hard even to agree on a clearly delimited basic meaning of a word. A staircase can certainly be understood as a set of steps, but how many steps need there be before one can talk about a staircase? How far can different sets of steps be separated before speakers start talking about multiple staircases? Given an average size of a step, how much can an individual step depart from this size before it is no longer referred to as a part of the same staircase? Similar considerations apply for many other parts of a building. Pillars, for instance, can gradually merge into walls; upstands become balustrades; alcoves have to be of a certain size (but what size?) to be conceived of as a space in their own right. All of this is relevant to Wang's (2011) notion of *cognitive identity*, according to which a wide range of cultural, social, and individual factors determine the extent to which a phenomenon is perceived in terms of a specific significance.

Considerations such as these are common in an architect's everyday life, and they also relate directly to cognitive linguistics research. Whereas the meanings of words were previously understood as sets of features needing to be determined by lexicographers, researchers now agree that they are best described in terms of prototypes or abstract schemas that do not necessarily or directly fit any deterministic description. (See, e.g., Rosch, Mervis, Gray, Johnson, and Boyes-Braem 1975.) The word 'bird', for instance, typically triggers the association of a common exemplar that speakers would encounter regularly in their own culture; in the United States this might be a robin. Birds deviating substantially from the features of a robin, such as penguins, would still be understood as birds, but they take longer to come to mind, and their features (e.g., being unable to fly) would not be considered as decisive for birds.

When considering the elements of a building, we can assume that words such as 'corner', 'staircase', 'pillar', and 'balustrade' are associated with a number of basic spatial features according to the speakers' cultural background. However, even if architects, clients, and users share the same culture, their conceptual backgrounds will differ substantially, as we have seen. Thus, it is not at all clear that the spatial features subconsciously associated with each of these words would be similar for them—and this may not be clear in a discussion about architectural design until it is made explicit by some turn of the conversation that requires clarifying such subtle details.

The Triangular Cognition and Communication System of Architectural Design

To represent the complexity of mindsets involved in the architectural design process as illustrated in the previous section, consider a triangular cognition and communication system with the following three vertices (figure 13.1):

• the architects' cognition and design processes, including their abstract functional concepts of design space, individual objectives, creativity and innovation
• the users' intuitions and needs concerning spatial appropriation and ease of wayfinding, and their perception and experience of the spatial setting as a whole
• the clients' views of the architectural challenge, including economical, functional, and aesthetical considerations.

These three vertices of the triangle enclose design as a conceptual target to which each of the vertices is related in a different way. Moreover, the vertices are interconnected by edges symbolizing conceptual perspective-taking and communication and interaction among architects, users, and clients. All these stakeholders employ different kinds of discourses when it comes to discussing spatial experience and configurations.

Let us take a closer look at the vertices and edges of this triangle. To set the stage, consider the principal phases of design as defined by the RIBA Plan of Work 2013,[1] which provides a first impression of the uneven distribution of roles in the design process. In phase 0, Strategic Definition, architects identify the design goals and requirements in communication with the clients. Phase 1, Preparation and Brief, involves developing the project's objectives and outcomes and constraints on the final design. These general goals are specified in further detail in specific phases to be carried out by the architect, called the Concept Design, Developed Design, and Technical Design phases. The Construction phase is followed by

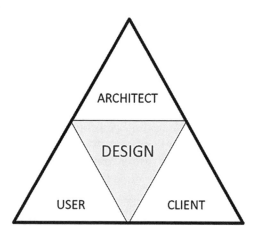

Figure 13.1
Cognitive agents involved in the architectural design process.

Handover, Close Out, and In Use. In this process, clients are prominent in the initial design phase(s), defining desired outcomes, requirements, and constraints. Users do not emerge before the construction is completed. Nevertheless, they may be implicitly present, as it is these stakeholders who will ultimately evaluate the end product, either encountering no issues with the building (the outcome anticipated by the client and architect) or encountering a number of unanticipated problems. The triangle of cognitive agents involved in the architectural design process outlined above represents an abstraction of a range of possible configurations. In the case of the design of a complex public building, the triangle is simplified since roles need not be held by individuals. Architects and clients could be groups or teams, and users may be masses of people who do not know one another. Also, users may fall into different subgroups, such as inhabitants (permanent users, e.g. teachers and airport employees) and visitors (temporary users, e.g. students and air travelers). Typically, inhabitants and visitors will have fundamentally different ways of using a building, implying different perspectives on the design layout. Furthermore, subtasks of the design process, such as producing documents, involve further people with different backgrounds and perspectives on the process—engineers, town planners, and experts on specific aspects of a building (e.g, energy consultants, sustainability consultants).

In the case of designing private buildings, the main roles of user and client may be represented by just one person. If that is the case, both roles are relevant, and they may sometimes be in conflict. As a user, the person will want to feel at ease in the building and appropriate it comfortably. As a client, the person will wish to focus on financial and other pragmatic constraints. Though comfort and affordability need not be mutually exclusive, their combination often poses a challenge to be addressed by the skilled architect through communication with the person holding the dual role of client and user.

Depending on circumstances, there may be further people involved whose roles fall between the three main roles, so as to support and facilitate communication between them. In the case of complex buildings, a client advisor (see www.architecture.com) may provide a link between the client and the architect, and a facility manager typically operates between client and user. A link between architects and users is sometimes facilitated through the process of participatory design. Thus, not only the vertices but also each of the edges of the triangle may be elaborated and enhanced in various ways. (See figure 13.2 for the more complex case.) The fact that established links exist between the different roles highlights the importance of reconciling the diverse conceptual perspectives involved.

Taking an abstract view on the three vertices of the triangle, the architects are the experts in charge of the design process and play the most prominent role. The clients are also experts; some design issues cannot be

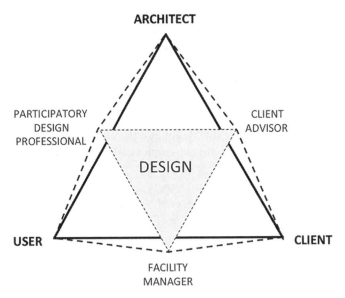

Figure 13.2
Negotiated vertices.

resolved without them. Users seem to play the weakest role; they are "naive" participants rather than experts, and throughout the design process they rarely have a say. However, at least in the case of complex public buildings, although there can be architect teams and client companies consisting of more than one person, the number of people using the building will far exceed the number of experts involved in planning the building. After construction, they will be the ones most involved with the building. Arguably, therefore, their role is the most important of the three.

The User Perspective

People visit and inhabit publicly accessible buildings for any number of purposes, largely depending on a building's functions, be it a transport terminal, hospital, conference center or office space. A common requirement is that a building's users need to be able to find their way through the building. From the perspective of cognitive science, wayfinding and navigation (Montello 2005) are addressed in terms of a range of cognitive functions and subtasks, including locomotion, orientation, path planning, spatial reasoning, and spatial memory. Visitors who have little knowledge about a specific building have to rely on cues from the environment for route planning and route following. (For a taxonomy of navigation tasks, see Wiener, Büchner, and Hölscher 2009.)

Users experience a building in a sequential fashion while moving through it, viewing the building from an egocentric perspective, perhaps guided by signs. Although this process may be further supported by wall-mounted maps giving an overview of the building's structure, this experiential perspective differs fundamentally from the allocentric perspective of floor plans and elevations primarily adopted by architects (Le Corbusier 1931/1986; Werner and Long 2003).

Obviously, efficient and intuitive signage is an aid to successful navigational (Arthur and Passini 1992). Beyond signs and maps, ease of wayfinding is influenced both by a building's structure and by cognitive strategies and spatial abilities (Carlson, Hölscher, Shipley, and Conroy Dalton 2010). With respect to a building's structure, wayfinding is affected mostly by factors such as the overall complexity of the corridor and room layout, the degree of visual distinctiveness of places, and visual access between decision points (Weisman 1981). Here, spatial features such as corners become elements of the wayfinding process. While finding their way and making navigation decisions, building users often strive to understand its logic and its structure. This process involves such perceptual cues of geometry as lines of sight and the number of local movement choices (Haq and Zimring 2003; Wiener, Hölscher, Büchner, and Konieczny 2012), as well as semantically rich characteristics (wall materials, textures, lighting, width of hallways) and meaningful landmark objects that serve as cues to the destination (Frankenstein, Brüssow, Ruzzoli, and Hölscher 2012).

Since building users necessarily start by orienting toward local features sequentially as they experience them, developing a comprehensive cognitive map of a complex building can take a long time, depending on how much of the building has been directly experienced and over what period of time. For some people this inherently complex cognitive task is more challenging than for others, as humans differ in their spatial abilities and navigational styles (Wolbers and Hegarty 2010). Research in this area has identified a range of wayfinding strategies adopted by individuals, such as orienting primarily toward better-known central parts of a building (Golledge and Spector 1978) and attempting to find short-cuts between floors (Hölscher, Meilinger, Vrachliotis, Brösamle, and Knauff 2006). The route-choice strategies of a particular user develop over time and may change as the users becomes more familiar with the building. Such changes in movement range and route choice are indicators of the user's appropriation of the building.

The Client Perspective

A client may be an individual or the board of directors of a large institution (for example, a multinational company). In either case, two of the primary requirements of clients are that the design represents value for money and that any concomitant risks (particularly financial ones) are minimized. After concerns about the initial investment, the next immediate and general concern is that the building be fit for its purpose. These *basic or expected needs* of clients are represented in the classic project-management triangle (Atkinson 1999) in terms of the differing requirements for the money/time/quality triad of constraints of the construction project. Beyond the expected concerns that most clients might have of any construction project (scope, cost, time, risk, quality), there may be *articulated or demanded needs*, especially with respect to expectations of how the end users of the building might behave in, use, or interact with the space.

The ways in which clients foresee a building being used will depend strongly on the type of building (e.g., hospital, airport, residential, etc.), and therefore such aspects of the design will play a greater or lesser role according to building type. One example where a specific expectation users have of clients might become a *specified need* (i.e., a need articulated in the design brief) is in the design of an airport, where the clients may have clear and well-defined expectations of how users will be guided through the building and, where appropriate, separated into different types of users (departing and arriving travelers, for example). For the design of a shopping mall, the expectations of the clients could be quite different—the clients might wish to increase the likelihood that shoppers will enter certain stores, that certain routes where high "footfall" is required will be prioritized, and that, in general, people will linger and hence become more likely to make purchases. A third example might be the design of an office environment, where clients wish to promote a strong collaborative culture among employees, facilitated by fluid, barrier-free movement throughout the whole office environment. However, as Kamara, Anumba, and Evbuomwan (2002, p. 4) point out, "the business need underpinning the decision to commission a project can also conflict with the wishes and perspectives of other components within the client body. For example, a corporate decision to rationalise space through open-plan offices might conflict with the users' need for privacy." Therefore, despite the clients' apparent disposition to take into account the needs of the users via the building design brief, there may arise situations in which the two sets of needs (the clients' and the users') are in conflict, or in which the clients' perception of the user perspective does not correspond to the users' actual views.

The Architect Perspective

The design process can be viewed as consisting of a series of tasks involving analytical tasks, acts of synthesis, and evaluation. These different tasks are frequently cyclical and will be interspersed with decision-making events.

Whether the task is to design a small bathroom or an entire city block, designers begin their work with the client and the design brief, an early statement of goals. Analysis and research follow, and brainstorming sessions allow for the generation of early ideas and design solutions. Sketches, diagrams, and simple drawings visually assist the conceptualization of these solutions. These help architects in the definition of their aesthetic vocabulary, their problem-solving processes, and complex manifestations of visual thinking. It is over early drawings that the architect develops a personal conversation. Ideas form sketches, and sketches help form new ideas. Representational tools assist architects in the translation of abstract ideas into concrete design solutions. In graphically communicating their proposals, both among team members and to the clients, architects gradually move from explorative ideas (also known as the solution space) to the precise definition of the building and the finalization of schematic design. Design decisions made by the architects during this transition restrict the solution space; input or feedback given by other architects or the clients result in re-expanding, redefining, or further narrowing the solution space. The more aligned the perspectives of architects and clients are, the faster they can reach a design solution and move to design development; the more diverging their views are, the more times the architects will have to re-expand the solution space and propose new schematic designs.

Notably, with the exception of situations in which the client is also the user, architects rarely receive input in their design solutions from users. Also in relation to the client, nothing guarantees the establishment of successful communication. In fact, cases of exceptional architect-client communication are rather few. Among those, one of the most notable is the close collaboration of the Dutch architect Gerrit Rietveld and his client, Truus Schröder, in the design of the Schröder house (Friedman 2007); Schröder held the roles of client and user. The degree to which her needs were accommodated by Rietveld is magnificently captured by numerous thoughtful details—for example, the elegant mail slot of the front door and the small shelf for her eyeglasses, carefully positioned near her bedside. The Schröder story is a bright exception. Most often, architects' ideas are guided by their own ideals and beliefs, previous experience, personal desires, aesthetic preferences, and common-sense judgments.

The creative process remains obscure. In the words of Glaser (1996), it is rather "esoteric, highly specialized, full of internal rituals, and hard to understand from the outside." This process led Banham (1990) to call architecture a "black box" that would be "at the risk of destroying itself as an art in the process" if it were to be "opened up to the understandings of the profane and the vulgar."

Within this complex, cyclical, self-reflective process, how do architects conceptualize the role of the user? In the introduction to his book on the relationship between the architect and the user, Till (2009) suggests that many architects view the user as little more than a contaminant corrupting their pure environment, the unadulterated end product of the complex design process described above. One piece of evidence for Till's view is the frequent absence of buildings' users from architectural photographs. This extreme view is, however, one that would be vehemently denied by many practicing architects who *do* profess to put users at the heart of their design endeavors. Clearly, there is a broad spectrum of attitudes, ranging from architects committed to participatory design (design processes that actively involve the end user in early stages of the design) to those who could be stigmatized as being dismissive of the end user, as Till suggests. It seems reasonable to assume that most architects are somewhere in the middle of this spectrum. They would like to think that they take the users' wishes and needs into account (and would take offense to the suggestion that they regard them as mere contaminants), but they probably would not go so far as to involve end users directly in the design process. Indeed, it simply "may not be possible to include most perspectives, particularly that of users, in the decision-making process" (Kamara et al. 2002).

Instead of direct consultation, architects often try to put themselves into the shoes of the user in order to consider the users' experience of being inside and moving around the completed project. With respect to many experiences inside a yet-to-be-realized building, this approach is probably "good enough" most of the time. For example, Peponis, Zimring, and Choi (1990) point out that architects use specific design features to support wayfinding, without assuming a "one-shot" approach that works in all building settings. They give the example of including a central atrium, which can help convey a sense of the building's structure as well as offer direct visual access to other floors. Staircases and elevators that are strategically connected to the atrium provide support for orientation and efficient movement decisions.

Particularly during a complex design process, architects may adopt different perspectives depending on relevance at different stages (Tenbrink, Brösamle, and Hölscher 2012). Conceptual shifts between perspectives may come along with systematic and perhaps subtle shifts in the language used to refer to the same spatial phenomena. Thus, language use reflects how thoughts adopt new directions, highlighting the diversity of perspectives as well as the impracticality (or impossibility) of considering all of these in parallel.

A major obstacle for architects when imagining the user perspective lies in the fact that the majority of a building's users (especially first-time visitors) have only partial knowledge of the building in which they are walking around, whereas the architects know nearly everything about the building (since it is the product of their own imagination and creativity). This makes it difficult for architects to disregard their expert knowledge in order to take on the role of a naive user. It is generally challenging to estimate other people's knowledge and adapt communication styles accordingly (Bromme, Rambow, and Nückles 2001). For example, architects were found to severely overestimate knowledge of contemporary architecture in non-experts (Rambow 2000), related to the specific ways in which everyday concepts and names are used in the architectural domain (Forty 2000).

The Seattle Public Library is a good example of a building in which fundamental discrepancies have arisen between users and architectural thinking. The architecture team, led by the architects Rem Koolhaas and Joshua Prince-Ramus (Kubo and Prat 2005), provided strong cues for navigating the building's ten stories—most prominently, brightly colored escalators. Unfortunately, these cues are valid only for navigating to some of the floors; it may be necessary to take less readily available routes to other destinations. As a result, users sometimes need to resist the attraction of obvious route choices in order to choose the correct access to important locations and even entire floors (Carlson et al. 2010). Though Koolhaas and his colleagues clearly considered the users' behavior and tried to anticipate their intentions, actual behavior observation in the Seattle Public Library revealed serious wayfinding challenges for users.

Educational Implications

Clearly, as we have shown, communication among architects, clients, and users may be problematic. What can be done to mitigate that? Initiatives such as the Royal Institute of British Architects' "best client" awards and public outreach programs aiming to educate the public about architecture (see http://www.londonopenhouse.org/) go some way toward encouraging dialogue between architects and their clients and users. Arguably, however, the easiest group to reach are the architects themselves, since enhancement of communication and mutual understanding could form part of the standard architectural education. Some scholars have observed the lack of empathy architects show for human real-world needs and have noted that the way architecture is taught distances architects from serving people (Bandini 1997).

Architectural education promotes experimentation with form, new materials, technologies, innovative representation and simulation techniques. What often escape architecture curricula are strategies to enhance students' sensitivity toward human issues (Thakur 2006)—pedagogical methods for better understanding and communicating with clients and users. Architectural work is too permanent and too complex, one might argue, to accommodate everyone's desires. Nevertheless, this observation is not sufficient to justify why architects are so dismissive of well-established methods available for addressing people's needs, while embracing case-based learning almost exclusively (Wright 1996; Akin 2002). The potential of other educational methods certainly should be explored.

One method that is currently being pioneered is to translate spatial cognition research into architectural education. The challenge is basically one of helping architects "put themselves into the shoes" of a client or a user. One method occasionally used in architecture schools is to set up fictitious scenarios in which students interview a person posing as a client. Another method is to provide a rich and detailed description of an idealized user, similar to the concept of a persona in product design and HCI. It clearly helps architects to put themselves into the shoes of their user if they have a clear concept of who their user might be.

Another approach, pioneered by Gehl (1971) and Whyte (1980), is to encourage architects to observe how people use and inhabit the built environment on an everyday basis. In-depth ethnographic research can significantly inform design decisions, or even help shape the design brief. If we augment this approach with input from spatial cognition research, we can move from simple behavioral observations to teaching architects how to conduct cognitive walkthroughs: to "role play" a user, performing a simple task in a real environment and noting assumptions made and problems encountered while performing it. Cognitive walkthroughs can serve both as means of ideation and techniques for validation. This method can easily be combined with visits to real environments or buildings in which users are known to have navigational or wayfinding problems. "Direct experience" exercises can be supported or augmented by more traditional lectures and by paper-based analytic exercises.

At the end of the design phase, when students typically present their design to their peers and tutors for assessment, the client/user perspective can be reintroduced and integrated into the traditional design "crit." This may be achieved by undertaking cognitive walkthroughs in virtual simulations of the building, and by asking "naive" users (not the students) to undertake simple explorative tasks in the building and to express their impressions, assumptions, or difficulties aloud. This approach, which requires relatively sophisticated virtual reality, was put to good use in a recent experimental educational program (Schneider et al. 2013).

Conclusion

Starting from general observations about the role of cognition and conceptual perspectives in communication, we have discussed a cognition and communication triangle representing the architectural design process. By clarifying the different perspectives of people involved in this process, we have highlighted the fundamental conceptual discrepancies that must be overcome for successful communication to be achieved. Though the triangle shows equal vertices, the situation is further complicated by the fact that each role can be filled in many different ways. Also, the relative importances of the roles are not equal, and neither are the edges of the triangle. Arguably there is no need for users to understand the architect perspective to the same extent as vice versa; the architects' purpose of designing a building for future use and appropriation seems to be thwarted in a fundamental sense by a lack of understanding of the user perspective.

A number of promising (though largely unconnected) steps toward supportive intervention have been taken, such as establishing clear roles for client advisers and using participatory design methods. In view of the rich empirical and theoretical background gained across relevant disciplines, such as cognitive science, cognitive linguistics, and design cognition, we suggest that the time is ripe for a more fundamental integration of insights in architectural training and design processes, along the lines suggested in our final section. Conceivably this will provide a further step toward the ultimate aim of architectural design: to incorporate the dreams of individuals across all three roles—architects, clients, and users—while incorporating their diverse concepts and ideals.

Note

1. The design process described by the Royal Institute of British Architects (RIBA) and the one provided by the American Institute of Architects (AIA) share the same basic stages. Sources: http://www.architecture.com/Files/RIBAProfessionalServices/ Practice/RIBAPlanofWork2013Overview.pdf   and   http://www.aia.org/aiaucmp/ groups/aia/documents/pdf/aias077491.pdf.

References

Akin, Ö. 2002. Case-based instruction strategies in architecture. *Design Studies* 23: 407–431.

Arthur, P., and Passini, R. 1992. *Wayfinding: People, Signs, and Architecture.* McGraw-Hill.

Atkinson, R. 1999. Project management: cost, time and quality, two best guesses and a phenomenon, its [sic] time to accept other success criteria. *International Journal of Project Management* 17 (6): 337–342.

Bandini, M. 1997. The conditions of criticism. In *The Education of the Architect: Historiography, Urbanism, and the Growth of Architectural Knowledge*, ed. M. Pollak. MIT Press.

Banham, R. 1990. A black box: The secret profession of architecture. *New Statesman and Society* 12 (October): 22–25.

Bromme, R., Rambow, R., and Nückles, M. 2001. Expertise and estimating what other people know: The influence of professional experience and type of knowledge. *Journal of Experimental Psychology. Applied* 7 (4): 317–330.

Carlson, L., Hölscher, C., Shipley, T., and Conroy Dalton, R. 2010. Getting lost in buildings. *Current Directions in Psychological Science* 19 (5): 284–289.

Clark, H. H. 1996. *Using Language*. Cambridge University Press.

Cuff, D., and Robertson, E. 1982. Words and images: The alchemy of communication. *Journal of Architectural Education* 36: 8–15.

Evans, V. 2009. *How Words Mean: Lexical Concepts, Cognitive Models and Meaning Construction*. Oxford University Press.

Forty, A. 2000. *Words and Buildings: A Vocabulary of Modern Architecture*. Thames and Hudson.

Frankenstein, J., Brüssow, S., Ruzzoli, F., and Hölscher, C. 2012. The language of landmarks: The role of background knowledge in indoor wayfinding. *Cognitive Processing* 13 (1): 165–170.

Friedman, A. 2007. *Women and the Making of the Modern House*. Yale University Press.

Gehl, J. 1971. *Life Between Buildings: Using Public Space*. Island.

Glaser, M. 1996. Design and business: The war is over. *AIGA Journal of Graphic Design* 14 (3): 45–46.

Golledge, R. G., and Spector, A. 1978. Comprehending the urban environment: Theory and practice. *Geographical Analysis* 10: 403–426.

Haq, S., and Zimring, C. 2003. Just down the road a piece: The development of topological knowledge of building layouts. *Environment and Behavior* 35: 132–160.

Hölscher, C., Meilinger, T., Vrachliotis, G., Brösamle, M., and Knauff, M. 2006. Up the down staircase: Wayfinding strategies and multi-level buildings. *Journal of Environmental Psychology* 26 (4): 284–299.

Kamara, J. M., Anumba, C. J., and Evbuomwan, N. F. 2002. *Capturing Client Requirements in Construction Projects*. ICE.

Kubo, M., and Prat, R. 2005. *Seattle Public Library: OMA—Rem Koolhaas*. Actar.

Le Corbusier. [1931] 1986. *Towards a New Architecture*. Dover.

Montello, D. R. 2005. Navigation. In *The Cambridge Handbook of Visuospatial Thinking*, ed. P. Shah and A. Miyake. Cambridge University Press.

Peponis, J., Zimring, C., and Choi, Y. K. 1990. Finding the building in wayfinding. *Environment and Behavior* 22 (5): 555–590.

Rambow, R. 2000. *Experten-Laien-Kommunikation in der Architektur*. Waxmann.

Rosch, E., Mervis, C. B., Gray, W., Johnson, D., and Boyes-Braem, P. 1975. Basic objects in natural categories. *Cognitive Psychology* 8 (3): 382–439.

Schneider, S., Kuliga, S., Hölscher, C., Conroy Dalton, R., Kunert, A., Kulik, A., et al. 2013 Educating architecture students to design buildings from the inside out— Experiences from an research-based design studio. In proceedings of the Ninth International Space Syntax Symposium, Seoul.

Tenbrink, T., Brösamle, M., and Hölscher, C. 2012. Flexibility of perspectives in architects' thinking. In proceedings of symposium on Spatial Cognition for Architectural Design, New York.

Thakur, A. B. 2006. Architecture Pedagogy: Psychological, Social, and Other Emergent Issues in the Design Studio. Available at http://diginole.lib.fsu.edu.

Till, J. 2009. *Architecture Depends*. MIT Press.

Wang, W. 2011. On the notions of cognitive entities and cognitive identities in architecture. Keynote lecture at symposium on Spatial Cognition for Architectural Design Symposium, New York.

Weisman, J. 1981. Evaluating architectural legibility: Wayfinding in the built environment. *Environment and Behavior* 13 (2): 189–204.

Werner, S., and Long, P. 2003. Cognition meets Le Corbusier—Cognitive principles of architectural design. In *Spatial Cognition III*, ed. C. Freksa, W. Brauer, C. Habel, and K. F. Wender. Springer.

Whyte, W. H. 1980. *The Social Life of Small Urban Spaces*. Conservation Foundation.

Wiener, J. M., Büchner, S. J., and Hölscher, C. 2009. Taxonomy of human wayfinding tasks: A knowledge-based approach. *Spatial Cognition and Computation* 9: 152–165.

Wiener, J. M., Hölscher, C., Büchner, S., and Konieczny, L. 2012. Gaze behaviour during space perception and spatial decision making. *Psychological Research* 76 (6): 713–729.

Wolbers, T., and Hegarty, M. 2010. What determines our navigational abilities? *Trends in Cognitive Sciences* 14: 138–146.

Wright, S. 1996. Case-based instruction: Linking theory to practice. *Physical Educator* 53 (4): 190–197.

14 Exploring the Nature and Development of Expertise in Geography

Roger M. Downs

Experts and Expertise

Excelling in academia

Experts abound in areas from the familiar and quotidian to the recondite and unusual; the advice of experts is sought, if not always followed. Experts are targets of humor, admiration, and disdain. Owing to the characterization of experts as people who know more and more about less and less, there is ambivalence in popular reactions.

Reactions from academics are equally mixed. Niels Bohr saw an expert as "a person who has found out by his own painful experience all the mistakes that one can make in a very narrow field" (Coughlan 1954, p. 62). Werner Heisenberg offered a positive gloss: "An expert is someone who knows some of the worst mistakes that can be made in his field, and how to avoid them" (Capri 2011, p. 181). Expert status is based on everything from publications and performances to testimonials and awards. Bohr was awarded a Nobel Prize in 1922, Heisenberg in 1932.

What constitutes an expert in geography or in any other area of human achievement? Experts are seen as authoritative and credible as a consequence of the knowledge and skills they bring to bear on a focused area of achievement. Knowledge and skills develop through intensive training and prolonged experience in transitioning from novice to expert.

Why it is important to understand expertise

Many disciplines have generated bodies of scholarship on the nature and development of expertise. To its disadvantage, geography has not done so. Geography needs systematic studies of expertise for two reasons.

First, expertise offers a framework for understanding what we do collectively as a discipline and how we do it as individual practitioners. It is a way of understanding the discipline's history, the making of scholars, and the power and beauty of geography's way of thinking. We can convey to others what happens, how, and why when we practice geography at different points along the expertise continuum. Second, expertise offers guidelines for what should be fostered in the next generation. "What students should know" and "what students should be able to do" are mantras of the standards movement that dominates K–12 education in the United States (Geography Education Standards Project 2013). Geography education can be tailored to meet the needs and capacities of people along the expertise continuum.

Approaches to expertise

In this chapter, I approach expertise from three perspectives: that of cognitive science, using theories, methods, and findings to capture the general nature of expertise; that of geography, using cognitive science to explore the particular characteristics of geographic expertise; and that of a case study, using think-aloud protocols and pedagogy to illustrate expertise in geographic problem solving. I then make a case for a systematic long-term effort to understand geographic expertise.

The Cognitive Science Approach to Expertise

Development of the approach

Over the past 50 years, there has been a multidisciplinary program of research on the nature and development of expertise, beginning with Chase and Simon's (1973) theory based on chess. The work was motivated by the development of expert systems in artificial intelligence, the analysis of organizational decision making, and the design of science education (Ericsson, Charness, Hoffman, and Feltovich 2009). As a consequence of these roots, research has been dominated by a blend of cognitive psychology approaches with computer science modeling approaches. Results have been theoretical and practical in areas such as education and expert system design, with ultimate validation in the success of computer chess programs, such as IBM's Deep Blue, in beating human world chess champions.

There is general agreement on the properties of expertise that transcend particular domains and on the properties of problems in different domains.

General characteristics of expertise

Among the domains of knowledge and achievement in which work on expertise has been done are games (e.g., chess, bridge, Go), sports (e.g., golf, tennis, swimming), professions (e.g., medicine, radiology, law), technical skills (e.g., electronics and computer programming), disciplines ranging from physics and chemistry to economics and history, and the visual arts and music. (For summaries, see Cooke 1992 and Ericsson et al. 2009.) The synthesis in this chapter draws on Chi 2006, Cooke 1992, Ericsson 1996, Ericsson et al. 2009, and Hoffman 1992.

Evidence suggests that the superior performance of experts is not a function of brain size, neurophysiology, or neuropsychology. Expert performance is domain specific: There is little or no transfer of expertise from one domain to another. Experts have a drive to excel. They differ in ability (or talent), motivation, and experience, although the weights and combinatory effects of these factors are debated. Even within their domain of expertise, experts do not always perform at the highest level; they have blind spots, they make errors, they sometimes are inattentive, they are subject to overload, and they may be locked into tried-and-true approaches that are not always appropriate.

Experts differ from non-experts in several ways. One distinction is in the approach to problems. Experts undertake a systematic and deep qualitative analysis of a problem, seeking understanding before attempting a solution. Understanding comes from breaking problems into manageable pieces, using underlying principles and concepts to build representations of the problem space, ignoring surface features, and identifying constraints. When undergraduate students and advanced graduate students in physics were asked to sort physics problems into categories, undergraduates sorted on the basis of surface features and specific words, whereas graduate students sorted on the basis of often implicit underlying principles (Chi, Feltovich, and Glaser 1981). Despite the time they spend analyzing problems, experts are faster in solving them. Physics experts could solve mechanics problems more accurately than novices in less than one fourth the time (Larkin, McDermott, Simon, and Simon 1980).

Another distinction between experts and non-experts is in the organization of knowledge. Though experts tend to know more, the form of their knowledge is more important than the quantity. They see domains as comprising conceptual chunks of related ideas, often in the form of typical patterns of relationships. The chunks are connected, which ensures fast retrieval of concepts and patterns. The classic demonstration of chunking came from chess. Chess masters could memorize chess pieces on a board in a few seconds with near-perfect accuracy, whereas novices could correctly replace only five or six pieces. If the same pieces were randomly placed on the board, masters and novices did not differ in performance (de Groot 1966).

Pattern-based conceptual knowledge makes it possible to learn new information quickly. Experts have well-learned procedures for solving problems such that it becomes automatic to see it that way and do it this way, again leading to speed in problem solving. The expert's superior memory, both short-term and long-term, is due to a combination of automaticity and chunking.

Throughout problem solving, experts engage in continuous self-monitoring and regulating of thought. This metacognitive skill reduces errors, checks for failures to comprehend, provides judgments of problem difficulty, and allows for honest assessments of what the person does and does not do well.

Domain character

The general characteristics of expertise are manifested in problem solving in games, in music, and in science. In academic disciplines, there is a distinction between domains characterized by a preponderance of well-structured problems over ill-structured problems. The distinction is rooted in the work of Reitman (1965), who introduced the idea, Simon (1973), who established criteria for the typology, and King and Kitchener (1994), who examined the distinction in the context of critical thinking. A problem's structure affects the problem-solving process and therefore affects expertise.

The distinguishing characteristics are completeness of problem description and solution certainty (or decidability) (King and Kitchener 1994). Well-structured problems have clearly defined initial and goal states and explicit transformation rules connecting states. Solutions are based on principles and laws, and are derived from well-tested, often algorithmic procedures. Problems have definitive solutions with optimal solution paths, and criteria for determining solution correctness (Sinnott 1992). Problems in mathematics, logic, and physics have this character. Among the examples cited by King and Kitchener (1994) are converting units of measure between the English and metric systems, solving for x in an algebraic equation, and calculating the trajectory of a rocket's flight.

Ill-structured problems do not have well-defined initial states, goal states, or transformation rules. They contain unspecified or open constraints and factors whose interactions must be resolved. In view of the number, the complexity, and the uncertainty of these constraints and factors, resolving them is difficult if not impossible. There are few widely accepted principles and laws. Important concepts are open-textured and thus debatable. Thus, the conceptualization of an ill-structured problem is crucial to problem solving. Problems in social sciences, such as political science, and in humanities, such as history, typically are ill-structured (Carretero and Voss 1994; Leinhardt, Beck, and Stainton 1994). Among the examples cited by King and Kitchener (1994) are determining what really happened in the Hue massacre in Vietnam, judging the adequacy of a theoretical proposition, and deciding how to dispose of nuclear waste safely.

Whereas the structure distinction marks categorical extremes, in practice problems fall along a continuum, with a fluid boundary between extremes (Simon 1973). Problems may show both characteristics. Ill-structured problems do not easily decompose into subproblems. Decomposability adds a challenge because problems can be "well structured in the small, but ill structured in the large" (Simon 1973, p. 190).

The distinction is not a value judgment but a recognition of domain complexity and character. Although physics, for example, lies near the well-structured end of the continuum, it also contains problems that can be described as ill-structured. However, there is often a high degree of consensus among physics experts on how to break a problem into components and which principles are crucial to the solution. Conversely, ill-structured problems generate disagreement such that alternative solution processes lead to different outcomes. There are rarely definitive answers. Even if answers are obtained, there are not widely accepted tests of those answers. Thus, another skill in solving ill-structured problems is persuasiveness in presenting solutions.

Solving problems is intellectually demanding. Problems of one type are not inherently more or less challenging than problems of another type; they are challenging in different ways. Tools differ across disciplines. In physics, problem solvers can use mathematics, controlled experimentation, and formal logic; in history, problem solvers use verbal approaches and argumentation (Voss and Wiley 2006).

There is no reason to believe that findings from cognitive science do not apply to geography, although there is no empirical basis to substantiate such a belief.

Approaching Expertise in Geography

Identifying experts
Livingstone (1992) argued that geography is a contested discipline. Contests have been fought over what it is, how it should be practiced, and why it should be practiced. Debates about expertise have been absent from those

contests. The closest thing we have had to such debates are assessments of the relative stature of particular geographers.

How might experts in geography be identified? Years of practice and experience are necessary though not sufficient, and so experts are more likely to be older scholars. There is no evidence of prodigies in geography, except in the trivial sense of children who memorize information about places. Competitions such as the National Geographic Bee for middle-school students and the AAG World Bowl for college students reduce geography to declarative place knowledge with only minimal involvement of procedural knowledge. Experts are more likely to have degrees beyond the baccalaureate, although a higher degree is not a necessity. They are more likely to be working in academia or government departments and less likely to be working for research companies or in business. Unlike chess or sports, there are no competitions pitting geographers against one another in demonstrations of expertise. There are no benchmarks for world, national, or personal records against which performance can be assessed. There are no quantitative measures of speed or accuracy, although the significance of published works can be measured by indices of citation (Batty 2002; Wrigley and Matthews 1986).

Assessment of outstanding achievement occurs in several ways. One method uses grade-point average. A second acknowledges outstanding performances (e.g., an award for "best journal paper," a book award, a "best dissertation" award), or gives awards for sustained high-level performance over extended periods. The third is nebulous but powerful: informal word-of-mouth assessments leading to collective recognition of outstanding performance.

Awards for significant achievement are the most visible recognition of pre-eminence and, presumably, expertise. Interdisciplinary organizations recognize significant achievements. The National Academy of Sciences elects members on the basis of "their distinguished and continuing achievements in original research."[1] As of May 2013, sixteen geographers (including Foreign Honorary Members) are members of the Human Environmental Sciences section, one geographer is a member of the Economic Sciences, and one geographer is a member of the Environmental Sciences and Ecology section. The American Academy of Arts and Sciences elects scholars of "exceptional achievement" with "a wide range of expertise."[2] There are fifteen members of Class III.5 Archaeology, Anthropology, Sociology, Geography, and Demography. Ten geographers are members of both organizations. The American Association for the Advancement of Science recognizes "meritorious efforts to advance science or its applications."[3] In the Geology and Geography section there are 32 geographers. Membership of the three organizations overlaps. The Association of American Geographers, the American Geographical Society, the National Council for Geographic Education, and the National Geographical Society offer awards for distinguished and/or meritorious contributions in scholarship and service. It is reasonable to assume that many if not all awardees are experts.

Another strategy for identifying experts is via specialized literatures. There are "Who's Who" volumes, but visibility may not equate with expertise. The International Geographical Union has a "Who's Who in Geography" database. Entry is by self-nomination, with screening to avoid spurious entries.[4] Books identify great ideas and, presumably, great contributors (Hanson 1997). Textbooks identify major figures and contain biographic sketches describing their contributions. Again, one would presume that many of these people are experts. Histories of the discipline are built around significant contributions by geographers, and a presumption of expertise is reasonable.

Expertise is clearer in extra-disciplinary settings. Geographers are expert witnesses in legal contexts. Clark (1991) describes how qualifications are documented and challenged, discusses the role of expert testimony in court proceedings, and considers the value of geographic expertise. (See also Mitchell 1978.) Geographers are appointed as masters in legal proceedings. Morrill (1973 1976) describes why he was appointed to draft redistricting plans for the state of Washington. Of particular interest here is Morrill's (1973, p. 463) explanation of the selection of a geographer: "The court felt that political scientists would want to study the whole complicated history of conflict and decision-making in the case, but that the drawing of equal population regions was a technical task, subject to demographic and geographic rather than political criteria." Geographers advise presidents (Bowman 1921; Smith 2002), advise federal agencies (Kates 2011), and participate in policy debates (Turner 2005; Murphy 2006).

Identification of experts is neither easy nor without contention. Potential biases in selection processes, derivation of citation indices, and appearance in textbooks and histories are obvious. Even if we could arrive at a consensus list of experts, we would still need to capture what constitutes expertise. Commonalities in years practicing geography, occupational history, or publications are interesting but not revealing indicators of the nature of expertise.

Therefore, we need an alternative approach. I begin with a definition: "An expert in history is assumed to have a general and a specialized knowledge of history as well as facility in the skills of historical research and writing." (Voss and Wiley 2006, p. 569) If we substitute 'geography' and 'geographical' for 'history' and 'historical', the resulting statement is reasonable. However, it lacks specificity: What knowledge? What is the difference between general and specialized knowledge? Which research and writing skills? To answer these questions, we need to focus on expertise in action—that is, on how knowledge and skills are creatively brought to bear on geographic problems. In doing so, we should keep qualifications in mind. First, the effort should initially be descriptive, not prescriptive. Second, answers will be contingent on time and place. There are cultural variations in geographical practices in any period (Livingstone 1992). Third, geography encompasses natural-scientific, social-scientific, and humanist approaches. Particular geographers contribute different knowledge and skill sets, and there is no singular form of geographic expertise. Fourth, we must sample across the continuum from novices to experts. Fifth, we must adapt the characteristics of expertise to the particularities of geography. Doing so requires us to consider the position of geography along the problem-structure continuum.

Geography as a problem domain

Throughout geography's long history, geography and space have been inseparable at the most fundamental level. The areas of connection include subject matter (geography describes and explains the arrangement of people and things on Earth's surface), methodology (geography uses maps, spatial statistics, and geospatial technologies), and conceptual approaches (geography applies spatial analysis to study patterns and processes). The language of geography is inherently spatial in character: 'scale' (global to local), 'dimension', 'distribution', 'distance', 'proximity', 'direction', 'discontinuity', and so on. As a consequence, geography is similar to astronomy and architecture in that understanding of space and the use of spatial thinking are integral to its ways of operating. In the same way that the general concept of expertise becomes domain specific, so too do ideas of space and spatial thinking when they become part of the thinking process of a geographer. Therefore, expertise in geography is inevitably imbued with space and spatial thinking. The particular expressions of these ideas are a function of personal predilection, especially when it comes to choosing problems and questions.

My focus here is neither on the substantive nature of the discipline nor on ideologies. Expertise enables us to pose geographic questions and solve problems. Therefore, my focus is on the nature of questions and problems in geography, using the idea of problem structure.

Geography fits the characterization of an ill-structured discipline. With roots in natural science, social science, and humanities, geographic problems span the problem-structure continuum. Most problems in physical geography and most problems in Geographic Information Science (GIScience) lack the crystalline clarity of problems in mathematics or physics. Questions of humanistic geography closely resemble those of history, a paradigmatic ill-structured discipline.

As a contested discipline, geography has few laws and theories that receive unanimous approbation. Geography has flirted with traditions of exceptionalism and uniqueness, which makes agreement on problem definition, clear paths to solutions, and agreement on tests of solutions all the more unlikely. Geography's long-standing appreciation of the particularities of context pushes it to the ill-structured end of the continuum. There are few widely accepted curricular structures or dominant textbooks. Depending upon one's perspective, geography enjoys, or suffers from, fierce ideological debates that go to the heart of the discipline's ontology and epistemology. For multiple reasons, geography does not lean toward the well-structured end of the continuum.

Despite the connotations, the characterization of geography as an ill-structured domain is not a negative judgment. The intellectual challenge of becoming an expert is matched by the challenge of understanding that process.

Approaches to expertise

There are three ways of approaching expertise in geography: analysis of autobiographies and biographies, "how to" accounts, and empirical studies. Each approach has strengths and weaknesses. Through triangulation, the three approaches can provide a comprehensive picture of geographic expertise.

Autobiographies have the advantage of showing the mind at work and the disadvantage of doing so retrospectively, suffering from recollection biases. There are relatively few autobiographies by geographers. (For examples, see Buttimer 1983; De Blij 2000; Gould 1999; Gould and Pitts 2002; Haggett 1990; Tuan 1999.) Autobiographies are selective in their existence and in their contents. An autobiography exists when a life is of considerable interest to many and therefore is publishable. It presents a picture of the author as the author would wish to see himself or herself portrayed, not necessarily an accurate picture (Folkenflik 1993; Lejeune 1989; Moss 2001). As the personal equivalent of Whig history, autobiographies present the richness of intellectual life in terms of childhood, progression through formal and informal training, career, and scholarship. The Geographers on Film interviews, directed by M. W. Dow, are autobiographical in nature, answering semi-standard questions about the background, philosophy, and achievements of a few hundred geographers.

Generalizing from geographers' autobiographies is a challenge. In my reading, there are fascinating commonalties: in early life, play with maps, ownership of atlases, explorations into the local world; in formal education, the role of teacher-mentors and the encouragement of families; in early career, the struggle to identify and own an area of scholarship. However, the commonalties rarely offer insights into problem solving, challenges, obstacles, choices leading to breakthroughs, or the role of knowledge and skills. Autobiographies remind us of the human drive to excel, but they do little to help us understand the details of expertise.

Geography is well endowed with how-to accounts, overviews of research scholarship (Gomez and Jones 2010), guidance on undertaking a research project (Flowerdew and Martin 1997), guidance focusing on research in human geography (Cloke 2004; Hoggart, Lees, and Davies 2002), guidance in the use of qualitative methods (Hay 2005), and advice on how to write a dissertation (Parsons, Parsons, and Knight 1995). Phillips's (1976) distinction between "logic in use" and "reconstructed logic" offers a way of thinking about how-to accounts. Reconstructed logic is an idealized and prescriptive representation of the research process. Logic in use (that is, what actually happens) is rarely articulated, because the researcher isn't aware of the steps in the process. How-to accounts are interesting but not necessarily helpful for understanding how expertise operates during problem solving.

There have been few empirical studies of geographic expertise. Hoffman (1987) studied aerial photo interpreters as they engaged in image analysis of terrain. Bellezza (1992) analyzed college students' use of mnemonics in remembering regional geography information as a way of understanding knowledge structures. Both of those studies were conducted by psychologists, and in them there is little discussion of expertise in geography. Sheppard (1993) assessed the consequences of emphasizing the role of geographic expertise in the development of automated geography. Goodchild's (2007) discussions of volunteered geographic information and citizen science point to people operating at the non-expert end of the expertise continuum and yet playing important parts in the expansion of geospatial databases. There have been several studies of expertise in the interpretation of maps (Gilhooly, Wood, Kinnear, and Green 1988; Griffin 1983; Kulhavy, Pridemore, and Stock 1992; Montello, Sullivan, and Pick 1994; Thorndyke and Stasz 1980).

In sum, we know little about the nature or the development of geographic expertise.

A Case Study of Expertise in Geography

An empirical approach

We start with a blank slate in terms of systematic, empirically based accounts of geographic expertise. There are multiple approaches to understanding. Hoffman, Shadboldt, Burton, and Klein (1995, p. 132) cite three methods of eliciting knowledge—"analysis of the tasks that experts perform," "various types of interviews," and "contrived techniques"—and assert that "these can be paraphrased as: What do experts usually do? What do experts say they do? and What do they do when they are constrained in some new way?" All three categories are applicable to studying geographic expertise. Ericsson (1996, pp. 2–3) suggests that any method must generate performances by experts that occur "reliably in clearly specified situations with distinctive observable characteristics," that "should be reproducible under controlled conditions in the laboratory to allow for experimental variation and systematic observation of the mediating processes," and that "should be predictable and described by objective absolute measurements."

Essential tasks

Task choice is critical because experts do not always perform better than non-experts on all tasks in a domain (Ericsson 1996). Experts do, however, outperform non-experts on tasks reflecting the essence of their domain. What tasks might exemplify the essence of geography?

A conceptual answer is "a major research project, one that would be subject to debate." In attempting to give a practical answer, I will follow a well-worn path that accords with popular and professional opinions. Geography is about maps, and one of its essential tasks involves their interpretation. Map interpretation is taught in academic institutions at all educational levels, and also in the military. Textbooks either teach it explicitly or presume that the skill has already been learned. It is used for questions in the K–12 National Assessment of Educational Progress and in graduate-level examinations. It is the basis for sports such as orienteering and geocaching. Map interpretation is emblematic of geography, having face and ecological validity as a task that goes to the discipline's essence.

The task is based on Bunge's (1962) magisterial book *Theoretical Geography*. As an example of "pure spatial prediction," Bunge (p. 246)

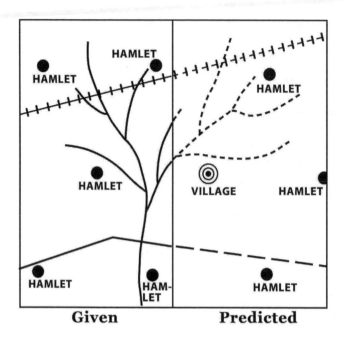

Figure 14.1
Bunge's original map-prediction figure.

presented a map in two sections, one given and one to be predicted (see figure 14.1), and asked "What will the adjacent sheet be like?" The answers for a railroad and a highway were based on extrapolation, the uncertainty increasing with distance from the given map. For the village, however, "No extrapolation is involved. Geographers predict a village because geographic theory demands it." As an extension of Bunge's procedure, I asked people along the expertise continuum to complete the missing map.

There are cognitive science parallels to this task. In exploring problem solving, Bartlett (1932) presented a nested series of sectional road maps, each succeeding map encompassing a larger area. Given a starting point, participants were asked to get to a destination to the northwest. As each map was presented, participants could go back to the starting point or could go to some intervening map to choose a different route. As parallels in geography, Lobeck (1956) used line-drawing maps and cross-sectional diagrams to pose and answer geomorphological questions about the causes of shapes and patterns on Earth's surface. Christaller's 1972 essay on the discovery of Central Place Theory described his use of road maps as the basis for sketching structural arrangements and patterns in the landscape.

I adapted the concept of map prediction as a basis for discussing expertise in educational contexts and in exploring expertise in research contexts. The task is ill-structured. Though there is a clearly defined initial state, the goal state and the transformation rules are undetermined, although the given map is a template with constraints. There is no obvious test to determine solution correctness. Since maps are highly selective models, there are many factors that could affect the solution.

The map-completion process

The following interpretation is based on discussions and think-aloud protocols that illustrate the nature of geographic expertise along the naive-expert continuum and the power and value of an empirical approach.

I made three changes to Bunge's map (figure 14.2), substituting the more familiar word 'village' for 'hamlet', adding a branch to the river system, and adding a key. In educational contexts, I have asked hundreds of people, ranging from fourth-graders to teachers, to complete the missing portion of the map, and then conducted a group discussion of geographical thinking. Classroom discussions took between 30 to 60 minutes. In research contexts, dozens of people, ranging from undergraduates with no background in geography to members of geography faculties, have completed the missing portion and used the think-aloud process (Ericsson and Simon 1993) to describe what they were doing and why they were doing it in that way. Interviewers requested explanations when participants did not spontaneously offer verbal descriptions. The sessions, which took approximately 30 minutes, were videotaped for coding and analysis.

Results

The map-completion problem can be decomposed into four elements, something that people with considerable amounts of geographical training did with ease. The numbered elements in figure 14.3 reflect different challenges in terms of knowledge and skill, not necessarily the sequence used to complete the map. I explained the responses to elements separately, although people with higher levels of expertise looked for and often failed to find interdependencies involving two or more elements of the map. The map must "make sense." In de Groot's (1966) classic study of chess, experts were no better than non-experts at remembering positions of pieces assigned randomly to positions on the board.

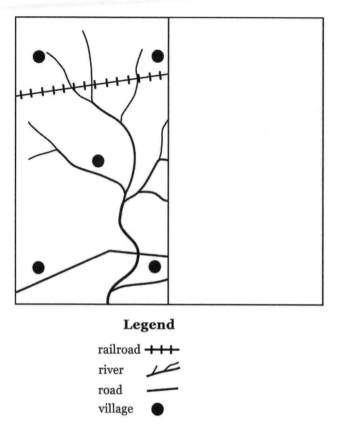

Legend

railroad ┼┼┼

river ↙↗

road ———

village ●

Figure 14.2
The revised map.

All participants made inferences on the basis of the given map, following Bruner's (1957) classic idea of "going beyond the information given." Drawing on their knowledge of maps, the world, and geography, they engaged in spatial extrapolation and interpolation.

The railway line is the simplest problem, something that even younger students solve because it involves straight-line extrapolation (figure 14.4). The reasoning behind the process, however, differs with expertise. The youngest students offered few or no geographic reasons for the line's being straight and continuing to be straight.

At this point in the study, there is evidence of a basic concept that underpins application of expertise to any problem involving spatial graphics: the distinction between graphic and geographic understanding. The lines can be treated as graphic marks to be extrapolated on the basis

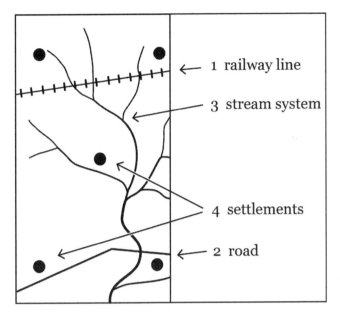

Figure 14.3
Decomposing the map problem into elements.

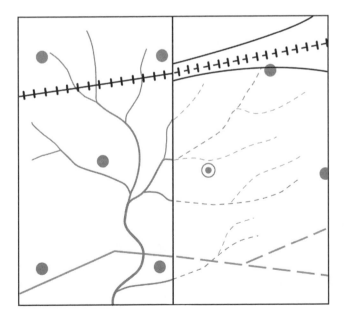

Figure 14.4
The railway line.

of shape. With increasing geographic expertise, lines are seen as graphic symbols representing real-world phenomena; the shapes and patterns of the lines reflect the properties of those phenomena. Understanding of graphic symbolism explains why preschool children commonly have difficulty understanding the symbolic meaning of graphic marks in map interpretation (Liben and Yekel 1996), and why even children as old as 8 or 9 years may be confused when symbols fail to share qualities such as color or shape with their referents (Myers and Liben 2008). Indeed, when questioned about the railway line, younger students believed that the cross-hatching indicated railroad ties, showing a failure to understand either the conventions of graphic symbolism or spatial scale. Participants with greater expertise recognized that, with increasing distance from the predicted map, railway lines may deviate away from the route shown in the given map, and offered explanations in terms of movement toward settlements or deviations as a function of topography (which was only implicit in the map). Even this apparently simple problem demonstrates the intellectual bases of domain-specific expertise in geography.

The road is more complex because of the bend on the given map (figure 14.5). Recognizing the complexity indicates geographic expertise in that it involves understanding that roads (and railway lines) follow paths of least resistance (geodesics). Deviations from a straight line have a cause in geographic space. However, there is a choice in completing the road on the predicted map. If someone believes that the cause on the given map is not repeated on the predicted map, the answer is a straight-line extrapolation. If the cause is repeated, there are multiple options for the predicted path, depending on the cause. People with geographic expertise offer reasons for routes, such as the influence of terrain (hills, marshes, rock types), the role of land ownership in either pulling the route toward or pushing it away from the owner's land, or the desire to cross a river at right angles to minimize bridging costs. Knowledge of a general principle—the minimization of distance—is applied to the particular shape of a geographic space.

The streams require considerably more understanding. (See figure 14.6A.) People with expertise recognize two things. First, streams form an integrated system, and therefore principles of stream ordering can be applied to establish linkages between stream elements. (See figure 14.6B.) There are systematic relationships among stream order and number, length, and basin area. Second, streams fall into types on the basis of patterns and the underlying geology. In this case, the stream system is

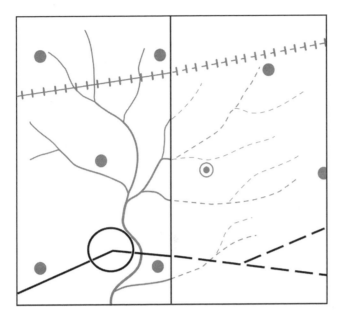

Figure 14.5
The road.

dendritic (figure 14.6C). With these two pieces of knowledge, it is possible to generate the stream pattern on the predicted map (figure 14.6D). Experts can go further in terms of inferences, knowing, for example, that dendritic streams typically develop on relatively homogeneous rocks without strong contrasts in resistance and in areas of relatively gentle slopes. Experts, therefore, describe the land in both halves of the map as sloping gently from the top right to the bottom left corner. Experts and non-experts often attribute cardinal directions to the map even though there is no graphic indicator. For people with less geographic expertise, the top is north because that is "how maps are." People with more expertise recognize that assignment of north as the top of the map is conventional and not necessary, although they too believe that by convention the top of the map is most likely to be north.

The villages require considerable geographic expertise. (See figure 14.7A.) The problem can be solved in three ways. In the first strategy, villages are seen as scattered without any underlying pattern, and therefore villages can be scattered without any underlying geographic logic in the predicted map. In the second strategy, the triangular lattice is seen in the villages in the given map (figure 14.7B), and this pattern can be extended to the

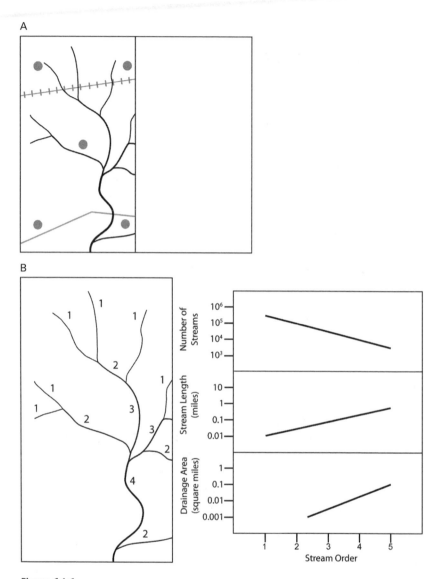

Figure 14.6
Predicting the stream and river pattern. A: the rivers and streams on the given map.
B: stream systems and properties. C: stream types. D: completing the stream and river
system on the predicted map.

C

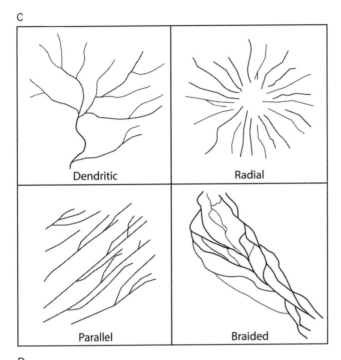

D

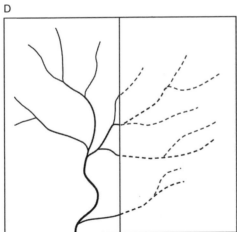

Figure 14.6
(Continued)

predicted map (figure 14.7C). These two strategies are graphic, not geographic. In the third strategy, the triangular lattice is seen as reflecting a central place hierarchy, and thus extension into the predicted map is driven by theory (figure 14.7D). At this point, the existence of a town can be inferred from theory, which adds a novel element to the predicted map and illustrates the power of geographic thinking. The three types of problem solving represent different levels of expertise. School students typically use the first strategy; only a few of them use the second. People with considerable expertise employ the third strategy, because they recognize the underlying patterns and principles.

The preceding analysis is based on elements taken separately. However, at higher levels of expertise, participants look for and fail to find expected connections between elements. There is not, for example, a strong connection between the route of either the road or the railway line and the locations of the settlements, something that would be expected from geographical principles. Thus, some participants produced extrapolations for the road and the railway line that made direct connections to the settlements. There were arguments for stronger connections between the settlements and the stream system. Among those with the highest levels of expertise there was a recognition that, although decomposition into separable elements was necessary, reassembling the elements into an integrated and geographically coherent landscape is a critical step.

The nature of geographic expertise

The characteristics of geographic expertise that emerge from the instructional and research versions of the task are remarkably consistent with the general properties of expertise that cognitive science has identified.

There are multiple strategies that are used in problem solving. For an expert, a typical sequence would be as follows: Decompose the map into functional elements; look for patterns in the elements; look for exceptions; extrapolate and/or interpolate elements; look for connections among elements; modify patterns to accord with what makes geographical sense and is aesthetically pleasing. Cross-cutting the strategies is the difference between using logics based on graphic considerations and using logics based on geographic principles. The latter are typically used by people with considerable expertise, the former by novices.

The role of knowledge is fundamental. Experts access deep knowledge structures quickly, identifying the stream system as dendritic or the settlements as a central place network. They offer detailed explanations of underlying geographic principles, talking about rock strata in the case of

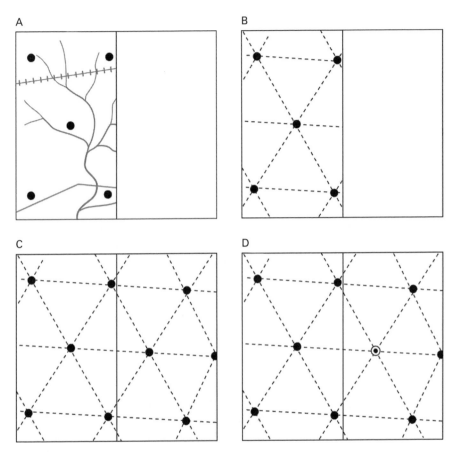

Figure 14.7
Predicting the villages. A: the villages. B: the pattern of villages on the given map. C: completing the pattern of villages on the predicted map. D: adding the town to the predicted map.

dendritic streams or about different k values in the case of the central place system.[5] All participants expressed feelings of being challenged, frustrated, and satisfied. For school students, there was a sense of triumph and satisfaction on completing the map exercise. Solving problems is not a neutral and impersonal process. Experts saw the map as simplistic and lacking essential information, which led to some annoyance and frustration. Despite this, they saw coherence to the landscape depicted on the two halves of the map. That coherence, as in something making sense, is captured by Bunge's comment about the existence of the village (in this case the town): "geographic theory demands it."

Principled knowledge is a hallmark of expertise. This simple task taps into knowledge of shortest paths in transport systems, the patterns and processes underlying stream systems, and the logic of settlement patterns. Theories and principles generate expectations. Those expectations lead to predictions for various elements, but those elements must be mutually adjusted to be intellectually and aesthetically satisfying.

Conclusion: Strategic Approaches to Understanding Geographic Expertise

Strategies for studying geographic expertise

We can turn to other disciplines for models to study expertise. In view of geography's tripartite structure, we can turn to physics (Van Lehn and van de Sande 2009) as a model for physical geography, to political science (Voss, Carretero, Kennett, and Ney Silfies 1994) for social-science versions of human geography, and to history (Leinhardt et al. 1994) for humanistic approaches to geography. Analysis of the literature of each of these disciplines indicates the scale of the effort needed in time, resources, and approaches.

Several things are clear. First, we need a range of approaches (e.g., case studies of problem solvers across the expertise range; focused studies using a small set of tasks; reviews of biographies and autobiographies). Second, we need to mix cross-sectional with longitudinal studies. Geography has little experience with longitudinal studies over months, let alone years or decades. Third, we need to apply findings to the design of expert systems for education at all levels. Mounting such efforts would be comparable in time and resources to those devoted to the National Center for Geographic Information and Analysis, which has successfully developed GIScience since 1988 with funding from the National Science Foundation.

Tasks for studying geographic expertise

In cognitive science, chess has been a domain for studying expertise: "Because of its unique properties—particularly its rating scale and method of recording games—chess offers cognitive psychologists an ideal task environment in which to study skilled performance. It has been called a *Drosophila*, or fruit fly, for cognitive psychology." (Charness 1991, p. 39)

Geography needs a set of tasks—a geo-*Drosophila*, so to speak—for studying geographic performances. Tasks should be arrayed along two continua: from ill-structured to well-structured and from novice to expert. Tasks should be ecologically valid, rich in possibilities, challenging, interesting, meaningful, amenable to think-aloud protocols, and limited in number to ensure a focused database.

Developing tasks will be crucial to systematic studies of expertise. As examples of tasks, people could be asked to identify the projections underlying maps, to complete a "Where's Waldo?' task as an assessment of understanding GIS operations, to link cross sections and geomorphological features, and to interpret landscapes in topographic maps.

The problem of problem selection

The task I used and those I have suggested relate to the essence of geography in that the knowledge and skills required for their solution are central to geography's way of thinking. In that respect, they tap directly into expertise. In another sense, they miss one hallmark of expertise: identification of worthwhile problems. Getzels (1979, p. 167) argued that "very little is known about how problems are found and formulated."

Three of the stages of Kuhn's (1962) normal science were deciding which problems were worth pursuing, considering how to approach them, and recognizing what would constitute an acceptable solution. The latter two stages are characteristic of expertise, and yet the first stage distinguishes the truly great scholar from the expert. Indeed, "finding the productive problem may be no less an intellectual achievement than attaining the productive solution" (Getzels 1979, p. 168).

Birch (1977) saw the pursuit of excellence in geography as being a function: "problem solving, believing it to be the most general test of intellectual excellence" (p. 428) and "the necessary relationship in scholarship between the achievement of excellence and the clarity of formulation of the essential problems at issue" (p. 426).

Understanding how and why someone sees a problem, especially in an area not considered problematic, is crucial to accounts of expertise. As cognitive scientists recognized, problem finding is not subject to scientific manipulation. At best, it is the province of biographies and autobiographies. At worst, it remains a mysterious ability—one to be admired but not explained.

Rationales for studying geographic expertise

Understanding the nature of geographic expertise—its character, the differences between novices and experts, and the links to the history of the discipline—is a necessary first step, one that will be rewarding in its own right.

However, as has happened in cognitive science, the next step—understanding the acquisition of expertise—is critical for geography at all levels. By understanding how expertise is acquired, we can design programs to share the power and beauty of doing geography. But designing curricula, textbooks, software, and pedagogical approaches requires benchmarks for expected and desired levels of performance. Assessing progress and providing feedback are essential. What should an 18-year-old know and be able to do, in contrast to an 8-year-old? What levels and types of knowledge and skills are expected of a graduate student completing a doctorate?

These are not questions "just' for geography education. They go to the heart of understanding geography as a way of thinking, something that is of theoretical, practical, and emotional importance to all geographers. This is the reason why geography needs to embark on a systematic, long-term program of research on expertise.

Acknowledgments

I would like to acknowledge the work of Valerie Sebestyen in preparing the figures and that of Lynn Liben in commenting on numerous revisions of the manuscript.

Notes

1. See www.nationalacademies.org/memarea/.

2. See www.amacad.org/about.aspx.

3. See www.aaas.org/aboutaaas/fellows/.

4. See www.igu-online.org/site.

5. The k value refers to the structural arrangement between, in this case, the villages and the town. A k value of 3 would see three villages related to the town; values of 4 and 7 also would be possible.

References

Bartlett, F. C. 1932. *Remembering: A Study in Experimental and Social Psychology.* Cambridge University Press.

Batty, M. 2002. The Geography of Scientific Citation. Available at http://www.casa .ucl.ac.uk.

Bellezza, F. S. 1992. Mnemonics and expert knowledge: Mental cuing. In *The Psychology of Expertise: Cognitive Research and Empirical AI*, ed. R. R. Hoffman. Springer.

Birch, W. 1977. On excellence and problem solving in geography. *Transactions of the Institute of British Geographers, N. S.* 2 (4): 417–429.

Bowman, I. 1921. *The New World: Problems in Political Geography.* World.

Bruner, J. S. 1957. Going beyond the information given. In *Contemporary Approaches to Cognition*, ed. J. S. Bruner, E. Brunswik, L. Festinger, F. Heider, K. F. Muenzinger, C. E. Osgood, et al. Harvard University Press.

Bunge, W. W., Jr. 1962. *Theoretical Geography.* Gleerup.

Buttimer, A. 1983. *The Practice of Geography.* Longman.

Capri, A. Z. 2011. *Quips, Quotes, and Quanta: An Anecdotal History of Physics.* World Scientific.

Carretero, M., and Voss, J. F., eds. 1994. *Cognitive and Instructional Processes in History and the Social Sciences.* Erlbaum.

Charness, N. 1991. Expertise in chess: The balance between knowledge and search. In *Toward a General Theory of Expertise: Prospects and Limits*, ed. K. A. Ericsson and J. Smith. Cambridge University Press.

Chase, W. G., and Simon, H. A. 1973. The mind's eye in chess. In *Visual Information Processing*, ed. W. G. Chase. Academic Press.

Chi, M. T. H. 2006. Two approaches to the study of experts' characteristics. In *The Cambridge Handbook of Expertise and Expert Performance*, ed. K. A. Ericsson. Cambridge University Press.

Chi, M. T. H., Feltovich, P. J., and Glaser, R. 1981. Categorization and representation of physics problems by experts and novices. *Cognitive Science* 5: 121–152.

Christaller, W. 1972. How I discovered the theory of central places: A report about the origins of central paces. In *Man, Space, and Environment: Concepts in Contemporary Human Geography*, ed. P. W. English and R. C. Mayfield. Oxford University Press.

Clark, W. A. V. 1991. Geography in court: Expertise in adversarial settings. *Transactions of the Institute of British Geographers, N. S.* 16 (1): 5–20.

Cloke, P. 2004. *Practising Human Geography*. SAGE.

Cooke, N. J. 1992. Modeling human expertise in expert systems. In *The Psychology of Expertise: Cognitive Research and Empirical AI*, ed. R. R. Hoffman. Springer.

Coughlan, R. 1954. Dr. Teller's magnificent obsession. *Life*, September.

De Blij, H. J. 2000. *Wartime Encounter with Geography*. Book Guild.

de Groot, A. D. 1966. Perception and memory versus thought: Some old ideas and recent findings. In *Problem Solving: Research, Method and Theory*, ed. B. Kleinmuntz. Wiley.

Ericsson, K. A. 1996. The acquisition of expert performance: An introduction to some of the issues. In *The Road to Excellence: The Acquisition of Expert Performance in the Arts And Sciences, Sports And Games*, ed. K. A. Ericsson. Erlbaum.

Ericsson, K. A., and Simon, H. A. 1993. *Protocol Analysis: Verbal Reports as Data*. MIT Press.

Ericsson, K. A., Charness, N., Hoffman, R. R., and Feltovich, P. J., eds. 2009. *The Cambridge Handbook of Expertise and Expert Performance*. Cambridge University Press.

Flowerdew, R., and Martin, D. 1997. *Methods in Human Geography: A Guide for Students Doing a Research Project*. Longman.

Folkenflik, R., ed. 1993. *The Culture of Autobiography: Constructions of Self-Representation*. Stanford University Press.

Geography Education Standards Project. 2013. *Geography for Life: The National Geography Standards*, second edition. National Council for Geographic Education.

Getzels, J. W. 1979. Problem finding: A theoretical note. *Cognitive Science* 3: 167–172.

Gilhooly, K. J., Wood, M., Kinnear, P. R., and Green, C. 1988. Skill in map reading and memory for maps. *Quarterly Journal of Experimental Psychology: Human Experimental Psychology* 40: 87–107.

Gomez, B., and Jones, J. P., III. 2010. *Research Methods in Geography: A Critical Introduction*. Wiley.

Goodchild, M. F. 2007. Citizens as voluntary sensors: Spatial data infrastructure in the world of Web 2.0. *International Journal of Spatial Data Infrastructures Research* 2: 24–32.

Gould, P. 1999. *Becoming a Geographer*. Syracuse University Press.

Gould, P., and Pitts, F. R. 2002. *Geographical Voices: Fourteen Autobiographical Essays*. Syracuse University Press.

Griffin, T. L. C. 1983. Problem solving on maps—the importance of user strategies. *Cartographic Journal* 20: 101–109.

Haggett, P. 1990. *The Geographer's Art*. Blackwell.

Hanson, S., ed. 1997. *Ten Geographic Ideas That Changed the World*. Rutgers University Press.

Hay, I. 2005. *Qualitative Research Methods in Human Geography*. Oxford University Press.

Hoffman, R. R. 1987. The problem of extracting the knowledge of experts from the perspective of experimental psychology. *AI Magazine* 8 (2): 53–67.

Hoffman, R. R., ed. 1992. *The Psychology of Expertise*. Springer.

Hoffman, R. R., Shadboldt, N. R., Burton, A. M., and Klein, G. 1995. Eliciting knowledge from experts: A methodological analysis. *Organizational Behavior and Human Decision Processes* 62 (2): 129–158.

Hoggart, K., Lees, L., and Davies, A. 2002. *Researching Human Geography*. Edward Arnold.

Kates, R. 2011. *Gilbert F. White 1911–2006*. National Academy of Sciences.

King, P. M., and Kitchener, K. S. 1994. *Developing Reflective Judgment: Understanding and Promoting Intellectual Growth and Critical Thinking in Adolescents and Adults*. Jossey-Bass.

Kuhn, T. S. 1962. *The Structure of Scientific Revolutions*. University of Chicago Press.

Kulhavy, R. W., Pridemore, D. R., and Stock, W. A. 1992. Cartographic experience and thinking aloud about thematic maps. *Cartographica* 29: 1–9.

Larkin, J., McDermott, J., Simon, D. P., and Simon, H. A. 1980. Expert and novice performance in solving physics problems. *Science* 208: 1335–1342.

Leinhardt, G., Beck, I. L., and Stainton, C., eds. 1994. *Teaching and Learning in History*. Erlbaum.

Lejeune, P. 1989. *On Autobiography*. University of Minnesota Press.

Liben, L. S., and Yekel, C. A. 1996. Preschoolers understanding of plan and oblique maps: The role of geometrical and representational correspondence. *Child Development* 67 (6): 2780–2796.

Livingstone, D. 1992. *The Geographical Tradition: Episodes in the History of a Contested Discipline*. Blackwell.

Lobeck, A. K. 1956. *Things Maps Don't Tell Us: An Adventure into Map Interpretation*. Macmillan.

Mitchell, J. K. 1978. The expert witness: A geographer's perspective on environmental litigation. *Geographical Review* 68 (2): 209–214.

Montello, D. R., Sullivan, C. N., and Pick, H. L. 1994. Recall memory for topographic maps and natural terrain: Effects of experience and task performance. *Cartographica* 31: 18–36.

Morrill, R. L. 1973. Ideal and reality in reapportionment. *Annals of the Association of American Geographers* 63: 463–477.

Morrill, R. L. 1976. Redistricting revisited. *Annals of the Association of American Geographers* 66: 548–566.

Moss, P., ed. 2001. *Placing Autobiography in Geography*. Syracuse University Press.

Murphy, A. B. 2006. Enhancing geography's role in public debate. *Annals of the Association of American Geographers* 96 (1): 1–13.

Myers, L. J., and Liben, L. S. 2008. The role of intentionality and iconicity in children's developing comprehension of cartographic symbols. *Child Development* 79 (3): 668–684.

Parsons, A. J., Parsons, T., and Knight, P. 1995. *How to Do Your Dissertation in Geography and Related Disciplines*. Chapman and Hall.

Phillips, B. S. 1976. *Social Research Strategy and Tactics*, third edition. Macmillan.

Reitman, W. R. 1965. *Cognition and Thought*. Wiley.

Sheppard, E. 1993. Automated geography: What kind of geography for what kind of society? *Professional Geographer* 45 (4): 457–460.

Simon, H. 1973. The structure of an ill-structured problem. *Artificial Intelligence* 4: 181–201.

Sinnott, J. D. 1992. A model for solution of ill-structured problems: Implications for everyday and abstract problem solving. In *Everyday Problem Solving: Theory and Application*, ed. J. D. Sinnott. Praeger.

Smith, N. 2002. *American Empire: Roosevelt's Geographer and the Prelude to Globalization*. University of California Press.

Thorndyke, P. W., and Stasz, C. 1980. Individual differences in procedures for knowledge acquisition from maps. *Cognitive Psychology* 12: 137–175.

Tuan, Y.-F. 1999. *Who Am I? An Autobiography of Emotion, Mind, and Spirit*. University of Wisconsin Press.

Turner, B. L., II. 2005. Geography's profile in public debate "inside the Beltway" and the National Academies. *Professional Geographer* 57 (3): 462–467.

Van Lehn, K., and van de Sande, B. 2009. Acquiring conceptual expertise from modeling: The case of elementary physics. In *The Development of Professional Performance: Toward Measurement of Expert Performance and Design of Optimal Learning Environments*, ed. K. A. Ericsson. Cambridge University Press.

Voss, J. F., and Wiley, J. 2006. Expertise in history. In *The Cambridge Handbook of Expertise and Expert Performance*, ed. K. A. Ericsson, N. Charness, P. J. Feltovich, and R. R. Hoffman. Cambridge University Press.

Voss, J. F., Carretero, M., Kennett, J., and Ney Silfies, L. 1994. The collapse of the Soviet Union: A case study in causal reasoning. In *Cognitive and Instructional Processes in History and the Social Sciences*, ed. M. Carretero and J. F. Voss. Erlbaum.

Wrigley, N., and Matthews, S. 1986. Citation classics and citation levels in geography. *Area* 18 (3): 185–194.

V   Epilogue

15   Learning to Live with Spatial Technologies

Michael F. Goodchild

The report *Learning to Think Spatially* (National Research Council 2006), which is cited in many of the chapters in this book, has as its subtitle *GIS as a Support System in the K–12 Curriculum*. My own interests in spatial thinking are similarly grounded in GIS (geographic information systems; my use of the term in what follows encompasses all technologies that manipulate geographic information, which I define as geographically referenced information about the surface and near-surface of the Earth), and in almost 40 years of teaching, researching, and writing about the topic. I have been eager to understand the role of that powerful technology in building our knowledge of the geographic world and in enabling our human activities within it, and how that role will evolve as the technology continues its very rapid growth. In thinking about how to structure this epilogue, and how to help to bring the book to a close, it seems to me that GIS can provide a useful framing, a means of linking contributions that have extended well beyond the respective scopes of geography and psychology.

A distinction is often drawn between training in GIS, with its emphasis on how to manipulate the software to achieve certain objectives, and education in GIS, with its emphasis on the underlying principles that are implemented in the software's construction and guide the reasoning of an intelligent user. Recently it has become commonplace to refer to those principles as geographic information *science* (Goodchild 1992). In the early days of GIS, the user interface was clumsy and hard to learn (until the 1990s, commands had to be typed in a prescribed syntax, for example—so GIS labs were often very frustrating for students. At the end of a year-long course sequence at the University of California at Santa Barbara, I liked to give the students a task that would be personally rewarding and would help them to forget the pain of the previous months. A "fly-by"—a simulated flight over the Santa Barbara area—was suitably rewarding, and could be used to impress family members and friends. But in 2005, with the release of Google Earth, it suddenly became possible for a 10-year-old child to generate a fly-by in 10 minutes, without any background knowledge of geography or GIS, or indeed without post-primary education in any academic discipline.

More broadly, during the past decade, there has been a steady erosion of the need for GIS training, as more and more GIS functions have become available behind easy-to-use interfaces. Owners of smart phones can now find points of interest and solve wayfinding problems without any of the training that is still needed to replicate these functions in a state-of-the-art GIS. But the underlying principles are still the same, and the need for education in GIScience is as strong as ever. As the report *Learning to Think Spatially* (National Research Council 2006) shows, it is easy to be misled by the powerful GIS tools that are now available to everyone. The earlier *How to Lie with Maps* (Monmonier 1991) is a masterful compendium of how maps can mislead and misdirect, and Wood (1992), Wood, Fels, and Krygier (2010), Harley (2001), and many others have documented the hidden agendas that lurk beneath what may appear to be an objective presentation of information about geography.

GI *systems* are no more and no less than tools. When directed by thoughtful users, they can be very powerful. Use of GIS is, thus, a collaboration between machine and mind, rather than a service performed by a machine. My reaction to the 2005 release of Google Earth, and to the many other developments that have increased the engagement of the general public with GIS, has been to ponder exactly what might be meant by "thoughtful." What should a well-educated user know when approaching GIS? How have my own thought processes been modified by four decades of exposure to these systems?

As will be abundantly evident to anyone who has sampled the pages of this book, or followed the growing literature on spatial thinking, the answer lies in spatial skills. The objectives of the 2006 NRC report were to show that spatial skills were essential to survival in modern society and that these skills could be enhanced through exposure to GIS. A thoughtful user of GIS is one who thinks spatially—more specific, one who comes to GIS armed with an understanding of spatial concepts and of how they are instantiated in the geographic world. In my own case, these skills originated in an early education in mathematics, especially in geometry; in a first degree in physics, with its emphasis on processes embedded in space and time; in a lifetime of exploring and navigating through the complex underground spaces of caves; and in decades of developing, working with, and explaining GIS.

Thinking with GIS

GIS can be defined as a set of computer-based tools for acquiring, compiling, storing, analyzing, visualizing, and sharing geographic information—essentially, for performing any conceivable function on geographic information that can be represented in a computational procedure (Longley, Goodchild, Maguire, and Rhind 2011). If spatial skills are important to intelligent use of GIS, it follows that the designers and developers of GIS, as well as its users, should have them. The consequences of not having spatial skills are easy to illustrate. The 2006 NRC report, for example, cites the now-well-known case of an article in the magazine *The Economist* in which a map was used to show the range of missiles being developed by North Korea. Since any flat map must distort, a circle drawn on the map will not generally connect points equidistant from its center. Figure 15.1 shows a closely related example: a screen shot from an online mapping service sponsored by a US federal agency. The representative fraction, or "scale," of the map is shown at the top of the screen and has been enlarged. No map, however extensive the area represented, can have a truly constant scale, so it is normal to round the value rather than express it to eight significant digits, as here. But this map uses a version of the Mercator

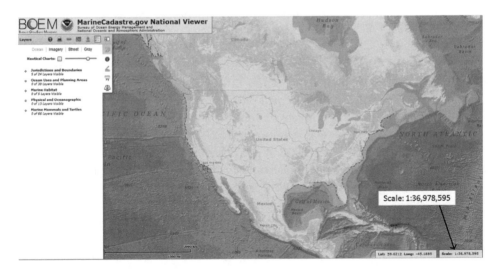

Figure 15.1

A screen shot from the marine cadaster viewer (csc.noaa.gov/mmcviewer) of the National Oceanic and Atmospheric Administration. Note the annotation at the lower right corner: "Scale: 1:36,978,595."

projection, and from the bottom edge to the top edge of the map the representative fraction, which is proportional to cos(latitude), changes by a factor of roughly 2. Clearly what happened here is that the software was coded by a GIS programmer who lacked a basic understanding of the relationship between the three-dimensional globe and the flattened two-dimensional map, copied the scale of the Mercator projection at the equator from a readily accessible source, then evaluated and displayed it to the maximum precision of the machine. We must conclude that the federal agency's own experts were unaware of the problem when the service was launched, and that users of the map are similarly unaware if no protests have been made.

Much has been written in the past few decades about the use of GIS for scientific discovery and decision support (see Longley et al. 2011), but comparatively little has been written about its use by people lacking the basic knowledge needed for successful manipulation of geographic information. That basic knowledge may well be lacking in those who design and develop software, or in those who use that software in everyday life. Many of the chapters of this book have addressed the enhancement of spatial skills through learning and education. To ensure that the designers and developers of GIS software have those skills requires more, however. It requires recognition of the importance of spatial skills in the relevant curricula and job descriptions, detailed documentation of exactly what those skills entail, and a method of determining whether a candidate possesses those skills.

GIS tools are now readily accessible through personal devices. Among their applications are locating points of interest, businesses, and friends; searching for conveniently located services; obtaining navigational directions; mapping crime, outbreaks of disease, and personal travel; and publishing maps. Though it is tempting to hope that exposure to such tools will enhance users' spatial skills, it is also possible and perhaps even likely that reliance on such tools erodes a user's memory of geographic detail. In the past, memory was essential to navigation, but today the services of personal devices are making paper maps and street guides increasingly obsolete. Moreover, in a world in which spatial search services are available everywhere, at all times, many of the principles of spatial organization that have long eased the task of navigating from memory become redundant. Services that rely on impulse, such as convenience stores and fast-food restaurants, no longer have to be located conspicuously in order to be discovered, and high-end specialty stores, such as jewelry stores, no longer have to cluster in space, as more and more of their business is conducted online.

Consider a university campus and the wayfinding tasks of the students, faculty members, and staff members. At the University of California at Santa Barbara, for example, science and engineering can be found by heading toward the rising sun, and the humanities by heading away from it. Professors of geography can be found by locating the geography building. But as scholarship becomes more and more collaborative and interdisciplinary, as personal devices make it easier and easier to interact in virtual space, and as those same devices make complex wayfinding easy, such elaborate spatial organization becomes less and less necessary. Far from providing a straightforward fix to a simple problem, therefore, GIS services are likely, in the long term, to support fundamental changes in the way society is organized, and in how society interacts with its environment.

To date, GIS has focused largely on outdoor spaces, where geography can be usefully represented in only two spatial dimensions, and where the fixed nature of many features means that representations that ignore time can be useful. These limitations are steadily disappearing, however—in part because of the increasing availability of time-dependent information from such novel sources as GPS tracking and social media; in part because of the increasing positional accuracy and spatial resolution of more conventional geographic information; and in part because of the drive to provide wayfinding services in the complex three-dimensional spaces of buildings and mines where GPS signals are typically unavailable.

It seems reasonable to suppose that eventually we will be able to navigate everywhere, not only outdoors, by using services available through personal devices; that we will be able to determine the up-to-the-minute locations of everything, including moving things, to decimeter accuracy, and to query their properties; and that concerns about privacy, confidentiality, and surveillance will loom larger than ever.

Spatial Skills: A Personal Assessment

In this section, if I can be allowed a little personal reflection, I propose to explore the evolution of my own spatial thinking, first through the need to navigate successfully through complex cave environments and then through four decades of research and teaching with and about GIS.

Cave navigation

Caves arguably present among the most challenging navigational problems. They are three-dimensional, they are geometrically and topologically complex, and the consequences of navigational failure can be extreme. Although most known caves have been mapped, the maps are rarely helpful to navigation. Often one must rely on very detailed three-dimensional knowledge in order to find one's way through complex mazes that are hard to represent effectively in two dimensions. Moreover, the caving community frowns on unsightly and intrusive aids to navigation, such as string, arrows, or colored tape. Instead cavers learn a number of reliable heuristics and use them individually or in combination. Most caves are formed by flowing water. Since the direction and the speed of water's flow can often be inferred from sculpted markings on cave walls, it is possible to navigate consistently upstream or downstream even where the formative stream has long since disappeared. If a cave has multiple entrances at different elevations, there will be a consistent convective air flow that can be followed. Cavers also learn to look backward at critical points, so that a return route can be recognized. Most useful, perhaps, are the mental representations that cavers create and use to navigate. I find, for example, that the memories I stored decades ago, when I was physically much stronger than I am now, are now inadequate, because they omit many of the features that are now important to me. Decades ago I would not have bothered to remember a ten-meter flat-out crawl in a stream that today seems at or beyond my physical limits.

My GIS support system

Like many others, I began my exposure to computerized maps and GIS with the assumption that little background knowledge was needed to apply them effectively. When I first encountered GIS, in the early 1970s, I had no knowledge of the principles of geodesy, cartography, or photogrammetry. Yet in the intervening forty years I have come to recognize that certain principles can be important to effective application of GIS, and that those principles can be as important in this domain as the second law of thermodynamics is in physics, or the periodic table in chemistry.

Over the past few decades I have devoted much of my time to discussing the potential of GIS in every part of the academy, from the humanities to engineering, and have learned how many patterns of thought that are by now instinctive to me are unusual and almost alien to others. When faced with interpreting geographic information, for example, such as the variation in some socioeconomic parameter over the fifty US states, my first instinct is to make a map, whereas in my experience many social scientists would never think of a map as a research tool. Shown a scatterplot of such information with some distinct outliers, I first want to know where those outliers are found on the map, so as to be able to search my own mind for geographic associations that might suggest an explanation.

Consider these three statements:

"Isla Vista is the most crowded urban area in the United States." (This is a widely cited belief in the UCSB community.)

"North Carolina has 301 miles of coastline." (source: Beaver 2006)

"Black Rock Playa (home of the Burning Man festival) is the second-largest flat region in the Northern Hemisphere." (source: http://www.burning man.com)

Since there is no official definition of the geographic limits of Isla Vista (no polygon, in GIS terms), there is no way to confirm or deny the first statement. The literature of fractals (e.g., Mandelbrot 1967) makes the second statement meaningless, since the length of a natural feature such as a coastline is a function of scale, rising as the scale becomes finer, and often at a predictable rate, until the definition of coastline breaks down. The third statement is also meaningless in the absence of any rigorous definition of "region" and any way of enumerating them: the number of such unspecified "regions" in the Northern Hemisphere is simply infinite. Though all three statements are consistent with principles of English syntax, none stands up to critical examination by an experienced spatial thinker.

Figure 15.2 shows the statistical significance of mortality counts among white American males of cancers of the respiratory system between 1950 and 1969, by county. The eye is immediately drawn to the red areas, where mortality is significantly above the national average, and begins looking for patterns and associations with remembered facts about the geography of the United States. Why, for example, is the rate so high in two adjacent counties in western Montana—because Butte and its mining industry are nearby? Why do Chicago, Detroit, and Buffalo have relatively high rates but not Minneapolis–St. Paul or Seattle? Why are the rates so high in certain coastal counties where shipbuilding was concentrated during World War II—could it be because of the heavy use of asbestos?

Many other principles have been cited at various places in this volume, most comprehensively by Karl Grossner and Donald Janelle. I will not try to provide a complete enumeration of the principles I have found most

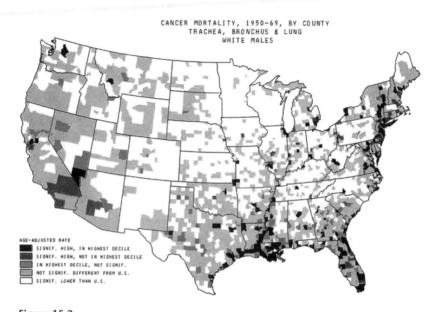

CANCER MORTALITY, 1950-69, BY COUNTY
TRACHEA, BRONCHUS & LUNG
WHITE MALES

AGE-ADJUSTED RATE
SIGNIF. HIGH, IN HIGHEST DECILE
SIGNIF. HIGH, NOT IN HIGHEST DECILE
IN HIGHEST DECILE, NOT SIGNIF.
NOT SIGNIF. DIFFERENT FROM U.S.
SIGNIF. LOWER THAN U.S.

Figure 15.2
Statistical significance of respiratory cancer mortality among white males in US counties, 1950–1969.

useful in my own research and have emphasized in my teaching, but perhaps one more example will be helpful. The modifiable areal unit problem (MAUP), first defined by Stan Openshaw and Peter Taylor, stands as one of the most important foundations of geographic information science. Briefly, it deals with the analysis of data aggregated to geographic regions. It states that the results of any analysis will depend on the precise delimitation of those regions, and will change when the regions are changed. Though it is tempting to think that changing region boundaries is analogous to taking a different sample, Openshaw and Taylor showed that the sampling metaphor was inappropriate and unhelpful. (See Openshaw 1983.)

Figure 15.3 shows an example, using population density for the state of California. On the left, counties are colored according to the 1990 population densities published by the US Bureau of the Census. But county boundaries were laid down over 100 years ago and bear little relationship to the geographic realities of today's California. The Mojave Desert, for example, is largely unpopulated, but according to this map the parts of it that lie in Los Angeles, Riverside, and San Bernardino counties have exactly the same population density as the heavily populated parts of those

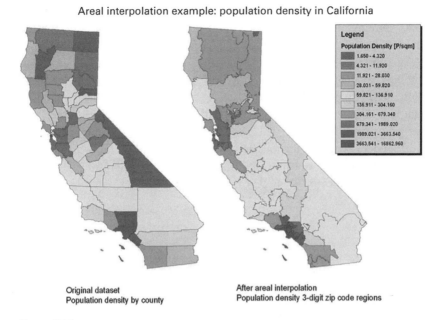

Figure 15.3

Population density for California in 1990. Left: as published by county. Right: estimated for three-digit ZIP codes.

counties. On the right, population density has been estimated for regions defined by the first three digits of the ZIP code, using area-weighted interpolation (Goodchild and Lam 1980). Because three-digit ZIP regions are smaller in areas of high population density and larger in less populated areas, this map provides what is clearly a better approximation to the true population distribution of California. (There are still problems, of course; and ironically, area-weighted interpolation assumes uniform population density in the source areas.) The MAUP underlies many applications of geographic information, and I have learned to be instinctively critical of any analysis of aggregated data.

Conclusion

I have tried in this short contribution to identify some of the ways in which GIS provides a framework for discussion of spatial skills and their role in working with geographic information. I have also argued that geographic technologies will become even more important as the spatial organization of society changes, and as people place greater reliance on these tools.

Recent developments, including smart-phone apps and online services, have demonstrated that it is possible to develop geographic information and to work with it without having a basic understanding of the nature of geography or well-developed spatial skills. Yet there are abundant examples of how easy it is to misuse and misinterpret geographic information. Enhancing spatial skills through learning and education—the central purpose of this book—can help by ensuring that developers and users have an understanding of how to interpret the results they obtain from apps and services. And as a distinct but less direct benefit, we know from abundant and replicated research that the level of development of spatial skills is a reliable indicator of success in science, technology, engineering, and mathematics.

References

Beaver, J. C. 2006. U.S. International Borders: Brief Facts. Congressional Research Service (http://www.fas.org/sgp/crs/misc/RS21729.pdf).

Goodchild, M. F. 1992. Geographical information science. *International Journal of Geographical Information Systems* 6: 31–45.

Goodchild, M. F., and Lam, N. S. 1980. Areal interpolation: A variant of the traditional spatial problem. *Geoprocessing* 1: 297–312.

Harley, J. B. 2001. *The New Nature of Maps: Essays in the History of Cartography*. Johns Hopkins University Press.

Longley, P. A., Goodchild, M. F., Maguire, D. J., and Rhind, D. W. 2011. *Geographic Information Systems and Science*, third edition. Wiley.

Mandelbrot, B. 1967. How long is the coast of Britain? Statistical self-similarity and fractional dimension. *Science, NS* 156 (3775): 636–638.

Monmonier, M. S. 1991. *How to Lie with Maps*. University of Chicago Press.

National Research Council. 2006. *Learning to Think Spatially: GIS as a Support System in the K–12 Curriculum*. National Academies Press.

Openshaw, S. 1983. *The Modifiable Areal Unit Problem*. GeoBooks.

Wood, D. 1992. *The Power of Maps*. Guilford.

Wood, D., Fels, J., and Krygier, J. 2010. *Rethinking the Power of Maps*. Guilford.

16   Teaching Space: What, How, and When

Nora S. Newcombe

Space in Mind is a wonderful title for a book, with many implications and connotations. Then, once we have savored the title, we get to the subtitle, *Concepts for Spatial Learning and Education*. This phrase strikes a more concrete and practical note. In fact, it delineates the central challenge for those of us who believe that spatial learning is exciting and that spatial education is an essential foundation for effective participation in modern technological society. What exactly are we advocating; what are we trying to teach? If we can answer this question, we can go on to consider further practical issues, such as how and when we should be teaching space. Knowing what to teach, when, and how would then provide the basis for constructing curricula, guidelines, and objectives.

We don't have all the answers yet, which is why this book is needed. But let's first applaud the fact that even considering such issues is a notable accomplishment. Not long ago, the very idea of spatial learning and education would have been considered odd. Spatial thinking was a neglected topic relative to other topics in the various disciplines that potentially address it. In cognitive and developmental psychology, there was much more interest in language acquisition, theory of mind, and memory. In education and educational psychology, there was more interest in the teaching of reading and mathematics and the study of student motivation. Many universities had abandoned their departments of geography altogether, and the study of geography in the K–12 system had been merged with the study of history to create social studies. In psychometrics and assessment, there were certainly tests of spatial ability, but those tests were rarely included in IQ tests, and there was no agreement on how the various tests fit together. Perhaps most problematic, over all fields and in the popular imagination, the inclination and ability to think spatially were widely regarded as fixed rather than learned, as difficult to change, and hence not as targets for intervention and education.

The situation has changed considerably in the last two decades, and at an accelerating pace. An early milestone was the publication of *Geography for Life* (Geography Education Standards Project 1994), a book that laid out the National Geography Standards for American K–12 education.[1] Probably even more important was the publication of *Learning to Think Spatially* (National Research Council 2006), a report written by an interdisciplinary panel that expanded a charge to consider the educational uses of geographic information systems (GIS) into a probing and comprehensive look at the development of spatial thinking. *Learning to Think Spatially* emphasized malleability and (I believe) included the first occurrence of the phrase "spatializing the curriculum." Subsequently, GIS became such a popular and economically important tool that learning to use it has been increasingly seen as vocationally relevant and valuable. Furthermore, scientific papers have appeared that support the importance of spatial thinking in achievement in the science, technology, engineering, and mathematical (STEM) disciplines (e.g., Wai, Lubinski, and Benbow 2009) and that show us that spatial ability is not fixed at all but rather is substantially malleable, improvements being both durable over time and generalizing beyond the trained skill (Uttal et al. 2013). Another recent indicator of interest in spatial learning and education was a 2012 retreat, held at the University of California at Santa Barbara, that resulted in a report titled *Spatial Thinking Across the College Curriculum* (Hegarty et al. 2013).

Excitement about the real-world relevance of spatial thinking is growing, and we are gaining confidence in the idea that children (and adults) can learn spatially and that there should be some kind of spatial education at a variety of ages and levels. But what is the best strategy for providing opportunities for spatial learning ?

Should Spatial Education Focus on Training Spatial Skills, or on Spatializing the Curriculum?

There are two strategies for supporting spatial learning, one of them focused more on individuals and the other more on curricula (Newcombe 2012). They are complementary and probably mutually reinforcing, but it is useful to keep them somewhat distinct as we consider ways to build on our educational investments and as we prioritize research to evaluate our efforts. In some contexts, at some ages, and for some skills, one approach or the other may be the more practical and the more cost-effective.

One approach to spatial education focuses on the spatial ability of individual students. The central idea of such an approach is to increase students' accuracy and ease in accomplishing spatial tasks, such as mental rotation, in advance of instruction in other subject areas for which such skills may be useful, such as mathematics or engineering. For young children, this end might be accomplished through play with puzzles and blocks and through art activities. For university students, we might encourage, or even require, participation in a course using workbooks, online displays, and homework. There is some experimental evidence that interventions of this kind can work to improve learning in science, technology, engineering, and mathematics (STEM), as well as improving spatial skills per se (Miller and Halpern 2013; Sorby 2009; Sorby, Casey, Veurink, and Dulaney 2013).

However, the study of how well individual interventions work is just beginning, and much more remains to be discovered. In particular, we need a more systematic approach to thinking about what spatial skills should be trained, and whether there are best practices regarding the sequence of trained skills. In addition, although there is evidence that training shows at least some durability and generalization (Uttal et al. 2013), we don't know whether its effects last longer than a few months, or whether they generalize widely. For example, is it easier to learn about plate tectonics after having mastered organic chemistry in the previous year? In fact, there are reasons for pessimism: initial effects of spatial training in the college physics classroom were not discernible after a few months (Miller and Halpern 2013), and organic chemists and geoscientists seem to have different sets of spatial skills (Resnick and Shipley 2013).

One terminological note about this approach concerns the words 'ability' and 'skill'. The individual-training approach often is construed as affecting students' spatial ability, which is why I used that term in introducing it. But 'spatial skills' is a better term, for two reasons. First, we shouldn't use a singular noun, because there are a variety of distinct spatial processes, even if they are correlated to an extent (e.g., mental rotation and perspective taking). Each process probably is best suited for different tasks; they may also provide alternative routes to achieving the same cognitive task. (See the chapter by Hegarty, Stieff, and Dixon in this volume.) Second, for most people, the word 'ability' brings to mind a mental entity that is fixed and innate, whereas skills suggests things that are contingent and malleable and thus sensible targets for education.

An alternative to the individual-training approach focuses on spatializing the curriculum. The curricular strategy has the distinct advantage of not requiring more time to be set aside, in an already busy day, for training in skills. With the K–12 curriculum and the university curriculum already full, there may not be room for a new subject called "spatial thinking." Instead, the usual material can be taught in a spatial way. For example, university students learning about "deep time"—about time spans of billions of years and how they are divided into categories—can be supported by a carefully planned spatial approach using principles drawn from what we know about analogical learning and category formation (Resnick, Shipley, Newcombe, Massey, and Wills 2012). The curricular approach also has the advantage of drawing attention to the importance of symbolic systems for communicating spatial information, including designing effective diagrams, graphs, and other visualizations (as elegantly shown in the work of Edward Tufte) and (just as important) teaching students how to read these spatial displays (Cromley, Bergey, et al. 2013; Cromley, Perez, et al. 2013). Furthermore, curricular changes may raise students' skill levels, thus combining the individual-training approach and the curricular approach.

Although spatializing the curriculum is a promising way to teach spatial thinking, there are many unanswered questions about the enterprise, as there are about individual training. We need to decide which curricula we should spatialize, at what developmental levels, and how, and then to evaluate the effects. (See the chapter by Hegarty, Stieff, and Dixon.) In addition, we need to be wary about (and thoroughly evaluate) whether students who have very low skill levels may be unable to cope with certain curricula and be deterred from persevering in very spatial disciplines (Uttal and Cohen 2012). If so, the training strategy focused on the individual may be an essential precursor to a spatialized curriculum for some students. Another kind of precursor could be at least one university-level course in spatial thinking, something of a hybrid between the skills and the curricular approaches. (See Sinton's chapter in this volume.)

What Spatial Skills? What Spatial Content?

There are theoretical and conceptual challenges for both the individual-training approach and the curricular approach. The question for the individual-training approach is what spatial skills we should aim to train. The challenge for the curricular approach is what spatial concepts we should aim to communicate. In short, for both strategies the challenge is to delineate how we conceptualize the spatial world. There have been many attempts to create a taxonomy or a typology, both for spatial skills and for spatial concepts. Arguably, there have been too many. Long lists of terms and ideas often overlap, creating a sense of confusion more than a sense of order.

Several chapters in this book (e.g., Atit, Shipley, and Tikoff; Hinze et al.) utilize a taxonomy that posits four kinds of skills and concepts. Developed in various disciplines and motivated by various kinds of evidence (see, e.g., Chatterjee 2008; Newcombe and Shipley 2014; Palmer 1978; Uttal et al. 2013), the taxonomy is based on two distinctions. The first distinction is between spatial skills and concepts that involve the internal structures of objects and those that involve the locations of those objects in the wider world. The internal structure of objects is adaptively useful for tool making and tool use, and the locations of objects in the wider world allow for successful navigation. Tool use and navigation are distinct adaptive functions, relying on distinct brain areas; tool use is largely a human adaptation, whereas navigation is a ubiquitous adaptive demand—a challenge solved in different ways by different species, but a challenge that must be solved to survive. However, navigation-based thinking can become uniquely human when it involves symbolic tools for thinking about distributions and interactions on the surface of the Earth and about their sources and meanings. (See the chapter by Goodchild.) The second distinction is between static representation of the two kinds of information (object structure or spatial location) and dynamic transformation of those representations (e.g., mental rotation of object structure, or perspective taking within an environment). Thus, this taxonomy suggests the existence of four categories of spatial thinking generated by crossing the two distinctions just discussed: intrinsic-static, intrinsic-dynamic, extrinsic-static, and extrinsic-dynamic. (See figure 16.1.)

In chapter 12, Grossner and Janelle take a different approach to the goal of a spatial taxonomy: bottom-up data mining rather than top-down theorizing, with a focus on concepts rather than on skills. Their table 12.2 lists ten basic categories of spatial concepts, with more specific spatial concepts nested within those ten categories, rather than the four categories generated by the two-distinction framework. It is interesting to ask whether their approach also shows evidence of the two distinctions we have just discussed, i.e., intrinsic-extrinsic and static-dynamic. It is possible that the table could be reconceptualized in terms of the distinction between object-focused intrinsic structure and environment-focused extrinsic relations and the distinction between static representations and dynamic transformation. Let's take a closer look.

The correspondence between the two approaches is most evident in looking at the first and second categories in Grossner and Janelle's table

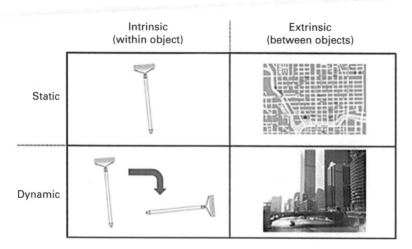

| | Intrinsic (within object) | Extrinsic (between objects) |

Figure 16.1
A 2 × 2 taxonomy of spatial thinking skills. Source: Uttal et al. 2013.

12.2. The category of spatial structures concerns extrinsic relations in the environment (e.g., region and landmark), whereas the category of spatial properties pertains to objects (e.g., size and, shape). Five other categories (space-time context, position, spatial dynamics, spatial relations, and representation) are also dominated by concepts pertaining to extrinsic relations. However, some very general terms (e.g., distance and spatial organization) can also be found nested within these categories. Such general terms apply to both within-object and between-object concepts. Similarly, there are two very general categories in that table that would apply across the intrinsic-extrinsic distinction. Spatial transformations are general dynamic changes, corresponding to the dynamic side of the static-dynamic dichotomy. Spatial principles are general analytic ideas, interestingly with an emphasis on analogical thinking.[2] Thus, it may be possible to map similarities across taxonomies, and ultimately arrive at a consensual definition and taxonomy that would be a boon to analyses. One initial test of the approach could be to sort the terms of Grossner and Janelle's table 12.2 into the 2 × 2 classification, with a fifth category received for overarching terms referring to principles and abstract entities (e.g., representation), and then to conduct a content analysis of texts to reveal how the terms clustered.

In fact, across all the chapters in this book we see that a challenge for the field is the need to compare taxonomies to establish similarities and differences, and determining which taxonomy is most useful, on theoretical, empirical, or practical grounds. Overall, the field of spatial education clearly needs a consensus regarding skills and concepts. Without such agreement, it is hard to develop training programs and guidelines, scope and sequence documents, and advice for parents, teachers, and policy makers. This book is an effort to meet this challenge by provoking the required debate and further empirical work needed to lead to consensus. However, a notable obstacle to this goal is the differing goals, methods, and vocabularies of the various spatial sciences. Work in computer science (see the chapter by Freksa and Schultheis), work in architecture (see the chapter by Tenbrink et al.), and work in linguistics (see Bateman and Lestrade, this volume) differ in many ways from the traditions in psychology and geography that I have briefly considered in this section. Bridging these conceptual and terminological barriers will require concerted and open-minded effort—what diplomats call, in a term of art, "frank discussion."

Action-to-Abstraction in Spatial Learning

Another challenge for making recommendations about spatial learning and education involves a long-standing debate concerning the role of embodiment in mental functioning. In this volume, Freksa and Schultheis and Hegarty, Stieff, and Dixon argue for a sequence in teaching space that begins with concrete and embodied action. Proposals of this kind go back at least to Jean Piaget, who argued that babies began with sensorimotor intelligence, and progressed through stages to symbolic and formal thought, and, in the case of spatial representation, to Euclidean accuracy. Freksa and Schultheis and Hegarty et al. would not embrace Piaget's stages or ages, but they do have the same basic (and intuitively appealing) idea of a sequence. Wang's work on four-dimensional spatial representations, reported in her chapter in this volume, makes the most radical proposal regarding a developmental sequence away from embodiment, suggesting that perhaps embodiment can be completely transcended.

For other researchers, however, space is necessarily embodied—that is, there is not a sequence at all, and there is no symbolic abstraction. (See the chapter by Waller.) Gibsonian theory, with its arguments that organisms are built so that they simply resonate adaptively to environmental affordances, is the root of many ideas along these lines. More recently, investigators have taken discoveries such as the perceptual basis of mental rotation (Farah 1988; Farah, Péronnet, Gonon, and Giard 1988) or the importance of inertial processing in navigation (Waller, this volume) to support the idea, and Barsalou (2008) has proposed a general approach to cognition along these lines.

One aspect of this debate is the question of whether or not humans (and members of other species) form cognitive maps. Debate continues, some researchers proposing that navigation uses partial information from snapshots and sensorimotor sequence memories (Foo, Warren, Duchon, and Tarr 2005; McNamara 1991; Shettleworth 2010; Tversky 1981) and others suggesting the existence of more integrated, survey-style representations (Chrastil and Warren 2013; Newcombe, Huttenlocher, Sandberg, Lie, and Johnson 1999). Individual differences may come into play here, with some people more able to form integrated representations than others (Ishikawa and Montello 2006; Weisberg, Schinazi, Newcombe, Shipley, and Epstein 2014), although in some studies all participants have converged on integrated representations after sufficient exposure, though with variations in initial inferences (Schinazi, Nardi, Newcombe, Shipley, and Epstein 2013).

The importance of embodied learning is undeniable, but in my view so too is the reality of symbolic representation. In cognitive development, this idea is sometimes called representational redescription (Karmiloff-Smith 1992). That is, our body-based interactions with the world can progress to internal spatial representations, which we can manipulate, transform, and discuss. The role in spatial learning of external representations, such as maps, diagrams, and graphs, shows this. In addition, there is strong evidence that gesture can help to support an abstraction process in spatial learning (Beilock and Goldin-Meadow 2010; Goldin-Meadow 2010, 2011), as can signing (Malaia and Wilbur, this volume), sketching (Ainsworth, Prain, and Tytler 2011; Forbus, Usher, Lovett, Lockwood, and Wetzel 2011), and concrete experience (Kontra, Goldin-Meadow, and Beilock 2012). But concrete experience does not always help (Kontra et al. 2012; Uttal, Scudder, and DeLoache 1997). An unanswered question is whether, when internal representations are formed, they are context-bound (i.e., domain-specific) or whether they can be applied in contexts and domains other than those in which they were learned. Can they eventually become completely abstract?

Conclusion

The study of spatial learning and education has blossomed in the past ten years. Yet there is much more that we need to know before we will be able to utilize this powerful kind of human thought fully. Future investigation will require a consensual inter-disciplinary taxonomy and a consensual vocabulary, one of the aims of this book. But much more is required. In particular, the infrastructure that supports scholarship in areas such as language acquisition and reading is scant in the area of spatial learning and education, and is uneasily dependent on the effort and the good will of a small group of investigators and universities. A partial list of what is in short supply would include high-profile journals, established societies with written rules of procedure and at least modest bank accounts, smaller sections of larger societies (e.g., the American Educational Research Association and the American Psychological Association), coverage in textbooks, undergraduate majors, graduate certificate programs, and targeted grant programs. However, the growth of the past ten or twenty years allows optimism that such an infrastructure will be built, and that ten years from now we will know much more than we do now.

Notes

1. A second edition was released in 2012. The chapter by Downs in the present volume provides background on spatial expertise in geography.

2. Some of the concepts in Grossner and Janelle's table 12.2, such as gravity, molecule, chirality, and ecosystem, are content-laden and nearly saturated with disciplinary meaning, thus highlighting how spatial concepts are strongly intertwined with other kinds of concepts.

References

Ainsworth, S., Prain, V., and Tytler, R. 2011. Drawing to learn in science. *Science* 333: 1096–1097.

Barsalou, L. W. 2008. Grounded cognition. *Annual Review of Psychology* 59: 617–645.

Beilock, S., and Goldin-Meadow, S. 2010. Gesture changes thought by grounding it in action. *Psychological Science* 21: 1605–1610.

Chatterjee, A. 2008. The neural organization of spatial thought and language. *Seminars in Speech and Language* 29: 226–238.

Chrastil, E. R., and Warren, W. H. 2013. Active and passive spatial learning in human navigation: Acquisition of survey knowledge. *Journal of Experimental Psychology. Learning, Memory, and Cognition* 39: 1520–1537.

Cromley, J. C., Bergey, B. W., Fitzhugh, S., Newcombe, N., Wills, T. W., Shipley, T. F., et al. 2013. Effects of three diagram instruction methods on transfer of diagram comprehension skills: The critical role of inference while learning. *Learning and Instruction* 26: 45–58.

Cromley, J. G., Perez, T. C., Fitzhugh, S. L., Newcombe, N. S., Wills, T. W., and Tanaka, J. C. 2013. Improving students' diagram comprehension with classroom instruction. *Journal of Experimental Education* 81: 511–537.

Farah, M. J. 1988. Is visual imagery really visual? Overlooked evidence from neuro-psychology. *Psychological Review* 95: 307–317.

Farah, M. J., Péronnet, F., Gonon, M. A., and Giard, M. H. 1988. Electrophysiological evidence for a shared representational medium for visual images and visual percepts. *Journal of Experimental Psychology. General* 117: 248–257.

Foo, P., Warren, W. H., Duchon, A., and Tarr, M. J. 2005. Do humans integrate routes into a cognitive map? Map- versus landmark-based navigation of novel shortcuts. *Journal of Experimental Psychology. Learning, Memory, and Cognition* 31: 195–215.

Forbus, K., Usher, J., Lovett, A., Lockwood, K., and Wetzel, J. 2011. CogSketch: Sketch understanding for cognitive science research and for education. *Topics in Cognitive Science* 3: 648–666.

Geography Education Standards Project. 1994. *Geography for Life: National Geography Standards 1994*. National Geographic Research & Exploration.

Goldin-Meadow, S. 2010. When gesture does and does not promote learning. *Language and Cognition* 2: 1–19.

Goldin-Meadow, S. 2011. Learning through gesture. *Wiley Interdisciplinary Reviews: Cognitive Science* 2: 595–607.

Hegarty, M., Newcombe, N. S., Goodchild, M. F., Janelle, D. G., Shipley, T. F., and Sinton, D. 2013. Spatial Thinking Across the College Curriculum. Final report of specialist meeting, Santa Barbara, 2012 (http://www.spatial.ucsb.edu/events/STATCC/docs/STATCC-Final-report.pdf).

Ishikawa, T., and Montello, D. R. 2006. Spatial knowledge acquisition from direct experience in the environment: Individual differences in the development of metric knowledge and the integration of separately learned places. *Cognitive Psychology* 52: 93–129.

Karmiloff-Smith, A. 1992. *Beyond Modularity: A Developmental Perspective on Cognitive Science*. MIT Press.

Kontra, C., Goldin-Meadow, S., and Beilock, S. L. 2012. Embodied learning across the life span. *Topics in Cognitive Science* 4: 731–739.

McNamara, T. P. 1991. Memory's view of space. In *The Psychology of Learning and Motivation*, volume 27: *Advances in Research and Theory*, ed. G. H. Bower. Academic Press.

Miller, D. I., and Halpern, D. F. 2013. Can spatial training improve long-term outcomes for gifted STEM undergraduates? *Learning and Individual Differences* 26: 141–152.

National Research Council. 2006. *Learning to Think Spatially*. National Academies Press.

Newcombe, N. S. 2012. Two ways to help students with spatial thinking in geoscience. In, *Earth and Mind II: A Synthesis of Research on Thinking and Learning in the Geosciences* ed. K. A. Kastens and C. M. Manduca. Special paper 486, Geological Society of America.

Newcombe, N. S., and Shipley, T. F. 2014. Thinking about spatial thinking: New typology, new assessments. In *Studying Visual and Spatial Reasoning for Design Creativity*, ed. J. S. Gero. Springer.

Newcombe, N., Huttenlocher, J., Sandberg, E., Lie, E., and Johnson, S. 1999. What do misestimations and asymmetries in spatial judgement indicate about spatial representation? *Journal of Experimental Psychology. Learning, Memory, and Cognition* 25: 986–996.

Palmer, S. E. 1978. Fundamental aspects of cognitive representation. In *Cognition and Categorization*, ed. E. Rosch and B. B. Lloyd. Erlbaum.

Resnick, I., and Shipley, T. F. 2013. Breaking new ground in the mind: An initial study of mental brittle transformation and mental rigid rotation in science experts. *Cognitive Processing* 14: 143–152.

Resnick, I., Shipley, T. F., Newcombe, N., Massey, C., and Wills, T. 2012. Examining the representation and understanding of large magnitudes using the hierarchical alignment model of analogical reasoning. In *Proceedings of the 34th Annual Conference of the Cognitive Science Society*, ed. N. Miyake, D. Peebles, and R. P. Cooper. Cognitive Science Society.

Schinazi, V. R., Nardi, D., Newcombe, N. S., Shipley, T. F., and Epstein, R. A. 2013. Hippocampal size predicts rapid learning of a cognitive map in humans. *Hippocampus* 23: 515–528.

Shettleworth, S. J. 2010. *Cognition, Evolution, and Behavior*, second edition. Oxford University Press.

Sorby, S. 2009. Developing spatial cognitive skills among middle school students. *Cognitive Processing* 10 (Suppl. 2): S312–S315.

Sorby, S., Casey, B., Veurink, N., and Dulaney, A. 2013. The role of spatial training in improving spatial and calculus performance in engineering students. *Learning and Individual Differences* 26: 20–29.

Tversky, B. 1981. Distortions in memory for maps. *Cognitive Psychology* 13: 407–433.

Uttal, D. H., and Cohen, C. A. 2012. Spatial thinking and STEM education: When, why, and how? In, *The Psychology of Learning and Motivation*, volume 57 ed. B. H. Ross. Academic Press.

Uttal, D. H., Meadow, N. G., Tipton, E., Hand, L. L., Alden, A. R., Warren, C., et al. 2013. The malleability of spatial skills: A meta-analysis of training studies. *Psychological Bulletin* 139: 352–402.

Uttal, D. H., Scudder, K. V., and DeLoache, J. S. 1997. Manipulatives as symbols: A new perspective on the use of concrete objects to teach mathematics. *Journal of Applied Developmental Psychology* 18: 37–54.

Wai, J., Lubinski, D., and Benbow, C. P. 2009. Spatial ability for STEM domains: Aligning over 50 years of cumulative psychological knowledge solidifies its importance. *Journal of Educational Psychology* 101: 817–835.

Weisberg, S. M., Schinazi, V. R., Newcombe, N. S., Shipley, T. F., and Epstein, R. A. 2014. Variations in cognitive maps: Understanding individual differences in navigation. *Journal of Experimental Psychology. Learning, Memory, and Cognition* 40: 669–682.

Contributors

Kinnari Atit, Temple University

John Bateman, University of Bremen

Ruth Conroy Dalton, Northumbria University

Ghislain Deslongchamps, University of New Brunswick

Bonnie Dixon, University of Maryland

Roger M. Downs, Pennsylvania State University

Christian Freksa, University of Bremen

Michael F. Goodchild, University of California, Santa Barbara

Karl Grossner, Stanford University

Mary Hegarty, University of California, Santa Barbara

Scott R. Hinze, Northwestern University

Christoph Hölscher, ETH Zurich and University of Freiburg

Alycia M. Hund, Illinois State University

Donald G. Janelle, University of California, Santa Barbara

Sander Lestrade, University of Amsterdam

Evie Malaia, University of Texas, Arlington

Daniel R. Montello, University of California, Santa Barbara

Nora S. Newcombe, Temple University

David N. Rapp, Northwestern University

Holger Schultheis, University of Bremen

Thomas F. Shipley, Temple University

Mary Jane Shultz, Tufts University

Diana Sinton, University Consortium for Geographic Information Science

Mike Stieff, University of Illinois, Chicago

Thora Tenbrink, Bangor University

Basil Tikoff, University of Wisconsin, Madison

Dido Tsigaridi, Harvard University

David Waller, Miami University

Ranxiao Frances Wang, University of Illinois, Urbana-Champaign

Ronnie B. Wilbur, Purdue University

Kenneth C. Williamson, Texas A&M University

Vickie M. Williamson, Texas A&M University

Index